Housing AMERICA

Mobilizing Bankers, Builders and Communities to Solve the Nation's Affordable Housing Crisis

Jess Lederman, Editor

PROBUS PUBLISHING COMPANY
Chicago, Illinois
Cambridge, England

To the pioneers of affordable housing, who have struggled and survived through a dozen lean years. Their words are a challenge and an inspiration and a message of hope.

Table of Contents

SECTION VI: CRITICAL ISSUES IN AFFORDABLE HOUSING

Contributing Authors

Amy S. Anthony is president of Housing Investments, Inc., an affiliated company organized from the Housing Group of Aldrich, Eastman & Waltch, Inc., which manages over $5 billion in client capital secured by $10 billion in real property. Ms. Anthony was previously secretary of the Massachusetts Executive Office of Communities and Development, where she developed affordable-housing programs that received national awards. In 1987 she was named to the National Housing Task Force that developed recommendations for renewed federal investments in affordable housing.

Mary Brosnahan is executive director of the Coalition for the Homeless, The nation's oldest and most respected homeless advocacy group. She graduated from Notre Dame in 1983 and worked as a film publicist and editor before joining the Dukakis presidential campaign, where she served as lead press advance person. Ms. Brosnahan has been with The Coalition since 1989.

Barbara Bryan has been involved in affordable-housing development and finance for over 10 years, and is currently assistant director of multifamily finance for the National Association of Home Builders. Ms. Bryan coordinated the NAHB-Fannie Mae Affordable Housing Initiative, and works with builders and local builder associations nationwide to support their activities in affordable housing. She received a degree in urban studies from Trinity College in Washington, D.C.

Judith A. Calogero, executive director for the New York State Rural Housing Coalition, has worked in the affordable-housing field for 13 years. In 1983, as assistant director of the Albany County Rural Housing Alliance, Inc., she oversaw a project that received the New York State Commissioner's Award for Excellence in housing development. Ms. Calogero holds a master's degree in planning and urban studies from Rensselaer Polytechnic Institute.

Rick Cohen is vice president of The Enterprise Foundation, a charitable organization building a national system of housing for very-low-income households. He is well known in the planning and development field for his design of "linkage" programs, in which market rate developers contribute to the cost of building affordable housing. Mr. Cohen is the author of numerous books and articles on this and related topics.

Millard Dean Fuller is an author, a lawyer, a former millionaire and the founder of Habitat for Humanity International. He has won numerous awards including the Martin Luther King, Jr., Humanitarian Award. Aided by volunteers such as former President Jimmy Carter, Mr. Fuller's ambition is nothing less than "the elimination of poverty housing in the world" (see attached reprint from *Time* magazine).

Rosalie Genevro has been executive director of the Architectural League of New York since 1985. Trained as an architectural historian, she has written the history on public housing in New York and served as research director of Advisory Services for Better Housing, a non-profit housing consulting firm. Projects carried out under her direction at the Architectural League have included studies on public school design and the relationship of park and infrastructure development.

Bertrand Goldberg is an internationally acclaimed, award-winning architect. Among his many achievements, Mr. Goldberg designed new solutions for public housing in the Raymond Hilliard Housing Center on Chicago's south side and many other projects dealing with low-cost housing, including the production of prefabricated housing during and after WWII. Mr. Goldberg currently resides and works in Chicago.

Barbara A. Gordon is executive director of the Lake County [Illinois] Community Action Project, the county's largest social service, economic and housing development non-profit corporation. She is the recipient of numerous awards for agency and volunteer work locally, statewide and nationally. Mrs. Gordon is vice president of the Federal Home Loan Bank's Community Investment Advisory Council-Illinois/Wisconsin and is a director on the Bank of Northern Illinois, N.A. and is a member of its CRA Committee. She received her M.S. in Human Service Administration from Spertus of Judiaca College, Chicago.

Gloria Guard, executive director of People's Emergency Center in Philadelphia, Pennsylvania, is the recipient of several awards, including the United Way's Executive Director of the Year, of which she was the very first recipient. She developed a unique facility for homeless families that has become a model for shelters around the country. Ms. Guard holds a double Master's degree from Bryn Mawr College and serves on numerous non-profit boards. She has a broad range of experience working with anti-hunger, addiction, and women's health programs, as well as programs geared towards aiding and housing people with AIDS.

Bruce C. Gunter is president of the

non-profit affordable housing developer Progressive Redevelopment, Inc., the largest non-profit housing developer in the city of Atlanta, GA. PRI focuses primarily on developing single-room occupancy (SROs) for "working homeless individuals" and limited equity cooperatives for low-income families. Mr. Gunter serves on the board of Habitat for Humanity International.

William Jones is the founder and president of Neighborhood Preservation Coalition of New York State, Inc., executive director of the Housing and Neighborhood Development Institute, Inc., and a member of the Federal Home Loan Bank Affordable Housing Advisory Council.

Thomas L. Kenyon is president of the National Alliance to End Homelessness, and serves on the boards of numerous charitable organizations. Previously, he was executive director of the Fund for Educational Advancement. Prior to that, Mr. Kenyon spent over 20 years in the private sector, primarily in the area of international education.

George Knight is executive director of Neighborhood Reinvestment Corporation. He is responsible for guiding NRC to assist 145 local affiliate programs in revitalizing 290 neighborhoods in over 140 cities. Previously, Mr. Knight worked for Booz, Allen & Hamilton, where he specialized in real estate finance and urban development. He received a M.A. with honors from the University of Chicago and a Master of Divinity from McCormick Seminary in 1969.

Richard D. Koller is president of RDK, Inc., a Bethesda, MD-based real estate consulting company engaged in commercial real estate loan sales and acquisition. Prior to forming RDK, Inc., Mr. Koller was affiliated with the National Association of Realtors where he launched the first industry-wide initiative to develop a commercial secondary mortgage market and spearheaded the association's affordable housing finance activities. Mr. Koller is credited with helping to create the RTC affordable housing seller-financing program. Prior to joining NAR, Mr. Koller earned an MBA in finance and real estate from George Washington University and is a former staff assistant to the Vice President of the United States.

Michael D. Lappin is president and chief executive officer of Community Preservation Corporation, a consortium of 43 major savings and commercial banks and seven leading insurance companies. It is the nation's foremost non-profit housing lender. Mr. Lappin joined CPC as a lending officer in 1975 after working for five years in the policy research and neighborhood preservation department of New York's Housing Development Administration. He received a master's degree in international relations from the American University in Washington, D.C., and studied philosophy at the Graduate Facility of the New School for Social Research and at the New York University Graduate School of Business.

Martin D. Levine is Fannie Mae's senior vice president for low- and moderate-income programs. Previously he spent nine years in the Congressional Budget

Office, most recently dealing with programs on housing and community development. Mr. Levine earned a Ph.D. in political science from Michigan State University.

Stuart M. Lopes is executive vice president for GE Mortgage Insurance Companies, the nation's leading private mortgage insurance group. He previously worked for Fannie Mae. Mr. Levine received an MBA from George Washington University.

F. Lynn Luallen is president of The Housing Partnership, Inc., and earlier served as executive director of Louisville Housing Development Corporation. Mr. Luallen held the position of executive director of Kentucky Housing Corporation for two terms, where he was responsible for the development of several innovative affordable-housing programs. He has served two terms as president of the National Council of State Housing Agencies, and received special recognition by that organization for his efforts to create national awareness of the need for affordable housing in the United States.

Felice Michetti was appointed commissioner of New York City's Department of Housing Preservation and Development (HPD) by Mayor David N. Dinkins in March, 1990. As commissioner, she oversees New York City's housing agency with a workforce of some 4,700 employees and an annual budget of $500 million. Ms. Mitchetti has devoted 17 years to public service as a housing and planning professional. She joined the New York City Department of City Planning in 1973 and, in 1979, moved to HPD where she rose through the ranks serving first as assostant commissioner for rehabilitation and subsequently as deputy commissioner for the Office of Property Management. Immediately prior to her appointment as commissioner she served as president of the New York City Housing Development Corporation and first deputy commissioner of HPD, a post in which she was responsible for developing and implementing the city's 10-year, $5.1 billion housing program. A summa cum laude graduate of Fordham University and the Fordham University School of Law, she is an attorney and admitted to practice before the New York Bar.

Sarah Minier is communications and training coordinator for the New York State Rural Housing Coalition. In addition to writing and editing articles for print media, she has written and produced dozens of educational videotapes and films, which have won nine national and international awards, most recently from the International Festival of Scientific Films in Shanghai, China. Ms. Minier received her M.A. and B.S. degrees from the University of Wisconsin-Madison.

Keith Rolland is a communications professional in Philadelphia, Pennsylvania. He works with the Federal Reserve Bank of Philadelphia in the Community and Consumer Affairs Department, writing and editing consulting reports, publications and articles on public-private partnerships in low-income communities. Mr. Rolland also organizes informational meetings for two banking councils. Previously, he started and directed a clearinghouse and reporting service on community development news and investments.

Nan P. Roman, vice president for policy and programs for the National Alliance to End Homelessness, has been involved in low-income housing since 1976. Prior to her current position, Ms. Roman served as director of community services for Friendship House, and as assistant to the director of the National Association of Neighborhoods. She received a master's degree in cultural anthropology from the University of Illinois.

Judith Ann Serrin is director of admissions, placement and special programs for the Columbia University Graduate School of Business. She has taught journalism at Columbia and other universities, and earlier worked as a reporter for the Detroit Free Press. Ms. Serrin is a member of Phi Beta Kappa and received her M.S. in journalism from Columbia University.

Dwight A. Sewell is the chairman and director of the Maine State Housing Authority. He has worked in the housing field for 25 years in a variety of posts, including state director of the Farmers Home Administration.

Muriel T. Watkins developed the RTC's Affordable Housing Disposition Program to create homeownership and affordable rental opportunities for low- and moderate-income families through the sale of foreclosed real estate. Ms. Watkins has more than eight years experience working with the sale of distressed real estate both residential and commercial. She is a planner by training with a background in community development finance.

Mary Lee Widener is President, CEO and one of the co-founders of Neighborhood Housing Services of America, Inc. NHSA's primary function is to operate a secondary market for the revolving loan funds of NHS organizations. Mrs. Widener played a key role in expanding the NHS network of nonprofit organizations from three in 1971 to 176 that exist today. Currently, she chairs the Affordable Housing Council of the Federal Home Loan Bank of San Francisco.

Mark A. Willis is president of Chase Community Development Corporation, and previously served as deputy commissioner for development with the New York City Department of Housing Preservation and Development. He has held numerous other posts within New York City government. Mr. Willis received a J.D. from Harvard, and an M.A. and Ph.D. from Yale.

Introduction

Jess Lederman
Author and Private Investor

Working on *Housing America* was an exciting and inspiring experience. When I began this project in the fall of 1990, however, I was deeply pessimistic about the future of housing in the United States. The ranks of the homeless were swelling, housing affordability was declining, and federal support for housing had been drastically cut. If all this was happening during a decade of robust economic expansion, what bleak fate did this suggest for housing during the slower growth that this country would surely experience in the 1990s?

The results of my research point to hope and not despair. Americans have responded to the housing crisis in a heroic manner. They have made up for some of the lack of federal funding through energetic and creative efforts, often developing unique and ingenious solutions on minimal budgets. The thirty chapters of this book tell the story of the builders and bankers, the rabbis and ministers, the local politicians, community developers and volunteers who have joined forces to make the American dream of decent housing and affordable homeownership come true. Some of the people and programs described in *Housing America* operate for profit, some are driven by religious conviction, and others are motivated by the simple and compelling desire to take charge of their lives, to make their communities better places for themselves and their neighbors. Whatever the motivation, they are all making a significant difference. They are what makes this country great.

It is my hope that the detailed information and case studies contained in this book will provide an inspiration and example for those who are looking for ways to help others, and for those who need help themselves.

THE CRISIS IN HOUSING

Many people question whether any such thing as a housing crisis exists at all. After all, the United States is an affluent country with an enormous housing stock. The deductibility of mortgage interest represents a significant federal subsidy for housing. Some have even argued the hundreds of billions of dollars of mortgage debt that are issued every year are counterproductive, fueling wasteful speculation by developers and crowding out more productive corporate investment.

Of course, there are flaws in all these arguments. While it is true that, statistically, there are sufficient housing units nationwide to provide shelter for every American, the excess supply isn't necessarily in the right location, available at the right price, or suitably structured to satisfy the demand from low-income people. Similarly, the federal tax break represented by mortgage interest deductibility is most beneficial to those with the highest incomes, and excess speculation has typically been concentrated on luxury rather than affordable housing.

The housing crisis can be divided into two broad categories. First, there is the poorest portion of the population that does not have access to decent permanent shelter of any kind, and for whom the port of entry tends to be rental housing. Second, there is the portion of the population that is currently renting, but aspires to homeownership. Statistics reveal that the number of people in both categories increased in the 1980s.

Few would dispute the observation that homelessness is a much greater problem in the 1990s than it was in the 1970s. The causes of homelessness are many and varied, but the phenomenon certainly reflects the failure of the economic expansion of the 1980s to "trickle down" to the lowest economic classes, as well as the profound cutbacks in federal housing programs under the Reagan ad-

ministration. The People's Emergency Center in Philadelphia, Pennsylvania, is typical when it reports that the number of homeless people using its facilities in 1983 was three times the average level of the 1970s. By 1987 the number had doubled again. It is estimated that as many as two million Americans experience homelessness every year. The number of people who live on the edge of homelessness increased as the economy softened in the early 1990s; in 1991 there were 4.8 million poor people who paid more than 50 percent of their income for rent. Those are 4.8 million people who are only one setback away from homelessness.

The most recent U.S. Census study informs us that more than one half of all households were unable to qualify for the purchase of a median-priced home, and the National Association of Homebuilders reports that homeownership rates declined in the 1980s for the first time since the Second World War. Consider also the plight of young Americans, as analyzed by William C. Apgar of the Joint Center for Housing Studies at Harvard University:

"Housing prices are unlikely to ease during the 1990s . . . For younger families attempting to buy a first home, however, stable but high prices mean that their opportunities to become owners are still limited . . . Rapid growth of the young adult population in the 1970s checked wage growth for many entry level jobs. Rising divorce and increased incidence of teenage pregnancy have added to the number of economically disadvantaged single-parent households."[1]

Apgar goes on to note that between 1974 and 1988 the real income of households headed by individuals less than twenty-five years old fell by 28 percent. This has greatly reduced the percentage of young families who have the financial means to become first-time home buyers.

Of course, simply reciting these statistics does not prove that there is a crisis. One might accept the need to do something about homelessness, but argue that homeownership is another, less important matter. Sure, it would be nice if everyone owned his or her own home, but is homeownership per se a critical national objective?

A full answer to this question is beyond the scope of this book, which focuses on practical solutions, rather than theoretical or philosophical discussions. However, a few points can be made. Homeownership levels have a major effect on the overall economy in general, on home prices in particular. I spent much of my career providing financing for high-cost housing for affluent families, and was always acutely aware that the upper-income market is primarily a *trade-up* market. The family trading up must be able to sell its lower-cost home to a new first-time home buyer. If the number of young first-time home buyers declines, the effects ripple up and reduce the appreciation potential of higher-priced housing. But this is only the narrowest "what's in it for me" argument. Many of the contributing authors to *Housing America* have seen the dramatic effect that homeownership can have on individuals and communities. As Millard Fuller, the charismatic head of Habitat for Humanity International has said, "The pride, dignity, and responsibility of homeownership have renewed individuals and families—often transforming them."[2] Homeownership has been the traditional vehicle through which

Americans have built wealth and gained a stake in their communities. Communities with a higher percentage of homeowners tend to be more stable and productive, less beset by crime and despair. One does not have to build a complex econometric model to become convinced that eliminating homelessness and increasing homeownership thus yield economic benefits and a better quality of life for all Americans. The more difficult question is, how do we accomplish these goals? That is the subject of this book.

HOUSING AMERICA

Most of the organizations represented in *Housing America* would enthusiastically support increasing the budget for government-supported housing programs, and would deny that their own efforts, no matter how significant, can make up for the shortfall in federal funding. I agree with this position. Former President Bush's phrase, "a thousand points of light" might be an inspiring slogan, but it can also be seen as a convenient way for government to turn its back in the naive hope that volunteer efforts can solve all our social problems. As with wise investments in science and education, the social and economic returns from increased investment in housing can be tremendous. Focusing on the current budget deficit—the overwhelming stumbling block in the current political environment—is incredibly short-sighted, because these are the investments that we *must* make to ensure long-term growth and prosperity.

The problem, of course, is that the federal government has a splendid track record of wasteful expenditures. In contrast, waste is something you will not find in any of the private initiatives described in this book. They have figured out how to produce maximum results with minimum dollars. To quote Millard Fuller once more, they "offer a hand up, not a handout."[3] Surely these are qualities that both liberals and conservatives, Democrats and Republicans, can endorse wholeheartedly. What this suggests to me is that when we once again decide to reinvest in housing, as surely one day we must, many of the programs in *Housing America*, and other programs modeled on them, will be the ideal conduits for increased federal spending. If this is the case, then the hard times that we are currently experiencing will at least have produced something of value.

SECTION I: FINANCING AFFORDABLE HOUSING

The inspiration for *Housing America* was an extraordinarily productive symposium sponsored by the National Association of Realtors (NAR) on the financing needs of low- and moderate-income Americans. While I was not in the habit of thinking of the NAR as a leading force in the affordable housing movement, it is in fact playing a valuable role as a catalyst for action and a conduit for information. Chapter 1, which was written as a result of the NAR symposium, provides a comprehensive overview of state-of-the-art techniques and critical issues in affordable financing. One of the most important conclusions that came out of the symposium was that traditional financing vehicles are often inappropriate and waste scarce capital resources. For example, most mortgage revenue bond programs provide shallow subsidies to borrowers for a 30-year term. However, many borrowers need deeper subsidies in the early years, and may in fact need no

subsidy at all after five or ten years, due to rising incomes. A more effective program would provide deeper up-front subsidies where needed, and then recycle subsidy dollars to new borrowers as old borrowers achieve self-sufficiency.

Much affordable financing does not necessarily require below-market interest rates and government or charitable subsidies, and several of the chapters in Section I deal with organizations that operate for profit. Each of them has learned to tailor its analysis and services to the unique characteristics of the low-income sector. Private mortgage insurers such as General Electric Mortgage Insurance Co. (Chapter 2) make low-down-payment loans possible for conventional (i.e., non-FHA/VA) loans. Both GEMICO and Chase Community Development Corporation (Chapter 3), which lends in the New York metropolitan area, have succeeded largely through the application of enlightened loan underwriting standards that remove "suburban blinders" and take into account the realities of urban environments. Both organizations have proven that there need be no conflict between the goals of supporting affordable housing and economic development and making a profit. In fact, Chase CDC has yet to have a loan become delinquent, and GEMICO's extensive analysis concludes that "if all other factors are equal, lower-income borrowers are more likely to make their house payments on time [than higher income borrowers]." These findings are not really surprising; they simply underscore how valuable homeownership is to low-income Americans.

Community Preservation Corporation (CPC, Chapter 4) is a nonprofit lender that operates in New York, but they provide an excellent model that could be replicated throughout the country. CPC uses a layered approach to financing, emphasizing market rate lending wherever possible, and thus leveraging valuable subsidy dollars. Their most important innovation has been to develop a highly efficient, streamlined approach to loan origination that makes affordable housing projects practical to the many smaller for-profit and nonprofit developers who were previously shut out of the complex and time consuming requirements imposed by government and private sector funding sources. These developers have become CPC's core clients, and through them CPC has financed over 28,000 affordable housing units without incurring a single loan loss.

The Federal National Mortgage Association (Fannie Mae, Chapter 5), is chartered by Congress but is publicly owned and operates for a profit. Fannie Mae has made all of the underwriting adjustments that Chase and GEMICO have made, and it has experienced a similar degree of success. The role that Fannie Mae plays in the low-income market, however, is a good example of the way that the sophisticated financial technology developed by Wall Street is being applied to affordable housing. Fannie Mae is what is known as a secondary market conduit, meaning that it buys mortgage loans from originators and either packages them into securities for resale to institutional investors or finances the purchased loans through the sale of debt. A typical loan purchased by Fannie Mae is originated by a lender like Chase and is often covered by private mortgage insurance. Fannie Mae's purchases allow lendable funds to recycle, vastly increasing the supply of affordable mortgage money. Neighborhood Housing Services of America (Chapter 6)

plays the same role, albeit on a much smaller scale, in the nonprofit sector, and specializes in more heavily subsidized loans.

Section I concludes with a discussion of the role that pension funds can play in affordable housing. Although their current involvement in low-income projects has been negligible, pension funds control two trillion dollars of assets; even a minuscule percentage of that money could make an enormous difference to the market for affordable housing. While it is highly unlikely that pension funds will ever provide meaningful amounts of below-market financing (for fiduciary reasons alone), there is no reason why they cannot be used as a market-rate resource in the layered financing approach mentioned above. This suggests that they will be providers of debt, rather than equity, and might best be used as a takeout for seasoned, low-risk loans. Chapter 7 provides a number of specific steps for identifying and accessing pension fund money.

SECTION II: DESIGNING, DEVELOPING, AND BUILDING AFFORDABLE HOUSING

The six chapters of Section II examine the efforts of architects, builders, and developers who are working to provide affordable ownership and rental housing. One of the themes that underlies the best work in this area is that we must challenge many of the preconceptions, rules, and regulations that govern much of our thinking about housing in general. For example, both for-profit and nonprofit builders see density restrictions (which restrict the number of units that can be built on a given lot size) as one of the primary hindrances to the development of affordable housing. In an era of limited subsidies, it is difficult to acquire land at below-market prices; but by increasing density allowances, we can sharply reduce the cost of land per unit. This is particularly important in expensive markets, such as San Francisco, where Bridge Housing Corporation (Chapter 11) has built some of the most elegant and affordable high-density housing in the country.

A willingness to break with tradition is also reflected in the designs discussed by the Architectural League of New York in Chapter 8. These are plans for affordable housing units located on vacant lots in New York City that were previously thought to be too small to support any housing at all. Additionally, they reflect the challenges that architects must face in meeting the special needs of many sectors of the low-income population, including single-parent families, extended families, and medical support facilities.

One of the reasons that housing projects of any sort fail is that they focus myopically on bricks and mortar, ignoring the needs of the residents and the social dynamics of the community. Bertrand Goldberg, one of this country's eminent architects, addresses this point in Chapter 13 when he states that "the developer we need for the future is one who can build new neighborhoods . . . [which] can provide extensive mixed use and make identity of the individual possible within a community environment." A large part of Bridge Housing's success can be attributed to its emphasis on mixed-income developments, where residents living in market-rate and affordable units are neighbors. Not only does this promote a more stable society than one in which low-income residents are

segregated from the rest of the population, but it also offers an ingenious solution to the affordability problem: cash flow from market rate units is used to subsidize low-income units.

Successful nonprofit builders and developers have learned to marshal every available resource in order to accomplish their goals. Progressive Redevelopment, Inc. (Chapter 10), located in Atlanta, Georgia, has thrived because of its extraordinary skill at obtaining subsidized front-end financing, including charitable donations, grants, low-interest loans, tax credits, government programs, and conventional bank financing. Habitat for Humanity (Chapter 12), an international organization that has received considerable media attention thanks to the involvement of former President Jimmy Carter, does not accept government funding because it does not wish to compromise its autonomy. Instead, Habitat for Humanity has developed a highly successful program that constructs single-family housing through a reliance on donated land and materials and volunteer labor. Like many of the best affordable housing programs, recipients play a significant role in the process, helping to build their own homes and paying for them with long-term loans.

I am not aware of any organizations that are entirely independent in their efforts to produce affordable housing. Most low-income housing in fact involves a partnership of the public and private sectors, and of for-profit and nonprofit operations. Chapter 9 discusses a wide range of affordable housing initiatives that commercial homebuilders are pursuing throughout the United States. Typically these involve a partnership between the homebuilder, who provides invaluable expertise, and a non-profit housing sponsor.

SECTION III: FEDERAL, STATE, AND LOCAL GOVERNMENT PROGRAMS

While the federal government receives more than a little criticism within the affordable housing community, it nevertheless plays an immensely import-ant role in affordable housing. Chapter 14 discusses the initiatives of the Depart-ment of Housing and Urban Develop-ment (HUD) under Jack Kemp. Kemp came to the helm as part of the Bush administration, and thus inherited an ag-ency that had already suffered massive cuts under the Reagan administration, and was further weakened by mismanagement under its previous leadership. Kemp brought enthusiasm and creativity to the job, but only limited increases in funding. For example, one of HUD's initiatives (the "NIMBY" report) called for numerous sensible reforms (in-cluding the modification of zoning requirements that would allow for higher density, and thus more affordable hous-ing), but did not provide for any additio-nal federal spending.

The savings and loan scandal and the resulting bailout under the auspices of the Resolution Trust Corporation (RTC) normally bring only dark thoughts to mind. But the good news is that, out of the wreckage of this monumental disas-ter, 18,000 single- and multifamily homes are being made available as affordable housing (Chapter 15). RTC was given a special mandate by Congress to maximize the availability of residential properties for low- and moderate-income people. The agency has wisely chosen to involve existing public agencies and non-profits to let eligible buyers know about available units, or to obtain below-market financing in conjunction with the sale of its properties.

State housing finance agencies (HFAs) have played an important role in afford-able housing over the past two decades, primarily through their use of mortgage revenue bonds and low-income housing tax credits. Chapter 16 provides summaries of innovative programs offered by fifteen state HFAs. As dis-cussed above, mortgage revenue bonds offer only shallow subsidies, and as fede-ral support disappeared and affordability problems worsened, HFAs had to devise creative, low-cost solutions to meet growing needs. This is illustrated in Chapter 17, which uses a series of case studies to show how the Main State Housing Authority went well beyond its original charter to help its homeless and disadvantaged constituents.

In New York City, crime, poverty, the reduction in federal funding, and a deteriorating housing stock compound the problems of homelessness and affordability. Chapter 18 details how the municipal government has responded to these challenges with a multitude of creative housing initiatives, including the reconstruction of city-owned vacant buildings, and the use of below-market loans to encourage private renovation.

SECTION IV: NEIGHBORHOOD DEVELOPMENT ORGANIZATIONS

In September of 1991 the *Wall Street Journal* featured a front-page article high-lighting the success of nonprofit com-munity development organizations in revitalizing America's inner cities. While

there are thousands of such organizations, and their strategies and tactics vary widely, all have one thing in
common: their success is dependent on
securing the widest possible participation
of institutions throughout their community. Effective community development
organizations (CDOs) are invariably
partnerships between the public and
private sector, between nonprofit community organizations, bankers, builders,
investors, and local government. CDOs
are playing an increasingly critical role in
affordable housing in this country.

The first two chapters of Section IV
discuss two large nonprofit institutions
that are known as community development intermediaries. Neighborhood
Reinvestment Corporation (NRC) (Chapter 19), which is funded primarily by
Congress, and the Enterprise Foundation
(Chapter 20), which relies on private
donations, work with hundreds of CDOs
throughout the United States. Neither of
the two intermediaries will go into a
community and start a CDO from
scratch; there must be substantial evidence of local interest and ready and willing sponsors. Once these ingredients are
in place, however, the intermediaries can
use their experience to help a CDO to
quickly become operational and effective. Both NRC and Enterprise help nascent CDOs with planning and training,
and provide technical and financial assistance. Each CDO typically faces unique
challenges in its community, and the
intermediaries are skilled at tailoring
solutions to local needs, rather than
applying an inflexible national model.

The final three chapters of Section IV
provide a look at three specific CDOs.
The Housing Partnership, Inc. (HPI),
located in Louisville, Kentucky, is an ex-

cellent example of an organization
whose success is premised on partnership with institutions and individuals at
all levels of the community. Chapter 21
illustrates the full range of an ambitious
CDOs' activities by including HPI's
detailed 1991-1992 plan. The Housing
and Neighborhood Development Institute (Chapter 22) offers an inspiring
example of how much even a small CDO
can accomplish on a limited budget. The
Lake County Community Action Program in Waukegan, Illinois (Chapter 23),
operates in a pocket of poverty in the
midst of one of America's most affluent
counties. Its story demonstrates how a
CDO succeeded by appealing to the enlightened self-interest of local bankers,
and by using strong leadership to overcome the natural inertia and conflict inherent in forging an effective partnership
with the private sector.

SECTION V: HOUSING FOR THE HOMELESS

The first four chapters of this section
describe organizations dedicated to ending homelessness. The National Alliance
to End Homelessness (Chapter 24) and
The United Way of America (Chapter
25) are both national organizations,
while the Coalition for the Homeless
(Chapter 26) has primarily focused its
efforts within New York State, and the
People's Emergency Center (Chapter 27)
operates a homeless shelter in
Philadelphia, Pennsylvania. While they
use a variety of approaches to achieve a
similar end, several common themes
emerge. For example, both The National
Alliance and the Coalition were formed
in reaction to the proliferation of the
homeless during the early 1980s. Initi-

ally, their efforts were reactive—stopgap measures to alleviate suffering, such as the distribution of food and clothing and the provision of temporary shelter. Gradually it became clear to everyone involved in the struggle that the focus must be on solving the causes, and not simply the symptoms, of homelessness. Thus the Alliance has provided support for several efforts to increase the supply of SRO (single-room occupancy) housing, while the Coalition has tended to focus on class action suits that uphold the obligation of cities and states to provide decent shelter for the disadvantaged.

Many organizations have recognized that one of the most effective things we can do is to prevent people from becoming homeless in the first place. To this end both the United Way and the Alliance have programs providing emergency financial assistance to families in danger of eviction or foreclosure.

All of the organizations represented in Section V have come to the firm conclusion that far more is required than bricks and mortar and monetary assistance. Social services are an important element in all effective programs for the homeless. In order to help people achieve independence, services such as child care, legal aid, job counseling, and medical assistance must be provided. By using all of these resources, one program of the United Way aims to get people out of shelters, into apartments, and to be totally self-sufficient within eighteen months. Not surprisingly, the bottom line cost of such programs, which solve the underlying problems rather than simply covering up the symptoms, is far less than the cost of continuing to rely on temporary measures.

Section V concludes with a case study of the People's Emergency Center, which was forced to relocate its homeless shelter in 1987. It details the Center's efforts in finding an appropriate site, obtaining community and political support, raising money, and designing and building the facility.

SECTION VI: CRITICAL ISSUES IN AFFORDABLE HOUSING

Section VI presents an examination of three critical issues in affordable housing. Housing for the elderly is an increasingly important topic, because the over-65 age group is growing at two-and-one-half times the rate of the overall population. Chapter 28 explores several different aspects of this issue, including housing design and financing.

Employers in New York, Los Angeles, and other high-priced markets often find it difficult to attract—or in some cases retain—good workers without providing some form of housing assistance. In certain instances the only solution has been relocation to a lower-cost market. Chapter 29 discusses a number of less drastic approaches to solving this problem, including programs that subsidize employee housing payments and reduce the cost of new construction in the company's area.

The problems of housing the urban poor have often taken the spotlight in discussions of homelessness and affordability. However, in some parts of the country poverty has increased at a more rapid rate in rural rather than urban areas, and housing for the rural poor is a very real concern. Rural housing problems are compounded by vexing problems such as lack of access to transportation and health services that are more readily available in America's cities.

Chapter 30 analyzes the activities of the New York State Rural Housing Coalition, which acts as an advocate for the rural homeless and impoverished.

ENDNOTES

[1] "Changing Demographics and the Housing Outlook to the Year 2000," William C. Apgar, Jr., September 10, 1990, presentation to the National Association of Realtors.

[2] "Habitat for Humanity: Changing the World One House at a Time," Millard Fuller, President, Habitat for Humanity International.

[3] "Habitat for Humanity," ibid.

Section I

Financing Affordable Housing

Chapter 1

Financing Affordable Housing: State-of-the-Art Techniques and Critical Issues*

Richard D. Koller
President
RDK, Inc.

INTRODUCTION

Annually, the Real Estate Finance Division of the NATIONAL ASSOCIATION OF REALTORS® sponsors a credit issues conference for industry leaders to address pressing issues. The sixth annual real estate finance roundtable, called the Symposium on Real Estate Finance, took place in September of 1990 and focused on the financing needs of low- and moderate-income Americans, including first-time home buyers. The resulting report of the Symposium, *Practical Solutions to Affordable Housing Finance Problems,* continues to reflect the thinking of the industry today on the subject of afford-able housing finance. The thoughts and ideas expressed throughout the report have become, and will remain, part of U.S. public and private policy formation during the coming years. This chapter of *Housing America* is adapted from Practical Solutions and, as a result, reflects the opinions of the program participants, not necessarily policy positions of the NATIONAL ASSOCIATION OF REALTORS.®

The NATIONAL ASSOCIATION OF REALTORS® wishes to thank Jess Lederman for his work during the planning of the 1990 Symposium. The association is particularly proud that the Symposium

---

*Statistics as of 1990.

Richard Koller formerly managed the National Association of Realtors Affordable Housing Finance Iniatives.

contributed to the development of the Resolution Trust Corporation's seller-financing program (see Chapter 15), which is opening the door to homeownership to many more Americans than had been previously possible.

SUMMARY

First-time and low- and moderate-income American home buyers are increasingly unable to make the leap from renting to homeownership, the traditional means by which American families gain a stake in their communities and save for retirement. The spiraling cost of homes nationwide during the 1970s and 1980s combined with lagging growth of personal income has left America with significant need for affordable housing, which has become increasingly hard to produce. For the second quarter of 1991, the NATIONAL ASSOCIATION OF REALTORS® reported that potential first-time buyers had only 79 percent of the income to quality for the purchase of an "average" U.S. home. Current low mortgage interest rates are neither a panacea for housing affordability nor signal a permanent change in the industry.

Mortgage credit for low- and moderate-income Americans is the single greatest hurdle to affordable housing. Historically, affordable housing finance has focused on synthesizing down payments and stretching qualification ratios. Little attention has been given to what could be called the "term of assistance," which could significantly increase available funding without sacrificing current levels of housing support. Rather than providing permanent 30-year assistance, affordable housing finance programs should be geared to the period of need since household income, especially for the first-time buyers, tends to increase over time and at some point homeowners who got into their homes with public assistance may no longer need or be "entitled" to public support. It is vital for the benefit of the greatest number of people and the effective utilization of scarce capital resources that lenders—public and private—replace long-term-oriented programs with short-term need-based assistance.

Traditionally, "affordable," as in affordable housing, has meant the cost of a home is affordable to families earning incomes not exceeding 115 percent of local median income. Given the disparity between the dollar amount of income median-income families earn and the amount of that income that can be used for housing according to even "liberalized" underwriting guidelines, it is clear there is great need to either minimize the cost of units to be sold into this segment of the market or devise creative ways to pay for existing homes or both. Whether one believes true affordable housing—not just comparatively low-cost housing—can be produced without subsidies is not relevant. What is relevant is that affordable housing be built through whatever means and resources can be marshalled to produce it.

Further, affordable housing should not fall victim to financial institutions' regulatory reform. Affordable housing should be a national priority. What's more, in terms of credit risk, affordable housing is in many instances less speculative than other types of development given existing and projected demand for it during the 1990s. In fact, according to Marty Levine, senior vice president for low- and moderate-income housing at Fannie Mae, affordable housing and community lending have been a profitable activity for his company from the start.

ANALYSIS OF THE PROBLEMS AND ISSUES

Policy and Program Options for the Federal Government

During the 1980s, federal support for housing programs gave way to other national priorities. As a result, the number and diversity of federal programs and funding available to encourage homeownership declined. What's more, last decade's scandals at the Department of Housing and Urban Development (HUD) caused the cancellation of programs once considered vital to the well-being of the housing industry and Americans in need of housing assistance. Restoration of home ownership as a national priority is an important domestic social (and economic) goal.

Inasmuch as there is little, if any, money available to fund new programs at any level, the federal government is providing leadership and support for public/private partnerships and other entities working on affordability programs. HUD's Joint Venture for Affordable Housing (JVAH) was a highly successful demonstration program with state and local governments and private sector participants that utilized regulatory reform, streamlined processing, innovative land planning, and financial enhancements to produce 176,000 affordable housing units across the country during 1988 and 1989 at a cost to the federal government of only $5 million. Via JVAH, HUD established a process by which affordable housing can be developed profitably anywhere in the country.

Also in 1989, President Bush directed Secretary of Housing and Urban Development, Jack Kemp to study government regulations that (unnecessarily) increase the cost of housing in America. The resulting Commission on Regulatory Barriers to Affordable Housing (CRBAH) recently issued its report, *Not in My Back Yard*, which found, among other things, that local housing regulations are adding as much as 35 percent to the price of homes (see Chapter 14). *Not in My Back Yard* is a useful guide for serious review and reconsideration of municipal housing and environmental regulations. Unnecessary or poorly conceived regulations can be as much a barrier to homeownership as income and home price levels.

There is much more to be done. While the JVAH and CRBAH have identified problems and mapped possible solutions, HUD must continue to forge ahead. HUD leadership on employer-assisted housing, for example, would be valuable. Decentralization of decision making from Washington, D.C., to local HUD offices would likely create more efficient utilization of government resources and make the field offices active resources for, and partners in, the development of low-cost housing.

Programmatically, the federal government's role is to develop new and sustain existing programs that promote housing affordability. The overhaul of existing and recently canceled mainstay programs should be a priority. So should be the development of a consolidated, federal government real estate owned (REO) sales program, including properties from HUD, RTC, and the Department of

Veterans Affairs (DVA), which would be coordinated with state and local housing agencies. Further, there would be much to be gained from standardizing and establishing reciprocity between government, government-sponsored enterprises, and private sector lenders and insurers for the acceptance of, for example, project approvals to eliminate duplications of effort and increase loan processing speed.

Single-Family Housing

One program that deserves reconsideration is the investor segment of the FHA 203(b) program, which was canceled in response to investor defaults on Federal Housing Administration (FHA) insured mortgages. Tightening underwriting for investor purchases under 203(b) would cure the default problem. The assumption of old, low-interest mortgages on properties where loan-to-value ratios (LTVs) have dropped to, say, 50 percent, would pose little, if any, risk to HUD. Newer loans might require additional interest-bearing security, such as pledged certificates of deposit (CDs), and LTVs below 75 percent.

Allowing investors back into 203(b) could immediately reduce HUD's REO inventory and increase the number of rental housing units available nationwide. Ultimately, some of these homes might become ownership opportunities for first-time and low- and moderate-income families. FHA will insure investor loans on its REO through the Section 203(k) program, setting a precedent for re-extending 203(b) to investors. What's more, RTC REO is eligible for FHA 203(b) insurance if new property carries a standard new-home warranty (existing property doesn't require such a warranty). The Department should re-examine

its policies and goals for continuity and relevance in the current market.

With the banishment of investors from 203(b), HUD has stepped up its efforts to market the 203(k) purchase/rehabilitation program. Results and comments from the field are mixed. The industry applauds the existence of a program in which owners and investors can obtain purchase and rehabilitation financing insurance in a single package, but universally bemoan the administrative burden attached to making 203(k) loans, which limits its effectiveness. Despite this, according to Ken Crandall, chief architect in the Single Family Division at HUD, interest in the program is increasing. Crandall expects the current 550 (approximately) 203(k) lenders nationwide to originate $100 million in 203(k) loans in 1991, up from $49 million in 1990 and $24 million in 1989. Many of these loans will end up in Ginnie Mae pools.

Previously, suggestions have been made to offer incentives to lenders to engender more support for the 203(k) program. One was to extend CRA credit for 203(k) loan production in the first-time and low- and moderate-income market. Second, an internal HUD-based reward system for lenders who meet pre-established affordable housing goals could be established. For example, the Department could guarantee expedited mortgage insurance premium (MIP) certificate processing for firms reaching pre-set targets in the first-time and low- and moderate-income lending.

It should also be noted that approved nonprofits are eligible for a 10 percent price discount on all HUD foreclosed property.

Specific programs aside, the federal government's role in mortgage insurance should be maintained. As to whether actuarial soundness for the Mutual Mortgage Insurance fund is necessary is up for debate, as is whether FHA should be used to deliver a subsidy or if subsidies should be directed exclusively toward down-payment assistance. It is imperative to the low end of the market that the federal government at least maintain its role while debate on these subjects continues.

Multifamily Housing

During the 1990s, the ongoing affordability of the nation's low- and moderate-income multifamily housing stock will be in jeopardy as the agreements that keep them low cost expire. Low- and moderate-income rentals are an integral part of the housing ladder and critical to the accumulation of down-payment funds. Private and nonprofit owners of multifamily property already "in the system" might be willing to extend their existing government contracts in return for new mortgage insurance which would allow them to refinance and "cash out" of their buildings during the current credit crunch. However, both groups have cited red tape and interference by HUD as reasons to abandon the programs even if it means realizing a lower profit on their investments. Every effort must be made to maintain a stock of low-cost rental units.

At a time when the federal budget is stretched to the limit, it is important to note that the above ideas for increasing the reach and effectiveness of HUD programs do not require large amounts of up-front capital. They are, in concept, revenue neutral. Recapturable/recoverable rental housing subsidies would be welcomed by the industry as would

participating debt arrangements between the government and owners. The concept of government as an equity partner, not a subsidizer, is the idea for the '90s.

U.S. Income Tax Policy

Individual Tax Policy

Prior to 1986, the U.S. tax code encouraged homeownership by maximizing the value of homeownership-related tax deductions. In 1986, with the passage of the Tax Reform Act of 1986 (TRA '86), Congress increased the code's standard deduction to a level that all but eliminates the tax reduction value of homeownership for first-time and low- and moderate-income households.

There have been multiple suggestions made as to how to remedy this problem and renew federal support of homeownership through tax policy. The suggestions include: (1) front loading homeownership tax benefits by accelerating deductions into the early years of the mortgage, where the greatest need for assistance and the least ability to use the current tax code to advantage co-exist. Under this concept, such an acceleration would be counterbalanced in the out years; (2) expanding the use of tax credits, which have greater value to lower-income families than mortgage interest deductions; (3) authorizing tax-advantaged savings accounts for the specific purpose of accumulating down-payment funds; and (4) institutionalizing tax incentives, such as low-income housing tax credits, for investors to produce affordable rental housing. Uncertainty equates with risk in the capital markets, drives down the value of tax credits and inhibits investment. Syndicators report a decline in tax credit value from the recent lengthening of the holding period on new projects.

Tax credit legislation, and all legislation like it, should be enacted for periods greater than one year. The country cannot afford unnecessary disruption in the development of new affordable rental housing, the first rung of the housing ladder on which aspiring homeowners save for housing down payments.

Funding for these ideas could come from two recommended sources: (1) the reduction of tax benefits that flow from the purchase of luxury housing, where the lion's share of tax benefits accrue. As a policy matter, at least some of those benefit dollars should be redirected to first-time and low- and moderate-income Americans; and (2) disallowing consumer credit from being categorized as homeownership debt in order to qualify consumer spending for tax deductions. This is a loophole that must be closed under any circumstances.

Finally, because the current tax structure virtually eliminates any value of tax benefits to the first-time home buyer, and because elderly homeowners have tremendous home equity and can benefit from mortgage interest deductions, an incentive program should be designed to encourage the elderly to finance first-time and low- and moderate-income home purchases.

Corporate Tax Policy

A small but perhaps important step could be taken with regard to the Internal Revenue Service (IRS) definition of "accepted business expenses." The U.S. tax code specifies so-called acceptable expenses and should be modified to include mortgage assistance to employees through employer-assisted housing programs. Subsequent employee housing benefits could be tax-free to both parties and provide an impetus for employers to explore the benefits of a housing program for their employees.

Along the same lines, the IRS should authorize Employee Home Ownership Plans (EHOPs), which would allow corporations to access loan funds for employee mortgages by using company stock as loan collateral. With the collateral, EHOP lenders would be able to provide loans, on whatever terms they desire, to the company's employees and get the same 50 percent tax write-off available to Employee Stock Ownership Plan (ESOP) lenders under the tax code. The genesis of the ESOP write-off was congressional desire to boost employee ownership in their companies. The same sort of thinking is appropriate for EHOPs, where employees would own a share of their neighborhoods. It is not a large leap to see the benefits that could accrue to our inner cities if EHOPs and enterprise zones worked together.

Tax-Exempt Bonds

Federal tax policy should be amended to allow states with bond financing needs beyond their limits to obtain excess bond authority from another state(s). The allocation system might be changed so states needing extra funding could apply to the federal government for permission to use bonds not being utilized by other states. As an alternative, states should be given the ability to trade or sell excess bond authority.

A particularly effective bond-driven housing program is mortgage credit certificates, known as MCCs. Mortgage credit certificates are federal income tax credits issued through state housing agencies to eligible first-time home buyers. They are created solely out of a state's federal mortgage revenue bond (MRB) allocations.

Authorized by the Tax Reform Act of 1984, MCCs have the effect of increasing buyers' income (and purchasing power) by several thousand dollars, making first-time housing more affordable. Eligibility is determined by an applicant's income relative to local median income and housing cost. The reduction in tax liability is a percentage of the mortgage interest paid for the year, usually between 10 percent and 30 percent. MCCs are dollar-for-dollar reductions in tax due to the federal government and are therefore much more valuable than "above-the-line" tax deductions which translate to less than 100 percent tax reduction value.

Michigan has a very successful MCC program that operates until funding is exhausted each year. Since 1986, the Michigan Housing Development Authority has issued in excess of 8,000 MCCs worth nearly $308 million. Michigan MCCs carry a 20 percent tax credit. To date, approximately 80 percent of MCC loans have been made to first-time home buyers and 28 percent of all loans have gone to single females or female heads of households. MHDA estimates its MCC program provides an equivalent mortgage interest rate reduction of 2.5 percent. The key to Michigan's success has been lender enthusiasm for the program, which requires minimal documentation and provides application approvals in as little as 48 hours.

Policy and Program Options for State Housing Authorities and Finance Agencies

The states have responded to the decline in federal housing programs during the last decade by developing a variety of their own funding vehicles and programs. The most notable of these is, perhaps, the taxable housing bond, which is commonly used to supplement tax-exempt bond proceeds. Taxable bonds are sold by state housing authorities and backed by the taxing power of the state. Principal and interest on loans made from the taxable bond proceeds are paid to the housing agency and continuously recirculated into new loans. The original bond debt to create the loan pool is usually repaid from the state's general bond fund.

The State of California pioneered the use of taxable bonds and has approved multiple issues totalling more than $550 million. Of those funds, $300 million has gone into affordable housing, including new construction, $200 million for rehabs (including acquisition loans) and $50 million specifically for first-time home buyers. The new construction and rehab programs are administered through the California Department of Housing and Community Development and the first-time buyers program is done through the California Housing Finance Agency. To date, 349 affordable ownership units have been awarded and an additional 1,200 are in the pipeline. More than 2,600 rental rehab units have also been produced using taxable bond debt.

State-specific secondary-market programs have been used successfully to provide an outlet for nonconforming residential real estate loans held by state lending institutions, creating liquidity for loans that would have otherwise been moribund in portfolio. In return for the opportunity to sell these loans, lender participants perform a community or social service.

The Vermont Housing Finance Agency (VHFA), in concert with a consortium of Vermont state bankers and Fannie Mae, invented the Green Mountain Mortgage Market, dubbed "Sugar Mae," to increase statewide investment in affordable housing. The Vermont Housing Finance Agency issues state tax exempt housing bonds to fund the purchase of nonconforming product originated and held by Vermont lenders. These loans are pooled by VHFA, and credit enhanced and securitized by Fannie Mae before being sold into the secondary market. In return, selling lenders reinvest 50 percent of the loan sale proceeds into affordable housing. Such a program is a viable option for raising capital—from an existing source—in states where a substantial amount of capital is tied up in nonconforming loans.

The Rhode Island Housing and Mortgage Finance Corporation (RIHMFC) Lease/Purchase Initiative uses below-market state funds to finance housing purchases (existing and new construction) by nonprofits that, in turn, lease the units to prequalified future buyers. During the lease period, buyers make payments to an escrow account to build a 2.5 percent down payment for the house. In the case of new construction, the construction loan from RIHMFC is retired with below-market gap financing from local lenders and nonprofits. The gap financing is repaid within a maximum of two years from the proceeds of a 30-year fixed-rate mortgage provided by RIHMFC, once the buyer is fully qualified. The second 2.5 percent of the down payment may come from any source, including gifts. Ninety-five percent LTV mortgage insurance is provided through General Electric Mortgage Insurance Company. Fannie Mae purchases the first mortgages.

The State of Connecticut Trust Funds' Yankee Mac program, which started in 1981 and was just recently replaced, made available, as needed by market conditions, state pension fund dollars for below-market-rate mortgages to home buyers purchasing homes in the state. Total program volume totalled out about $500 million, with zero defaults. In 1986 Yankee Mac restructured its portfolio of pass-through certificates into a now common CMO/REMIC and sold it for a substantial profit. California and New Hampshire have similar programs.

Yankee Mac was a pioneer in the business of pension funds lending on residential real estate, and as such, faced limitations that are no longer necessary. In August of 1991, the state launched the second generation of Yankee Mac called the State Treasurers Affordable Residential (STAR) Mortgage Program, which takes advantage of the latest technology in the mortgage-backed securities market. The new program will originate 30-year mortgages on Connecticut homes at 50 basis points below Fannie Mae's current rate. The program will utilize Fannie Mae's Community Home Buyers Program underwriting (including the "3/2" up to 15 percent of a pool), except there will be no income limitation. The conforming loans will be pooled, securitized by Fannie Mae, and swapped back to the State on a regular basis. Jumbos will either be held in portfolio or sold to a conduit. Maximum LTV on conforming loans will be 95 percent. Maximum on jumbos will be 90 percent.

The new program is greatly simplified

and will provide greater liquidity and an unlimited ability to originate 95 percent LTV loans (with private mortgage insurance). Preference will be given, in the following order, to: beneficiaries who are first-time buyers; beneficiaries who are not first-time buyers; and then all other buyers purchasing a home in Connecticut. Refinance loans may be considered.

The State of New Jersey may soon have a unique source of funding for affordable housing that doesn't rely on taxes or bond issues and is revenue neutral. State Assemblyman Robert Franks has introduced a bill that would allow participating counties to pool residential rental security deposits into revolving funds that would make loans to affordable housing developers. County participation would be optional. Participating counties would name a board of trustees and undertake a self study of their housing needs and proportion loans accordingly. Loans would be made to public and private organizations at below market rates for no more than 20 years. Security deposits would be protected by a mandatory reserve account and interest on the deposits would accrue at the same rate as mandated under present law. The total amount of security deposit money statewide in New Jersey approximates $1 billion.

Another new concept is that of the state mortgage insurance programs to minimize the cost of mortgage insurance. State mortgage bond programs often require private mortgage insurance to protect against defaults on their high LTV loans. The cost to buyers of "retail" private mortgage insurance produces a "Catch-22" for program borrowers, who

are, by definition, among the least able to pay nonsubsidized mortgage insurance costs. Conversely, those who can afford private premiums are less likely to be eligible for state-sponsored funding. In addition, insurance on low-down-payment loans (95 percent or higher) for very low-income buyers often carry a substantial risk premium. The result is a limitation of the benefits of state housing bond programs.

At the state level it is also feasible to establish an information clearinghouse for use by organizations wanting to advance affordable housing. The private, nonprofit Community Information Exchange (CIE) in Washington, D.C., provides a national-level model for those wishing to spread the word on affordable housing and community economic development programs.

Other ideas that might be pursued at the state level include: neighborhood assistance programs (state-sponsored tax incentive programs that provide tax credits to businesses providing capital and other resources to distressed communities); tax-free (state tax only) mortgage revenue bonds; state second mortgages (soft seconds); state subsidized interest rates; and state funding for housing rehabilitation and conservation.

PROGRAM AND POLICY OPTIONS FOR MUNICIPAL GOVERNMENTS

Even with limited municipal government taxing capability, there are a number of finance-related concepts available to benefit affordable housing at the local level.

Tax Increment Financing (TIF) raises development/redevelopment funds through the use of bonds later retired from the incremental tax revenue generated from the improved property. There need not be any interruption in the pre-existing property tax stream. Generally, the "value-added" portion of the property taxes is used exclusively to first retire the bond debt before being added to the general property tax fund. TIF financing allows municipalities to fund development without incurring substantial costs.

During the 1980s, Madison, Wisconsin, used TIFs to finance more than 250 affordable housing units and various commercial projects in formerly blighted areas of its downtown. Madison officials view the TIF vehicle as gap financing for projects in the public interest that could not be done "but for" the utilization of TIF funds. The maximum city investment is capped at the present value of the expected incremental tax stream to the city over a period no longer than 23 years (by law). Madison has seen an increase in property values of more than $200 million in TIF districts.

Other avenues of fund raising are also available to municipalities. Depending on the amount of funding needed to reach jurisdictional goals, municipal housing bonds could provide some or all of the funding needed for a particular project or be used to leverage state, local or philanthropic money. Local government has within its purview the ability to modify property and transfer tax rates or rules and the passage of special taxes to serve particular purposes. For example, property tax relief for low-income people and projects may be the difference between housing and no housing for local citizens. Local jurisdictions can also use a system of fees and fee waivers to promote low-cost housing production. While unilateral local action is limited by funding constraints, creative use of these options alone could go a long way to meet community needs.

THE ROLE OF PUBLIC/PRIVATE PARTNERSHIPS

The public sector role in affordable housing may be severely limited for years to come. In turning to the private sector for social programs, one will find that it will, by nature, limit the amount of capital invested in perceived low-return investments. However, even with these limitations, a powerful result is possible when the public and private sectors combine. The following concepts and examples are illustrative.

Much has been done and continues to be done through public/private partnerships to develop programs that minimize mortgage payments and/or stretch qualifying incomes for first-time and low- and moderate-income home buyers. The Federal National Mortgage Association's Community Home Buyers Program and the Federal Home Loan Mortgage Corporation's Home Affordability Program relax underwriting criteria and down-payment requirements for first-time and low- and moderate-income home buyers.

The Federal National Mortgage Association, or Fannie Mae, has long been the leader in first-time and low- and moderate-income housing finance. To date, Fannie Mae has purchased more than $2 billion in low- and moderate-income loans and has recently announced a $10 billion commitment to be fulfilled by July 1993. Fannie Mae's low- and moderate-income programs span all facets of the business including public finance (bonds and tax credits), single and multifamily community lending, equity investment, and other specific programs designed to serve particular purposes. The Community Home Buyers Program, which incorporates liberalized underwriting and down-payment requirements with home ownership education, serves as the basis for many of its current programs. Fannie Mae also has recently announced its commitment to purchase $1 billion in employer-assisted home loans over the next three years as part of its "Magnet" program.

The Federal Home Loan Mortgage Corporation (Freddie Mac) has its own community home buyers program, called the Home Affordability Program (HAP), which is similar to Fannie Mae's program. Freddie Mac goes a step further than HAP with its "Michigan Initiative," which includes a sweat equity component and allows gift down payments up to 2.5 percent LTV. Despite Freddie Mac's $500 million commitment to the Michigan Initiative and the innovative underwriting it utilizes, the program has not been successful and has been undergoing revision.

Opportunities exist for affordable housing proponents to develop "challenge dollar" programs whereby federal, state, and local public and private organizations pledge certain amounts of matching dollars to supplement those already available for a particular purpose.

Innovative servicing may be yet another way to drive down costs associated with mortgages. By recognizing the differences between "A", "B," and "C" quality credits and adjusting servicing techniques to better address each, it may be possible to reduce the number of expected foreclosures and therefore the cost of mortgages and mortgage insurance across the board. While this is obviously not feasible below the national level, it would be possible for the mortgage insurance and lending industries to undertake an empirical study of the characteristics of various credit quality loans. It may be that modifications such as contacting borrowers before payments are due, immediately after a payment becomes late, and providing immediate counseling, as has been tested in isolated cases with positive results, could prove highly successfully in driving down the delinquencies that cause mortgage interest rates and insurance premiums to rise.

Employers, public and private, and labor unions in increasing numbers, are instituting employer-assisted housing programs to help employees purchase homes. Employers have found that it is necessary, on one hand, to offer such an incentive to attract and retain high-quality workers in high-cost urban areas of the country and, on the other hand, found that doing so makes for a happier, more stable and more productive work force. Employer-assisted housing programs are considered a "wave of the future" as an employee benefit and could become a major tool in combating the high cost of housing in urban America.

Recirculating capital pools, known as Community Loan Funds, Revolving Fund (loan) Pools, Mortgage or Rental Assistance Pools, or Benevolent Loan Funds, are pools of low-cost or free money made available by community-oriented sources which is loaned to buyers who need it to afford a home. The funds are recirculated among new buyers as they are repaid, thereby creating a long-term source of funds.

Housing trust funds, a similar concept, are capital pools funded from any continuous source, such as real estate ownership taxes (residential or commercial) or development fees, transfer taxes, or special taxes levied by governments to fund particular housing activities.

Community Land Trusts (CLTs) are nonprofit organizations that hold property in perpetuity for affordable housing. Land trusts build, rehab or renovate improvements on the property and lease or sell them to families at or below local median income for, usually, periods of 99 years. As nonprofit unleveraged landowners, CLTs eliminate the cost of land from the occupant's monthly payment, making such housing affordable for even the lowest-income families. Should a land trust close, ownership of all property is transferred to the nearest CLT. Land trust boards of trustees must be comprised of one-third tenants or owners.

Community land trusts utilize a unique qualifying process that requires prospective renters and buyers to donate their services to the trust for a period of time before becoming eligible for a home of their own. Upon getting a home, they are required to perform ongoing maintenance to their own and other trust properties each year. This builds a sense of community among land trust families and drives down the cost of ownership for all. Sweat equity is ultimately recognized as part of the down payment.

Financial, credit and homeownership counseling may be required. Closing costs must be paid from the buyer's own funds in cash at settlement. Return on owner's equity upon resale of a CLT property is capped using a formula that recognizes the amount of equity invested, improvements made, and market appreciation.

Similar to land trusts are mutual housing associations (MHAs) which are private, nonprofit 501(c)(3) (tax status) partnership organizations that develop new and rehab existing affordable housing. Mutual housing is cooperative; members, who do not have to be residents, pay a fee to join. Monthly housing costs are based upon property operating costs only, which have been minimized through the utilization of subsidies and grants from the public and private sectors. Residents of mutual housing associations are guaranteed a home for as long as they wish to stay. The majority of the board of directors is constituted of residents and potential residents. Unlike Community Land Trusts, MHAs are not committed to holding a particular property in perpetuity for affordable housing. They can move as necessary to larger or smaller facilities as needs dictate. Neighborhood Reinvestment Corporation, a national nonprofit organization, brought the mutual housing association concept to the United States from Europe and now provides direction and assistance to associations across the country.

"Linked deposits" tie socially minded individuals' bank deposits to community development loans (in this case, low-cost mortgages), thereby utilizing the banking system to underwrite mortgage credit. Investors earn a market or negotiated rate of return on their deposits, which are made available only for stipulated credit purposes.

On the local level it is possible to identify and rehabilitate existing homes and buildings that would be suitable for first-time and low- and moderate-income housing. Even the most cash-strapped municipalities can begin an affordable housing program if projects are begun on a one-at-a-time basis.

Credit Quality

No discussion of affordable housing can be complete without a discussion of credit quality, the basis of which is the integrity of the borrower. Lending experience has shown there are two types of people—good credits and bad credits—and they extend across all socioeconomic classes. Income is not the sole determinant of whether one will or will not pay his or her debts.

Knowing this, and given our ability to obtain and analyze data, the industry ought to be able to identify the common threads between good credits and bad credits and, perhaps, someday institutionalize 100 percent LTV loans. Ultimately, the industry might be able to move away from it emphasis on down payments and toward borrower creditworthiness.

Citizens and Southern National Bank, in conjunction with the Atlanta Mortgage Consortium (AMC), has developed a program to identify good credits and maximize the help the consortium can give them. Management at C&S has found that a "right-minded" buyer, with counseling and homeownership training is an excellent risk. Citizens and Southern and AMC have found the time spent at the front end is costly, but the return, in terms of limiting foreclosures, is very good.

PROFILE: NCNB COMMUNITY DEVELOPMENT CORPORATION

NCNB Community Development Corporation, the nonprofit community development subsidiary of NCNB National Bank of North Carolina, sells $85,000 homes (according to an NCNB CDC value-equivalency formula) for $65,000 to first-time and low- and moderate-income home buyers.

The keys to NCNB's program are strict management of development soft costs and innovative financing for buyers. Soft cost savings are derived from pre-selling units (no marketing costs), city write-downs on development parcels, the use of standardized project and unit plans, and the elimination of a developer's entrepreneurial profit on the project.

NCNB's financing structure utilizes a below-market first mortgage with an "elastic" (soft) second mortgage from local governments in Charlotte and Raleigh, North Carolina. NCNB CDC arranges 65 percent LTV first-mortgage financing through NCNB Mortgage Corporation at 75-100 basis points below market for its buyers. Local governments provide 35 percent LTV soft seconds at whatever rate and term are required to drive the borrower's monthly housing expenses down to 30 percent of gross monthly income. The 30 percent figure is NCNB's definition of "affordable" for individuals earning 50-80 percent of area median income. Interest rates on seconds have been as low as 2 percent with terms as long as 30 years. Credit and homeownership counseling is arranged by each city, either through a municipal government agency or the involvement of expert community groups. NCNB National Bank receives Community Reinvestment Act credit for the CDC's work.

The greatest obstacle to efficient first-time buyer and low- and moderate-income development, according to Dennis Rash, NCNB CDC's president, is maintaining a pipeline of ready purchasers. Qualifying low-income buyers (debt consolidation, cleaning up of credit records, obtaining divorces, establishing independent credit for female heads of households) is time-intensive. NCNB intends to build a continuous pipeline of 50-60 prepared buyers in the future to fuel its construction plans.

NCNB's focus on affordable ownership emanates from its belief that homeownership opportunity is the single strongest motivator for, and in, urban renewal. Owners have, by design, a long-term interest in revitalized neighborhoods, which continually build community commitment to affordable housing. The constraint in NCNB's development model is not production speed, but, rather, pipeline. A steady flow of buyers will allow production in Charlotte and Raleigh to grow to as much as 75 ownership opportunities per year in the near term.

Based upon its model, NCNB plans to develop additional affordable housing nationwide.

THE INFLUENCE OF FIRREA AND CRA ON AFFORDABLE HOUSING

The Financial Institutions Reform, Recovery and Enforcement Act of 1989, known as FIRREA, was a sweeping reform of existing law relating to all facets of thrift institution activity, including lending limitations and enhancements to the Community Reinvestment Act of 1977. Changes in these two areas are having a significant influence on the availability of funding for low- and moderate-income housing.

The Financial Institutions Reform, Recovery and Enforcement Act

While FIRREA has had a net positive impact on the thrift industry, the law does have two drawbacks that need to be addressed. The 100 percent capital requirement on apartment and single-family home construction imposed by FIRREA has all but eliminated thrift lending to multifamily affordable housing developers. A reduction in this requirement, specifically to bolster first-time and low- and moderate-income housing, significant enough to spur this segment of the market would be important to the resurgence of affordable multi- and single-family projects, rental and purchase. The same logic flows to the "Loans to One Borrower" rule, which limits the percentage of capital a thrift can lend to any one customer. Since strong demand for housing at the lower end of the spectrum is evident throughout the country, a waiver of or adjustment to the Loans to One Borrower provision to accommodate affordable housing, could be safe, useful and beneficial. An extension of the "credit crunch" to this seg-ment of the market is not warranted.

The Community Reinvestment Act

The Community Reinvestment Act of 1977, commonly referred to as CRA, was enacted by Congress to encourage banks to lend equitably throughout their communities. CRA was a response to redlining, the practice of not lending in particular geographic areas, which is interpreted as tantamount to discriminat-ing against particular income and ethnic groups.

Under FIRREA, CRA ratings and rat-ing criteria, which were previously con-fidential, are now made public after a

bank's regular regulatory examination. However, CRA does not dictate specific actions, activities, products or services necessary to satisfy the community reinvestment requirement. Generally, that which a bank offers or provides with regard to CRA is negotiated in consulta-tion with community groups who prov-ide information about community needs. This dialogue also provides some protec-tion from community protest about what is ultimately offered. It is important to note that the Act requires all CRA activit-ies of the bank to be consistent with safe and sound operation of the institution.

Four federal regulatory agencies are responsible for CRA examinations and enforcement: the Federal Deposit Insur-ance Corporation (FDIC), the Federal

Table 1.1

Rating	Definition
Outstanding	Record of meeting community credit needs. Explicit lending guidelines actively promoted and overseen by senior management and board members. Monitoring methods well documented.
Satisfactory	Supportive, but less comprehensive, program of determining demand for loans to neighborhood borrowers.
Needs to Improve	Inadequate program of assessing loan demand and services offered. Poor record of loan approval in low-income neighborhoods.
Substantial Noncompliance	Community needs rarely, if ever, considered by management and board. No viable neighborhood lending programs and little contact with community groups.

Reserve Board, the Comptroller of the Currency; and the Office of Thrift Supervision (OTS).

Currently, banks are rated as Outstanding, Satisfactory, Needs to Improve, or Substantial Noncompliance. Once issued, the law requires CRA ratings to be accompanied by a statement from the institution describing its community, the products it offers to meet community needs, and a self-evaluation of its CRA performance.

Compliance with CRA is measured by assessment factors in five "performance categories": ascertainment of community credit needs; marketing and types of credit extended; geographic distribution and record of opening and closing offices; discrimination and other illegal credit practices; community development activities. Copies of all rating-relevant material must be available, at a cost not to exceed the cost of reproduction, at the bank's main office and most of its branches.

The public disclosure amendment is specifically designed to place regulatory and public pressure on banks. Positive CRA ratings are critical to institutions with expansion plans because CRA performance has become a key factor in obtaining government approval for acquisitions, mergers, and new branches. In addition, socially conscious private investors, public agencies and local governments are now choosing depository institutions on the basis of CRA ratings. However, according to one account, it's been estimated that, through 1988, about 98 percent of financial institutions have received above-average CRA ratings. Institutions have become sensitive to the issue and are willing to

develop viable programs to meet the community needs.

CRA Sample Programs

Pittsburgh, Pennsylvania

In 1989, Mayor Sophie Masloff instituted the Pittsburgh CRA, a modified system which exceeds the CRA requirements set by the federal government. Using the Act's Neighborhood Investment Rating System, the city of Pittsburgh has transferred its $300 million in bank deposits to the five highest CRA ranked banks in the city. The city will revisit its ratings bi-annually, allocating its funds to those banks which have a strong history of investing in Pittsburgh's needy neighborhoods and the capability to provide the best cost structure and quality of service to the city.

Increased competition for city deposits has spawned concomitant investment in Pittsburgh's low- and moderate-income neighborhoods. As a result, Masloff has requested all municipal authorities and the public school system to adopt the city's system. In all, Pittsburgh's total deposits equal nearly one billion dollars.

Massachusetts

On January 15, 1991, the Massachusetts Bankers Association announced a $400 million initiative to increase bank investment in the state's lower-income areas. The intent of this multifaceted state-wide plan is both to encourage bank investment in low-income areas and to convince Massachusetts bankers to comply with all the state and federal CRA requirements.

The association identified the following four major "areas of need" for low-income neighborhoods: access to capital; increased mortgage lending; access to basic banking services; and the production of affordable housing. Next, three new corporations, the Massachusetts Housing Investment Corporation (MHIC), the Massachusetts Community and Banking Council (MCBC), and the Massachusetts Minority Enterprise Investment Corporation (MEIC) were created to address these needs.

Although start-up has been delayed by tax and legal issues, a mortgage fair held early in 1990 attracted 1,200 potential home buyers, 175 of whom were enrolled in bank-sponsored first-time home buyers classes.

Washington, D.C.

Citicorp Savings Bank of Washington awarded a $20,000 grant to Neighborhood Housing Services (NHS, see Chapter 6), a neighborhood-based organization that strengthens communities by rehabilitating and revitalizing housing. The grant will be used to create a multimedia resource center on home repair and housing issues in the District's troubled Petworth neighborhood. NHS plans to produce home-repair videotapes, books on housing issues, and displays comparing different qualities and styles of materials, such as paint, flooring and roofing tiles, to educate homeowners. The NHS staff also plans "hands-on" displays with plumbing and electrical fixtures.

Crestar Bank N.A. of Washington, D.C., has developed an innovative benefits program for potential buyers that requires less income to qualify for a loan, less cash for closing, utilizes local-government-subsidized second mortgage loans, and allows flexibility in the funding of closing costs. Programs like Crestar's, however constructed, are valuable resources in the community.

The Metropolitan Washington Airports Authority has adopted a policy of linked deposits to encourage the banking community to reinvest in the local, small, disadvantaged business community. In December of 1990, the MWAA advertised in the *Washington Post* for local, "outstanding"-rated banks to participate in the immediate investment of $7,785,000 of Authority funds. Such programs are increasingly common.

Future Directions for CRA Lending

Under CRA, lending institutions could work with the federal agencies and investment banking community to develop a program to securitize affordable-housing and other social-purpose/public-benefit loans into "CRA-qualified" mortgage securities. Such a system would move CRA loans out of lender portfolios and increase funding for community investment without a parallel increase in institutionally held assets.

Further, CRA credit could be attached to the affordable disposition of REO and other types of community benefit activity. This action would create an additional supply of affordable housing opportunities, provide a rational incentive for banks to reduce prices and qualification terms for the purchase of REO, and increase the safety and soundness of the institution by selling nonperforming assets.

Increasing Affordability through Low-Down-Payment Loans: the Role of the Mortgage Insurance Industry

Stuart M. Lopes
Executive Vice President
Risk Management
GE Capital Mortgage Corporation

The essential business of mortgage insurers is to help more people buy truly affordable homes. Without mortgage insurance (MI), most lenders wouldn't take the risk of providing mortgage loans with low down payments. Since the private MI industry began in 1957, we have helped make home ownership possible for millions of Americans.

In recent years, we've heard a lot of bad news about the prospects for affordable housing. During the 1980s, U.S. home ownership levels dipped for the first time in decades, particularly for people under age 35. Delinquencies and foreclosures rose to record levels. Regional housing recessions, increased consu-mer debt, and lower savings all worked together to make home ownership harder to achieve for people with low or moderate incomes.

But we in the private mortgage insurance industry have begun to focus on the good news: we can make housing more affordable for low- and moderate-income home buyers. We are discovering new ways to balance the need for affordable housing with the financial risks of mortgage lending. Let's begin by looking at a specific example of the challenges we're facing today.

Joanne Davis[1] carries a gun and, as a member of the Cleveland police force, she knows how to use it. Her beat covers half a dozen neighborhoods in the inner city. These neighborhoods are lined with row houses and small businesses, the kind of streets where children bounce balls on the sidewalks while adults relax on their stoops. As in any city, the quality of neighborhoods can change quickly. Joanne knows which streets are safe and which are not. She knows the parks and the shops, and where to find the best delis and restaurants. She also knows where to find the slums and crack houses, and it's her job to make those neighborhoods safer. Joanne loves Cleveland and is committed to her job. Recently she decided to buy a house on her beat.

Glenda Strader[1] is a mortgage loan underwriter for GE Capital Mortgage Insurance. Her job is to examine mortgage loan files, review information on borrowers and properties, and decide whether GE will insure the loan against default. On one particular day, Glenda's stack of files includes a loan for Joanne Davis. When Glenda opens that file, she sees the basic information illustrated below.

GE's underwriter is troubled by the appraiser's comments. She is wary about the adjacent commercial property, knowing that it might affect the value of nearby residential properties. The descriptions of loitering and boarded-up windows are even more disturbing. This modestly priced house could be in a deteriorating, high-crime neighborhood—not a good mortgage risk. The underwriter also is concerned about the borrower's debt ratio, which is slightly higher than the level recommended by GE's guidelines.

This is a tough case for Glenda. She isn't familiar with the property, and the strengths of the loan application must be weighed against potentially risky factors. Glenda is tempted to dismiss the loan immediately, knowing that a rejection could be supported. **She also knows that every insurance application we decline may represent a missed opportunity for revenue and profit.**

That missed opportunity has triggered important changes in the mortgage insurance business. Today we're insuring loans that we didn't know how to handle only a few years ago. GE and others in the mortgage insurance industry have

---

Borrower name: Joanne Davis

Annual income: $33,000

Appraised value/sales price of home: $55,000

Down payment: $2,750 (5%)

Total monthly debts as a percentage of monthly income: 39%

Borrower credit: No negative reports.

Appraiser's comments: Subject property is located beside a commercial establishment; observed loitering on nearest street corner. House appears to be in good repair, but two buildings on the next block have boarded-up windows.

begun to remove the "suburban blinders" that threaten to restrict our business unnecessarily and shut out potential homeowners from the market. We recognize that there is tremendous demand for affordable housing from low- to moderate-income people who can handle the responsibility of a mortgage. And we're beginning to explore ways to meet this demand profitably.

Did GE's underwriter approve Joanne Davis's loan for insurance? Let's leave that question open until we have addressed some of the broader issues of balancing risk management with housing affordability.

The Business of Affordable Housing

By now it should be clear that mortgage insurers are necessarily concerned with home *purchases* versus renting. While we recognize the plight of the homeless as a major national concern, such severe housing problems are beyond the scope of our business. We focus on employed people with low-to-moderate incomes, particularly first-time home buyers who might otherwise be shut out of the market.

As stated at the outset, affordable home ownership is the business of mortgage insurers. To understand why, consider the basic mechanics of mortgage insurance and why mortgage lenders need it.

For most home buyers, saving enough money for a down payment is the greatest barrier to home ownership. Traditionally, mortgage lenders have required a down payment of at least 20 percent of the home's purchase price. However, lenders will approve a mortgage with a smaller down payment if the loan is covered by mortgage insurance. Essentially, mortgage insurance helps people buy homes with a low down payment by protecting lenders from severe financial loss if the loan is not repaid. To be eligible for private mortgage insurance, the home buyer must make a down payment of at least 5 percent of the home's value. (In some cases, part of the down payment may come from a gift or certain kinds of loans. See "Other Innovations" below.)

Even though mortgages are secured with the purchased properties, it isn't easy to recover losses on low-down-payment loans. There are many expenses associated with a loan default. Interest accumulates during the delinquency period and then during foreclosure—a period which may last a year or more. Other costs include legal fees, home maintenance and repair expenses, real estate brokers' fees and other closing costs. These costs generally total 15 percent to 20 percent of the loan amount or more. After these expenses are paid, the lender may be left with a net loss. This loss is magnified if the foreclosed property is resold for less than its original sales price.[2]

The risk of loss is greater on loans with a small down payment. This makes sense intuitively. First, the more money a borrower has invested in a property, the less likely he or she is to default on the loan and lose that investment. Second, the higher the down payment, the lower the monthly payment. This may mean less financial strain on the home owner's budget.

Our experience at GE confirms that lower down payments are associated with higher risk. When a borrower defaults on a loan, the lender submits a claim for payment. Figure 2.1 shows GE's claim rates on loans with various down-payment sizes in relation to an index of GE's average claim rate. From 1987 through June 1991, we were 58 percent more likely to receive a claim on loans with a down payment of 10 percent or less. The claim rate declined steadily with larger down payments. With a 20 percent down payment or more, GE-insured loans were 21 percent less likely to result in a claim.

Our business is managing risk; we aren't looking for risk-free loans. All loans—regardless of the borrower and the property—carry a risk. However, we are looking to insure *reasonable* risks. It's our job to constantly define and redefine "reasonable risks" based on the best information available. And the more competent the MI industry becomes at managing these risks, the better we can support loans that make housing more affordable.

MANAGING THE RISK

Who Is at Risk?

Obviously, lenders, mortgage insurers and investors are concerned about the financial risk associated with mortgage loans—i.e., that the loan won't get repaid. But we haven't lost sight of the

---

Figure 2.1   Mortgage Insurance Claim Rates

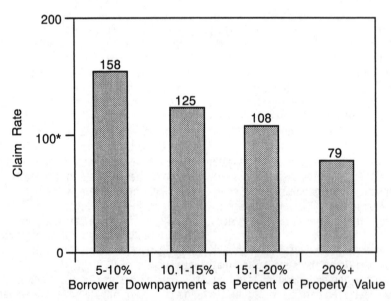

*100 = Index of overall GE Mortgage Insurance Company claims rate for mortgages originated 1987 through July, 1991.

fact that the home buyer also runs a risk—the risk of losing the home. For a person with a modest income, that risk may be more meaningful. When low- to moderate-income people manage to achieve homeownership, they may place a high value on it. They're also more likely to buy a home to obtain decent shelter, rather than for status or as a short-term investment.

Thus, the mortgage insurer, the lender and the home buyer each stand to lose when the loan defaults. The MI company will be obligated to pay the claim for loss. Loan servicing income is curtailed, and the claim payment may not be sufficient to cover all of the lender's losses. The borrower, of course, may lose his home and its equity. So in a very real sense, homeowners, lenders and mortgage insurers share a common interest in ensuring that the risks we accept on a loan are reasonable, both when the loan is approved and into the future.

Striking a Balance

Lenders and MI companies assess risk by underwriting loans. Underwriting is the process of collecting and analyzing information on the borrower and the property to decide whether the loan represents a reasonable risk. There's nothing new about this process; lenders have always underwritten loans with varying degrees of strictness and formality.

However, underwriting and risk management are more complicated than they used to be. Following World War II, the United States enjoyed nearly three decades of economic prosperity. As a country, we reaped the benefits of low interest rates, moderate inflation and low unemployment, along with high housing appreciation and income growth. Increasing home values and a strong economy helped borrowers avoid loan defaults. Inflation served to mask poor underwriting. When a default did occur, the property often could be sold for more than the original purchase price. Thus, loan defaults were not a major concern. Nationwide foreclosure rates stayed well below 1 percent, leading many lenders to become complacent about loan quality as they sought to increase market share.

All of this began to change in the early '80s. Inflation slowed down and interest rates shot up. The 1981-82 recession was accompanied by severe problems in some of the nation's basic industries, and unemployment rose to nearly 10 percent. Consumer debt levels increased, and people found it harder than ever to save money.

In an effort to help make home ownership more affordable, many lenders developed new loan instruments. Adjustable-rate mortgages became popular, and some of these genuinely helped home buyers. However, there were also higher-risk loans, such as those that allowed loan balances to actually increase (negative amortization). Borrowers with certain kinds of negatively amortizing loans risked owing more on their houses than the original loan amount. The risks were exacerbated by high unemployment and regional economic problems. It didn't take long before these conditions produced the inevitable: skyrocketing foreclosures and delinquencies, resulting in lost homes and lost money.

This experience provided a much-needed impetus to improve risk management in the housing finance industry. Now there is a general awareness that "the good old days" are over, and we can't go back. As a whole, we in the housing finance business have recognized that mortgage loan instruments require certain safeguards. We have learned to control the dangers of negative amortization, and we know that adjustable-rate mortgages need sensible interest rate caps (maximum interest rates allowed within a defined period of time). We're becoming more experienced in monitoring the economy and projecting regional economic conditions. As we've stopped relying on inflation to cover mistakes, our underwriting has improved tremendously. And we recognize that providing mortgage loans to unqualified borrowers doesn't serve anyone well in the long run.

Nevertheless, because of larger economic issues, mortgage lending remains a risky business. The savings and loan crisis has jolted the entire financial services industry, making us even more aware of the need for sound risk practices. Local and regional markets are always in a state of flux, requiring constant vigilance and the ability to adapt quickly to changes. Taken together, all of these factors have spurred better risk management among mortgage lenders, insurers and investors.

At the same time, the "crunch" in affordable housing has produced new market demands and imperatives. Congress has directed insured financial institutions to serve the lending needs in their communities, as evidenced by the newly strengthened mandates of the Community Reinvestment Act (CRA). The Act requires depository institutions to address credit needs in *all* sectors of the markets they serve when it is possible to do so profitably. This mandate has posed a challenge for mortgage lenders, who must strike a balance between complying with CRA and prudently managing risk.

Underwriting as an Art

One way that MI companies are helping lenders comply with CRA is by constantly improving our ability to assess and manage risk. Since the MI industry began in 1957, it has helped nine million families buy homes with small down payments. We've learned a lot by underwriting these loans, and our knowledge is helping us better serve low- to moderate-income borrowers.

How do we decide whether a loan poses a reasonable risk? Our business would be easy if we could pin loan defaults down to one or two factors, but that isn't the case. Every mortgage loan is unique, and a variety of factors may contribute to default. Among the most important items we examine are:

- Down-payment size (as a percentage of property value)

- Potential for property appreciation or depreciation

- The borrower's willingness to pay

Other factors that may affect the risk of a loan include the purpose of the loan (e.g., a primary residence versus a vacation home), the type of mortgage instrument (e.g., fixed interest rate versus adjustable interest rate), the source of down-payment funds, income ratios, and the borrower's job stability.

Underwriting, then, is the process of examining each of these risk factors, weighing and balancing them as a whole, and determining whether the loan represents an insurable risk. The process is facilitated by specific underwriting guidelines. For example, there are guidelines for assessing a borrower's debt situation that are standard throughout the industry.

In the aftermath of the 1980s' loan default boom, underwriting guidelines became more restrictive and were applied more rigidly. In fact, many lenders and mortgage insurers became "matrix" underwriters, so called because underwriting was performed as quantitatively as possible under absolute guidelines and formulas. For example, if a borrower's debt-to-income ratio was even one percentage point higher than the prescribed level, the loan might automatically be disapproved. This kind of restriction can be programmed into underwriting software so that the underwriter's computer refuses to proceed with the steps necessary to approve the loan.

Although GE uses computers to assist with underwriting, we don't allow them to make our decisions. Increasingly, we have recognized that underwriting is an art, not a science. If a loan falls outside the guidelines of one item, it may have other compensating factors that make us comfortable with the risk. Our underwriting philosophy has evolved to recognize that no single characteristic of the borrower or the property determines the overall quality of a loan.

What's so wrong with matrix underwriting? After all, it saves time and provides consistent results.

It's true that a matrix approach makes underwriting decisions simpler. Perhaps we could even replace our underwriters with machines. But given that we want to insure any loan that makes sense, we must rely on the good judgment of our underwriters. No one has developed a machine that can process all the combinations of relevant factors that result in a common-sense underwriting decision.

A balanced approach to underwriting not only helps maintain our profitability, but also it is the key to serving lower-income borrowers. We want our lenders to show us any loan that makes sense from a risk perspective, regardless of the price of the house. As we dig deeper into available data on lower-income borrowers, we're discovering that they may represent some of the lowest-risk loans we insure.

Exploding the Myths

Assume that we have two potential home buyers. The first one is a successful businessman who owns a restaurant in a medium-sized city. He makes $120,000 a year, and he wants to buy a stylish home in the suburbs. The second home buyer lives in the same city and, in fact, has lived there all of his life. He is a high-school teacher who earns $30,000 a year, and he wants to buy a home in the modest neighborhood where his school is located. Both buyers plan to make a 5 percent down payment. All other things being equal (creditworthiness, debt ratios, etc.), who represents the greatest risk for a lender and mortgage insurer?

Contrary to what one might expect, our experience indicates that the high-school teacher is the best bet. In fact, if all other factors are equal, lower-income borrowers are generally more likely to make their house payments on time.

Figure 2.2 shows delinquency rates by

borrower income range for GE-insured loans that were originated from 1987 through June 1991. The delinquencies are indexed to GE's overall average delinquency rate. As shown in the figure, borrowers with annual incomes less than $40,000 were 8 percent less likely to become delinquent on their loan payments. In fact, **the lowest income group had the best record on delinquencies.** Other income groups hovered around the overall average, with the exception of the highest income group. For borrowers with an annual income of $100,000 or more, the delinquency rate was 58 percent higher than average.

Similarly, industry experience shows that higher loan amounts also pose a greater risk of default. According to a 1989 study conducted by the MI industry trade group, Mortgage Insurance Companies of America (MICA), as the loan amount increases, the risk of default also increases. The study was based on an analysis of more than 500,000 loans insured by all private mortgage insurers between 1979 and 1987. The results showed that loans between $90,000 and $105,000 are 7 percent more likely to default than loans under $90,000. Loans between $106,000 and $130,000 are 16 percent more likely to default. This stair-

---

Figure 2.2   Mortgage Delinquency Rates

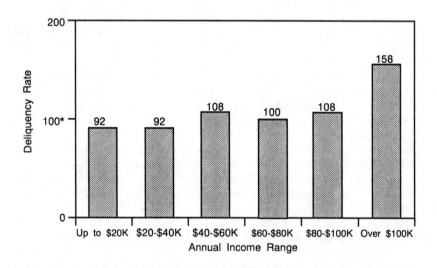

*100 = Index of overall GE Mortgage Insurance Company claims rate for mortgages originated 1987 through July, 1991.

step progression continues as loan balances rise, reaching a peak for loans over $188,000, which are 56 percent riskier than loans under $90,000.[3]

To understand why high-income, high-balance loans are riskier, it is important to remember that people need houses for shelter. Higher-income people have more options for satisfying that need. For example, when they have trouble making their mortgage payment, affluent home owners may figure it makes sense to default and bear the short-term expense of moving to a more modest home. Moving may not be feasible for people with low and moderate incomes; they generally have fewer attractive options for housing. Thus, even during times of economic strain, homeowners with low-to-moderate incomes may have greater incentive to continue paying their mortgages.

Understanding the Borrower

GE's experience in Boston provides a good example of the connection between income levels and risk. As everyone knows, during the past few years property values in Boston have softened. To help cushion the risk of declining property values, many lenders and mortgage investors are requiring higher down payments from home buyers in the Boston area. Some lenders and MI companies are no longer considering 95 percent loan-to-value (5 percent down payment) loans.

During this economic downturn, GE's Boston office has continued to underwrite low-down-payment loans. We believe that high-quality business continues to exist among low- to moderate-income home buyers, even in a soft market. And when we underwrite these loans, we look beyond the numbers. We weigh and balance every risk factor and actively look for information that will help us approve the loan.

One important factor is a borrower's personal ties to the metropolitan area. We notice how long the borrower has lived in the area and whether he or she has family members who live nearby. It's harder to walk away from a house when you're attached to the larger community. It's less likely that you'll default on a loan if you have close family members who might offer assistance. Borrowers' proximity to their place of employment also makes a difference. The closer they live to their jobs, the more comfortable we can feel about their loans.

Consider this example. In 1988, GE insured five low-down-payment loans in a condominium project located near Boston. Within a year or two, the value of those condos plunged significantly. Many of the condo occupants walked away from their loans. Dozens of units went into foreclosure. But the five borrowers that GE insured are still living in their condos and making their mortgage payments—in spite of the fact that their mortgage balance is higher than the current value of the property.

Why do those borrowers decide to stay? We can't explain it with absolute certainty, but our knowledge of the borrowers and the city provides enough clues to build a plausible theory. When underwriting those loans, we analyzed all the traditional risk factors: credit, property, job stability and income ratios. We also found additional information. The borrowers are natives of the area, and probably have relatives who live nearby. They have good job stability in local businesses. And, because they have lower incomes, this housing represents fundamental shelter. Boston rental rates have remained relatively high, even during the recession. Moving is expensive, and these borrowers can't easily walk down the street and find cheaper housing. Finally, because of their ties to the community, these borrowers appear less likely to turn in their keys and walk away. This additional knowledge helps us say yes to a low- to moderate-income home buyer and underscores our philosophy of insuring every loan that makes sense.

This example highlights the importance of knowing a community. Increasingly, we have recognized that even the most sophisticated underwriting can lead to erroneous conclusions without specific knowledge of local economic conditions and trends. To take it a step further, good risk management also requires greater knowledge of local communities. We need to understand more about borrowers than just their underwriting ratios. These are areas where we in the MI industry realize we need help.

Assuming Risk in Local Markets, Nationwide

There's an interesting paradox in the MI business: on the one hand, the need for affordable housing affects individuals and families in the individual communities. All housing is local, as the saying goes. On the other hand, nationwide risk dispersion is crucial in safely assuming the particular risk of any one mortgage. Most mortgage insurers operate on a national basis, which provides the geographic dispersion necessary to protect policyholders during regional economic cycles.

Few, if any, individual mortgage lenders or investors could accomplish this dispersion on their own.

Broad risk dispersion is particularly relevant to our ability to support low-down-payment lending. It would be much more difficult to insure 95 percent loan-to-value loans in soft markets, such as Boston, if we weren't also insuring higher-down-payment loans in stronger markets. We can maintain overall quality in our insured business through a dispersion of borrower types, collateral types, price ranges, down-payment sizes and property locations. Risk dispersion is a fundamental tenet of risk management.

This risk dispersion allows us to accept risks that few locally based operations could assume. At the same time, we understand that *local knowledge is essential for good risk management.*

Loan underwriters understand that it's an important part of their job to know their market areas. GE has 29 branch offices located all over the country, which allows us to provide underwriting service that is geared toward the needs of particular markets. As often as possible, our underwriters spend time with appraisers and others knowledgeable about the local market. These efforts are greatly aided by our Regional Risk Managers, who monitor broader economic trends in each of seven regions, collect market data and provide our underwriters with detailed analyses on loan performance and property value trends.

This continuous monitoring of the real estate market is essential for a company that holds risk in every part of the nation. However, as a nationwide company, we recognize that our strength lies in our ability to spot trends in broad regional markets. When it comes to detailed knowledge of local markets, we must rely on the expertise of the people who live and work in those areas. More and more often, we have turned to community lenders, state and local housing agencies, and grass roots housing organizations.

These local organizations have a vital role in expanding housing opportunities in their communities. If we are to be most effective in helping more people buy homes, neither the government nor local groups nor national corporations can do it alone. We must combine financial strength, risk dispersion and commitment to affordable housing with detailed knowledge of local markets.

SHARING RISK THROUGH PARTNERSHIPS

What do you get when you cross a profit-driven mortgage insurance company with a community-based, not-for-profit group dedicated to housing lower-income people?

The short answer is "more" — more affordable housing and more quality business. That's what happened in 1989 when GE teamed up with the National Training and Information Center (NTIC, formerly known as National People's Action). In 1989, GE and NTIC, in conjunction with Fannie Mae, began housing demonstration programs in Chicago, Cleveland, Indianapolis, Philadelphia, and St. Louis. These "Home Lending Programs" provided low- and moderate-income families with greater access to mortgages and reduced their cash costs at loan closing.

This venture caused at least a few ripples in the industry. Since 1972, the NTIC has been known as an aggressive group that vigorously championed housing causes for low-income people. GE is known as a practical, profit-motivated corporation. Some people thought the two organizations made strange bedfellows.

But we in the MI industry had already begun to recognize that there was no conflict between our goals and those of the NTIC. The NTIC had the local market expertise and the motivation to help people move into homes they could really afford to own. Fannie Mae was willing to buy the loans—a big plus for the lenders who would originate the mortgages. And GE had the capital and the expertise to underwrite the risk, which we found to be a reasonable one. A partnership among the three of us made sense.

By this time, GE was already involved in other innovative partnerships as well. In November 1988, we announced our first risk-sharing program with the New Hampshire Housing Finance Authority. This deal was quickly followed by similar agreements with the housing finance agencies of Massachusetts, Rhode Island, and Pennsylvania. Under each of these programs, the agency agreed to assume a portion of the risk, thereby creating the first co-insurance agreements for mortgage revenue bond programs. In return, GE not only reduced the price of insurance, but also offered more flexible underwriting guidelines. The lower MI premium means that borrowers pay less cash when the loan closes. Less restrictive guidelines allow more low-income borrowers to qualify for a mortgage.

As of June 1991, GE had insured

more than 7,000 loans in risk-share programs. The delinquency rate for that portfolio has been the same as that for our overall business, less than 2 percent.

These risk-share programs represent a significant start in making housing more affordable in the participating states. They also have alerted us to the potential for expanding affordable housing through similar types of partnerships in the future.

Reducing Risk Through Education

As the MI industry has strengthened its focus on affordable housing, we've also taken a harder look at the home buyer's role in reducing risk. Buying a home is often a confusing, stressful process. Home buyers at *any* income level may feel overwhelmed by the decision and all the complications that may surround it. For lower-income, first-time buyers, these stresses may be magnified. As these buyers get caught up in the home-buying process, they may be tempted to buy more than they can truly afford. On the other hand, they may give up on ownership prematurely.

Although it's hard to prove quantitatively, we believe that well-informed buyers are more likely to make good home-buying decisions. To help mortgage lenders provide consumer education, GE and Fannie Mae joined forces to develop the **Community Home Buyer's Program**. The program reduces the income needed for a borrower to qualify for a mortgage, and enables closing costs to be financed with an unsecured loan. In addition, the program waives the usual cash reserve require-

ment, and allows borrowers to establish their credit through nontraditional methods of credit verification, such as records of rent and utility payments.

To be eligible to participate in the Community Home Buyer's Program, borrowers are asked to complete a course on home buying. The course includes such practical information as how to estimate an affordable housing price and monthly mortgage payment. It also covers topics such as home inspection, the loan closing and how to develop a personal budget. The most recent version of GE's program includes worksheets and a case study that give home buyers an opportunity to test their knowledge. For maximum flexibility, lenders may offer either classroom instruction or a "Home Study Guide" that can be completed independently by participants and reviewed by the lender.

We're also incorporating buyer education in other targeted programs. For example, in cooperation with Freddie Mac, GE recently agreed to insure loans for a special affordable housing program offered to AFL-CIO members. That program includes an educational component that covers much of the same material offered in the Community Home Buyer's Program.

Another outgrowth of the Community Home Buyer's Program is the **Community Home Improvement Loan**. This loan program expands the range of housing choices for low- to moderate-income buyers by allowing them to combine the price of a house and the cost of repairs into one insured, long-term loan, as long as the repairs do not exceed 30 percent of the house's value after improvements. The program is administered by the lender, who oversees the improvement process and the release of improvement funds from escrow.

Because the data is so recent, it's too early to make any definitive statements concerning the performance of the Community Home Buyer's Program. However, the preliminary indications look promising. For the 1,573 Community Home Buyer's loans ($145 million) that GE had insured as of July 1991, the delinquency rate was only six-tenths of 1 percent. We are betting that an informed borrower is a better borrower.

Other Innovations

Because saving enough money for a down payment often poses the greatest barrier to home ownership, we've also looked for new ways to ease that burden for lower-income buyers. One particularly popular option, also available through the Community Home Buyer's Program, is a "3/2" plan. Under this plan, borrowers may make a down payment of only 3 percent from their own funds. The remaining 2 percent of the down payment may be financed through an unsecured note or a cash gift from an immediate family member.

Another way GE has helped reduce cash requirements is through our **Easy One** premium plan. Generally, home buyers must pay closing costs of 3 to 6 percent of the loan amount, including the mortgage insurance premium. These costs can hit lower-income buyers particularly hard. In our standard coverage program for 95 percent loan-to-value loans, buyers pay one percent of the loan amount for the first-year premium and one half of 1 percent on renewal pre-

miums. With Easy One, the buyer pays only six-tenths of 1 percent for the first year and for each year thereafter. On a $60,000 loan, this means that the borrower saves about $250 in closing costs. Combined with the other features of the Community Home Buyer's Program, this MI program can make a real difference to lower-income borrowers.

Even with this type of assistance, some borrowers still have difficulty finding the cash required to close a loan. To help them, we're exploring ways to offer a lease-purchase program. In this program, the potential home buyer makes monthly payments into an escrow account in addition to his rent. Within a year or two, the escrow funds may be drawn out to help make a down payment on the house. This allows the borrower to enjoy the benefits of living in the home while providing a structured way to work toward ownership. Although we're still experimenting with this program, we believe it's an option worth pursuing, particularly in areas where housing prices are above average. Strong nonprofit groups are a key to this program's ultimate success, since they typically buy and lease the home while the purchaser accumulates a down payment.

What's Ahead?

Although we're proud of the programs described above, we recognize that they're only a beginning. There is tremendous untapped potential for finding ways to increase home ownership safely and profitably. Affordable housing represents an ongoing challenge, and we expect to continue addressing that challenge through the '90s and on into the next century. The task is a formidable one that will surely evolve with future business developments, but there are several actions we are focusing on today:

(1) Keep a fresh perspective and remain open to changes.

The first challenge that we at GE faced was making our organization receptive to loans that look different. There's more uncertainty and more work involved in underwriting loans with unfamiliar collateral or borrower characteristics. Managers must continuously support and reward underwriters for rising to the challenge. On a nationwide basis, CRA requirements have done much to produce positive actions in the lending industry, and we believe the continuing demand from consumers also will serve as a catalyst. But we must constantly work to keep affordable housing issues at the forefront and base our decisions on hard facts rather than conventional wisdom. In short, we must remain open to new ways of doing business.

(2) Sharpen our underwriting and analysis.

The better we become at underwriting, the more loans we will be able to insure for low- and moderate-income buyers. We will continue to analyze loan performance, monitor markets and re-evaluate our view of reasonable risks. The moment we think we have a handle on risk issues, the world changes. We must learn to see the world as it is—not as we want it to be—and to expect constant change.

(3) Expand our ability to work with housing finance agencies and community groups.

To serve the low- to moderate-income market fully, we need local market knowledge and skillfully packaged public subsidies to complement our underwriting skills. Affordable housing specialists in housing finance agencies and nonprofit development companies offer the knowledge, resources and practical capabilities we all need to make a significant difference in bringing more affordable homes to the market.

As we continue to support and sponsor affordable housing programs, we will not yield on loan quality. Our initiatives must be based on sound risk management principles that contribute to the profitability of the company. On the other hand, we also recognize there are more subjective, long-term payoffs, too. None of us wants to live in a society where our teachers, fire fighters, and police officers can't afford to buy a house.

Which brings us back to Joanne Davis, the Cleveland police officer described at the beginning. GE's underwriter might have rejected the Davis loan, but she decided to investigate further. She contacted an appraiser who was familiar with Cleveland's inner-city properties, and he agreed to take a look at the house. When he reported back, he had unearthed some facts that weren't in the loan file.

First, Ms. Davis's proposed house was located beside a post office on a bustling street. As with many post offices, the nearby corners were common gathering places for local residents. That explained the sinister-sounding "loitering" that was referred to in the first property appraisal. The appraiser also explained the boarded-up windows. The subject neighborhood was on its way up economically, and renovations were taking place. There was crime in the area, but it was concentrated in an area nearly ten blocks away, in an entirely different neighborhood. In the second appraiser's opinion, the house was worth its sale price.

In addition to these facts, GE's underwriter had additional information: Ms. Davis's obvious commitment to the city and her job. Overall, there were enough risk-compensating factors to mitigate concern about a high debt ratio, and GE approved the loan for insurance.

Our decision on Joanne Davis's loan had less to do with underwriting guidelines and formulas than experience and common sense applied to the particular facts of her case. Our underwriters evaluate loans one by one, person by person. In the final analysis, there is one fundamental way to measure our success in this business: by the number of people we help buy homes they can truly afford.

Endnotes

1. "Joanne Davis" and "Glenda Strader" are fictitious names. The loan discussed is based on an actual underwriting case, though names and other particulars have been modified.

2. Much of the information on mortgage insurance and lender losses was drawn directly from the Mortgage Insurance Companies of America *1990-1991 Factbook and Membership Directory*.

3. "Capital Update," Mortgage Insurance Companies of America, December 1989.

Chapter 3

The Chase Community Development Corporation: A Model of For-Profit Affordable Housing Lending

Mark A. Willis
President
The Chase Community Development Corporation

INTRODUCTION

The Chase Community Development Corporation (CCDC) provides financing for the development of low- and moderate-income communities, primarily in the New York metropolitan area. Envisioned from the start as a separate, for-profit business, this subsidiary of the Chase Manhattan Corporation offers a wide range of products for both housing and economic development. Although legally allowed to make equity investments, it has primarily limited itself to the role of lender. Since its establishment in the summer of 1989, it has grown rapidly to encompass five business units and some 40 employees, making it one of the largest bank community development corporation (CDC) in the country. By focusing narrowly on this specialized marketplace, the CCDC has already been able to commit over $300 million, well ahead of plan based on Chase's initial pledge to commit $200 million over the first five years.

The mission of the CCDC is simple and straightforward: to support housing and economic development in low- and moderate-income communities. This is not just another bank CDC, because it takes its mission one step further. For the CDC, community development lending is more than just making loans in a community. Therefore, in addition to seeking to increase Chase's share of this particular marketplace, the CCDC also seeks to expand the size of that marketplace. Through education, it makes bank financing more accessible to people who may never before have thought that they

37

could borrow enough money to buy a home. Through its special focus on community-based development, it has helped to strengthen and expand the role of community groups and tenant organizations in the development of their neighborhoods. And through innovative approaches to structuring deals, it has been able to bring financing to projects that would otherwise have been unbankable. With no minimum loan size and a unique knowledge of local neighborhoods and of government programs, the CCDC has been able to turn into reality projects that had previously only been dreams.

Not only has the CCDC been able to become an active lender, but it has also demonstrated that lending in this marketplace can be done without sacrificing portfolio quality or ability to earn income. Key to the ability of the CCDC to lend effectively and profitably has been its establishment as a business unit with a narrowly defined marketplace, its ability to tap and build upon the strengths of other parts of Chase, and its highly motivated and skilled staff. Before going into detail on each of these elements, it is important to understand how the CCDC has structured itself to be able to offer a set of products carefully tailored to carry out its mission.

THE STRUCTURE OF THE CCDC

To serve each of the major areas within its marketplace, the CCDC established five distinct operating units: Residential Mortgages, Third-Party Lending, Direct Lending, Community-Based Development Lending, and Small Business Lending. Each has its own expert knowledge and product mix to maximize the

CCDC's ability to support housing and economic development in low- and moderate-income communities. The following sections set forth the different approaches of each of the units.

Residential Mortgage Unit

The first unit is the Residential Mortgage Unit, which offers 15- and 30-year fixed-rate home mortgages to purchasers of one- to four-family homes, cooperatives, and condominiums. The CCDC originally held all its loans in its own portfolio but has since forged a strong relationship with Fannie Mae (see Chapter 5), which has been willing to stretch its regular programs to match the lending policies of the CCDC. Presently, the CCDC sells most of its loans to the secondary market. Rather than act as a constraint, this utilization of the secondary market has only strengthened the CCDC's ability to tailor its products to respond to the varying characteristics of the many and diverse communities in the New York metropolitan area. By developing a close working knowledge of these communities and a close working relationship with Fannie Mae, the CCDC has been able to help many borrowers who might not otherwise have been served. And, for those few loans which cannot qualify under the secondary-market criteria, the CCDC can easily accommodate them in its own portfolio.

One way that knowledge of the community has been utilized is the recognition of so-called Sou-Sou accounts in the West Indian community. These accounts have long existed and are an informal way of pooling savings. Money from these accounts should be eligible for meeting the down-payment requirements for a home loan, but the standard mortgage banking rules preclude such a use unless the money has been in a bank account for at least two months. The CCDC led the way for change and now accepts money taken directly from Sou-Sou or similar types of accounts for the down payment. The result has been the development of a unique market niche for the CCDC in the Caribbean-American home ownership communities in central Brooklyn (Bedford-Stuyvesant, Bushwick, East New York, Brownsville, etc.). But the CCDC did not quit there, it reached out to encourage Fannie Mae to also accept money paid directly from Sou-Sou accounts.

The two organizations have continued to cooperate in finding ways to accommodate other unique aspects of the New York metropolitan region market. Armed with its extensive knowledge of the local housing stock, for example, the CCDC has been able to work with Fannie Mae to accept three- and four-family homes, and to eliminate any limits on the proportion of the loans going to two-family homes, bringing their treatment in line with that of single-family homes.

In addition, the CCDC's home mortgage products conform to the basic features of Fannie Mae's standard Community Home Buyer's Program. These features include as little as 5 percent down and a waiver of the normal requirements for cash reserves to cover monthly expenses. Also, the applicant's borrowing power is enhanced by raising to 33-38 percent the acceptable percentages of the borrower's gross income that is available for, respectively, housing costs and total debt costs including housing costs. The program also allows credit histories to be created from payment records for rent or utility bills when the borrower does not have a formal credit history established. As a result of this last option, the CCDC has been able to increase by about 10 percent the potential pool of borrowers for whom it has been able to make home ownership possible.

To ensure that its products are as accessible as possible, the CCDC has taken some additional steps on its own. First, it has waived the application fee and limited the commitment fee to 1 percent, thus reducing the up-front cash requirements. Second, it maintains all of the processing and underwriting in-house and in one location, providing the CCDC with complete control of the approval process. And third, the CCDC has consciously kept its origination unit small, allowing it to offer personal attention. Such attention can often be critical, especially if problems exist with the borrower's credit file. The CCDC gives the borrower the time and support to correct erroneous data or to provide explanations which mitigate the existence of any past credit problems.

A review of the characteristics of approved borrowers speaks for itself. Of those who are purchasing existing homes, some one-third rely at least in part on money from a Sou-Sou or equivalent account. Co-borrowers are common and the relationships among them do not fit the standard mold. While a number of the loans are made to single individuals or married couples, as many as three quarters of these loans involve at least one co-borrower who is not a spouse. These co-borrowers are generally part of the extended family: a brother/sister, an aunt/uncle, a father/mother, a son/daughter.

The Residential Mortgage Unit is constantly seeking to identify new sources of business. It conducts one to two educational seminars a month in conjunction with local churches and community groups to broaden the market for home mortgages. Many people in low- and moderate-income communities have not had any previous experience in selecting a home or in applying and qualifying for a loan. These seminars provide valuable information to facilitate the process of buying a home. The unit is also looking for new outlets for its products to make them more available to its target marketplace. One approach now being explored is to work with community development credit unions, which can then offer the CCDC's specialized mortgage products to their members.

Besides residential mortgages the unit also offers construction financing for the rehabilitation of vacant one- to four-family row houses auctioned by the City of New York. This product is part of the Urban Home Loan Program which was started by Chase in 1981. Some one hundred buildings (over 300 units of housing) have been restored to the city's occupied housing stock as a result of this special rehabilitation program.

The unit constantly seeks ways to improve its existing products and to develop new ones. Recently, it helped Fannie Mae develop its moderate rehabilitation program, which the CCDC is offering as a way to fix up "handyman specials." It is also working on products for residential properties that have commercial uses on the first floor and to expand its existing one- to four-family products to cover the kind of six-family homes that characterize the housing stock in a number of New York City neighborhoods.

Not surprisingly, portfolio performance for this unit has been excellent. Home buyers in the CCDC's target neighborhoods value their newly achieved piece of the American dream and fight hard to preserve it. Moreover, a unique type of risk diversification is achieved within the portfolio by having loans backed by multiple co-borrowers each with their own independent earning power. Although most of the loans are not very old, the preliminary results are very encouraging. None of the home mortgages in Chase's portfolio have been delinquent, let alone in default. And the performance of the inherently riskier construction loans made under the Urban Home Loan Program has been marred by only one pre-existing problem loan that resists all efforts to help the borrowers get back on track.

By paying attention to the characteristics of the many different and diverse neighborhoods in the New York City metropolitan area, the residential mortgage unit has seen its business grow rapidly from its inception to a volume presently running at a rate of $50 million a year.

Third-Party Lending Unit

This unit lends to not-for-profit or government-sponsored financial intermediaries which have developed an expertise in serving markets that overlap with those of the CCDC. Rather than view these organizations as competitors, the CCDC sees them as vehicles to offer products and services to meet needs which it cannot satisfy itself either because demand is so high or because the intermediary can provide the service more efficiently. Generally, lines of credit are advanced to capitalize loan funds, allowing the organization to re-lend the funds to individual projects. These advances are made at rates below market levels but above the unit's cost of funds, permitting the intermediary the option to add on a spread to cover its operating costs.

The CCDC is currently involved with five such intermediaries. The best-known multibank consortium is the Community Preservation Corporation (CPC), which also includes savings banks and insurance companies. CPC was set up specifically to work in partnership with government, and over its 18-year history has helped rehabilitate over 33,000 units of low- and moderate-income housing in New York City. Chase was one of the driving forces behind the creation of CPC in 1974, and it continues to participate actively on CPC's board and mortgage committee. Other recipients of CCDC dollars include a fund to finance the moderate rehabilitation of small mixed-use buildings administered by the local office of Neighborhood Housing Services (see Chapter 6); a bridge loan pool to allow local community organizations to do gut rehabilitations of multifamily residential properties under the auspices of LISC (Local Initiatives Support Corporation) and the Enterprise Foundation (see Chapter 20); and a small business loan fund overseen by the economic development corporations in each of the five boroughs of New York city.

Through this special unit, the CCDC has developed an important expertise in the establishment and ongoing monitoring of multibank consortia and loan funds. As with its regular loan portfolio, the CCDC seeks to make sure that the money goes to projects which are properly structured to allow the project to be completed and the loan to be repaid.

In those cases where the loans are likely to be riskier, the CCDC advises the group on how best to structure its program with, for example, a special reserve which can provide the banks with additional security. To date, the portfolios of all of the financial intermediaries with whom the CCDC deals have good track records. Such success results from hard work and constant vigilance on the part of the staff.

Direct Lending Unit

The Direct Lending Unit and the Community-Based Development Unit (further described in the following section) mainly provide construction financing for a wide range of projects: residential/commercial/mixed-use; new construction/rehabilitation; rental/for sale. Both of these units have specialized lending teams that can make projects happen. They know the neighborhoods and the government programs which provide grants and low-interest loans. Without subsidies, many of the projects would not be feasible in the low- and moderate-income communities in the New York metropolitan area.

The CCDC also offers permanent financing with its capacity to hold such loans in its portfolio enhanced by the availability of mortgage insurance from both the state and the city. The state program works through the State of New York Mortgage Agency (SONYMA) and the city program works through the Rehabilitation Mortgage Insurance Corporation (REMIC). With the help of these programs, the CCDC is now able on practically all multifamily rental and cooperative properties to commit on the permanent loan at the same time it commits on the construction loan. It is one of three banks that has recently been approved to originate insured permanent loans for sale to the main New York City employees' pension fund. By reducing the risk on permanent loans, these mortgage insurance programs have also helped to encourage construction lending.

SONYMA is also supporting the development of neighborhood shopping strips by offering mortgage insurance, which makes it possible for the city pension system to buy these loans. As a result, the CCDC has been able to expand its capacity to make construction loans on these projects in neighborhoods where commercial development is lagging behind the redevelopment of the housing stock.

The Direct Lending Unit itself deals with for-profit developers, both large and small. Its projects tend to be larger, on average, than those done by the Community-Based Development Lending Unit, but both units work with many of the same government programs (e.g., the New York City Housing Partnership Program, the New York City Vacant Building Program, the programs of both the New York State Urban Development Corporation—UDC—and the New York City Economic Development Corporation to promote the development of neighborhood commercial strips).

The Direct Lending Unit has worked closely with the New York City Housing Partnership to open up new opportunities for minority firms in the city's homebuilding industry. The CCDC helped establish a special program set up by the Housing Partnership to make it possible for minority firms with limited experience, often only as subcontractors, to graduate to the role of developer/builder. This unit took the first loan through to closing, paving the way for the other lenders. Since the program utilizes a wide range of government and private resources, these initial negotiations proved critical in resolving the details of the relationships and obligations of the parties.

The CCDC's underwriting of these projects has focused on ensuring a conservative but adequate budget. Minimizing both direct and indirect costs is an essential part of providing affordable housing. The level of the borrower's commitment to the project is also critical and so on many of its projects the CCDC requires equity of 10 percent of the hard costs. This approach has resulted in a portfolio that has performed well, with a number of projects already completed and the loans repaid. Most of the projects have come in at or below budget, with any overruns limited in scope and easily covered by the borrower.

Community-Based Development Lending Unit

This unit deals with projects that involve community-based development organizations either as the developer or as a member of the development team. By establishing this separate unit, the CCDC has signalled its strong interest in developing a close working relationship with such groups, who are trying to strengthen their neighborhoods. This lending unit welcomes and in fact encourages community-based development organizations to seek out informal financial advice as early in the development process as possible, thereby allowing the unit to become an active force in neighborhood development. Since many of the projects undertaken by these types of organizations have multiple layers of financing, early involvement by the CCDC in structuring these layers can be crucial to their ultimate success. While the unit is not equipped to provide extensive technical assistance, it can help a group explore alternatives before any of the loan or grant conditions have been cast in stone. Those who can use this type of input most effectively are groups with previous development experience.

In addition to doing individual projects one at a time, this unit has also worked directly with government to leverage government dollars through generic types of programs. As a result the CCDC has helped increase access to government funds for a wide range of local groups, those who had previously been Chase customers as well as those who had not. For example, the CCDC worked with New York City's Department of Housing Preservation and Development and with the Community Service Society to become an official and integral part of the Ownership Transfer Program, which helps tenant and community organizations buy and rehabilitate multifamily buildings. Recently, while looking for ways to work with the city to provide housing for the homeless, this unit developed a new product to provide startup loans to not-for-profit groups that were selected to run transitional homeless shelters. By working closely with the city's Human Resources Administration, the unit developed a set of documents which have been used for three such loans, with a number of additional applications now being processed.

Development of a close working relationship with community-based organizations and with government has yielded a portfolio that continues to perform well.

Small Business Lending Unit

This offers loans to small businesses providing employment or services to the residents of low- and moderate-income neighborhoods. The loans are guaranteed by the Small Business Administration (SBA) and are structured according to the uniqueness of each business need. A close working relationship has been established with local business development organizations, chambers of commerce and community groups. Through these organizations and through educational seminars, the Small Business Lending Unit is able to build strong community linkages and thereby generate small business loan activity. In combination with the loans for the construction of housing and commercial strips, this new product area strengthens the economies of low- and moderate-income neighborhoods, improving the health of the region's economy as a whole.

KEYS TO SUCCESS

Key to the success of the CCDC is its establishment as a business unit with a narrowly defined marketplace, its ability to tap and build upon the strengths of other parts of Chase, and its highly motivated and skilled staff.

A Narrowly Focused Business

The initial decision to establish the CCDC as a for-profit business unit was one of the most critical determinants of its success. It has allowed the CCDC to develop a clear market identity within the low- and moderate-income market-place. For-profit and not-for-profit developers recognize it as a highly pro-fessional source of market-rate financing readily available for use on its own or in conjunction with government programs. While the CCDC cannot offer any sub-sidized money itself, it can and does pro-vide advice as to other possible sources of such financial assistance (including the philanthropic area of Chase).

The focus on the "bottom line" also helps to ensure that the borrower gets the maximum benefit from seeking financing from a bank. With its no-non-sense professionalism, the CCDC car-efully evaluates the feasibility of every loan application. While the CCDC would like to do every deal, it knows that it cannot. Instead, it tries to identify poten-tial problems as early in the process as possible. Straight answers, while not necessarily welcomed, are in the end al-ways appreciated since it saves the applicant time and effort. Once the pro-blems have surfaced, the borrower can then decide whether to focus on restructuring the deal or move on to a new project.

Since profitability depends on the loan being paid back, the staff cannot afford to delude itself on the viability of a project. This approach is not only critical to the CCDC but also to the borrower and the community. Allowing, for example, a community group to start a project which, right from the beginning, does not have a good chance of success is doing a disservice to everyone involved. If the project fails, the not-for-profit group will be hurt, the community will lose a project it needs, and the govern-ment will see support for its programs reduced.

The for-profit mandate also helps to clarify the way the staff and the long-term outlook for the CCDC is judged. The CCDC and its staff are evaluated on much the same bases as other line oper-ations of Chase. For its staff members, this focus on a business approach allows them to be judged for their ability to generate business and to make loans that will be paid back. For the long-term out-look for the CCDC, the issue becomes mainly one of whether it remains profit-able. As long as it does not become a net drain on the overall organization, it will continue to receive recognition for its success and retain the support it needs to continue its work. If it should lose money, it will see its support diminish rapidly. The CCDC, however, is not ex-pected to match the same rate of pro-fitability as other areas of Chase since its deals, by their very nature, are smaller and more complex.

The narrow business focus also keeps the CCDC aggressively searching for ways to serve its marketplace. The organ-ization actively reaches out both to potential borrowers who may not be aware of its skills and to government officials who are trying to design new programs which can successfully lever-age public funds with private capital. As-sessment of community needs is a natu-ral part of the everyday activities of the CCDC.

Chase's approach to serving the low-and moderate-income community market has also freed the CCDC of responsibilities that could have diverted its attention and thereby impaired its ability to carry out its mission. For example, the CCDC has not been asked to bear the responsibility for handling either philanthropic contributions to local organizations or regulatory responsibilities under the Community Reinvestment Act. These tasks are handled by other areas of the Bank which have their own expertise. The president of the CCDC is, however, a member of the Community Development and Human Services corporate responsibility subcommittee and of the Bank's Community Reinvestment Committee.

Leveraging Chase Strengths

As for being able to take advantage of the Chase connection, the most important ingredient has been the highly visible support of top management. Chase has a proud history of concern for and involvement in the welfare of its local community, and the decision to create the CCDC grew out of this tradition and the recognition that Chase's future is inextricably tied to the continued vitality of the region. With many of Chase's employees and customers living in low- and moderate-income neighborhoods, no one doubts the importance of the CCDC's mission. Senior management at Chase sees the CCDC as a way to strengthen New York as a place to live and work, and this message is conveyed clearly and often to the whole organization. The resulting high profile has translated into a high level of cooperation throughout Chase, expediting the CCDC's efforts to open up new avenues for serving its target community.

One area where early support was critical was in the establishment by the CCDC of its own credit policy. Many of the projects that fit the CCDC's mission simply could not fit the Bank's standard parameters for lending. Rather than having to treat each loan as an exception, the decision was made to develop a credit supplement that would allow as a matter of policy the vast majority of projects that the CCDC would do. Rules were changed in recognition of the fact that many of the CCDC's deals are simply different, with many layers of financing, higher combined loan to values, and a host of restrictions imposed by government regulations. Through a process of education the CCDC was able to show that change did not necessarily mean higher risk. Deals done by the CCDC often have protections that so-called market deals do not and cannot have. For example, rehabilitations of occupied housing obviously have no marketing risk, and even rehabs of vacant buildings essentially face unlimited demand at subsidized rent levels. Moreover, the CCDC's projects generally enjoy political and community support, which helps smooth the government approval processes and can be critical if unanticipated problems require further public involvement. In fact, once the government has invested funds in a project, it will help to restructure projects that run into unexpected problems, thereby providing an additional layer of security to the loan.

High-level support has also helped the CCDC marshal the skills and energy of other parts of Chase, freeing it to focus more intensively on the provision of products tailored to its target market. The CCDC has been able, for example, to take advantage of Chase's experience as a real estate lender, with the head of that department having been the initial chair of the CCDC. The result has been easy access to the administrative and technical services already developed for that department. Other specialized services have also been readily available. For example, the servicing and selling of home mortgages in the secondary market have been supplied by Chase Home Mortgage Corporation. The close working relationship that has been developed with the rest of Chase is perhaps best demonstrated by the ability of the CCDC to participate its loans to the Bank when its level of capitalization would otherwise limit the size of the loan it could make. (All officers of the CCDC are also officers of the Bank.)

Cooperation from the local retail network has also been extensive, allowing the CCDC to tap into the extensive knowledge of neighborhoods and of customers that exists in the branches. Taking advantage of this knowledge requires a two-way flow, with the CCDC offering to the branches its special mix of products for low- and moderate-income communities and with the branches in return referring customers and providing feedback on the applicability of these products to the customer base.

Skilled and Motivated Staff

It has taken more than the right corporate environment to set the stage for success. It has also taken the right mix of people, from both the public and private sectors. All of the staff share a special characteristic: a commitment to helping low- and moderate-income communities. The deals done by the CCDC are not easy, but the effort is rewarded in the

end by the palatable impact on people's lives. The extra amounts of time, patience, and understanding required to structure and close the deals is inherent in the types of projects being undertaken. They tend to be smaller and more complex than those done in other parts of Chase. They often involve many layers of financing from different government agencies combined with philanthropic grants. And many of the borrowers lack the sophistication and experience of long-time developers.

Essential to underwriting the CCDC's loans are basic lending skills, and all of the lending officers of the CCDC staff have that training, with some loan officers having more than 25 years of experience in this field. As with all loans, it is important to identify as many of the risks up-front, thereby decreasing the likelihood of surprises later on. Lending officers must know what to look for on the site once construction has started, helping to ensure that the project is completed on time and on budget (they regularly make unannounced visits). This skill is especially important for the CCDC's types of deals. In most cases, the market or the restrictions that come with government money limit any upside potential, and so a project cannot be salvaged by inflation or speculative increases in rents or sales prices. The project must be completed on time and on budget if the financing is going to work.

The loan officers for the CCDC also have highly specialized knowledge of the low- and moderate-income neighborhoods, of the community groups working in those neighborhoods, and of the relevant government programs—all of which are important ingredients to make deals work. Familiarity with a neighborhood and the development taking place there is a prerequisite for judging the viability of a project. Also, good contacts with many of the community groups allows the CCDC to tap their knowledge as well as bring them into the project, if appropriate, to make it work. Knowledge of government programs is also important since so many of the loans are done in conjunction with city, state, or federal funds (New York City alone is in the middle of a $5.1 billion ten-year housing plan [see Chapter 18]). This knowledge can be learned, but it also helps that some of the staff also comes from government. They, therefore, understand from first-hand experience the regulatory and bureaucratic environment faced by government officials and so can work effectively to overcome these institutional barriers.

Even with all these tools, success is not guaranteed. The staff must also have the vision to see how best to put all the pieces together into a bankable deal. Only recently, a community group came to the CCDC with a deal that would provide much-needed housing in the South Bronx. The application had been rejected by a number of other financial institutions. Rather than dismiss the request based on the written proposal, the CCDC staff sat down with the community group and with the two churches which were also putting in money. After a number of discussions, a whole new approach was developed which satisfied the needs of all the parties. The ability to find creative ways to make the project viable while bringing the CCDC's risk down to an acceptable level is the CCDC's idea of how to provide innovative financing.

SUMMARY

By setting up and then providing high-level support to a separate, narrowly focused business unit, Chase has been able to rapidly build a company serving a wide variety of the housing and economic development needs of low- and moderate-income communities. The CCDC has come a long way in its first four years of existence and it provides a model for how organizations such as Chase can do well by doing good.

Chapter 4

The Community Preservation Corporation: a National Model for Financing Affordable Housing

Michael D. Lappin
President
The Community Preservation Corporation

INTRODUCTION

The success of The Community Preservation Corporation (CPC) has been its ability to develop and expand a lending market for small owners and contractors who produce low-cost housing as their primary business—and to do so without engaging in concessionary underwriting or pricing. With this approach, CPC has demonstrated that neither safety, soundness, nor earnings need be compromised for the sake of producing affordable housing. Based on this, CPC has put together resources totaling more than $755 million from institutional investors to finance this market. How CPC has accomplished this, and what lessons can be applied to affordable-housing markets across the country, are the subjects of this chapter.

WHAT IS CPC?

CPC, a private, not-for-profit mortgage lender, has been financing affordable housing in the New York City metropolitan area for 18 years. An independent organization, CPC is sponsored by almost 50 of New York's major commercial and savings banks and seven New York-based insurance companies.

Established in 1974 in response to the rapid deterioration of housing in New York City's low- and moderate-income neighborhoods, CPC has financed the construction or rehabilitation of more than 32,000 affordable housing units, representing public and private investment of about $1 billion, through January 1993. To date, CPC has not incurred any loan losses.

CPC makes construction and permanent loans, drawing upon two types of credit facilities: an unsecured line of credit for secured construction loans, provided by its sponsoring banks, and a variety of credit agreements to purchase either long-term mortgages originated by CPC or notes secured by pools of long-term mortgages, also originated by CPC. An investment committee made up of senior bank lending officers and the president of CPC sets the corporation's lending standards and approves individual loans made from these credit sources.

CPC earns fee income from loan originations, spreads on construction loans, and servicing fees on permanent loans and on other funds it manages. Originally capitalized by contributions from its sponsors, CPC has for the last 12 years supported itself from its operating revenues. Accumulated surpluses and reserves from prior years now total approximately $10 million. CPC's ability to generate surpluses has been important, both in supporting and expanding its lending activities and in demonstrating the long-term viability of lending for affordable housing.

CPC was set up as an independent organization for several reasons. First, the business it planned to pursue was regarded as highly risky, given the fact that a number of New York City's once-stable neighborhoods had experienced rapid decline in the years immediately preceding CPC's creation. Spreading the risk among a large number of banks would mitigate the misgivings that individual institutions might have about the uncertainties of such lending.

Second, CPC intended to work very closely with government to carry out its goals. CPC's loan underwriting would

have to reflect the monetary value of a variety of public programs, such as tax exemption and abatement programs, various subsidy programs, and eligibility for rent increases—which would in turn require a mastering of the complex regulations governing these programs. The uncertain loan volume and the small size of individual loans, coupled with such complexities, argued against the creation of affordable-housing programs by all but the largest banks.

Third, CPC would act as a bridge between government and the financial community. As a loan originator, CPC could identify the regulatory and administrative obstacles that impede investment in affordable housing. CPC could then work with government to overcome these obstacles, thereby creating a climate that would encourage investment. As a spokesman for the financial community, CPC would help government understand the requirements for private investment. At the same time, CPC would inform its sponsoring banks about workable public programs and assist the banks to lend in the affordable-housing market.

While CPC's founders had a clear vision of their goal—to finance the rebuilding of New York City's deteriorating neighborhoods—their understanding of exactly how to accomplish this came only with actual experience in the marketplace. CPC's discovery of a new market of small owners who had little or no access to financing was not anticipated. Rather, it was a by-product—albeit the critical one—of CPC's efforts to bring efficiency and predictability to the process of financing the development of affordable housing.

MARKET BARRIERS TO AFFORDABLE HOUSING

While many lending institutions have long recognized the need to finance affordable housing, a number of market barriers have obstructed this goal. They include:

- The small size of many deals means that income to the originator cannot cover staff costs.

- Complex government subsidies add further to processing costs by requiring specialized staff resources to deal with an array of public programs.

- Most affordable-housing developers are inexperienced and undercapitalized, which augments risk and drains staff time.

- Neighborhood risk is perceived to be high.

- Debt and equity investments in multi-family rental housing (in which many lower-income families live) have been inhibited by certain regulatory and legislative actions:

  - Risk-based capital requirements, imposed initially on banks, and extended to savings and loan institutions by the Financial Institutions Reform, Recovery and Enforcement Act of 1989 (FIRREA), assign a 100 percent risk-weight to multifamily mortgages, making it more expensive for regulated lenders to invest in multifamily housing than in other products.

  - Various provisions of the Tax Reform Act of 1986 reduced the eco-nomic incentive to make equity investments in rental housing.

- Secondary-market outlets for affordable housing debt are very limited.

CPC has sought to deal with these issues by employing a four-step approach: (1) organizing the government process; (2) merging this streamlined government process with sound loan origination procedures; (3) adding credit enhancement; and (4) attracting the participation of secondary-market players.

ORGANIZING THE PROCESS OF PUBLIC PROGRAMS AND PRIVATE FINANCING

To deal with the first three market barriers identified above—small deals, complex government programs, and inexperienced developers—CPC has worked with government to organize a process that creates access for low-cost builders, both for-profit and non-profit, to government programs and private financing. Three examples illustrate this process.

Example I: The moderate rehabilitation of occupied rental housing

The crisis that led to the creation of CPC was the deep recession in New York City's economy in the mid-1970s. During the previous decade the city had a net loss of half a million jobs, primarily in the manufacturing sector. The consequent weakened housing demand severely affected the maintenance of the city's older rental housing stock. Building income could not keep pace with operating costs, repairs were deferred, and upgrading of mechanical systems was not even considered, as cash flows could hardly support current day-to-day operations, let alone new debt. The result was the rapid deterioration of the city's already marginal low- and moderate-income neighborhoods. By the mid-seventies, New York was losing roughly 25,000 dwelling units a year to abandonment.

CPC's and the city's response to these conditions was to focus on preserving the housing that was still occupied in neighborhoods bordering the areas of abandonment. CPC and the city identified two such neighborhoods: Washington Heights/Inwood in upper Manhattan, and Crown Heights in central Brooklyn. Their housing stock consisted almost entirely of multifamily rental buildings constructed in the early 1900s. These buildings were, for the most part, privately owned and fully occupied, with deterioration occurring in their aging physical plants. What was needed was investment to replace plumbing, boilers, roofs, and windows, and to upgrade electrical systems, at a cost of $10,000 to $15,000 per unit, while maintaining occupancy of the units. If a way could be found to arrest decay in these quintessential New York City neighborhoods—and avoid the far greater cost of replacing these units should they become abandoned—similar methods could be applied throughout the city.

When CPC attempted to make investments to support this preservation strategy, two problems emerged: the complexity of the government programs available to encourage apartment building rehabilitation, and the general lack of sophistication among the owners of such housing.

Three basic public programs were available to support building rehabilitation: rent increase authority, rent subsidies, and real estate tax abatement and exemption. Each program was complicated in its own right and was administered by a different city department. In order for these programs to leverage investment, their economic value had to be understood and incorporated into the mortgage underwriting. In addition, the certainty of benefits and their timing had to be coordinated. Rent increases and real estate tax benefits had to be obtainable to support the new debt that financed the rehabilitation, and rent subsidies had to be available to assist those households that could not afford the resulting rent increases.

If these programs were complicated to experienced owners, they were altogether baffling to the unsophisticated property owners in CPC's two target neighborhoods. Most of these owners, many of whom were immigrants and new to the real estate business, had little experience with government programs, and even less with rehabilitation. Furthermore, many of the owners had bought their buildings with privately arranged mortgages, and they had limited experience with financial institutions.

To overcome these problems, CPC and the city worked to simplify and combine these programs and, where possible, to integrate them with the loan origination process. Accordingly, to eliminate the duplicative data requirements of the programs, several innovations were developed: the application for a rent increase following rehabilitation was combined with applications for construction and permanent financing; public commitments for rent subsidies were combined with the private financing commitment, and the same documentation used to obtain real estate tax abatement and exemption was used to obtain rent increases. Hence, CPC became a "one-stop shop" where owners could obtain these crucial public supports as well as their private financing.

Left to their own devices, most of these inexperienced owners would have great difficulty in obtaining, let alone coordinating, these necessary elements for rehabilitation. Since CPC assumed a key role in obtaining the public benefits, it could reliably incorporate the economic value of these benefits into its mortgage underwriting.

At the same one-stop shop, CPC offered counseling to owners regarding rehabilitation. Specifically, it provided owners with construction specifications for common renovation items such as plumbing, heating, and windows. Additionally, as CPC gained experience, it developed a strong working knowledge of construction prices, contractor abilities, and other important aspects of the market that could help it to guide owners. While CPC was careful not to slip into the role of developer, the soundness of the advice it provided set the tone for the industry.

What were the results of these efforts?

In Washington Heights/Inwood, CPC financed the in-occupancy rehabilitation of more than 7,500 units over a decade, in a manner that was affordable to the existing tenants and created no displacement. These units represented more than 10 percent of all the housing in that area and probably about 30 percent of the deteriorated units. Perhaps the best measure of CPC's success is the fact that CPC now does very little financing in Washington Heights/Inwood; the neighborhood has once again become an investment area for local banks, which are now financing the rebuilding of the area.

Example II: Substantial rehabilitation of deteriorated buildings and "gut" rehabilitation of vacant buildings

As public resources for housing expanded, so did the CPC-New York City relationship. At the same time, CPC expanded its lending to include all of the city's nonluxury areas. Utilizing one percent financing, made available through the city's Participation Loan Program (PLP), CPC created a joint funding process whereby market-rate private funds are combined with these very low interest public funds to produce a below-market blended interest rate. The reduced debt service enabled CPC and the city to broaden their financing activities to include more badly deteriorated occupied buildings, as well as vacant buildings, many of which were owned by the city through tax foreclosures. (The city initially used Federal Community Development Block Grant funds and later its own capital funds to finance PLP.)

CPC and the city built upon the streamlining efforts described in Example I to utilize these new resources efficiently. CPC and the city developed pre-approved cost standards and specifications for construction, standardized debt instruments, and standardized legal agreements for loan servicing and subsidy provisions. Up-front agreement in these areas allowed financing and subsidy applications to be combined in one document, as were funding commitments. While the city and CPC each exercise separate approval authority, once approval has been granted, CPC is authorized to represent both parties during construction and advance city funds escrowed with CPC at the construction closing. CPC and the city were thus able to expand their joint efforts to rebuild more deteriorated areas (such as Harlem and the South Bronx) by providing simplified access for unsophisticated owners through an expanded version of the one-stop shop.

Having suffered through a recession in the seventies, by the late eighties the city's economy was expanding rapidly, and the need for additional affordable housing had become critical. The abandoned housing the city had taken over during the previous decade was now seen as a resource to meet these new housing demands. In 1987 CPC and the city developed the Vacant Building Program for the restoration of several hundred of these buildings, located primarily in Harlem and the South Bronx.

The Vacant Building Program expanded upon previous city and CPC initiatives. Properties were sold to new owners for $1, financing subsidies were provided to keep rents low, cost standards and specifications were pre-approved, and deed restrictions to main-

tain long-term affordability were subordinated to the private debt. CPC served as the loan originator and manager of construction on behalf of itself and the city. The simplified process attracted small developers, who rehabilitated the buildings and now manage them. In the program's first four years, some 6,000 units were created. The apartments are rented by households earning between $15,000 and $25,000 annually.

Example III: The Poughkeepsie Experiment

The one-stop approach need not be confined to large cities, but can also be applied to small localities. In the city of Poughkeepsie, in New York's Hudson Valley region, clusters of small deteriorated properties (two to eight units) containing owner-occupied and rental housing are a blight on several downtown neighborhoods. A similar linking of public programs with private funds is now being developed, which will enable small, inexperienced owners to go to a single place to obtain their private loan commitments, public subsidies, and other benefits. This program differs from the previous examples because here, for the smallest deals, the one-stop shop is the city's Office of Property Development, not CPC. For these deals, owners will receive commitments for both public and private funds from the city, in accordance with preapproved standards and documentation. In order to ensure that appropriate standards are adhered to, CPC trains its own and the city's staff regarding both underwriting standards and processing requirements. The city certifies to CPC that it has adhered to all preapproved policies and procedures, with CPC monitoring such certifications.

This approach promises to overcome what has been a major obstacle to rehabilitating these buildings in the past—the difficulty faced by small owners trying to obtain both public and private financing on their own.

Result: Cost Savings

It is important to note that in each of the three examples discussed, the one-stop shop approach worked in a well-defined market where more fundamental issues—such as land use, density, and environment—were not at stake. This left primarily processing issues to grapple with. A strong public commitment to deal with these processing issues (as noted in the three examples), plus the involvement of a private sector partner with strong financial resources and expertise, were key to streamlining the process.

Maintaining this simplified procedure over the long haul has proved difficult and sometimes impossible. As the crisis that prompted the initial public-private effort fades, programmatic resources may diminish, as well as the commitment to new, streamlined procedures.

Where such procedures have worked, as noted above, processing times have been reduced by as much as a year. This efficiency translates into a significant savings of carrying costs for the borrower, which in turn translates into increased affordability of decent housing for lower-income households and increased leveraging of scarce government funds.

The reduction in processing time resulting from a simplified process, com-bined with CPC's specialized knowledge and hands-on assistance, opened the market to small owners and builders. More players in the market leads to increased price competition—which inevitably results in dramatically lower development costs. For example, development costs for both moderate and substantial rehabilitation done through CPC have been running at about one-half the amount spent on comparable federal government Section 8 Moderate and Substantial Rehabilitation projects.

The developers who succeeded under the federal government programs were those who could navigate their way through complicated mazes of government regulations, and who also had the financial staying power to withstand long delays. With CPC's approach, which streamlines much of the complicated process, the developers who succeed are those who know how to negotiate the lowest costs for quality work and run a construction job efficiently and effectively.

ORIGINATING BANKABLE LOANS

The need for affordable housing is a vast national problem requiring vast financial resources that government alone cannot provide. To generate significant amounts of private funds, lenders much achieve market rates of return and be protected from inordinate risks. An affordable-housing program that requires private institutions to lend at below-market rates, or on concessionary terms, will generate neither long-term institutional support nor a significant volume of lending.

CPC's lending programs are market-rate: borrowers pay a market rate of interest to CPC, and CPC, in turn, passes on a market rate of return to its participating lenders. By providing a reasonable profit to lenders, CPC creates an economic incentive for their continued participation in affordable-housing lending.

The bedrock of CPC's efforts is underwriting loans that conform to bankable standards. Specifically, loan-to-value (LTV) and debt service coverage ratios are not concessionary. If either the LTV is too high and/or the debt service coverage ratio is too low, public subsidies can be used to augment CPC funds. The crux of CPC's approach is to find the piece of the affordable-housing investment that is bankable. Using private funds for that portion further reduces the need for public subsidies.

Where public subsidies are involved, they are in all respects subordinate to any permanent financing provided by CPC. This point can be illustrated in two ways. First, CPC's permanent loans are always secured by a first lien on the property, with any public financing in a subordinate position. Second, any deed restrictions (such as income eligibility) that come into play by virtue of using public monies and/or land are subordinate to the private financing. Therefore, should a foreclosure become necessary, the first mortgage lender has a "clean" mortgage to foreclose on. While CPC has never exercised this subordination feature, it has nevertheless been critical to gaining access to permanent mortgage investors.

Additionally, CPC requires tangible evidence of a borrower's commitment. During construction, borrowers are generally required to make a reasonable up-front equity investment, calculated as a percentage of total development costs. (In the case of nonprofit developers, a portion of the equity may be publicly funded.) CPC's intimate knowledge of construction costs, along with its close scrutiny of the borrower's development budget, ensures that the borrower's equity is real and is not funded from the proceeds of an overfinanced project.

With such up-front equity, CPC has created a financially sound way to do business with developers whose financial statements alone would not demonstrate their creditworthiness. Further protection from construction-period risk is derived from a 10 percent letter of credit and from CPC's 10 percent retention on construction draws.

Together, these policies serve to mitigate the risks inherent in building affordable housing. The combination of a significant up-front equity investment, a letter of credit payable to CPC in the event of borrower default, and CPC's retention on construction draws creates greater incentive for the borrower to complete the job, instead of walking away from it.

CREDIT ENHANCEMENT

Replicating CPC's program requires appropriate credit enhancement. In spite of the sound underwriting that CPC strives to achieve, this type of lending is not without risk. In fact, the neighborhoods in which this housing is located feel economic downswings and social problems more keenly than others. It follows that, in order for such loans to be made by a primary lender, and sold to the secondary market—on more than a token basis—properly structured credit enhancement must be in place.

Accordingly, New York State developed a system of mortgage insurance to share the risk of investment in low- and moderate-income neighborhoods. By doing so it recognized that the rebuilding and preservation of these neighborhoods requires a massive investment that cannot be made by government alone. Mortgage insurance has proved to be a highly efficient use of public funds to leverage private funds for the support of affordable housing.

The State of New York Mortgage Agency (SONYMA) makes mortgage insurance available in blighted or distressed areas of the state. Generally SONYMA insures only a portion of the loan amount, and maintains reserves equal to one-fifth of the insured amount. Let us suppose, for example, that 50 percent of the loan amount is insured by SONYMA. A reserve of 20 percent of the insured amount is maintained. This means that SONYMA can credit-enhance a $1 million loan by creating a reserve of $100,000.

The features of SONYMA's multifamily mortgage insurance program that have been critical to its acceptance among institutional investors include the following:

The program is funded from a surcharge of 25 cents per $100 on the state's mortgage recording tax, as well as from premiums, fees, and interest earnings generated by SONYMA's Mortgage Insurance Division. The tax surcharge is remitted to SONYMA as it is collected, making this a highly reliable source of funding. Furthermore, the payment of

claims is not an obligation of the state, but, rather, is supported by this dedicated tax. SONYMA is required to reserve 20 cents for every $1 of mortgage insurance coverage to which it has committed. If reserves are depleted and SONYMA is unable to meet all outstanding insurance claims, the agency is legally obligated to use any funds that subsequently become available to pay prior claims before underwriting any new policies.

SONYMA provides top-loss insurance for mortgages made in blighted or distressed areas of New York State. Top-loss insurance, also referred to as first-loss insurance, is superior to a standard loss-sharing arrangement, whereby any losses would be shared, say on a 50/50 basis, among all the parties that are at risk. SONYMA insurance, on the other hand, covers 100 percent of losses, up to 50 percent or 75 percent of the outstanding mortgage principal amount, depending on whether and to what extent the property was rehabilitated with the mortgage proceeds. (Coverage may go as high as 100 percent of the mortgage principal amount if the mortgage is made or purchased by a public employee pension fund.)

SONYMA's loss recovery mechanism is clear and certain. SONYMA operates with a Master Mortgage Insurance Policy to which a participating lender becomes a party. The master policy generally provides for SONYMA to pay out claims once the insured lender has taken title to a property through foreclosure. At SONYMA's option, it may agree to make quarterly payments of principal and interest for up to two years after a loan is four payments in arrears. In the case of mortgages originated by CPC and sold to New York City or State employee pension funds, SONYMA has agreed to certain special loss recovery procedures. These include:

- Mandatory periodic payments prior to foreclosure, and

- Monthly, rather than quarterly, periodic payments.

CPC, as the largest user of SONYMA insurance, has never experienced a failure by SONYMA to meet its insurance obligations.

The above factors contributed to SONYMA's acceptance by New York City and State public pension funds. In 1984 the New York City Employees Retirement System and the Police Pension Fund entered into historic agreements with CPC to purchase permanent whole loans originated by CPC on a forward-committed basis. To arrive at a market yield, the pension funds compared a SONYMA-insured mortgage to U.S. government-insured mortgage instruments that the pension funds routinely buy (specifically, Ginnie Maes) in terms of (1) the security itself, (2) prepayment assumptions, (3) liquidity, and (4) miscellaneous structural features. The conclusion reached was that SONYMA-insured mortgages are sound investments, but that they should be priced to produce a higher yield than mortgages backed by the full faith and credit of the United States government.

The Teachers Retirement System of the City of New York subsequently agreed to participate in the program as well, bringing the total current commitment to $350 million. In 1991, CPC completed negotiations with the New York State Common Retirement Fund leading to a similar commitment in the amount of $50 million, which represents the first part of a $200 million authorization.

The provision of credit enhancement by local government opens up opportunities all around. Access to institutional investors is created for borrowers who would not otherwise have such access. Banks, pension funds, and other institutional investors that otherwise would not be able to invest in affordable housing at acceptable levels of risk are able to do so prudently. Governments can use their subsidy dollars to leverage private investment in neighborhoods where this would not otherwise occur.

THE SECONDARY MARKET: AN OPPORTUNITY FOR NEW FEDERAL INVOLVEMENT

National credit sources find it difficult to invest in affordable housing, given the vast number of markets throughout the country. The recent experiences of the Federal Home Loan Mortgage Corporation (Freddie Mac) and the Federal National Mortgage Association (Fannie Mae) illustrate the problem.

During the 1980s, Freddie Mac invested billions of dollars in moderate- and middle-income multifamily buildings in New York City. Freddie Mac's national underwriting standards did not fully account for local market conditions, operating costs, and the inexperience of owners. Freddie Mac's lack of familiarity with local market conditions has resulted, in many cases, in overstated building values and troubled loans.

Fannie Mae, on the other hand, has

invested very little in these neighborhoods. While protecting itself from the risks inherent in financing affordable housing, Fannie Mae also missed some opportunities for solid housing investments. These examples illustrate two sides of the same coin: inadequate market knowledge produces inadequate housing results.

Others, such as the Federal Housing Administration (FHA), who have sought to underwrite local loans, have imposed elaborate processing requirements, producing lengthy delays and exorbitant costs. The result of this approach has been virtually to miss the market of smaller-scale projects, carried out by small for-profit and not-for-profit developers, that has represented the core of CPC's lending business.

These experiences suggest a new role for these national programs: the reinsurance of properly constituted local mortgage insurance programs. Specifically, the national agencies could underwrite the local mortgage insurance rather than getting involved in underwriting individual mortgages.

Under such a reinsurance system, each national agency—Fannie Mae, Freddie Mac, FHA, or a regional Federal Home Loan Bank—would make the offer to reinsure local programs structured along the lines of SONYMA. Hence, the national agencies would establish guidelines for the capitalization of loss reserves, for top-loss coverage, and for loss recovery procedures. If these guidelines were adopted by a local insurance program, that program would become eligible for reinsurance by the national agencies.

The local insurer, armed with specific knowledge of the local market, would specify standards for underwriting individual loans. These loans need not be only for multifamily housing, but may be for other types of affordable housing for which there is no secondary market (for example, group homes or two-family homes with ground-floor commercial space). Care in establishing such guidelines would be encouraged by the local insurer's first loss position, should loan defaults occur.

The knowledge that it is possible to create a Fannie Mae or Freddie Mac mortgage-backed security—the equivalent of triple-A paper—with acceptable state mortgage insurance in place, should serve as a powerful incentive to local governments to set up programs modeled after SONYMA.

This approach can create the essential preconditions of a secondary market: volume and uniformity. A simplified loan origination mechanism, such as CPC's one-stop-shop approach, can open the market to a small army of affordable-housing developers to create volume. Uniformity is produced, not in the individual investments, but in the standardized insurance programs that credit-enhance the mortgages.

After several years of effort, CPC recently entered into a program with Fannie Mae that incorporates the above approach. Under this program, Fannie Mae has agreed to securitize $50 million of multifamily mortgages, originated by CPC in accordance with agreed-upon underwriting standards, and supported by a junior lien also originated by CPC but held by separate investors. Such a program should create an opportunity to revolve the commitment authority of banks and institutional investors that participate in CPC lending activities. The greater security, combined with the greater liquidity of federally backed paper, should result in a reduction in required yields, and reduce the cost of this type of financing.

CPC—A NEW LENDING INSTITUTION

CPC is a new type of lending institution. Its only business has been the financing of affordable housing. This specialization has led to a detailed understanding of the various affordable-housing markets, including both the characteristics of viable projects and the nature of housing producers. On the latter point, in particular, CPC has acquired familiarity and experience with small, less experienced owners and builders. CPC has streamlined its own processing, and that of government subsidy providers, to improve accessibility for small producers. The lower costs of these builders are a powerful aid to affordability. They have also enabled CPC's business to expand to its present annual pace, with financing of about 2,500 apartments annually.

CPC's ability to achieve this owes much to its multibank sponsorship. First, such sponsorship gives it strong access to government as a representative of the financial industry. With such access it can help shape those public programs that can leverage investment in affordable housing as noted above.

Second, such broad-based sponsorship permits CPC to maintain its focus on affordable housing issues for the long term, and not merely respond to changing institutional and regulatory constraints affecting such lending. Such a long-term focus is essential, since the development of new markets—and the lending products tailored to such

markets—requires a prolonged effort, as is the case with other types of lending products. Furthermore, the company must be given time to develop a sound financial base, enabling it to develop the expertise, staff resources, and career paths that are needed to successfully deal with its area of business.

Third, such sponsorship can buffer the institution from the shifting financial fortunes of individual members.

In this time of increasingly centralized banking systems, we are in danger of losing the knowledge and decision-making infrastructure necessary to provide credit to our affordable-housing markets. As lending decisions become further removed from the markets themselves, the availability of needed credit is sure to become less certain.

The creation of separate lending entities like CPC could fill part of this potential vacuum. If this is desired, bank regulatory policies, banking statutes, and other laws and regulations must be examined with respect to incentives that could be provided for the creation of such new businesses.

AFFORDABLE HOUSING FINANCE: A ROUTINE EVENT

The lessons CPC has learned during its 18-year history have relevance beyond New York City's borders. The key is to open up the credit markets, both primary and secondary, to the small owners and builders who can produce affordable housing most economically, but require access to capital to do so. The first step in the process is to create the necessary infrastructure to make government programs accessible. Effective utilization of government supports must then be melded with a loan origination process that is both efficient and practical, resulting in loans that make economic sense for participating private sector lenders. The addition of mortgage insurance that is locally underwritten and financed would allow for the creation of investment-grade securities attractive to the secondary market.

By paving the way for institutional investors to invest in low- and moderate-income neighborhoods, we can rebuild our cities in the same way we built our suburbs, using FHA and Veterans Administration insurance, following World War II. The ultimate goal now with respect to multifamily housing—as it was then with respect to single-family housing—is to transform investment in affordable housing from an extraordinary event to a routine one.

Chapter 5

Fannie Mae's Affordable Housing Initiatives: Historical Perspective and Future Prospects

Martin D. Levin
Senior Vice President
Low- and Moderate-Income Housing
Federal National Mortgage Association (Fannie Mae)

INTRODUCTION

As the Adams Morgan neighborhood in Washington, D.C., moved upscale in the mid-1980s, with trendy restaurants and high-priced homes, most residents and businesses welcomed the change. But life worsened for apartment residents at 1201-1207 Champlain Court, in the Reed-Cooke section of the community.

Their buildings were left open to squatters and drug users. In an attempt to force residents out, tenants say the landlord refused to make needed repairs. "When it got cold, sometimes we had heat, sometimes we didn't. You had to get up early enough to heat your water on the stove so you could take a bath

before you went to work," said tenant Thelma Williams.

But rather than leave, seven tenants dubbed themselves "the last holdouts" and decided to purchase the building. They wanted to organize a limited-equity cooperative—a type of housing in which each tenant is a shareholder in a corporation that owns the building.

The tenants believed the co-op was their best chance to improve their living conditions and preserve affordable housing in the neighborhood, where the price of homes had soared.

After a five-year struggle to arrange financing and rent subsidies and complete extensive renovation, the tenants took control of their building, now known as the Champlain Court Cooperative. The residents met regularly to determine how they would run and maintain the co-op, and many became more active in community affairs.

The co-op venture was one of six affordable-housing developments to receive a $25,000 grant from the Fannie Mae Maxwell Awards of Excellence Program for the Production of Low-Income Housing. The awards, an annual program at Fannie Mae, recognize groups from around the country for their efforts to create and preserve affordable housing. The Champlain co-op project succeeded because the residents were able to tap into a network of nonprofit community organizations, government entities and private businesses that work in partnership to meet affordable-housing needs.

Partnerships like the one set up at Washington's Champlain Court are a major part of a nationwide emphasis on supplying affordable housing for those of lesser means. As direct federal support for the rehabilitation or construction of new housing for lower-income families declined during the 1980s, lenders, states, local governments, nonprofits, and other private corporations increasingly stepped in to develop creative ways to make rental housing more affordable and make mortgages more accessible to those with modest incomes.

FANNIE MAE'S ROLE IN THE HOME MORTGAGE MARKET

Sitting right in the middle of those housing partnerships and the national housing market is Fannie Mae. At the end of 1990, it was a $430 billion company—the nation's largest investor in home mortgages.

To understand Fannie Mae's role in the nation's mortgage market, and why and how the company is supporting partnerships like the one at Washington's Champlain Court, it's helpful to take a brief look at the history of the federal government's role in promoting home ownership and affordable housing.

Not until the Great Depression did the federal government take a major role in the mortgage finance business. The Hoover administration intervened in housing finance in 1932 chiefly to save the sinking financial system. About 50 percent of the nation's primary-mortgage lending institutions, with more than a quarter of all mortgage assets in default, were failing. Hoover and Congress established the Federal Home Loan Bank system with 12 regional banks. The banks got money from the Treasury and made survival loans to savings institutions, secured by home mortgages.

Then came President Franklin Delano Roosevelt with his sweeping financial reforms and social programs for a nation he saw as one third "ill housed, ill clad, and ill nourished."

The Housing Act of 1934 was the centerpiece of the administration's reformation. It created the Federal Deposit Insurance Corporation, the Federal Savings and Loan Insurance Corporation, and the Federal Housing Administration to encourage savers to keep their deposits in the institutions. The federal government began insuring mortgages for up to 20 years. Spread-out monthly payments allowed average Americans, for the first time, to own a home almost as cheaply as renting one.

The FHA mortgages marked the birth of widely available, fully amortizing long-term mortgages (20 years). Thus a policy originally based on saving a bankrupt financial system turned out to be one of the great pieces of social policy in the nation's history. From 1940 to 1990, the homeownership rate for the nation went from roughly half of all households to almost two-thirds.

As part of the 1934 Housing Act, Congress also authorized the FHA administrator to create profit-making "national mortgage associations." These companies were to make a secondary mortgage market for primary-market lenders, principally thrifts and mortgage companies. In February 1938, the FHA Administrator created Fannie Mae as a taxpayer-supported agency, thus making a secondary mortgage market where lenders could sell FHA mortgages. It was the birth of the world's first secondary mortgage market—a concept now spreading to other nations.

Although it began as a taxpayer-supported agency, Fannie Mae's ownership has evolved through several changes in its federal charter. In 1954, Congress made Fannie Mae a mixed-ownership company—part government and part private ownership. Congress and the Johnson administration privatized the company by law in 1968. At the same time, the Government National Mortgage Association (Ginnie Mae) was created as a federal agency to support government subsidy programs. Fannie Mae began to focus on the purchase of conventional mortgage loans not insured by the federal government.

Fannie Mae's success at making a secondary market, mainly for mortgage bankers, led thrift institutions to persuade Congress to establish another secondary-market institution to provide liquidity for them. Hence, the Federal Home Loan Mortgage Corporation, or Freddie Mac, was established in 1970. Today, Freddie Mac has evolved into a privately managed, shareholder-owned company like Fannie Mae, and is Fannie Mae's major competitor in the secondary market. Both companies compete for the same primary-market customers—thrifts, mortgage companies, commercial banks—and for the same investors in our debt, mortgage-backed securities and equity.

Figure 5.1 illustrates how Fannie Mae interacts with mortgage lenders and investors in the secondary market. Fannie Mae conducts its business in two distinct ways:

1. It buys home loans from banks, savings and loans, and other lenders for our mortgage investment portfolio, which stood at $109 billion at the end of June 1991.

2. It also buys pools of mortgages from lenders and packages them into Mortgage-Backed Securities, or MBS, for sale to investors. Investors buy MBS with Fannie Mae's guarantee that they will receive the timely payment of principal and interest. Fannie Mae MBS have gained broad acceptance since their introduction in 1981; 10 years later, there were more than $300 billion of the Company's MBS outstanding.

The primary and secondary mortgage markets have evolved over the last 50 years into a highly efficient system for

Figure 5.1   How Fannie Mae Has Provided over $600 Billion to
              Finance Homes for 13 Million Families over the Past
              52 Years

1. Home buyers go to a local lending institution for
mortgage loans to purchase a home. These lenders
           make up the "primary market."

↓

2. The lending institutions keep the new mortgages
as investments or sell them to investors, such as
Fannie Mae. These investors make up the
             "secondary mortgage market."

↓

3. By purchasing home mortgages, Fannie Mae
provides local lenders new funds to make more
home loans, thereby assuring home buyers a
continual supply of credit. In 1989, secondary
market investors purchased 75% of all mortgages
             originated in the U.S.

↓

4. Fannie Mae can keep the loans in its own
investment portfolio, financing those loans by
the sale of bonds to investors. Alternatively,
Fannie Mae can package the loans into securities
(Mortgage-Backed Securities) for other investors.
FannieMae guarantees the timely payment of
monthly principal and interest on the
          Mortgage-Backed Securities.

↓

5. The cycle begins again as lenders make
        other loans to home buyers.

providing low-cost financing for housing. In the decade of the eighties, Fannie Mae and Freddie Mac provided financing for an estimated eight million low-, middle-, and moderate-income home buyers.

FINANCING FOR LOW- AND MODERATE-INCOME HOUSEHOLDS THROUGH FANNIE MAE'S STANDARD PROGRAMS

Both Fannie Mae and Freddie Mac are restricted to investing in loans for low-, moderate-, and middle-income Amer-icans. The maximum amount of a home mortgage the companies can buy is set annually under a formula established by law. For example, the mortgage cap in 1991 was $191,250. Few loans are purchased at that level, however. The average one-unit first-mortgage loan Fannie Mae purchased or securitized in the first six months of 1991 was $90,560—affordable to families of mod-est means.

The story is the same for the rental properties the company finances. The typical unit Fannie Mae financed through its conventional multifamily program in 1990 carries a rent affordable to households with income below the area median.

FANNIE MAE'S SPECIALIZED FINANCING PRODUCTS FOR LOW- AND MODERATE-INCOME FAMILIES AND THOSE WITH SPECIAL NEEDS

In 1987, Fannie Mae supplemented its standard programs by creating a separate Office of Low- and Moderate-Income Housing that is responsible for developing and offering programs that meet special housing needs. It announced at the time that it was making the move to become a more vigorous force for housing for lower income families. Federal housing assistance did not keep up with the growing need in the late 1970s and 1980s. This resulted in greater demands for affordable-housing programs from lenders, states, local governments, and community organizations and businesses. Fannie Mae's Office of Low- and Moderate-Income Housing was established in large part to support and encourage the efforts of these groups.

Homeless, low- and moderate-income families and first-time home buyers are staring across a widening affordability gap at their dream of a decent place to live.

• The rate of homeownership in the 1980s declined for the first time since the end of the Great Depression— from the high of 65.6 in 1980 to 63.9 in 1990.

• Estimates of the number of homeless range from 350,000 by HUD to 3 million by the National Coalition for the Homeless.

• According to the Neighborhood Reinvestment Corporation, a gap of some three million exists between the supply of low-income units and families who need them. By the year 2000, that gap is expected to widen to eight million—that's a housing shortage for 18 million people.

• Even if lenders offer 5 percent, 10 percent, and 20 percent down-payment options, only 22 percent of white renters and 4 percent of black renters have the income and wealth to qualify for a mortgage to purchase a typical starter home, according to a 1991 study by the Joint Center for Housing Studies of Harvard University.

• The homeownership rate for households in the 25-29 age group fell from 43.3 percent in 1980 to 35.4 percent in the second quarter of 1989. For households in the 30-34 age group, the rate fell from 61.1 percent in 1980 to 53.7 percent in the second quarter of 1989.

• There are in the range of 10 million people today, or about 3.8 million households, who either have inadequate housing or pay more than 50 percent of their income for housing and receive no housing assistance of any kind from the federal level.

Between 1987 and the end of 1990, Fannie Mae's Office of Low- and Moderate-Income Housing had committed more than $5 billion through specialized financing programs in communities across the nation. These commitments will serve approximately 90,000 lower-income families. Fannie Mae announced in March 1991 a $10 billion expansion of its low- and moderate-income housing programs. This expanded effort, which

Chapter 5

will serve 180,000 additional families, focuses the Company's efforts on the six areas described below.

1. *Low- and Moderate-Income Home Buyers*

For households of modest means, the three greatest barriers to homeownership are (1) accumulating the down payment, (2) establishing a credit history, and (3) managing housing expenses that often exceed standards permitted in traditional mortgage lending.

Since launching its community lending initiative in 1987, Fannie Mae has developed several "model" programs for home buyers, each designed to overcome the major barriers to home ownership. The basic model for home buyers involves combining market-rate first mortgages with subsidized seconds provided by a state or local government, or a nonprofit agency. The programs are done in partnership with lenders, mortgage insurers, public agencies, and nonprofit organizations across the country.

A significant new component, the 3/2 Option, was added to community lending in 1991 to make it easier for borrowers to accumulate the standard minimum down payment by combining their own resources with gifts or loans from others. For instance, under the 3/2 Option, home buyers may meet the minimum 5 percent down-payment requirement with 3 percent of the funds coming from their personal resources and up to 2 percent from a gift from a family member or a grant or unsecured loan from a nonprofit organization or public entity.

Other flexible standards recognize

that many borrowers have a long history of managing high rental payments, and therefore allow as much as 33 percent of monthly gross income to be used for mortgage payments. The traditional standard limits mortgage expenses to 28 percent of income.

Home buyers in this program may demonstrate their credit history through nontraditional means, including verification from utility companies and landlords.

Fannie Mae has committed more than $3 billion to community lending initiatives—commitments that will turn the dream of homeownership into reality for thousands of families who otherwise would have little or no chance of ever owning a home.

One of these home buyers lives in Fannie Mae's hometown of Washington, D.C. This example illustrates how the community lending program can work, given the right combination of organizations working for affordable housing. The story begins with a D.C. man suddenly becoming a single father of four. The family fell behind in its rent payments and soon found itself in the city government's transitional housing program. That's when MANNA Inc., a nonprofit housing developer and social service provider, came into contact with the family. MANNA enrolled the father into a program for prospective home buyers where he could learn budgeting, goal-setting, establishing savings plans, and other skills necessary to become a home owner.

Through MANNA's program, the father found a stable, good-paying job working for the city's transit authority. Ultimately, he saved the down payment necessary to buy a four-bedroom townhouse condominium in a project developed by MANNA through a public/private partnership. Fannie Mae bought the family's mortgage through its community lending initiative.

2. Employer-Assisted Housing

The high cost of housing in urban areas has made it difficult, if not impossible, for many wage earners to find affordable housing close to where they work. Employers in these areas have found that the lack of affordable housing undermines their efforts to attract and retain qualified employees. With labor force conditions tightening as a result of a maturing work force, employers are looking increasingly to offering housing benefits as a tool for recruiting and retaining employees.

Fannie Mae's employer-assisted housing initiative, called Magnet, allows employers to offer affordable-housing assistance in the form of down payments, closing costs, and/or monthly housing payments. The plan is flexible, with options that allow custom designing of a housing benefit plan to respond to the particular needs and market of the employer and employees.

Local lenders finance first mortgage loans under Fannie Mae guidelines for employees participating in employer-assisted housing programs. Fannie Mae then purchases the loans from the lender.

Here's an example of how the employer-assisted housing program has been put to use. A health care organization in a large East Coast city was having great difficulty recruiting and retaining nurses and lab technicians, in part because of the high cost of housing in the area. The hospital was spending $15,000 to $20,000 to recruit and relocate each new nurse and technician. The hospital decided to redirect that money to an employer-assisted housing program. Their reason was simple—doing so would save the hospital money while at the same time help recruiting efforts. The hospital found that by offering housing assistance, which induced staff to stay at least three years, it could reduce recruiting costs enough to completely cover the costs of the housing program.

3. Rural Housing

In rural America, families are more likely to live in poverty than those in our cities. With a significant decline in the number of affordable rural housing units over the past decade, their prospects for affordable housing are bleak.

In June of 1991, Fannie Mae and the Farmers Home Administration formed a partnership to help low- and moderate-income families in rural areas, through a new federally guaranteed loan program. The program features:

No down payment. This allows low- and moderate-income borrowers to finance 100 percent of their mortgage, except for closing costs.

Less qualifying income. Home buyers may qualify for a mortgage using up to 29 percent of their gross monthly income for housing expenses, and up to 41 percent for total debt. Typical ratios are 28 and 36 percent, respectively.

Below-market-rate mortgages for low-income borrowers. Farmers Home subsidizes lower interest rates on the guaranteed mortgages based on a formula that matches borrowers' income to their area's median income.

According to Farmers Home, a typical borrower served by the program is likely to be in his or her mid- to late twenties; a first-time buyer with a loan of approximately $50,000, who is a high school graduate with a family of three, living in a community of between 3,000 and 5,000 residents, earning between $20,000 and $30,000 annually.

4. *Elderly*

In 1989, older Americans represented about 12 percent of the population, and by the year 2030, when the "baby boom" reaches age 65, they will represent 22 percent of the population.

Even though home price appreciation has increased, many older homeowners are living on fixed retirement incomes and are "house rich but cash poor." Also, many are not physically or financially capable of repairing or maintaining their properties. Despite financial problems and difficulties with home maintenance, many elderly residents desire to remain in the homes in which they've lived for many years.

To meet the special needs of older Americans, Fannie Mae offers a variety of housing options, named Seniors' Housing Opportunities (SHO).

Each option allows elderly home-owners to maintain their independence and privacy. The SHO programs include financing for accessory apartments, homesharing arrangements, and sale-leasebacks.

Fannie Mae will also purchase reverse annuity mortgage loans originated as part of a HUD-sponsored demonstration to provide additional housing options for older homeowners. Under this demonstration FHA will insure 25,000 home-equity conversion mortgages (HECMs) that permit seniors to convert their home equity into spendable dollars.

5. *Lower Income Renters*

There is a growing shortage of affordable rental units for poor families. From 1960 to 1987, the number of units renting for less than $300 a month shrank by four million. Meanwhile, the number of families at the low end of the income spectrum who need affordable rental units at those prices grew dramatically.

One of the few sources supporting the construction or rehabilitation of rental units today is a program Congress authorized in 1986 to allow tax credits for corporations making equity investments in qualified low-income rental housing projects.

By 1990, Fannie Mae had made commitments to invest more than $160 million in qualifying projects located in numerous communities throughout the country. Fannie Mae announced in 1991, plans to commit another $150 million to tax-credit projects, investments which will help finance the development of more than 8,000 badly needed units of affordable rental housing for families, for the elderly, and for formerly homeless individuals and families.

6. *Public Finance Initiatives*

Fannie Mae works with state and local housing finance agencies (HFAs) to reduce the cost of mortgages that are financed with mortgage revenue bonds and to help HFAs increase the supply of low- and moderate-income housing in their jurisdictions.

Through 1990, Fannie Mae had purchased more than $87.5 billion of single-family mortgage revenue bonds from housing finance agencies. By selling bonds directly to Fannie Mae, HFAs reduce their borrowing costs and consequently can make mortgages available to home buyers at lower costs than would otherwise be possible.

Fannie Mae also provides credit enhancement for single-family tax-exempt mortgage revenue bonds by using Mortgage-Backed Securities (MBS) as collateral. For housing finance agencies, the benefit of credit enhancement is that it makes mortgage revenue bonds eligible for a "triple-A" rating, thereby reducing the HFAs' financing costs by eliminating the need for mortgage pool insurance, special hazard insurance, or debt service funds. These cost savings can then be passed on to the homeowner in the form of lower mortgage rates.

One of Fannie Mae's recent public finance transactions may become a model that could be adopted nationwide by housing finance agencies. Under this model—the Knoll

HomeStart initiative developed by the Treasurer of the Commonwealth of Pennsylvania, $100 million in funds were set aside to provide mortgages with flexible down-payment requirements and below-market interest rates for eligible home buyers in Pennsylvania. The Pennsylvania HFA will package the loans into MBS issued and guaranteed by Fannie Mae, and the MBS will then be purchased as an investment by the Treasurer. Although the interest rate is slightly below the long-term mortgage interest rate, it meets the Treasurer's overall return requirements.

OUTREACH TO HOUSING PARTNERS

Fannie Mae's extra efforts to support affordable housing do not end with these six initiatives. In fact, these initiatives were originated as part of other partnerships the company has formed with trade associations representing lenders and others in the real estate business, national nonprofit groups, and associations representing state and local housing finance agencies.

Here are a few examples of the additional partnerships Fannie Mae is involved with:

- In conjunction with the Enterprise Foundation, Fannie Mae has established an equity fund to finance rental housing projects that combine permanent shelter and social services for the formerly homeless and others with special needs.

- In 1991, Fannie Mae began an initiative with the U.S. Conference of Mayors, the National Association of Realtors, and Freddie Mac to develop a series of model affordable-housing partnerships in 11 cities throughout the country.

The Fannie Mae Foundation also supports the development of affordable housing in several ways. First, the Foundation's grants are heavily focused on low-income housing needs and the growing importance nonprofits have in providing solutions to our country's housing needs. One example of grants for low-income housing development is the Foundation's support of the Local Initiative Support Corporation, or LISC. In 1991, Fannie Mae awarded a grant of $450,000 to LISC to support their work with community development corpora-tions. LISC is using the grant, along with funds from other corporate sponsors, to provide non-profit housing developers with the start-up funds and technical assistance needed to acquire, renovate or build and sell single-family homes.

A second way the Foundation supports housing development is with its Annual Maxwell Awards of Excellence Program. Each year, the Foundation provides $25,000 grants to six organizations for outstanding affordable-housing projects. The six winners are chosen by an independent committee of low-income housing experts from a field of over 100 applicants. The Champlain Court project mentioned at the beginning of this chapter was one of the recipients of a $25,000 Excellence Award from the Foundation.

Chapter 6

Neighborhood Housing Services of America: Developing a Secondary Market for Affordable-Housing Loans

Mary Lee Widener
President
Neighborhood Housing Services of America, Inc.

In 1979, Antonio and Herlinda Mata were struggling to raise four children in a one-bedroom house. When they'd bought the house, their first, in 1970, they knew it was too small for their family. But it was all they could afford on Mr. Mata's income as a craftsman for a local bookbindery. They wanted the security homeownership would provide for their family. And they looked forward to the day when they would be able to add a room or find a bigger house.

Although Mr. Mata worked hard and steadily, the Matas' income was never large enough for a bigger house. As the children became teenagers, the family's overcrowding grew more desperate. Fin-

ally, the Matas approached the Neighborhood Housing Services (NHS) program in San Antonio. The NHS was able to help, providing a long-term, very low interest loan to add two bedrooms and another bathroom, and to repair the roof and foundation.

Because the NHS had made an important difference in their lives, soon both Mr. and Mrs. Mata were volunteering their time to the NHS partnership, working with their neighbors and with San Antonio's business leaders to see that others have the same chance for a better life that their family had. This work was strengthened when Neighborhood Housing Services of America purchased the Matas' loan, replenishing the NHS loan fund so it could continue to help the elderly, the disabled, single parents, minorities, and low-income families improve their homes, their neighborhoods, and their communities.

NHSA—THE CORPORATION

Neighborhood Housing Services of America, Inc. (NHSA) is a state-chartered, public charity, 501(c)(3) national corporation. It is a part of the NeighborWorks network of neighborhood revitalization organizations and is the sister corporation to the congressionally chartered Neighborhood Reinvestment Corporation (see Chapter 19). NHSA's mission is to strengthen private sector participation in the NeighborWorks network and to meet the liquidity needs of its revolving loan funds. NHSA's Board of Directors, Trustees, and staff represent the traditional resident-business-public sector partnership which is the foundation of all NeighborWorks organizations.

REVOLVING LOAN FUNDS

At the heart of the NeighborWorks network are the revolving loan funds of Neighborhood Housing Services (NHS) programs in 141 cities. Each uses the fund to make home repair loans at flexible rates and terms for residents who do not qualify for conventional financing, usually because their incomes are too low. NHS revolving loan funds recapitalize slowly because repayment schedules must be extended over many years to meet the ability of low-income borrowers to repay. These local loan funds need an infusion of new capital to keep pace with the demand to upgrade the neighborhood. Just as Fannie Mae and Freddie Mac buy loans from savings and loan associations and banks, NHSA provides a secondary market for NHS revolving loan funds.

NHSA purchases blocks of loans from local programs—with recourse—and sells notes backed by these loans to institutional investors, including insurance companies, savings and loans, and pension funds. NHSA makes the purchases at par—accepting the low yields without discounting the face value of the loans—and then seeks social investors to participate in providing these funds to the programs at charitable rates.

SOCIAL INVESTMENT LENDING

NHSA has met the challenge of keeping pace with the liquidity needs of the NeighborWorks network through a careful match of program needs with capital pools. This has been achieved through a blend of below-market-rate social investments from institutional investors and contributed funds (leverage dollars) from foundations, corporations, and the Neighborhood Reinvestment Corporation (see Figure 6.1). NHSA's end-loan financing through its capital pools reached $74 million as of September 30, 1992.

Beyond work with its own capital pools, in recent years NHSA has developed master commitment agreements for loan placements with other lenders. These include a $25 million agreement with Fannie Mae (see Chapter 5) and a $125 million agreement with a consortium of New Jersey lenders. Loan packaging by the NeighborWorks network

Figure 6.1

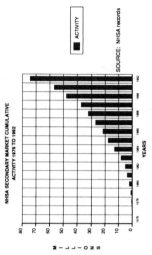

NHSA SECONDARY MARKET DEMOGRAPHICS
Median Incomes 1992 to 1991

YEARS

US MEDIAN
NHS MEDIAN

SOURCES:
U.S. Median: Bureau of Census
Money Income and Poverty
Status of Family and Persons
NHS Median: NHSA records
Note: Incomes are in 1990
constant dollar adjusted
for household size

*N*HSA's secondary market serves borrowers who do not meet conventional credit standards. Profiles on loans purchased by NHSA reflect borrowers at nearly 50 percent of U.S. median and a widening gap.

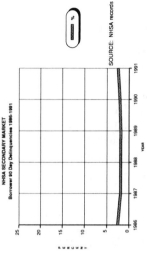

NHSA SECONDARY MARKET CUMULATIVE
ACTIVITY 1978 TO 1992

MILLIONS

YEARS

ACTIVITY

SOURCE: NHSA records

A steady growth in social investments has made possible a similar growth in NHSA loan activity, reaching a one-year high of $17.5 million in 1992.

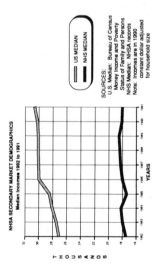

NHSA SECONDARY MARKET CUMULATIVE
INVESTMENTS 1978 TO 1992

MILLIONS

YEARS

INVESTMENTS

SOURCE: NHSA records

*N*HSA resources come from social investors who are willing to take a below-market yield on notes backed by loans from the NeighborWorks[SM] network and from grants for capital reserves from Neighborhood Reinvestment.

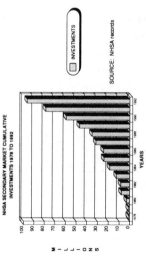

NHSA SECONDARY MARKET
Borrower 90 Day Delinquencies 1986-1991

PERCENT

YEAR

%

SOURCE: NHSA records

A minimal borrower delinquency rate has contributed to NHSA's flawless performance on its investments. NHSA has met all obligations to its social investors; they have experienced no losses, not even a late payment.

against these agreements has been substantial and approvals of those loan
packages exceed $108 million.

WHO IS BEING SERVED

The 163 active NeighborWorks organizations operate in 141 cities, counties, and towns, serving 297 neighborhoods containing slightly over 3 million
residents who live in 1.1 million housing
units. The neighborhoods are further
described by the following statistics:

- Forty-two percent of the households
  are owner-occupied; the national rate
  is 64 percent.

- Racial minorities comprise 39 percent
  of the population; Spanish-speaking
  ethnic minorities comprise 16 percent
  of the total population.

- Seventy-seven percent of the neighborhoods have median family incomes of
  less than 80 percent of their metropolitan area median.

  According to a 1989 survey by the
  Neighborhood Reinvestment Corporation,

- The average revolving loan fund
  borrower's family income is $18,100.
  This is 53 percent of the national median family income.

- Fifty percent of local revolving loan
  fund borrowers are female. Nationally,
  women head 15.5 percent of all
  households; 21 percent of all revolving
  loan fund borrowers are female heads
  of household.

- Eighteen percent of all revolving loan
  fund clients are over 64 years of age.
  Another 15 percent are 55 to 64 years
  of age. In 1988, less than 5 percent of

the conventional-loan clients were 55
or older.

CREATING THE NHSA
SECONDARY MARKET

A strong factor in all aspects of NHSA's
life is reliance on the creative energies of
its Board, staff, and friends. There was
no precedent for doing what we incorporated ourselves to undertake. Yet,
we were confident we could meet the
challenge of providing liquidity for the
revolving loan funds of NHS organizations. We felt that we had to
succeed because we could see that almost immediately after the first three
NHSs began operations, their success in
providing services to their neighborhoods
brought them up against the barrier of
limited loan funds.

Before passage of the Community
Development Act of 1974, foundations
were the only source of NHS loan funds.
While the small loan funds imposed a
limitation, each NHS possessed a uniquely powerful ingredient for success: a
governing board made up of a partnership of unlikely partners—residents of a
troubled neighborhood, representatives
of local financial institutions, and the
local government.

The partnership representatives were
united by their shared commitment to
success in upgrading a jointly selected
declining neighborhood. They had committed to each other to do all they could
to achieve their objectives. Neighborhood residents risked their limited
resources and incurred debt to improve
their homes, and risked their reputations
by encouraging their neighbors to do the
same. Business leaders contributed
management expertise and financial

support to the program's operations, and made conventional loans that would have been turned down were it not for their NHS partnership commitment. The local government sensitized all its departments to the neighborhood's needs, with cooperation ranging from the assignment of housing inspection staff to help identify home repair needs to active participation by police, sanitation, planning, and other departments—plus budgeting capital improvements such as sidewalk repairs, park installations, and lighting improvements.

Renewed confidence in the neighborhood could be expected to flow from such widespread commitments, and it did. Hardship situations could be expected to emerge as the rehabilitation activity got under way, and they did.

For example, one of the first clients of the NHS in Oakland, California, was a 90-year-old widow who had lived in her modest bungalow most of her life. Her children had moved out of the area, but she did not want to leave her home. However, the house needed major repairs and had become unsafe for her and a concern to the neighborhood. The NHS approached her to see if she needed help.

Mrs. Hart welcomed an inspection by the Oakland NHS rehabilitation specialist. He found that the house needed a new roof, foundation work, rewiring, and repairs in the kitchen to bring it to minimum health and safety standards. It also needed exterior painting. When she heard the recommendations, Mrs. Hart simply asked if she could get help in getting the work done and if it would be possible to add a small landing at the back door so she would have a place to put a rocking chair and sit outside.

The NHS staff helped her get contractor bids for the work and discussed financing with her. Mrs. Hart lived on a small Social Security income, and it was clear she would need special help. She carefully determined that she could pay $16.17 per month for a loan.

The Oakland NHS, following its normal policy, used its revolving loan fund to make her a loan for the repairs at her ability to pay. (NHS loans are made with acceleration clauses so that when the property changes hands the loan is repaid in full.) Her children were able to help pay for some of the repairs, reducing the amount she needed to borrow. The NHS also managed the rehabilitation. And when the work was completed, Mrs. Hart was able to celebrate in her rocking chair outside on her new back landing.

This loan, and the improved housing it made possible, benefited both the borrower and her neighbors. But the repayment schedule necessary to meet her ability to pay would not replenish the NHS's revolving loan fund soon enough to meet other residents' needs for affordable home repair loans. As the financial limitations of the loan funds created for hardship lending became an early reality, NHS boards were faced with a need to ration funds even before they could celebrate their success in turning a debilitating lack of confidence in the neighborhood into a heavy demand for rehabilitation loans and technical assistance. Out of this combination of success and frustration, the NHSA secondary market was born—conceived by NHS partners who wanted a reliable way to replenish their revolving loan funds.

The president of the NHS in Oakland, California, was then a financial industry representative from Great Western

Savings—Leslie N. Shaw. He captured the sentiment of all the partners when he said that a businesslike mechanism would have to be created to replenish NHS loan funds. His recommendations spurred development of a NHS loan purchase program, and Neighborhood Housing Services of America was incorporated to administer it. Many of the Board members, including its chairman, Robert O'Brien, Jr., are charter members and have served for the full 17 years of NHSA's existence. Most others have served for more than a decade and are past presidents of early programs, such as William Plechaty, NHSA's vice chairman and past president of the Chicago NHS; Clarissa Walker, past chairperson of the Minneapolis Southside NHS; Sophia Jeffery, chairperson of the Springfield, Massachusetts, NHS and chairperson of the National NHS Advisory Council; and Alphonso Whitfield, Jr., NHSA's Loan Committee chairperson and past president of the Newark NHS. The average term of all board members is nine years.

Within weeks of Mr. Shaw's recommendation, NHSA's founders approached the Urban Reinvestment Task Force, Neighborhood Reinvestment's predecessor, for grant support to enable NHSA to purchase loans from the local groups, which had been made to "unbankable" borrowers at terms based upon their ability to pay (terms that over the years have averaged 6 percent interest and 12-year maturities). Within months, a grant was approved and the loan purchase program established. The availability of such resources to the NHS organizations unleashed program activity which until then had been held back by uncertainty. Requests to NHSA to purchase loans quickly exceeded available resources.

With the help of the Ford Foundation's Louis Winnick and the Neighborhood Reinvestment Corporation under the leadership of William A. Whiteside, NHSA began work to turn its loan purchase program into a true secondary market. The NHSA board—made up of representatives of each of the NHS partners, including talented financial institution executives—worked closely with staff in designing the initial format, and key board members along with the chairman of the Federal Home Loan Bank Board participated in pivotal meetings with Ford Foundation representatives. Mr. Winnick enlisted the participation of the Equitable Life Assurance Society of the U.S. as the first purchaser of NHSA corporate notes, backed by the cash flow from NHS loans and other collateral. The Equitable's $1 million purchase, closed in May 1978, liquified NHSA's mortgage pool and allowed NHSA to buy a further $1 million in NHS loans. This successful process has been refined and repeated again and again since this initial note sale.

NHSA SECONDARY-MARKET OPERATIONS

NHSA's secondary market is built on the solid foundation of an active board of directors and board committees. The directors are aggressive in monitoring the health of NHSA and in assuring that the operations are responsive to the programs served.

Just as the revolving loan funds are the heart of the NeighborWorks network, NHSA's Loan Committee is the heart of the secondary market. Its members share the partnership strength of the NeighborWorks network, bringing to the same table leaders who know the day-to-day social and economic struggles of low- and moderate-income neighborhoods and leaders who understand the concerns of the financial industry.

NHSA's Loan Committee, chaired by Alphonso Whitfield, Jr., vice president and director of community investment for the Federal Home Loan Bank Board of New York, works diligently on policy development to keep pace with the network's changing needs. It then "rolls up its sleeves" and acts on hundreds of staff recommendations for loan approvals in the course of the secondary-market operations.

NHSA's Loan Committee mirrors the same resident-business-local government partnership that is the foundation of all NHS organizations. It is expressed in the lively participation of representatives from the three sectors at every level of our work. NHSA's loan policies reflect the insight of its members in the financing needs of the groups served by NHSA. That insight grows out of their own personal involvement as volunteers on local boards.

The challenge faced by the committee is one of constantly balancing the local financing needs with fiscal responsibility. Major policy changes that are called for to keep pace with network financing requests are considered and acted on by the full board. The decisions are not easy and are debated fully.

In one instance, the first-hand experiences of Mayor Joseph P. Riley, Jr., in attempting to push the upgrading of small apartment buildings in Charleston, South Carolina, brought him to make the motion that NHSA seek to establish the capacity to finance the rehabilitation of small apartment buildings. In another instance, it was the first-hand experiences of Alphonso Whitfield, Jr., as president of the Newark NHS and then-Director of Social Investments at The Prudential in attempting to push the upgrade of vacant lots and vacant houses in Newark that played a major role in the establishment of the NHSA first-mortgage program.

Beyond the establishment of specific lending programs, operational policies are monitored in relation to network needs. Sophia Jeffery, as chairperson of the National NHS Advisory Council, receives recommendations for policy changes from a Technical Advisory Group made up of network representatives. She brings the recommendations to the Loan Committee and the board as needed. A recent request was that NHSA's reserve requirements be changed to allow a higher leveraging of NHS loan portfolios through sales to NHSA. As a result, NHSA has agreed to reduce the reserve requirements.

The challenges of being a last-resort lender do not end with establishing policies and approving loans. Rather, the ongoing challenge is in assuring that the loan decisions will result in payback of the loans, as it is their cash stream that is the source of funds for payback of NHSA notes with social investors who are the ultimate funders of the secondary-market program. This challenge is met by NHSA staff. We see the staff's longevity as an important factor in its success.

NHSA's officers and secondary-market lead staff largely "grew up" with the program.[1] Their collective longevity with

NHSA is 82.83 years, averaging 11.83 years per person. Michael Balmuth, NHSA's senior vice president, heads the secondary market operations. Craig Galloway and Roypim Ramsey run day-to-day operations—purchasing approved loans and closing notes with social investors. NHSA's founding board chairman and treasurer, George Behymer, then-president of Home Federal Savings and Loan of Cincinnati, encouraged NHSA to establish a top-quality in-house computerized loan servicing operation early in its life. Ritchie Post, NHSA's vice president of finance, undertook that challenge and built a highly successful system for (1) reporting to the local program on the status of loans sold to NHSA, (2) NHSA's own financial statement requirements, and (3) reporting to social investors on the status of loans used as collateral to back their notes. Armed with monthly status reports, Edward Cullen, another long-time member of NHSA's staff, is able to be that friendly, nudging voice on the other end of the phone that has been so successful in encouraging programs to cure loan delinquencies.

The loan purchase procedure functions as follows:

- An NHS offers to sell a portion of its loan portfolio to NHSA under the conditions of a Loan Sale and Servicing Agreement, which provides that:

  - NHSA buys the NHS loans at par (without discounting),

  - the servicing relationship between the borrower and the NHS remains with the NHS,

  - should a loan become 90 days delinquent, the NHS will buy it back or replace it with a similar loan, and

- the NHS may sell NHSA not more than 50 percent of its loan portfolio, so that it always has this replacement capacity.

- NHSA buys the loans approved by its Loan Committee by utilizing capital it has received through grants and loans. After it has pooled a significant dollar volume in loans from a number of programs, NHSA is prepared to issue a corporate note backed by these loans.

- A social investor agrees to buy NHSA's notes in accordance with the terms and conditions of a Master Note Purchase Agreement at an interest rate several points below market. The costs to NHSA of each social investment placement is the difference between the approximately 6 percent average interest rate on the loans purchased and the higher—yet below market—rate on the notes sold, plus operating expenses and credit enhancements in the form of reserves and mortgage insurance. At a closing, the social investor receives the notes, NHSA receives cash (which it uses to buy further loans, starting the cycle over again), and a trustee receives the pool of loans which guarantees the notes, as well as the reserves.

- NHSs collect monthly payments on the loans they have sold, forward them to NHSA, and NHSA, in turn, forwards them to the trustee. The trustee makes quarterly payments on NHSA's obligations to the social investor from a combination of the monthly loan payments received and the reserve funds. The reserve funds serve a dual purpose, subsidizing the interest rate differential and serving as a cash-flow-guarantee fund to cover unanticipated shortfalls that could result from delinquent loans.

NHSA's secondary market operates in a fiscally sound, responsible manner. At the same time, it is responsive to the human and social problems that local NHS programs are working to solve. Very often, NHS loans rebuild lives at the same time that they repair homes.

When James Sullivan and his wife inherited their 110-year-old, two-family Brooklyn house from Mrs. Sullivan's family about 15 years ago, it needed many repairs and had a serious termite infestation. The foundation was sinking, and the first floor was uninhabitable. Mr. Sullivan said that walking on the first floor was like taking a ride on the cyclone at Coney Island. The Sullivans moved into the third floor, did some exterior work, and were saving for a new foundation, interior remodeling, and a central heating system.

Shortly after the Sullivans had completed exterior repairs on the house, Mrs. Sullivan became seriously ill. All their savings went to pay her medical bills. Her condition has improved, but she is in a nursing home and will require constant care for the rest of her life. Also, at about this time, the company Mr. Sullivan worked for went bankrupt, and he lost all his pension rights.

Mr. Sullivan did get another job, as a token clerk with the Transit Authority, but because of his age he won't work there long enough to earn an adequate pension. The house is his only asset. But it was in such poor condition that he couldn't rent the downstairs apartment. And because the house didn't have central heating, he couldn't find a conventional lender who would loan him the money to make the needed repairs.

One day a friend told him about NHS.

Mr. Sullivan made a loan application. He got the loan, and much more. The NHS rehab specialist helped him find a contractor and supervised the work. And the NHS deferred Mr. Sullivan's loan payments until after the apartment was rented, so that he could use the rent money to make the payments. But Mr. Sullivan tells his story best:

I'm very grateful to NHS because they not only helped me remodel my house, but in a very real sense they helped me remodel my life. I was looking forward to a very bleak future in that I had lost my pension. Now I'm working for Transit. I will be with them hopefully for another several years, but I do have an income from the house which, together with Social Security, means I will be able to live in dignity in my old age.

EXPANDING THE SECONDARY-MARKET PROGRAM

As NeighborWorks partners and supporters observed the importance of the NHSA secondary-market program to the NHS network and its effectiveness, their personal and institutional commitments to it grew. New social investments flowed from this increased sense of commitment, and significant corporate and foundation grants leveraged larger lending pools, enabling NHSs and mutual housing associations to reach a wider range of lower-income housing needs.

Personal executive leadership was key to the successful expansion of NHSA's loan purchase capacity. Chief executives of Equitable, Prudential, Aetna, Allstate, and Metropolitan showed confidence in the NHSA secondary market through significant new commitments from their companies and highly visible personal support. Federal Reserve Board governor J. Charles Partee, chairman of the Neighborhood Reinvestment Corporation, provided steady leadership, enabling the Corporation's grants and loans to NHSA to expand its loan purchase capacity.

As NHSA's capacity grew, the local programs increasingly counted on the NHSA secondary-market program as a ready source of capital. The NHSA board was presented with the ongoing challenge of expanding support to allow for continued growth of the NHSA secondary market, ensuring continued liquidity of the NHS network as an important national resource for lower-income neighborhoods. The board of directors sought to form a board of trustees who would undertake this challenge as their primary objective.

Long-time friends of the NHS network and World Savings Board members—Herbert Sandler, chairman and chief executive officer and Warren Widener, director and president of the California NHS Foundation—helped NHSA and the Neighborhood Reinvestment Corporation enlist NHSA's first trustees. Charles E. Lord accepted enlistment as founding chairman and a charter member along with chief executive officers from Safeway Stores, Allstate Insurance Company, and the Bank of America. They were joined by senior executives from The Standard Oil Company in giving enormous personal time developing strategies and enlisting support. They undertook a goal of bringing the NHSA loan purchase capacity to a level that would position it to meet the challenges of the 1990s. They achieved this goal by creating a significant upsurge in private support for the secondary market—both grants and social investments—through their own participation and through their success in attracting others. At the same time, they also worked to expand the amount of conventional lending in low- and moderate-income neighborhoods.

Social Compact

Throughout their work, NHSA's trustees and directors have been mindful of the broad-scale lending needed to achieve the neighborhood revitalization mission of the NeighborWorks network. They are aware that the demand on NHS loan funds (and thus the need for replenishment through NHSA loan purchases) is directly related to the degree of private-sector lending available in Neighbor-Works neighborhoods. This awareness was a factor in their decision to lead an effort to create a "Social Compact Between the Financial Services Industry and America's Neighborhoods," reaching beyond the NeighborWorks network.

Social Compact is a peer-to-peer consortium of banking, saving, and insurance leaders who are committed to making a special effort to reach low-income communities and to encourage others to be creative in reaching out to do community lending. NHSA is contributing the time of Lynn Reilly Whiteside, who is providing lead staff support to this effort. More than 220 financial services institutions have already joined the Social Compact. The Social Compact leadership group consists of:

Leland S. Prussia, Chairman; formerly, BankAmerica

David Ballweg, Community State Bank

Joe Belew, Consumer Bankers Association

Leland C. Brendsel, Freddie Mac

Diane M. Casey, Independent Bankers Association of America

Brian D. Dittenhafer, Collective Federal Savings Bank

Raymond H. Elliott, formerly, Federal Home Loan Bank of Boston

James R. Faulstich, Federal Home Loan Bank of Seattle

Wayne E. Hedien, Allstate Insurance Company

Howard Hodges, The American Bankers Association

James A. Johnson, Fannie Mae

Roger Joslin, State Farm Fire and Casualty

Preston Martin (Immediate Past Chairman), Western Federal Savings

James F. Montgomery, Great Western Financial Corporation

Robert B. O'Brien, Jr., Printon, Kane Group

Arthur F. Ryan, The Chase Manhattan Bank

Herbert M. Sandler, World Savings & Loan Association

Paul Schosberg, Savings and Community Bankers of America

Charles Lee Thiemann, Federal Home Loan Bank of Cincinnati

Membership in Social Compact is voluntary. Leaders pledge to commit significant resources to low- and moderate-income neighborhoods in their market areas. As an example of strong interest in the needs of low-income neighborhoods, responses were received from nearly all the companies invited to participate in a Social Compact survey of services and products. They have a combined asset base of $693.3 billion. Results were disseminated to over 2,000 community groups. They were also sent to all Social Compact members, along with names and telephone numbers of a contact person at each institution, so that networking can begin and institutions can share ideas to promote creativity in serving low- and moderate-income neighborhoods.

Social Compact has also developed a recognition program to honor institutions with outstanding records in reaching out to neighborhoods. This aggressive, positive attention to responsive lending is expected to increase the availability of conventional funds in neighborhoods across America.

THE NHSA CAPITAL POOLS IN THE 1990s

As the nonprofit organizations that make up the NeighborWork network grow in maturity, their capital needs not only increase, they also become more complex. NHSA and the Neighborhood Reinvestment Corporation work closely with the network to understand its needs. Neighborhood Reinvestment provides a wide range of organizational development, technical assistance, and training services. Neighborhood Reinvestment also helps NHSA build its capacity to respond more broadly to the network's nonconventional financing needs, including direct origination of multifamily loans on nonprofit-owned properties. As a result, at July 1, 1991, the list of investors in the NHSA secondary market had grown to include the following:

Allstate Insurance Company

Aetna Life Insurance Company

BankAmerica Foundation

Employers Insurance of Wausau, A Mutual Company

The Equitable Life Assurance Society of the United States

Board of Pensions of the Evangelical Lutheran Church in America

The John D. and Catherine T. MacArthur Foundation

The Metropolitan Life Foundation

The Mutual Benefit Life Insurance Company

The National Cooperative Bank Development Corporation

Neighborhood Reinvestment

Presbyterian Church (USA) Foundation

Downtown United Presbyterian Church, Rochester, New York

The Prudential Insurance Company of America

General Board of Pensions of the United Methodist Church

World Savings and Loan Association

NHSA LOAN PRODUCTS

The types of loan products and dollar level of the capital pools are reflected in the NHSA Secondary Market Loan Products chart (see Figure 6.2.)

NHSA's loan products grew out of the needs of the NeighborWorks organizations. All represent underwriting criteria which were negotiated to be responsive to the needs of neighborhoods in transition and lower-income borrowers. The loan products were also created to fill gaps in conventional and public loan products and to fit within a housing development framework.

NHSA offers five general loan products to the NeighborWorks network. Each product has been designed to meet a particular need and selectively access different social investors. A brief description of NHSA's loan products follows.

Revolving Loan Fund Home Rehabilitation Loans. NHSA purchases rehabilitation mortgages at par and with recourse from local NeighborWorks organizations. Typically, these are second-mortgage loans made by NHS organizations because the resident cannot qualify to borrow from other lenders such as commercial banks. The Equitable Life Assurance Society of the United States helped NHSA create its secondary market for rehabilitation loans in 1976, with a $1 million investment. Since then, Equitable has made three more investments, bringing its total commitment to $10 million. Other large investors include Allstate Insurance with $8 million, Metropolitan Life Insurance with $5 million, World Savings and Loan with $15 million, and Aetna Life & Casualty with $4 million.

First Mortgages. To help local NeighborWorks organizations tackle the problems of abandoned houses to provide homeownership opportunities, NHSA and The Prudential Insurance Company of America developed a first-mortgage secondary market. The Prudential has made two commitments totalling $12.5 million. NHSA recently expanded this

Figure 6.2   NHSA Secondary Market Loan Products (as of July, 1991)

NEIGHBORWORKS℠ MORTGAGE ACTIVITY

1-4 Units	Rehabilitation Second Mortgages with recourse
1-8 Units	First Mortgages with recourse
1-4 Units	First Mortgages without recourse
5-40 Units	First Mortgages without recourse
Development and Bridge Loans	
Local Government Mortgages with recourse	

NHSA CAPITAL POOLS

INVESTOR	TOTAL NOTES	INTERNAL REVOLVING LOANS AND RESERVES	
Mutual Benefit Life	$ 1.0 M	Neighborhood Reinvestment	$8.7 M
Equitable	10.0 M		
Wausau	0.5 M		
AEtna	4.0 M		
Allstate	8.0 M	MacArthur Foundation	2.0 M
Metropolitan	5.0 M		
World Savings	15.0 M		
Presbyterian Church	0.2 M	Presbyterian Foundation	0.3 M
Citibank	.1 M		
Prudential	$ 12.5 M		
Lutheran Church	0.5 M		
Methodist Church	2.5 M		
World Savings	$ 18.7 M		
Lutheran Church	$ 1.5 M		
Methodist Church	2.5 M		
National Co-Op Bank Development Corp.	$ 1.9 M		
Allstate	$ 10.0 M		

secondary market through a partnership with World Savings and Loan Association. World is providing $18.7 million in affordable first-mortgage loans in 45 NHS neighborhoods in 13 states. World has built the infrastructure to keep this pool replenished with additional funds as needed.

Multifamily Loans. Because homeownership is out of reach for so many people, improving and increasing the supply of permanent affordable housing is a necessary element in stabilizing low- and moderate-income neighborhoods. With a grant and loan from Neighborhood Reinvestment, NHSA created a new program to provide permanent financing for multi-unit or rental housing owned and managed by nonprofits or mutual housing associations. With able encouragement from George Knight, Executive Director of Neighborhood Reinvestment, the Board of Pensions of the Evangelical Lutheran Church in America agreed to be the first investor in this program, providing $1.5 million for multifamily loan purchases. Another $0.5 million will be used for problem property first-mortgage purchases. The General Board of Pensions of the United Methodist Church became the second investor, with a $5 million commitment. Half the funds are available for multifamily loans and half for first-mortgage purchases.

Facilitating Private-Sector Financing. In addition to providing its own direct financing to facilitate neighborhood revitalization, NHSA has helped nonprofit and for-profit developers obtain needed financing from a variety of other sources.

Fannie Mae Master Commitment. Under a master commitment agreement with Fannie Mae, NHSA helped place $15 million in financing for quality multifamily housing in NHS-NeighborWorks neighborhoods. The need for this commitment grew out of the Neighborhood Reinvestment Corporation's Apartment Improvement Program headed by Steve Tuminaro, founder of the program. It generated rehabilitation of more than 17,251 multifamily units under very sound and successful structures. Yet, financing for improvement of large apartment buildings remains one of the most difficult challenges in affordable housing nationally.

National Co-Op Bank Development Corporation. Because nonprofits find that difficulty in obtaining development financing is often the biggest stumbling block for complex housing proposals, NHSA put together a housing development initiative and brought on a small staff headed by Michael Johnson, an architect and experienced developer. One of his early objectives resulted in a commitment by the National Co-Op Bank Development Corporation to make $1.9 million available for development loans to the NHSs and mutual housing associations. As a result, NHSA makes short-term loans to NeighborWorks organizations to finance recoverable predevelopment costs, limited construction financing, and working capital gaps while permanent project financing is put into place.

New Jersey Urban Lending Program. NHSA initiated and is managing the New Jersey Urban Lending Program in partnership with the state of New Jersey, under the leadership of Ernest Baskette, Jr., NHSA's vice president. The program makes available $125 million in residential construction financing to stimulate development of low- to moderate-income housing in urban areas of New Jersey.

Under the program, the staff has packaged $108 million in construction loans that were approved by its consortium of lenders as a group or by its members. This program also broke new ground for NHSA, guaranteeing a loan to induce rehabilitation of a 67-unit apartment building the NHS neighborhood. It is an unqualified restoration success important to the life of the neighborhood. Since this was known to be a higher-risk endeavor than those usually undertaken by NHSA, no social investor funds were put at risk. Instead, the city of Newark became the first-line guarantor and is a full partner with NHSA and the developer in attempting to make the building a financial success in addition to its physical rebirth.

Local Government Secondary Market. NHSA has developed the capacity to purchase loans made by city governments to lower-income families. Allstate pioneered this product with a $10 million commitment and the city of St. Paul became the first city to close an $800,000 loan under the program.

TWO DECADES OF SUCCESS

NHSA's pioneering nonprofit secondary market has met with success beyond any imagined when it began. It is an organization that has learned to accept all neighborhood funding challenges with full expectation of success. After all, it has liquefied community loan funds of unbankable loans to families with incomes which average below the poverty level without a single loss to an investor in its entire history.

From its beginning, NHSA has benefited from highly experienced outside counsel provided by Fred Pillon, a partner with Gibson, Dunn & Crutcher.

Mr. Pillon also serves as general counsel to NHSA. He has assisted NHSA's officers to put in place structures that ensure that their fiduciary objectives are met. A solid system of safeguards is a distinguishing factor for the NHSA secondary-market program.

Starting at the local program level, each NHS is subject to an annual audit of its financial statements and internal controls by an independent external auditor. Also, once every two years, Neighborhood Reinvestment performs a programmatic, operational and organizational review of each NHS. If weaknesses or potential weaknesses are found through either the financial audit or the program review, then Neighborhood Reinvestment assigns field service staff to work with the NHS program, board and staff to iron out any problems.

Another level of security at the local level is provided by NHSA's policy of requiring a 50 percent reserve of assets in any NHS's revolving loan fund. NHSA buys NHS loans with recourse, assuring that each NHS has sufficient assets to substitute or repurchase any delinquent loan. NHSA's own computer system tracks such delinquencies. If an NHS is late in forwarding the monthly payments it collects for loans sold, NHSA staff will work with the NHS to get payments current.

In the event an NHS decides to dissolve and NHSA has purchased loans from it, the Loan Sale and Servicing Agreement between the NHS and NHSA remains a legal obligation. Since most NHS loans are made from Community Development Block Grant funds that the local city has granted under contract to the NHS, when the NHS dissolves, its loan assets and the legal obligation of the Loan Sale and Servicing Agreement revert to the city. In the few instances where the city has received loan assets back from the NHS, it has also undertaken the obligation of the Loan Sale and Servicing Agreement.

NHSA purchases loans from over 136 NHSs that are spread geographically across the country and assigns loans to each investor with an eye to geographical diversity, thereby insulating each from regional economic upheavals. NHSA also maintains a pool of current, paying mortgages for immediate substitution into an investor pool in the event a mortgage in the pool goes delinquent. If a mortgage is pulled out of the investor pool, the originating NHS either repurchases the mortgage or substitutes a new mortgage out of its reserve pool. Thus the loans in the investor pool are always nondelinquent.

Finally, all of NHSA's investments are over-collateralized, providing additional principal security and allowing excess cash flow to cover the possibility that the collections from an NHS may be slow. All the collateral (loans, cash, and investments) is held on the investor's behalf by a trustee who protects the investor's investment security, monitors NHSA's obligations, and makes all payments to the investor.

Because of its fiscal soundness and effectiveness, the NHSA secondary-market program enjoys top-level private sector support as well as congressional support to help build its capital pools. In addition, members of the Neighborhood Reinvestment Board of Directors have added their own volunteer efforts to the vote of confidence demonstrated by the private sector and the Congress. With such strong support, we fully anticipate continued success. This confidence is grounded in the high levels of creative energy that continue to flow into the secondary-market program from the entire NeighborWorks network and its supporters.

ENDNOTE

[1] Mary Lee Widener, president; Michael Balmuth, senior vice president; Ritchie Post, vice president; Ernest Baskette, Jr., vice president; George Behymer, treasurer; Zaretta Kimble, assistant secretary; Craig Galloway; and Roypim Ramsey.

Chapter 7

Pension Funds and Affordable Housing

Amy S. Anthony
President
Housing Investments, Inc.

With total assets of over $2 trillion, pension plans are a key source of investment capital in the United States. Over the past two decades, pension fund investors have committed significant amounts of this capital to the U.S. commercial real estate markets. Such investors now hold approximately $100 billion in real estate assets, up from just $17 billion in 1981. Only a small proportion of this capital, however, has been invested in the housing sector, primarily in the acquisition or development of market-rate, multifamily apartment projects. Affordable housing has not been an area of focus. This chapter will address some of the reasons why pension funds have been reluctant to make affordable-housing investments and outline some investment strategies and structures that may serve to encourage such investment in the future.

Despite their current substantial presence, pension funds are relative newcomers to the real estate capital markets. Until the mid-1970s, real estate was considered too risky to be appropriate for pension investing. Thereafter, as real estate as an asset class became more acceptable, investments were largely limited to the office, retail and, later, industrial sectors. Multifamily housing was the last to gain acceptance. Even today, very few funds have committed significant amounts of capital to multifamily investments.

There are a number of reasons for this. First, the capital requirements of housing projects tend to be far smaller than those of office buildings or shopping malls. Thus, funds can invest larger amounts per transaction in these other property types. For fund staffs, investment oversight is simplified if the task is to manage five $20 million investments rather than twenty $5 million investments. Second, multifamily investments are perceived to entail greater risks. The income stream is less certain because residential leases tend to be significantly shorter than commercial leases, and tenant turnover is higher. Property management requirements are more intensive, and the credit of prospective tenants is less certain.

Affordable housing is seen as suffering from all of these drawbacks, and more. Rightly or wrongly, the concept of affordable housing carries with it the perception of "subsidy," which, in turn, carries the perception of increased risk and reduced investment return. This is perhaps the most clearcut reason for funds' lack of interest in affordable-housing investments.

In order to combat this perception effectively, those seeking capital from pension funds need first to understand pension funds' objectives and operating procedures. In general, pension funds are long-term, risk-adverse investors. As fiduciaries acting on behalf of plan participants, pension funds are obligated to seek competitive, risk-adjusted returns. With regard to real estate, this means that proposed investments must offer returns that are comparable to those available from other asset classes, such as stocks or bonds.

Targeting Potential Fund Investors

A first step in increasing pension fund participation in affordable housing is to identify those funds likely to be most inclined to consider such transactions. While any fund that has a history of

housing investment should be considered, my experience leads me to believe that large public funds, *i.e.*, state or municipal employee retirement funds with sizable assets ($3 billion to $5 billion or more) will most likely take the lead in this area, for several reasons.

1. Many larger public funds have their own investment management staff—including, in some cases, one or more staff members who focus specifically on real estate investments. These people have the level of professional competence necessary to understand and analyze knowledgeably the relatively complex investment structures that are likely to be involved in affordable-housing transactions.

2. Large funds will have sufficient capital to invest and likely will be actively seeking ways to further diversify their overall investment portfolio.

3. State funds may have access to and contacts within intermediary agencies or groups (such as housing finance agencies or bank consortiums) whose participation may be key to the structuring of economically feasible transactions.

4. Some state funds may have a legislative mandate or public policy interest in making in-state investments or, even more specifically, in-state "economically targeted" investments. The number of funds making such investments is increasing, and the most common area of investment is housing. To date, pools of single-family mortgage financing that are available to "members" (*e.g.*, the class of beneficiaries served by the fund, such as teachers or public employees) have been the most common vehicles. The

availability of such capital has helped make single-family ownership more affordable for the targeted groups. However, the efficiency of the secondary market, which both dictates the rate of return required by pension investors and assures the ready availability of mortgage financing for most home buyers, limits the ability of most pension funds to be major participants in this area.

5. Finally, state funds simply have had more experience with housing-related investments than their private counterparts. Thus they are more familiar with the property type and less time will be required to educate them about housing investments.

In targeting and gaining access to these funds, owners and developers of affordable housing should make use of the funds' existing relationships with real estate investment managers and consultants. While some funds invest directly, most rely upon managers and/or consultants to identify appropriate opportunities, underwrite the investments and, in some cases, make the final investment decision. These intermediaries will not only respond to specific investment proposals, but can serve as advocates for proposals that they feel have merit.

Structuring an Investment: Risk and Reward

When underwriting an affordable-housing transaction, pension funds' primary concerns will be risk and reward. Thus, those who seek pension fund capital for affordable housing must persuade fund investors that the risks inherent in a proposed investment have been accurately identified, that the proposed investment

structure serves to minimize those risks, and that the returns expected adequately compensate the fund for the risks that remain. While pension funds are as likely as other investors to perceive the public relations potential of supporting a social benefit such as affordable housing, they also will be wary of the political implications of doing so. Private funds in particular are unlikely to respond positively to political pressure to make an investment or to "soften" their usual investment criteria. Investment proposals should show potential fund investors how the real investment risks have been reduced, not attempt to persuade them to accept a lower rate of return to serve a social purpose.

In almost all cases, pension fund investments in affordable housing will take the form of debt. Equity ownership generally entails higher risks, most notably an exposure to "first dollar risk of loss." For example, Figure 7.1 illustrates the capital structure of an unleveraged equity investment. If the property appreciates in value by 20 percent over the holding period, the investor will receive the entire benefit of that appreciation; similarly, if the property declines in value by 20 percent, the investor will bear the entire loss. In terms of risk, the investor is placed "at risk" for the first dollar of loss and is rewarded beginning with the first dollar of gain.

Figure 7.2 represents the position of a debt investor who has made a traditional first-mortgage loan for 60 percent of the property's value. In this case, if the property appreciates by 20 percent, the property owner will receive the full benefit of that appreciation. The debt investor will receive the return of its original investment, plus the agreed-upon rate of interest. However, if the property

Figure 7.1   Equity Ownership

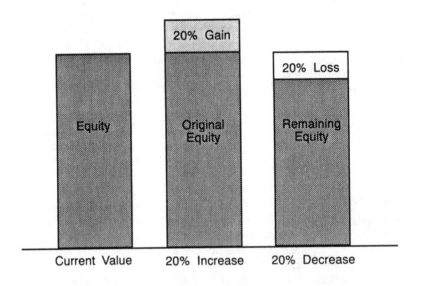

declines in value by 20 percent, the owner will suffer the loss, but the debt investor will still be entitled to its full principal and interest. Thus, the debt investor does not bear the first dollar risk of loss; only if the property decreases in value by more than 40 percent (and the debt investor is forced to foreclose) is the investor's capital threatened.

While pension investors may be willing to assume the higher risk/reward trade-off when the property involved is a "trophy" office building or retail mall, they likely will seek the greater security of debt in affordable-housing transactions. (Return through appreciation in value may also be contrary to the social goals of the affordable-housing program.) The addition of a second mortgage to the capital structure insulates the first mortgage holder (see Figure 7.3). Should property value decline and the borrower default, the holder of the second mortgage may step in and continue to service the first mortgage in order to protect its position. In the case of affordable housing, a second mortgage may be available from a governmental source such as a state housing agency or the Federal Home Loan Bank Board.

The timing of the debt investment also has risk implications. It is highly unlikely that pension funds will consider providing construction financing, which

Figure 7.2   Sixty Percent First Mortgage

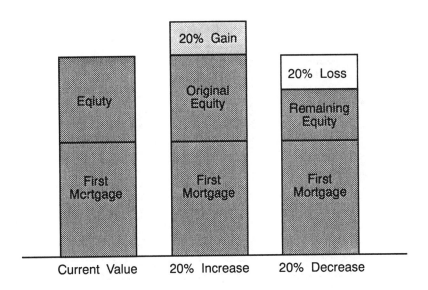

carries with it the risk that the project will be completed and leased on time and on budget. More appropriate to the risk profiles of most funds is "takeout" financing, *i.e.*, providing the capital required to repay the construction mortgage. Such financing is generally contingent upon the project's achieving certain leasing and/or income requirements.

More often, however (again, for reasons of risk), a fund may be interested in refinancing a project that has established a solid operating history, or in acquiring on the secondary market part or all of an existing, "seasoned" first-mortgage loan. In both cases, the property risks will have been reduced

because the project is completed and leased, and the borrower has a history of meeting its debt obligations.

These latter options also dovetail nicely with the objectives of traditional sources of development financing for affordable housing. In some locales, public or quasi-public agencies are available to provide construction and/or takeout financing for certain types of projects, or to offer interest rate guarantees or other "credit supports" to assist developers in obtaining (or affording) private market financing. These programs generally assume that the need for such assistance will be short-term, and that the owner/borrower will replace the

Figure 7.3   Sixty Percent First Mortgage + Thirty Percent Second Mortgage

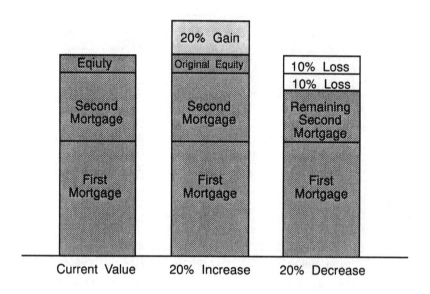

agency's capital with market-rate funding within three to five years so that the agency's funds can be recycled into further affordable development. At this stage in the operating history of the project, pension funds become a potential source for the replacement financing.

Reducing Risk

There are a variety of ways in which affordable-housing transactions may be structured in order to meet the risk/return requirements of pension investors. As noted above, a threshold requirement will be that the borrower have a significant amount of equity that

is "ahead" of the fund's invested capital (*i.e.*, at first risk of loss). In today's real estate environment, identifying investors willing to accept "first dollar" risk is extremely difficult. Returns on equity investments have fallen dramatically over the past few years, as the boom market of the mid-1980s has become the "bust" market of the early 1990s. In addition, virtually all of the tax incentives that so dramatically stimulated investor interest in real estate in the 1980s have been eliminated.

However, developers of affordable housing have an important advantage in this search for equity capital: the low-income housing credit. As one of the few tax shelters left, the credit is a strong incentive for taxable investors. The more equity that is raised, the more attractive the transaction to a pension investor. In general, it will be necessary to raise enough equity to meet 30 percent to 50 percent of an affordable project's capital requirements.

Pension funds will also be more inclined to consider investing in projects that have a strong debt service coverage ratio. This indicates that the project's net operating income is substantially higher than the amount necessary to meet the principal and interest payments on the proposed loan. For affordable projects, a ratio of 1:1.2 or better (meaning that net operating income is at least 120 percent of debt service requirements) likely would be necessary to allay a fund's fears of default. Again, the low-income-housing credit is an important factor. Tax shelter benefits are the major source of the equity investor's return; there is no expectation of current cash yield. Without the need to provide a current cash return to the equity investors, more of the property's cash flow is available for debt service. Thus, credits are often the key to making an affordable project economically feasible.

Another way to reduce the lender's risk is to propose a loan structure that requires a moderate rate of amortization for the mortgage principal. Most commercial mortgages require that interest be paid only currently, with all principal to be repaid at the end of the loan term. This leaves the lender's entire investment amount exposed for the full period of the investment. With an amortizing structure, the amount of the lender's capital investment, and thus that component of risk, is continually reduced over time. Amortization also helps to alleviate the debt investor's concern about an "exit strategy"—or how ultimately it will get out of the investment.

The ultimate risk in a real estate debt investment is that the borrower will default and the lender will end up having to operate or sell the property to recoup some or all of its investment. In this area, there is a benefit to affordable-housing investments that ought not to be overlooked. Generally, when a borrower defaults and title to the underlying property passes to the lender through foreclosure, the property's operating characteristics remain unchanged—except (of course) that there is no longer debt service to pay. Operating revenues remain the same, and to the extent that these revenues are insufficient to meet property expenses, the lender simply assumes the ongoing liability for operating losses. This is not the case with qualified affordable housing. There are two options for a lender that takes title to an affordable project to immediately increase the value of that project: (1) the lender may disregard the rental constraints and increase rents to market rates; or (2) the lender may keep the rental constraints in place and re-sell the low-income tax credits to other investors.

Model Investment

A typical affordable housing transaction designed to attract the attention of pension fund investors will have the following characteristics:

- The project will be sponsored by a private or nonprofit entity with a track record of successful affordable development.

- The project will be well-constructed,

in a stable neighborhood, and will have the potential for conversion to market-rate housing in the event of foreclosure.

- Leasing and management of the project will be handled by firms experienced in marketing and managing low-income housing.

- In order for such a project to be economically feasible and have the capacity to provide fund investors with the expected market rate of return:

- The developer's fees likely will be minimal or, if market-rate, contingent upon the operating success of the project.

- Equity financing will be provided by tax-motivated private investors attracted by the effective packaging of low-income housing credits.

Construction financing will be provided by a public or quasi-public agency at a below-market rate, or such an agency will provide some type of credit support that will lower the overall cost of traditional construction financing. Such an agency will also make available second-mortgage financing, if necessary.

SUMMARY

Pension fund investors have not traditionally been sources of capital for affordable housing. Nonetheless, given funds' increasing sophistication with regard to real estate investing, and their continued commitment of capital to market-rate projects, I believe there are opportunities to structure creative, mutually beneficial relationships. Pension funds will never become the source of subsidy that affordable-housing advocates constantly must seek; however, given today's environment—in which capital is difficult to obtain at any price—pension investors can play a critical role in maintaining the nation's supply of affordable housing.

Section II

Designing, Developing, and Building Affordable Housing

Chapter 8

Architectural Solutions for Affordable Housing on Small Sites

Rosalie Genevro
Executive Director
The Architectural League of New York

Much as they would like to, architects can't offer any magic to produce affordable housing. They can't provide capital, lower land prices, or negotiate labor rates. They can, however, contribute significantly to the quality, commodiousness, appropriateness, and efficiency of housing, and to making housing work as a building block of a desirable urban life. They can evaluate what is possible with available resources of land and evolving construction technologies and they can analyze the likely physical results of proposed zoning laws, design standards, and regulations for handicapped accessibility, energy efficiency, and landmark preservation. They can, in short, perform a variety of critical functions that should make them essential participants, not only in the design of specific housing projects, but in the design of housing programs themselves. Not since New York

State's Urban Development Corporation was reorganized and turned away from housing in the mid-1970s has a government agency systematically supported architectural research—and architecture *as* research—as a significant and worthy activity contributing to housing improvement.[1]

The Architectural League and the New York City Department of Housing Preservation and Development organized the "Vacant Lots" design study to reassert the usefulness and importance of design investigation as part of planning for housing programs. The design study addressed a particular issue—a rather untraditional one, in terms of standard housing practice: how to design low-income housing on small lots, in the interstices of the developed city. Since the late nineteenth century, housing reformers in New York had accepted

99

virtually as dogma that the city's standard 25-foot × 100-foot lot had to be aggregated into larger parcels to make possible economic dwellings with adequate light and air. By 1987, however, in the midst of its very ambitious 10-Year Plan for housing construction, the city was finding that it was running out of suitable large sites for development. In evaluating its resources, it found that it had thousands of scattered vacant sites that had been regarded as too small for housing investment. The Vacant Lots project set out to investigate whether these small sites could provide the basis for desirable development. An added spur was the idea that small builder/developers and community development groups could build small-scale projects. This would mean that a larger pool of builders would be capable of bidding on such projects, which should increase competition and lower prices to the city or other government funder.

Vacant Lots also served as an educational forum. Because of the decline in federal support for subsidized housing in the late '70s and early '80s, many younger architects have never been asked to work on low-income housing design at all. Vacant Lots was thus organized, in part, to provide a chance for interested architects to grapple with this unfamiliar set of design issues.

To serve its several purposes, the Vacant Lots study was structured to give a great deal of choice to participating architects and designers. Architects were invited to participate in an open call for entries issued by the League and NYC HPD in June 1987. When they registered for the project, they received a kit of materials—prepared by the project organizing committee of architects and an architectural historian, League staff

members, and an engineer from the Department of Housing Preservation and Development—describing the goals of the study, presentation guidelines, and background material on recent low-income housing design. Architects could choose to work on any one of ten sites, which represented a wide variety of neighborhood settings in four of New York's five boroughs. The three Bronx sites were a narrow through-block parcel (Site 1, Figure 8.1) in a mixed area of small apartment buildings and row houses, in an area of the South Bronx where a great deal of housing had been abandoned and ultimately demolished; a corner site (Site 2, Figure 8.2) slightly farther north, bordered on one side by a stand of once-substantial, now-abandoned masonry row houses, and on the other by a large apartment building substantially rehabilitated under Section 8 or one of the City's comparable renovation programs; and a lot (Site 3, Figure 8.3) in an area of large multifamily buildings mixed with what had once been urban villas but had long since been divided into apartments. The Brooklyn sites (4,

Figure 8.1   Site 1

5, and 6) are all in row-house neighbor-hoods. Site 4 (Figure 8.4) consists of two separated lots, each 20 feet × 100 feet; Site 5 (Figure 8.5) comprises four adjacent lots for a total size of 80 feet × 100 feet; and Site 6 (Figure 8.6) is one small lot, 22 feet × 100 feet. The sole Manhattan site, in Washington Heights (Site 7, Figure 8.7), is surrounded by six-story and higher multifamily buildings. Site 8 (Figure 8.8), in northern Queens, is a through-block site (40 feet × 195 feet) in a neighborhood dominated by

Figure 8.2 Site 2

Figure 8.3 Site 3

Figure 8.5 Site 5

Figure 8.4 Site 4

Figure 8.6 Site 6

one- and two-family attached houses. The even less dense area surrounding Site 9 (Figure 8.9) is built up mainly with one-family frame houses. The final site (Site 10, Figure 8.10), on the Rockaway peninsula in Queens, consists of two empty lots separated by a lot on which sits one of the area's typical three-story, two-family houses.

In addition to being able to choose among widely varying sites, architects were encouraged to think about how dwelling units and buildings could be de-signed to accommodate nontraditional households—single-parent families, extended families of several generations, groups of unrelated individuals, and individuals or families who need special health or other services. The architects were also told that they could propose solutions that violated the city's design guidelines for subsidized housing or required zoning variances, if they could show a compelling reason to do so. Our point of view here was that a fair number of the regulations with which

Figure 8.7 Site 7

Figure 8.9 Site 9

Figure 8.8 Site 8

Figure 8.10 Site 10

architects must comply have been built up through accretion rather than comprehensive analysis, and so sometimes result in contradictory directives or in overly cumbersome or restrictive rules which drive up costs for less than compensating gains. This, obviously, is a complex and debatable topic which requires much more systematic evaluation than we attempted for Vacant Lots. But our objective was to give architects as much free rein as possible to speculate and invent, within the already constraining limits of the small sites.

Seventy teams of architects created design proposals and submitted them to the League in September 1987. All of the projects were exhibited for several months in downtown Manhattan and in special presentations to a variety of city housing officials and other government representatives. The *Vacant Lots* catalogue, published by Princeton Architectural Press, reproduces all the projects, with explanatory texts.

The best designs produced for Vacant Lots can be grouped into three categories, based on the kinds of issues on which their authors chose to focus. These are, first, projects that directly addressed the issue of cost—either the cost of construction or the cost of occupancy; second, projects designed to serve tenants other than traditional families; and third, projects in which the urbanistic strategy and therefore the contribution of the project to improving its neighborhood are of primary interest. A small selection of the Vacant Lots proposals is presented here.

Design and Cost

There are several approaches to trying to reduce costs through design and construction that are all too evident in much subsidized housing: minimize any architectural ornament, or eliminate it altogether; use lower-cost materials, or alternatively, use materials that may have a relatively high initial cost but have a long-term, low-maintenance life and are so impervious to damage that they look institutional; make the forms of the buildings as simple and boxlike as possible, to cut down on the length of exterior wall and on construction time. Vacant Lots participants came up with some more-appealing alternatives.

The project by McDonough/Nouri Architects (now William McDonough Architects) for Site 10 in the Rockaways is a persuasive example of how attractive an extremely simple building can become in the hands of talented designers (Figure 8.11). The McDonough team accepted the basic type of housing in the area—two-family freestanding houses—but made one fundamental, enormously important change. Each family unit in a typical building in the neighborhood is created by dividing the building in half on its short dimension, thereby making two long, narrow, side-by-side units. The McDonough team decided instead to use a overall floorplan of two offset squares, with each square comprising one family's unit. What this accomplishes is to create rooms which are themselves closer to squares, an easier shape to furnish and a more appealing space to inhabit than a long narrow room. Such a plan also requires less space devoted to circulation, and reduces the length of party wall between the two units, thereby increasing aural privacy. Each unit has 22 feet of garden frontage, and the outdoor space of each lot is divided so that each family has an L-shaped parcel for their own use. The buildings are designed to

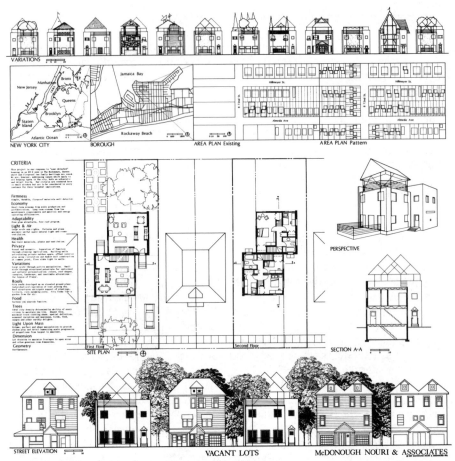

Figure 8.11 Project by McDonough Nouri and Associates

accommodate roof decks for each unit, and each tenant/owner can individualize a facade (one the street side, the other the garden). These houses are designed to be built of concrete block or tilt-up panels, whichever is cheaper given the place and scale of construction.

The project by Smith and Thompson Architects (Figure 8.12) for Site 7, in Manhattan, similarly uses a strategy of creating a simple, repeatable plan in which the dimensions and the placement

of kitchens and bathrooms have been designed to make construction easy, efficient and economical, thus making it possible for small contractors or even individuals to develop such sites. Smith and Thompson base their design on a 25-foot-wide module, the standard width of a New York lot. Fireproof construction, of masonry bearing walls and lightweight steel joists, permits a single-egress system. Materials for the facade—which the architects suggest could be fixed glass,

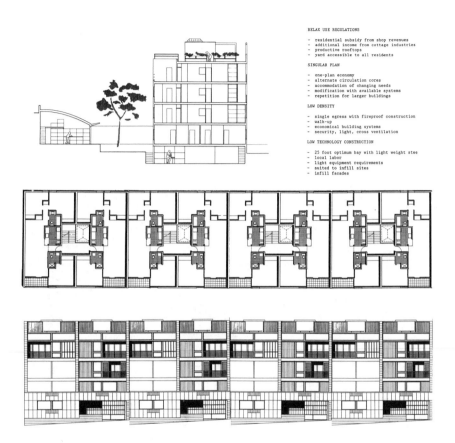

RELAX USE REGULATIONS

- residential subsidy from shop revenues
- additional income from cottage industries
- productive rooftops
- yard accessible to all residents

SINGULAR PLAN

- one-plan economy
- alternate circulation cores
- accommodation of changing needs
- modification with available systems
- repetition for larger buildings

LOW DENSITY

- single egress with fireproof construction
- walk-up
- economical building systems
- security, light, cross ventilation

LOW TECHNOLOGY CONSTRUCTION

- 25 foot optimum bay with light weight stee
- local labor
- light equipment requirements
- suited to infill sites
- infill facades

Figure 8.12 Project by G. Philip Smith, Douglas Thompson

corrugated or aluminum siding, insulated metal panels, or other inexpensive and readily available off-the-shelf products—could be chosen based on the surrounding neighborhood. Each floor of the walk-up building would contain a single apartment, with the service core running up through the middle. The apartment could be used as a large loft-like space, or divided into rooms with permanent walls or movable partitions, bookcases, or storage cabinets. On larger sites the plan could be flipped and repeated, with each pair of buildings joined to share a stair- and light well. The architects propose that a workshop be built at the back of the site to accommodate "simple low-capital occupations and trades." Rent from the workshop would contribute additional income to the building.

The project by Weiss/Manfredi Architects (Figure 8.13) for the Manhattan site proposes a concrete-slab building with large open floors that could be divided in a variety of ways for different types of tenants, possibly using tenant labor for the fitting-out of the apartments or rooms. The building forms a "U" around an internal courtyard that provides light and air to the tower at the back of the site and lower-rise block at the front. Bathrooms and kitchens are located off the "utility wall" running the length of the building. The architect's variations on how to divide the space range from single-room occupancy units with shared bathroom and kitchen space to large family apartments.

In their project for Site 2 in the Bronx (Figure 8.14), Bartholomew Voorsanger and his team focused on a different strategy to produce affordability: designing apartments as "starter units" that could be jointly owned by groups of unre-

Figure 8.13 Project by Marion Weiss and Michael Manfredi

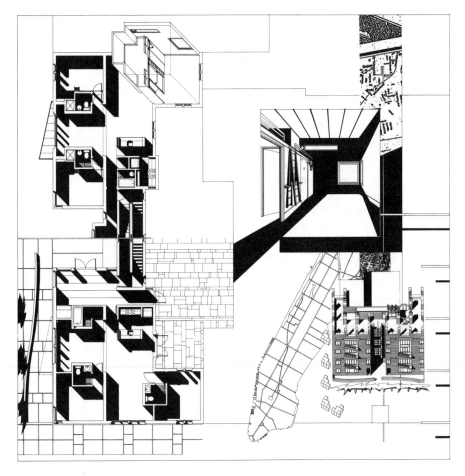

Figure 8.14 Project by Voorsanger and Mills Associates

lated individuals, in order to allow young, elderly, or low-income people to build equity and get the tax advantages of homeownership. Each "dwelling unit," of bedroom and bath, would be separately owned. Groups of three dwelling units would form an apartment, which would also include shared kitchen, dining, and living space. Eleven-foot ceiling heights in the dwelling units would allow residents to create loft spaces for sleeping, study, or nursery. The ground floor of the building has two two-bedroom apartments for handicapped residents, who would have access to the rear garden. The overall plan also envisions that each of the six apartments in the building above the ground floor would have exclusive rights to a defined area of the roof.

Housing for Whom?

As mentioned above, the Vacant Lots project encouraged architects to think about building and unit forms that would accommodate residents other than traditional families. New York has an enormous need for various types of group and supported housing; housing that will serve the clientele who lived in Single Room Occupancy buildings, residential hotels, or boarding houses when those forms were available; and housing for extended families, including the enormous number of immigrants who have poured into the city over the last decade.

In order to really investigate what particular groups of tenants need, several architects consulted social service providers or put together interdisciplinary teams to think through the program and design for their projects. Designers Gustavo Bonevardi and Lee Ledbetter, associated with planner Linda Baldwin, psychologist James Lay, and Morgan Hare, designed a residence for people with AIDS (Figure 8.15). Their project envisions a building with two zones: residential on the garden side of the building and public (service offices and treatment rooms) on the street side. Residents would each have their own room and bathroom, but would take their meals in a communal dining room. All residents' rooms would have balconies facing a garden. As proposed for Vacant Lots Site 1, which is a through-block site, the project would be made of two identical buildings, each serving 12 residents and sharing the garden. As did many of the Vacant Lots architects, this team envisioned their design as one which could be repeated on other small sites in other areas of the city. In this case, the design team proposes that the residential zone of the building could be taller, depending on

what zoning would allow, and the design of the public zone could be modified to fit other neighborhood contexts. They take note, however, that the small size of the facility serves many purposes: it makes possible the growth of a sense of community within the building for residents, makes the facility seem noninstitutional, and allows it to become integrated into its neighborhood. The design team suggests that this plan could serve any group of residents that needs an attended or supervised living situation.

Richard Hatch's proposal for Site 10 (Figure 8.16) in the Rockaways emphasizes that jobs are needed as much or more than additional housing in this neighborhood, which is isolated from Manhattan and other employment centers. He proposes what is really an update of a very old housing type: the workshop with housing above. His 1250-square-foot work areas would accommodate four to six workers and be accessible to step vans. The three-bedroom, duplex apartment above would include an outdoor terrace on the roof of the workshop. Hatch's hope is that making workspace and housing available on the same lot would attract entrepreneurs and spur a locally generated and sustainable revitalization of the area.

Housing and Urbanism

Some of the most visible affordable housing built in New York City in the last decade has conspicuously ignored the fact of its location in a city. Perhaps it is not surprising that in a period when public policy has been so ferociously anti-urban, cities should erode themselves from within by mimicking the housing forms of the suburbs and exurbs.

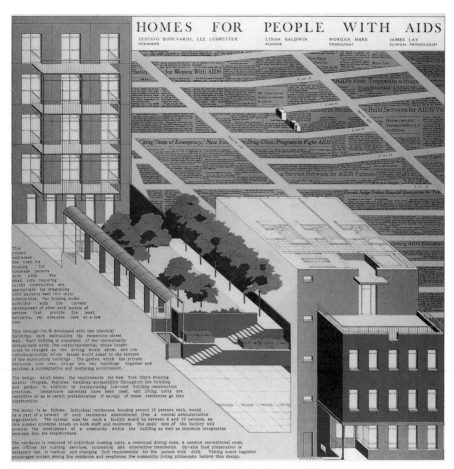

Figure 8.15 Project by Bonevardi, Ledbetter, Baldwin, Hare, and Lay

Charlotte Gardens, a group of factory-built ranch houses sited on cleared land in what was once a densely populated South Bronx neighborhood of multifamily buildings, is probably the most widely known and startling example. But the Nehemiah Homes, built in several locations in Brooklyn, also pay much more attention to accommodating automobiles and to creating private outdoor space than to any more-urban considerations such as making streets and sidewalks appealing and usable for pedestrians. The barracks-like design of the Nehemiah houses ignores the deadening impact, for example, of such decisions as making the corner houses the same as the others and not building on what too definitively become the placeless side streets of the development (Figure 8.17). Charlotte Gardens and the Nehemiah projects are defended by their supporters on the basis that they respond to the market preferences of their cli-

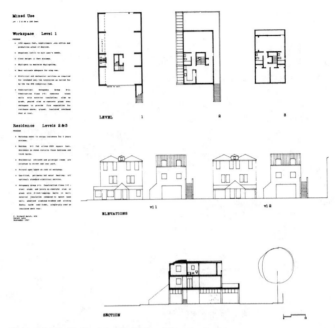

Figure 8.16   Project by C. Richard Hatch, Architect

entele, and, especially in the case of the Nehemiah Homes, that economics drives the site plans and overall design. While they may be economical measured in terms of initial cost, ranch houses and very low density row houses are profligate users of land and do not make efficient use of existing urban infrastructure, which includes not only water mains and sewer lines but public transportation and public schools.

The Vacant Lots project produced some thoughtful alternatives. For some of the denser neighborhoods, several appealing projects suggest how to insert new housing that would "repair" disintegrated blockfronts. In mixed and lower-density neighborhoods, the most stimulating ideas suggested how to accommodate cars without abandoning urbanity, and how to place a number of units on a site without losing a sense of connection between the units and the outdoors.

Nancy Hitchcock's and William Leggio's project for Site 2 (Figure 8.18) makes a very effective transition around a corner between a stand of row houses on one side and a large multifamily building on the other. The portion of the building abutting the row houses harmonizes with its neighbors, without copying them, and yet is completely integrated with the taller portion of the new building. The plans of both sections of the building are compact and well designed, with many of the apartments getting cross-ventilation and excellent exposure.

A project by the team led by Richard Plunz (Figure 8.19) for Site 1 is organized around a mews, or internal court.

Figure 8.17 Project by Nehemiah Homes

Access to apartments facing the street is through individual front doors on the street facade. Other apartments in the building are entered through a secure gate or door which provides access to the internal court, where the remaining individual front doors are located. This eliminates any internal common circulation space, and gains controlled outdoor space for common use. Plunz proposes that such buildings be two or three stories, to make possible the use of economic construction methods. The buildings could be built singly, in pairs sharing the court, or to fill a whole block.

The project by Deborah Gans, Brian McGrath, and Mark Robbins for Site 4 (Figure 8.20) proposes a very interesting combination of row- and courtyard-house types, which achieves desirable formal and social goals: it creates a supervisable outdoor play space, provides better light and ventilation to more rooms than in a typical row house, and makes possible a mix of unit sizes, from studio to three-bedroom, with the possibility of internal connections to accommodate extended families. The design provides four covered parking spaces for the eight apartments, without allowing the cars to dominate the landscape.

Daniel Heyden's and Robert Good-

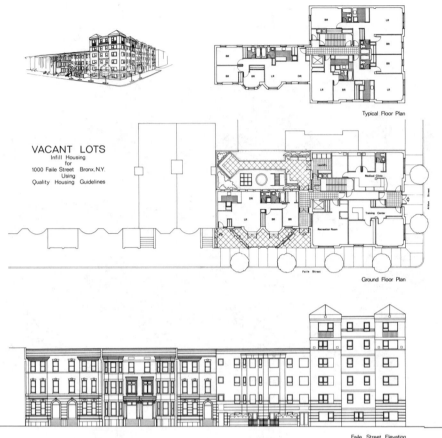

VACANT LOTS
Infill Housing
for
1000 Faile Street   Bronx, N.Y.
Using
Quality Housing Guidelines

Typical Floor Plan

Ground Floor Plan

Faile Street Elevation

Figure 8.18   Project by Nancy Hitchcock and William Leggio

win's design for the same site (Figure 8.21) takes a somewhat similar approach. In their higher-density scheme, the courtyard is landscaped rather than hardsurfaced, and cars use a single driveway along the side of the site to get to parking spaces at the rear of the building. As in the Gans/McGrath/Robbins project, there is a range of unit sizes, with the goal of accommodating different households of extended families.

The two through-block Vacant Lots sites elicited several proposals that re-

thought the traditional setup of a building facing each street with an open rear yard in between. A team led by Edward Mills proposed placing four "Villa Blocks" on Site 1 (Figure 8.22). Each three-story block would house three apartments. Three 30-foot × 30-foot gardens would separate the villas, and each villa would have a roof deck. For Site 8, Saunders/Heidel propose two two-story buildings at the street frontages, with a three-story building, smaller in plan, set midway through the block. Each of the

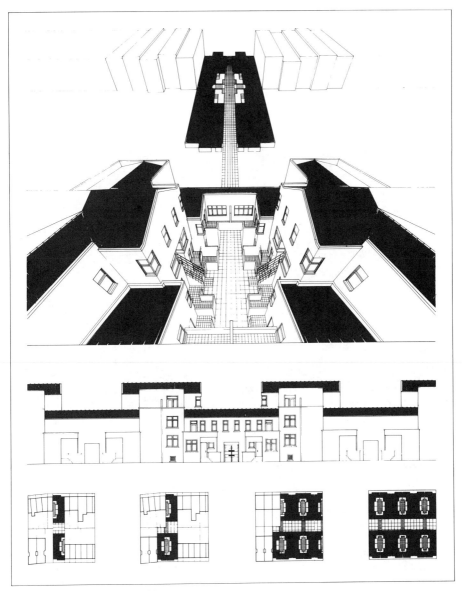

Figure 8.19 Project by R.A. Plunz

seven apartments on the site occupies an entire floor of one of the buildings, and each apartment except for the upper two in the mid-block building has its own designated outdoor space.

What did Vacant Lots accomplish?

Figure 8.20   Project by Gans, McGrath, and Robbins

None of the projects has been built yet. There is, as yet, no financing mechanism in the city's range of housing programs designed to support new construction on individual lots of such small size. But while it has been disappointing to the project participants and its organizers that none of the designs has been built, Vacant Lots was in fact conceived to generate ideas and to engage a number of designers in a process of investigation. The study project produced a body of im- ages and information that provide a gen- erous indication of the universe of possi- bilities offered by small sites, which should be helpful to housing officials and development organizations considering small-site development. The design study demonstrated that small sites can be put to good use and there are a lot of work- able design approaches that don't seem to have had wide application to date. A number of the projects suggest that small sites may have some intrinsic advan-

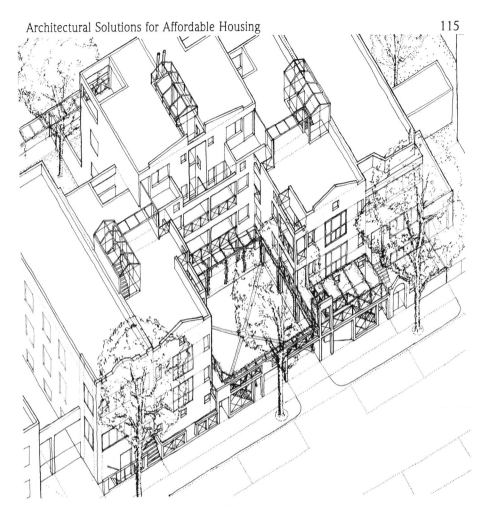

Figure 8.21   Project by Daniel Heyden and Robert Goodwin

tages—such as the possibility of using semi-skilled construction labor and little or no heavy construction machinery—that have been ignored or discounted when the focus has been on economies of scale and quantity production of units.

One of the most important lessons of the last quarter century of efforts at affordable-housing production—as well as of the same period's record in city planning and urban architecture—is that no one approach is a cure-all, or is even desirable when too universally applied. New York, and most other cities, have room for a wide variety of approaches to housing; the more different mechanisms and strategies at work, the better. Seeing small sites as a resource not only opens a new area of action for housing production, but also makes more likely the kind of fine-grained, place-specific building that makes cities interesting and desirable places to live.

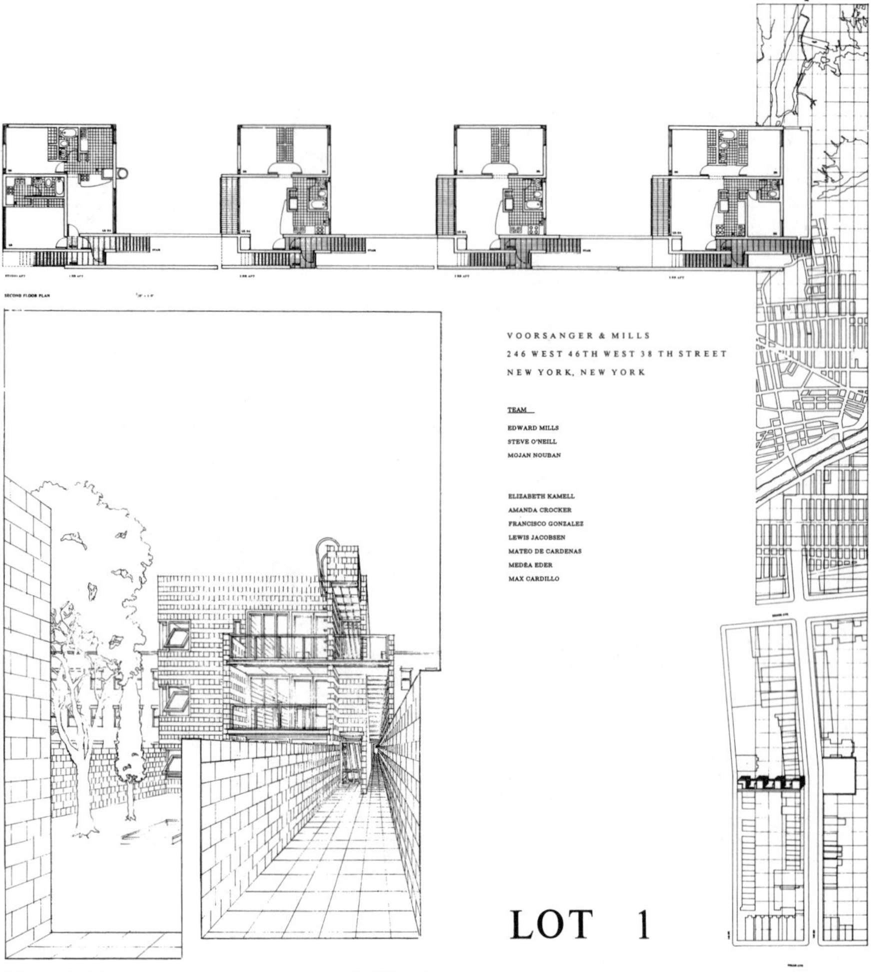

VOORSANGER & MILLS
246 WEST 46TH WEST 38 TH STREET
NEW YORK, NEW YORK

TEAM

EDWARD MILLS
STEVE O'NEILL
MOJAN NOUBAN

ELIZABETH KAMELL
AMANDA CROCKER
FRANCISCO GONZALEZ
LEWIS JACOBSEN
MATEO DE CARDENAS
MEDEA EDER
MAX CARDILLO

LOT 1

Figure 8.22 Project by Voorsanger and Mills Associates

ENDNOTE

[1] The Vacant Lots design study was organized by a committee of Elizabeth Adams, Paul Byard, Deborah Gans, Rosalie Genevro, Brian McGrath, Mark Robbins, Walter Whitcher, and Carol Willis.

LIST OF FIGURES

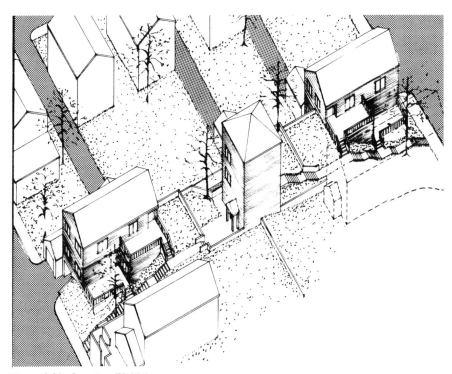

Figure 8.23 Saunders/Heidel

Figure 4 Site 4, East New York, Brooklyn (Photograph by Elizabeth Feeley)

Figure 5 Site 5, Brownsville, Brooklyn (Photograph by Elizabeth Feeley)

Figure 6 Site 6, Brownsville, Brooklyn (Photograph by Elizabeth Feeley)

Figure 7 Site 7, Washington Heights, Manhattan (Photograph by Elizabeth Feeley)

Figure 8 Site 8, Corona, Queens (Photograph by Elizabeth Feeley)

Figure 9 Site 9, Jamaica, Queens (Photograph by Elizabeth Feeley)

Figure 10 Site 10, Arverne, Queens (Photograph by Elizabeth Feeley)

Figure 11 Project by McDonough Nouri and Associates

William A. McDonough, partner-in-charge, Hamid R. Nouri, managing partner, Janet S. Roseff, Steve Pynes, Judy O'Buck Gordon, Joe Vance, Carl Finer

Figure 12 Project by G. Philip Smith, Douglas Thompson with Richard Kreshtool, Terry Van Dyne

Figure 13 Project by Marion Weiss and Michael Manfredi, Weiss/Manfredi Architects

Fig 14 Project by Voorsanger and Mills Associates

Bartholomew Voorsanger, partner-in-scharge; Kevin Gordon, associate; Randall Cude, Anne Elizabeth Perl, Enrique Colmenares, Satoshi Ohashi, Medea Eder, Eileen Delgado

Figure 15   Project by Gustavo Bonevardi and Lee Ledbetter, designers; Linda Baldwin, planner, Morgan Hare, consultant, James Lay, clinical psychologist

Figure 16   Project by C. Richard Hatch, architect

Figure 17   Project by Nehemiah Homes

Figure 18   Project by Nancy Hitchcock and William Leggio

Figure 19   Project by R. A. Plunz with Day, Flynn, Ho, Josephson, Rosenbaum, Smith, and Sollohub

Figure 20   Project by Deborah Gans, Brian McGrath, Mark Robbins

Figure 21   Project by Daniel Heyden and Robert Goodwin

Figure 22   Project by Voorsanger and Mills Associates

Edward Mills, partner-in-charge; Steve O'Neill, Mojan Mourban, Elizabeth Kamell, Amanda Crocker, Francisco Gonzalez, Lewis Jacobsen, Mateo de Cardenas, Medea Eder, Max Cardillo

Figure 23   Project by Saunders/Heidel

Chapter 9

The For-Profit Homebuilder's Perspective on Affordable Housing

Barbara Bryan
Assistant Director of Multifamily Finance
The National Association of Homebuilders

Homebuilders face numerous obstacles in efforts to produce housing affordable to moderate- and middle-income households in many regions of the U.S. Spiraling land costs, cumbersome regulatory reviews and permitting procedures, and rising impact-fee assessments add premiums to the cost of all housing, but affordable housing is least able to absorb these costs. The "Not In My Back Yard" (NIMBY) (see Chapter 14) or "no growth" syndrome reflected in vocal opposition to higher density affordable housing in many high-housing-cost areas adds costly delays and sometimes prevents development.

Even when builders are able to overcome these obstacles, they are increasingly faced with construction financing hurdles resulting from the stringent banking regulations and lending policies imposed in the early 1990s. Financing development of moderate-income housing is even more complicated as funds often must be layered from several subsidy sources to achieve affordability.

The National Association of Home Builders (NAHB) has been active in addressing the issue of housing affordability. Through research on cost-saving land development and construction techniques, demonstration projects such as the Joint Venture for Affordable Housing and the NAHB-Fannie Mae Affordable Housing Initiative, special task forces on financing affordable housing, and symposiums on how builders can address homelessness, NAHB provides policy-making input at the national level and disseminates information on affordable housing to member builders and local homebuilder associations.

THE JOINT VENTURE FOR AFFORDABLE HOUSING

The Joint Venture for Affordable Housing (JVAH) is a demonstration project undertaken in conjunction with the U.S. Department of Housing and Urban Development (HUD) to identify construction techniques, building-code modifications, and site-development regulations that can be used to reduce housing costs and promote affordability.

Under the demonstration, single-family housing developments were planned and built in 27 cities throughout the U.S. Developers, builders and local governments worked to review building codes and zoning regulations for requirements that add unnecessary costs to a home but do not necessarily add value. The documented cost savings achieved in the demonstration projects ranged from 2 percent to 30 percent per unit ($1,000 to over $15,000 in cost savings) compared to similar homes in the 27 communities.

The savings achieved in the JVAH demonstration projects can be attributed to four different sources:

• land-use regulations (changes in density restrictions),

• development standards,

• streamlined approval processing, and

• construction innovations in building the units.

MODIFYING LAND-USE REGULATIONS

The largest JVAH savings were attributable to changes in density and development standards. Reducing lot sizes, or raising the density, requires less land per house, thus reducing the land cost per unit. It also decreases infrastructure improvement costs and can provide more environmentally sensitive development.

Norcon Builders, developers of Covington Place, a JVAH demonstration in Greensboro, North Carolina, reduced costs through density increases. Although typical residential zoning for the area was three units per acre, Norcon received a variance to construct eight units per acre. When increased density was incorporated with reductions in street paving width and right-of-way and a unique surface stormwater drainage system, a savings of $7,653 per unit was achieved compared to typical Greensboro homes.

The Joint Venture projects show that well-planned higher density development can contribute to, rather than detract from, community attractiveness and livability in several ways. Increased common open space and preservation of a site's natural features can be incorporated into plans for higher-density developments through use of the cluster development technique. Reducing or eliminating setbacks from one or more lot boundaries using zero-lot-lines creates more usable side yards on smaller lots. Use of "Z lot" (zero-lot-line) configurations, which increase street frontage and decrease the garage's impact on the streetscape, can enhance the curb appeal of smaller lots.

Changing Land-Development Standards

Many communities still rely on outdated or excessive development standards, such as requiring local residential streets built to the same standard as major thoroughfares. For the demonstration projects, local officials cooperated with

Lakewood Apartments in Stafford County, VA were developed by Amurcon Corporation using the low-income housing tax credit. The property received an award from NAHB's Multihousing Council "The Edison Electric Institute Award for Best Affordable Low-Income Development."

builders and developers to allow certain changes in development standards. These included allowing construction of narrower streets with decreased pavement thickness, sidewalks on only one side of the street, substitution of grass swales for curbs and gutters, use of rolled curbs instead of vertical curbs, and use of less expensive and more effective sanitary sewer and water pipes.

By using a combination of these techniques, Cimarron, the Phoenix, Arizona, JVAH demonstration developed by Knoell Homes, was able to gain additional land to add 106 units to its original 149-unit plan for a 38-acre tract. Cost savings as a result were nearly $4,000 per unit.

Streamlining the Review and Approval Process

Streamlined review and approval was effective when it had the full cooperation of local officials. City or other local government staff must assume responsibility for examining the unnecessary time required for permitting, hearings, zoning exceptions, design approvals and construction reviews. The importance of these efforts in reducing housing costs lies in the fact that developers must pay interest each month on money they borrow to buy land, hold it until approvals are obtained and build homes. Delays represent real costs that are added to the price consumers pay for a home.

Some examples of fast-track processing in the JVAH projects include the
elimination of formal hearings for
changes, approval of most small projects
in "one-stop" processing, and combining
steps in the review process. The City of
Phoenix used the Cimarron demonstration project to review and modernize its
entire set of regulations and procedures
for land use and home construction. The
revised process saved three months of
time and $2,133 per unit, including
interest and overhead cost savings.

Construction Innovations

Most of the adverse cost impact of building codes comes in the interpretation of
codes and in inspection. Builders report
that building-code officials are reluctant
to depart from long-standing practices
and often feel little obligation to take an
active role in promoting housing
affordability. For their part, builders tend
to shy away from seeking acceptance of
new methods rather than face the
possibility of rejection or delay.

It was only with the full cooperation
of local governments in the Joint Venture
that many builders used construction
techniques now proven to be cost-effective. Direct construction savings in the
JVAH ran as high as $6,000 per unit.

Many of the techniques used in the
JVAH were based on optimum-value engineering developed and tested by
NAHB's National Research Center,
which allowed more efficient use of
materials and labor. These techniques
were used for building cost-saving wall
systems, clustered plumbing design and
use of durable, but less expensive, syn-
thetic pipes. Other innovative techniques
involved overall home design, floor fram-

ing and heating, ventilation and air-conditioning systems.

The Joint Venture for Affordable
Housing has increased the understanding
of builders and local officials of how cost
savings can be achieved through regulatory reform and innovative construction
techniques and passed on to home
buyers in more affordable homes.

NAHB–FANNIE MAE AFFORDABLE HOUSING INITIATIVE

NAHB and the Federal National Mortgage Association (Fannie Mae) are working jointly to develop models for financing housing for moderate-income
households. Under the Affordable Housing Initiative, NAHB solicited proposals
from member builders and local
homebuilders associations for development and financing of housing for moderate-income households in various
regions of the country. Projects with
potential for replication and local government contributions to enhance affordability were given selection priority.

In Austin, Texas, the Capital Area
Builders Association assisted the Austin
Housing Finance Corporation in identifying builders to submit proposals for infill
development in two urban neighborhoods located near downtown Austin. A
consortium of local banks was organized
to provide construction financing and the
city assembled parcels to reduce land
costs. City programs to provide rental assistance, down payments, and soft
second mortgages enhance affordability.
The initiative will produce 150 new
homeownership and rental units over a
three-year period. Eligible first-time
home buyers will receive low-down-pay-

ment mortgages under Fannie Mae's Community Home Buyers program.

In Norwich, Connecticut, developer Michael Franklin is building 51 homeownership units on a redevelopment area parcel overlooking the Thames River. In addition to providing land at below market cost and contributing a portion of infrastructure costs, the city, through its housing authority, is issuing 501(c)(3) bonds to provide construction financing. The Connecticut Housing Finance Agency will provide below-market-rate mortgages for half of the units, which will be made available to former residents of public housing with qualifying incomes. Fannie Mae has agreed to purchase mortgages issued by a local savings bank for the remaining units. Franklin has created an innovative SHARE loan program to provide second mortgages on the units, which are paid on a pro rata basis over 20 years and can be assumed by subsequent purchasers.

In Macon, Georgia, members of the Home Builders Association are working with a local, nonprofit Greater Macon Housing Corporation to produce 60 new energy-efficient homeownership units that will sell for under $40,000. The city is providing assistance to lower land acquisition costs, and a consortium of local banks is providing construction and permanent financing. Through an agreement with the Georgia Department of Corrections, inmates enrolled in a construction trades training program will provide panelized plumbing walls and other modular components that will be assembled on-site by local builders. Fannie Mae has agreed to provide flexible credit underwriting standards so that moderate-income households with minimal debt are able to qualify for

mortgages. The local bank consortium has agreed to hold a selected group of mortgages that do not meet requirements for sale to Fannie Mae.

Other NAHB-Fannie Mae Affordable Housing Initiative projects are under way in Florida, California, and Illinois.

HOME BUILDERS ASSOCIATION INITIATIVES

NAHB has over 750 local homebuilders association (HBA) affiliates across the U.S. Many are engaged in projects with organizations such as Habitat for Humanity (see Chapter 12) and Neighborhood Housing Services (see Chapter 6) that provide housing for moderate-income households. Other HBAs have formed affiliated nonprofits such as Home Aid, which was organized by the Building Industry Association of Southern California to develop transitional housing for the homeless and single-room-occupancy housing.

The Pennsylvania Builders Association (PBA), through its Division of Training and Education, has undertaken projects to rehabilitate vacant city-owned housing in Harrisburg and Johnstown. Labor was provided by trainees eligible under the Job Training Partnership Act, who receive instruction in a variety of building trades under the supervision of a full-time site superintendent provided by the PBA. Licensed subcontractors handle portions of the renovation requiring specialized expertise (e.g., plumbing, electrical). Funding for the projects came from the City Departments of Community and Economic Development. Renovated homes were sold to low-income first-time home buyers at prices under $35,000 per unit, with mortgages at below-market interest rates provided by the Pennsylvania Housing Finance Agency.

The Home Builder Association of Akron, Ohio, worked with the City of Akron to form the Urban Neighborhood Development Corporation (UNDC). UNDC acquires infill lots in central city neighborhoods and solicits bids from builders to produce units using one of several standard plans from UNDC. After the home is complete, the city pays the builder and sells the house to a first-time home buyer. In some cases, local lenders provide mortgage financing at favorable terms. This program focuses on neighborhoods which have experienced early stages of disinvestment and has been successful in stimulating home improvements by neighbors owning adjoining properties. The UNDC project has produced nearly 200 new units in Akron.

INDIVIDUAL BUILDER INITIATIVES

Many NAHB member firms have been active in the production of affordable housing using federal, state and local sources of financing to achieve affordability.

Dan Wilson, president of United Builders and Florida Low Income Housing Associates, in Crystal River, Florida, is active with other Florida HBA members in the Governor's Housing Partnership Task Force, which is developing moderate-income home ownership financing models using Community Development Block Grant (CDBG) funds, surtax-funded second-

A UNDC builder in Akron gave a simple contemporary finish to a UNDC standard plan. This house was sold to a first-time buyer for $45,000.

mortgage programs and local bank consortiums. Florida Low Income Housing Associates develops low-cost housing for farm workers and the elderly in high-cost areas of Florida, using low-income-housing tax credits, the Florida Housing Finance Agency SAIL second-mortgage program, and Farmer's Home Administration financing.

R. Randy Lee, a Staten Island developer, who has been involved in development of affordable and market-rate units in New York's outer boroughs, works in partnership with nonprofit housing sponsors to produce affordable housing. A recent example of his projects is the South Williamsburg Partnership Homes, 105 cooperative apartment homes in 35 townhouses developed under the auspices of the New York City Housing Partnership with Brooklyn Catholic Charities' Progress of Peoples Development Corporation as co-sponsor.

The first development in New York City to combine the cooperative form of ownership with modular home construction, South Williamsburg Partnership Homes features three-story, three-family townhouses priced from $41,000 to $91,000 and affordable to households in the $20,000 to $30,000 income range. Each apartment has a subsidy comprised of $15,000 from the New York State Affordable Housing Corporation New Homes Program, and $35,000 from New York City, $25,000 of which is provided through a cross-subsidy arrangement derived from sale of properties adjacent to the project site. A local bank provided construction financing and the New York City Housing Development Corporation will provide the below-market, tax-exempt permanent cooperative mortgage.

The development has been structured to provide for unique resale restrictions which provide that units can only be

This UNDC builder took basic design and gave it a simple, contemporary look.

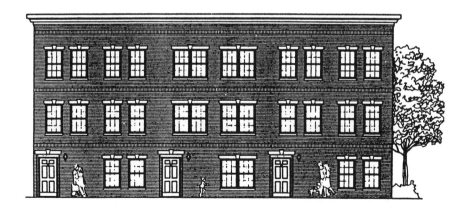

resold in the future to people whose family income is in the same percentage of median income as the current buyers'. For example, if the qualifying income for a particular unit today is $28,000, or about 80 percent of New York median, then the maximum resale price at any time in the future will be capped at a figure that would make it affordable to a family with 80 percent of whatever the New York median income is at that time. This unique resale formula allows a reasonable opportunity for a modest profit to be made, while, at the same time, keeping the units "affordable" in perpetuity.

As new financing mechanisms, such as FHA insurance for single-room-occupancy housing, are made available, increasing numbers of builders are able to address lower-income housing needs. However, a significant gap remains in the availability of financing compared to the need for moderate-income housing units.

NAHB members and senior officers of the association served on the HUD Commission to address regulatory barriers to affordable housing. It is their hope that the groundwork laid by the Commission report will stimulate state and local initiatives to reduce the high costs of excessive regulation on homebuilding that interfere with the production of affordable housing.

Chapter 10

Nonprofit Development in Atlanta, Georgia: Progressive Redevelopment, Inc.

Bruce G. Gunter
President
Progressive Redevelopment, Inc.

INTRODUCTION

During the late sixties, as much of the country was plunged into civic turmoil and racial strife, Atlanta managed a relatively peaceful integration, thus acquiring the reputation as "the city too busy to hate." Many credited enlightened leadership—black and white—for the transition. It was certainly true that in one sense the city was too busy raising tall skyscrapers and tending manicured lawns. Not all shared in the prosperity, of course, and there developed alongside the new skyline an impoverished core—by some measures, the second poorest central city in the nation. And so it was that when in July of 1990 the mayor of Atlanta, Maynard Jackson, intervened in a protest occupation of an abandoned downtown hotel by homeless squatters—some with families—it was widely expected that negotiations would be successful and further strife would be avoided. With a bold promise to establish a housing program of 3500 Single Room Occupancy (SRO) units, which would predominantly be affordable to the homeless, Mayor Jackson furthered the legacy of his predecessors. But he was moving against a pro-development ethic that had dominated Atlanta business and politics for decades, a mentality which was behind the removal of hundreds of affordable SRO units and the displacement of whole neighborhoods. As of this writing, one year later, not one of Jackson's promised SRO units has been built, and the civic tidal wave of enthusiasm that arose in the wake of the announcement that Atlanta would host the 1996 Summer Olympic Games threatens to further still the cries of the city's dis-

127

possessed. It was a dishearteningly familiar pattern for those who labored on behalf of Atlanta's homeless population. But the Mayor's promise signaled that this time might be different. A more sober assessment of the impact of the '96 Games recognized that, as the eyes of the world focused on the reality of such a stark contrast between rich and poor in Atlanta, the city's carefully nurtured image would suffer mightily. Hope began to surface that finally resources would be directed, regardless of their motivation, toward rebuilding and reclaiming Atlanta's impoverished inner-city neighborhoods. This hope was spurred on by the maturation of a creative non-profit community development sector, which had labored for years to develop decent, affordable housing with meager resources and no support from the "Big Mules," as Atlanta's power elite was known. One such organization was Progressive Redevelopment, Inc., known by its acronym PRI.

THE CREATION OF PROGRESSIVE REDEVELOPMENT, INC.

PRI began life as a neighborhood-based development organization, and, like other such groups, out of necessity employed a jack-of-all-trades approach to revitalize its host neighborhood—assembling financing, contracting out for construction, selling its own and renovated houses and apartment units, and, inevitably, serving as the political conscience of the community. The politics it played were hard-ball, for, more than anything else, PRI was a creature of its intense, almost messianic founder, the Reverend Craig Taylor, a Methodist minister, who knew that in a city long dominated by a banker-lawyer-developer

elite a more genteel approach would not begin to provide the vast resources needed to turn around the troubled South Atlanta neighborhood. Other grass roots development organizations had been around longer—notably Interfaith and Habitat for Humanity (see Chapter 12)—but their modest and hard-won successes did not provide the model to create the thousands of units that the city so desperately needed. Access to tens of millions of mortgage-loan dollars and seed capital from a myriad of sources of low-interest loans and grants was needed to augment the church/foundation grants combination that provided funding for but a few units at a time. A breakthrough occurred when, partly as a result of an aggressive media-driven and political campaign directed toward inducing the banks to lend more in poorer neighborhoods, a $20 million mortgage-loan pool called the Atlanta Mortgage Consortium (AMC) was organized. During the same period, the state of Georgia responded with a $5 million Georgia Housing Trust Fund for the Homeless, which provided very low interest 20-year loans to enable nonprofit developers to build affordable housing. PRI learned to stitch together a complex patchwork of grants, low-interest loans, tax credits, government programs and conventional bank debt for project financing. Together with a partnership approach to assembling a development team, the assembly of multilayered financing for community-based projects became PRI's modus operandi. Thus did a nonprofit join together with a public institution—the Trust Fund—and the private Atlanta Mortgage Consortium to create a hopeful new approach to developing decent, affordable housing in Atlanta. PRI began to move rapidly in a classic entrepreneurial response to satisfy an immense market need; its ability to satisfy that need was made possible by the provision of the right mix of resources.

After metamorphosing into more of a pure developer and legally incorporating as Progressive Redevelopment, Inc., in its first full year PRI produced 29 units of single-family detached housing in tandem with five different neighborhood development organizations, several of which PRI had helped organize as community land trusts. The following year PRI completed 21 more houses and assumed ownership of a small multifamily development. Toward the end of that year, PRI stepped into the role vacated by a bankrupt contractor to finish 41 units of what would later be organized as a limited-equity cooperative. It also introduced the organization to a precious and accessible source of equity capital—the Low Income Housing Tax Credit—that offered enormous potential.

THE EAST HILL STREET COOPERATIVE

The formation in 1991 of the East Hill Street Cooperative resulted from a spiritual collaboration of churches, neighborhood interests, local government officials, and several nonprofits, all of which PRI brought together. Except for a protracted delay with the construction lender, a not uncommon circumstance in these developments, the process proceeded "by the book" of community development organizing.

The former Woodgate Apartments, a 28-unit trouble spot in an otherwise fine, integrated community of small homes and old oak trees, had been repossessed by HUD, which left it sitting vacant for over a year. Using a particularly creative

financing technique, the church-sponsored Congregations for Affordable Housing garnered one-year, low-interest loans from its member churches and synagogues. One hundred thousand dollars accumulated in this matter served as the seed capital. Once the units were renovated and sold as a cooperative, the permanent mortgage, provided by the National Cooperative Bank, would be the source of funds that Congregations would use to pay off its promissory notes. PRI was selected to be the developer and promptly set about arranging the balance of the necessary financing.

SOURCES OF FUNDS FOR THE EAST HILL STREET CO-OP

$100,000	"Equity" from Congregations for Affordable Housing
250,000	Georgia Housing Trust Fund for the Homeless low interest loan
210,000	Rental-rehab grant from the local housing authority
345,000	Construction loan from a local bank
$905,000	Total acquisition and development cost

While construction was under way, joint organizing and marketing efforts by PRI and Congregations forged an initial board of directors for the nascent co-op. Able assistance from the county Community Development Office furthered the reclamation process, and the beginning of a new community took roots in their midst.

WELCOME HOME

While East Hill Street was gestating, PRI was tapped as the nonprofit developer for the largest new-construction, privately financed affordable-housing project to be built in Atlanta in perhaps ten years. All of the community organizing, the disputes with the banks, and the brick and mortar developments would appear in retrospect as skirmishes compared to the process that began with the occupation of the Imperial House and Reverend Taylor's part in negotiating its resolution. Another, very different, siege was about to begin.

Noel Khalil had tax credits in mind when he started punching his calculator after viewing the television coverage of Mayor Jackson making his vow to the homeless occupiers of the Imperial Hotel. He sought a financing scheme that would accommodate the $50 weekly rents which would be affordable even for the working homeless, typically day labor pool workers. Khalil was one of the most successful real estate developers in the city, and one of the few who had built in-town residential units. He also worked for one of the most powerful and successful black men in Atlanta — legendary Herman Russell—as CEO of Russell's development company, Gibraltar Land, Inc. Khalil offered his plan for an SRO to the Mayor which included a nonprofit partner to procure the equity in the form of tax credits and provide the necessary social services. Acting Housing Commissioner Paul Stange paired Gibralter with PRI and the planning for a facility that had no precedent in Atlanta began.

"Welcome House" was the name the

homeless had christened the derelict hotel that they called home for a short few weeks in that summer of 1990. And that was to be the name of the new SRI hotel that Khalil, Stange, and Taylor envisioned.

It was fortunate that no one told PRI just how difficult the project was to become or else a young Yale Divinity School graduate might never have been hired to staff the project. Mike Griffin wanted his first ministry to be in affordable housing, and PRI, with its roots in the church, made for a good place to start. Mike rounded out a dedicated core staff that included one other project manager, Fern Hatzenbuhler, a community organizer, Barbara King-Rogers, and the person that held it all together, business manager Lisa Columb. Bruce Gunter moved from his position as president of the board to executive director, bringing a business approach to complement the more activist proclivities of Craig, who moved to the board. Later, Kathy Davis was hired as property manager. It was a spirited group, one which persevered past missed payrolls, confounding development problems, and skeptical officials to advance a cause and business plan they knew to be both righteous, workable, and sustainable.

In the year that followed, a multilayered financing package was assembled in a cauldron of tense meetings with the downtown business community, last-minute arrangements on complex legal and financial issues, political posturing and more demonstrations. Many eyes were on the process, given the $4.3 million price tag and its downtown location in sight of City Hall and the State House.

SOURCES OF FUNDS FOR
THE WELCOME HOUSE

$1,400,000	Proceeds from syndication of Low-Income Housing Tax Credits
250,000	Georgia Housing Trust Fund low-interest loan
350,000	Federal Home Loan Bank "Affordable Housing Program" grant
500,000	Land donation by the City via 50-year ground lease
200,000	Grant from a local foundation
200,000	Letter of credit from a local foundation
1,400,000	Permanent, 20-year conventional mortgage
$4,300,000	Total cost of project

Since PRI's forte as an affordable-housing developer is the provision of a sufficiently subsidized capital structure on the front end, a word or two on these seven sources (actually eight, counting the construction/bridge loan necessary to fund the project until the tax-credit proceeds are placed) might be instructive.

The tax credits, allocated by the Georgia Housing and Finance Authority (GHFA), were syndicated by a subsidiary of the Enterprise Foundation (see Chapter 20), since no Atlanta business would step forward to buy them. A $1 per year

ground lease for the site, close by to a rapid rail MARTA station, was the next piece, offered by the city through its Urban Residential Finance Authority. The state, through the Trust Fund for the Homeless, (administered by GHFA) and again by property tax abatement, through act of the legislature, contributed other vital dollars. Grants were obtained through two sources: one federal, the "Affordable Housing Program" of the Federal Home Loan Bank, and one private foundation. Another foundation put up a letter of credit to guarantee the large operating reserve required by the equity partner.

As this is written, a full twelve months have been spent packaging these necessary funds, and, in fact, the permanent loan remains at the "tentative" commitment stage. PRI, Gibralter and a civic-minded architect carried the loan of salaries, overhead, and predevelopment costs incurred to date. Each funding source also generated its share of closing costs and paperwork. Despite 31 percent of the city's population living under the federal poverty line and an unequivocal written pledge made in writing by a popular and ostensibly powerful Mayor, the inevitable politics, turf wars, and "fate of downtown" arguments threatened the fragile financial framework of the project and contrived a pace of tortuous proportions. Still, not a spade of dirt has been turned. While most of the coterie of city officials, bankers and politicians continue to view the Welcome House as an eventuality, it has taken a process one official described as a "mini-Underground" (the $100 million entertainment complex built three years ago in the heart of the city) to provide a meager 209 rooms for the city's working homeless population.

There are the bright spots. With the pathways and partnerships forged by the Welcome House, the Commissioner of Housing has laid plans for the promised 3,500 units of SRO housing; the activist community has united to speak often with one voice; an Atlanta Neighborhood Development Partnership to target inner-city neighborhoods with money and expertise has been formed; and at least three neighborhoods most likely to be effected by the impending 1996 Olympics are rapidly organizing to engender their own revitalization. Meanwhile, the city's heretofore most successful affordable-housing developers, Habitat for Humanity and Charis Community Housing, are making their most ambitious plans yet. As for PRI, the multilayered financing template and joint-venture partnership model that it pioneered resulted in the development of 343 housing units in 1993 and has the organization primed to continue an ambitious program.

Looking Forward

PRI's mission always regarded affordable housing as a *means*, since the pathologies and deficiencies of skill, education and resources so endemic to inner city neighborhoods always meant that the provision of housing alone was not enough for a homeless or near homeless individual or family to latch on to the American dream. For this reason PRI has emphasized ownership, which meant wealth creation; fostering communities,

through housing cooperatives; and alignment with outside social service providers. PRI's current product line— SROs, transitional/multifamily housing, and owner-occupied co-ops—is designed as a "ladder" to allow upward movement from very low-income-level housing (SROs) to more-permanent housing (co-ops) in which families and neighborhoods can prosper together.

This is the approach embodied in PRI's plans for the future. The development of a second downtown SRO facility, currently under contract, combined with the Welcome House, will offer almost 300 rooms to approximately 500 individuals, with full access to health care, job counseling, drug and alcohol treatment, and exceptional access to transportation. Stringent management and tight security will be the indirect costs of delivering these services, all the while under the watchful eye of a wary if not antagonistic business community, which has a different vision for the downtown sector. The challenge that PRI does share with the business community is to develop the downtown area into a more healthy sector by providing a residential mix that can accommodate the sometimes conflicting agendas of upper-scale developments and dignified low-income housing.

Downtown, home to most of the area's homeless population, is one end of the spectrum. Different approaches are warranted in the neighborhoods. On the southern residential fringes, PRI has combined forces with a church-based job placement agency to provide decent transitional housing with complementary support services, such as day care, to formerly homeless individuals who are recently employed.

Finally, there are the cooperatives. PRI is nearing completion on its third limited-equity co-op, the Columns at East Hill, and will shortly begin work on a fourth, a 58-unit cooperative in the near vicinity. Many believe cooperatives will fill an important niche in the gap between ownership of single-family detached housing and rental-apartment housing.

Martin Luther King, Jr., perhaps Atlanta's most famous native son, spoke inspiringly about creating a "beloved community." As a crucible of the civil rights movement, the definitive challenge facing Atlanta is removing the cruel irony of having won the moral and legal victories of that movement only to see many of her citizens struggling this time to break free from economic bondage.

Welcome House was completed in December 1992 and is now leasing up on schedule. All parties involved in the process reported a great deal of satisfaction for a job well done.

Chapter 11

San Francisco, California: Bridge Housing Corporation

Jess Lederman
Author and Private Investor
and
Richard Koller
President, RDK, Inc.

Bridge Housing Corporation (Bridge), a nonprofit company, was formed in 1983, a time when high home prices, soaring interest rates and drastic reductions in federal and state programs were spelling disaster for housing in the Bay area. The market that Bridge faces today is still plagued by an extraordinary affordability gap. The median home price in 1990 was $292,000. The income necessary to qualify for a "starter home" in San Francisco is just shy of $100,000 per year. This is a level that is beyond the reach of over 92 percent of the city's residents, and, perhaps most significant, beyond the reach of 99 percent of San Francisco's rental population.

"In San Francisco, and throughout California, many renters have taken to viewing themselves as lifers, and they are not happy about that," says Don Terner, Bridge's dynamic president. "Further-more, both renters and owners are being pushed farther and farther out to the periphery of our region, forced to endure hellish commutes. They've left home at 6 A.M., they get to work at 8:30 and stand behind a lathe or sit at a typewriter and they're in no mood to be dealing with the real productivity aspects of their work. They labor through the day and then at 5 P.M. the same routine repeats itself. By the time they get home they're not fit to be with their family, their spouses, their kids. The notion of a productive, healthy economy is breaking down around the edges because people cannot find reasonably priced homes near their workplace."

AFFORDABILITY WITHOUT SUBSIDIES

Bridge was founded on the presumption

135

that federal and state subsidies for housing would be few and far between. The central question thus became: what new strategies and tactics could be developed to produce affordable housing?

Bridge found that the single most important variable in producing affordable housing without subsidies is *aggressive density bonuses*. The high cost of land is what drives up the cost of California housing, and Bridge buys land the way any developer does, at the going market rate. The key is to reduce the cost of land *per unit* by obtaining concessions on permissible densities during the public approval process.

"The most aggressive density bonus we ever obtained was on a piece of property that was originally entitled to 80 units," comments Don Terner, "and we were able to put up 167 units—a bonus of more than 100 percent. That may sound extreme, but this was a 10-acre site that was originally zoned at eight units to the acre, and to put 16 or 17 units to the acre for garden apartments on a 10-acre site is not a big deal. The key was that we had 87 units in that deal with a zero land cost."

"Basically, what we end up with is a project that serves a mixed-income market, with both affordable and market-rate units. The affordable units are those with a zero land cost. We add on top of that every financing bell and whistle we can think of. For example, we started out with tax-exempt financing and we still use that a bit. We're going now to federal tax credits made available to us under the 1986 tax reform act. We'll pick up any subsidy if and when we can find it, but that's not the day in, day out formula for production. The formula is: buy land, seek aggressive zoning concessions, layer on financing which will sometimes be concessionary given the affordable housing we're going to do, and finally, produce it at cost, not at a profit. You add all of that together, and we do have a way we've managed to succeed without a heavy reliance on subsidies."

AFFORDABILITY AND QUALITY

The mentality in California tends to be anti-growth. This works against affordable housing, resulting not only in restrictive zoning requirements, but also in an inherent suspicion that affordable housing will produce eyesores, drab housing that represents everything that the affluent Californian is trying to escape. The simple fact is that most middle- to upper-class homeowners don't want low-income neighbors.

Bridge found that the only way to address the overwhelming neighborhood resistance to affordable-housing projects—what HUD now calls the NIMBY syndrome (see Chapter 14)—was to produce high-quality units. The typical Bridge project is mixed-income, with perhaps 25 percent of the project representing affordable housing, and it is virtually impossible to tell the low-income from the market-rate tenants.

"We often encounter a great fear that you can't put very-low-income residents—from housing authority waiting lists—into an essentially market-rate development without a lot of tenant jealousy and a lot of strife," says Terner. "But that is simply not the case with our projects. I've walked some projects with lenders who voice these sorts of concerns, and I say, tell me who the very low income people are, point out what apartments they live in. And of course it can't be done."

"We build on a fair number of Cali-

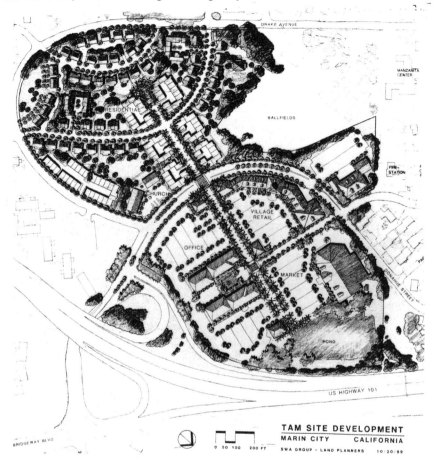

TAM SITE DEVELOPMENT
MARIN CITY   CALIFORNIA
SWA GROUP - LAND PLANNERS   10/20/89

fornia school sites because of state demographic changes, which have produced a number of surplus school properties. In one such development in Novato (a community in Napa County, north of San Francisco) we walked up a hillside to take a photograph looking down on the school site, and asked a woman if we could stand on her porch and take a photo of the project below. She peered at me over her glasses and asked 'Are you the people who developed the old Marian school down below?' I girded myself, expecting a stream of invective, and said yes. She said to me,

'Well, I've got to tell you, when they first proposed closing the school I was livid because it meant they'd have to bus my kids to the other side of town. But I figured, what the heck, we'd get a park out of the school site, and that might not be too bad. Then the town told us that they couldn't build a park, they couldn't afford to purchase the land. I was furious when I heard it was going to be a housing site. But when they said it was going to be a low-cost housing site, that was the end of the line. We were ready to lie down in front of the bulldozers to kill the project. I got my neighbors out there and

fought for two years, but you won. And I've got to tell you this, we look down on the project and we're kind of glad that you left the green area in the back which was the former athletic field, the way you clustered all the housing up front. And best of all, there are a couple of teenagers down there who come up the hill and baby-sit for my kids and there are some families there who we've become real friendly with. So I've got to admit that it's a nice job and I'm glad we didn't lie down in front of the bulldozers.

Come on in, have a cup of coffee, and anytime you want to take some photographs, come on up the hill.'"

Perhaps the most notable example of Bridge's success in combining quality and affordability is to be found in the affluent San Francisco suburb of Mill Valley. The Bridge development offers apartments renting for $300 to $600 per month, in contrast to nearby condominiums costing $350,000. Although the project initially met with strong opposition, it wasn't long before families

shopping for the upscale condominiums began coming into the development's rental office instead. In 1988 the Mill Valley project won the Urban Land Institute's award for excellence, not as the best nonprofit or best affordable project, but as the best small-scale residential development in the country.

"People often look at our projects and ask, 'Why does Bridge put swimming pools into low-income projects?'" says Terner. " 'Why, God forbid, do you put in hot tubs and health clubs? Surely this is the California mentality gone too far!' But the answer is simple. A typical Bridge development might start out as 20 percent affordable, and increase to as much as 35 percent or more as the

project's cash flow builds. But the key is that the majority of the units are market-rate. We've got to attract and keep market-rate tenants who are paying top dollar, so we have to offer the same kind of amenities that any market-rate development offers. After all, if they don't like our units, they can go down the street and rent at any number of other developments that have at least a perceived advantage over us, in that there are no low-income people living there. So we've got to have the hot tub and the pool, the health club and the wood-burning fireplace, and the washer/dryers in the units, not in laundries. Because if we don't keep the market-rate units filled, we've got to feed

these projects with our own cash. Furthermore, in our projects you have a mix of incomes, of races, of ethnicity, and you begin to develop healthy communities where there is no stigma, no label of 'low-income housing project.'"

Bridge's approach often results in projects that are actually less expensive than more traditional "bare bones" affordable housing. One dramatic example is a senior project with 125 units that rent for $390 per month. Across the street from the Bridge project is a church which runs a homeless shelter in its basement. The shelter takes people in at dusk, offers them a cot and a shower and a small meal, and then turns them out into the street the next morning. It costs the church $15 per night per person—$450 per month—to offer this temporary dormitory-style housing. By contrast, the Bridge units offer full amenity housing complete with balconies, dishwashers, and disposals, all for the equivalent of $13 per night. A typical Bridge project, it did not receive any subsidies, but features tax credits and a substantial density bonus.

PREVENTING WINDFALLS ON RESALES

Bridge's success in combining quality and affordability on for-sale units would seem to offer buyers a potential windfall on resale. For example, one Bridge for-

sale project featured units that were appraised at $400,000, but sold for only $99,000. Because of the overwhelming demand, the method of allocating units to prospective buyers was, appropriately enough, a lottery.

"The method that we use to prevent a windfall for the first lucky buyer in the lottery is fairly straightforward," according to Terner. "We put a sleeping second on the property. If we sell Bill Jones a unit for $99,000, and it's appraised for $400,000, then he takes a $301,000 sleeping second. He doesn't make any payments on the second, but when he sells the unit he has to pay off the debt with the proceeds."

"If Bill sells the unit in a couple of years for $425,000, he walks away with some appreciation on his equity, and we come away with $301,000 that we can use to make more affordable units. There are a number of ways that you can structure a sleeping second—you can put accruing rates of interest on it, or you can put in an equity kicker. You could deed restrict it, but the method we use keeps things simple—we just put in a second trust deed for the difference between the selling price and the appraised value."

THE NEXT STAGE: MIXED-USE/MIXED-INCOME

Bridge's most ambitious project, begun in 1990, is a development on 47 acres of prime property adjacent to the exclusive community of Sausalito.

"We're building what is essentially a small town," says Terner, "with 300 units of new housing, 300 rehabs, 292,000 square feet of commercial space, a park, a waterscape, an amphitheater, community facilities and a new freeway interchange. It's a very exciting project that takes what we're doing to the next step. We've been doing mixed-income, and this is mixed-use/mixed-income. The commercial space and 60 percent of the units that are market-rate will throw off income, allowing us to write down the cost of the affordable housing.

SUMMARY

Bridge Housing Corporation has built a substantial amount of rental and ownership housing that achieves an unprecedented blend of affordability and quality. They have done it while operating in one of the highest-cost and most overly regulated markets in the country. The key to their success has been securing the exemptions necessary to build high-density housing, and focusing on mixed-income developments in which cash flow from market-rate units can be used to subsidize affordable units. Theirs is a model which can be applied successfully in many American cities.

Chapter 12

Habitat for Humanity: Changing the World One House at a Time

Millard Fuller
President
Habitat for Humanity International

After 16 years of uplifting experiences and accomplishments, some setbacks, and considerable work and prayer, Habitat for Humanity can affirm confidently but humbly: we are part of the solution to the affordable-housing problem. We affirm this with confidence because our track record is conclusive. We affirm it humbly because our faith tells us that God has made this possible.

It's important to state openly and unashamedly at the outset that our Christian faith is the basic foundation of Habitat for Humanity's work. We believe that our mission is to put God's word of love into action and to dedicate ourselves to eliminating poverty housing and homelessness worldwide. We believe God has given us this work—or ministry—and has blessed us with accomplishments, and also with defeats, from which we learn. We believe that, if

we can remain true to our mission, Habitat for Humanity can change the world—one house, one family, one community at a time.

Established in 1976, Habitat for Humanity is an ecumenical Christian not-for-profit housing organization. Habitat's mission—and ultimate goal—is to eliminate poverty housing and homelessness from the world and to make decent shelter a matter of conscience and action. We believe we can best do this by witnessing to the gospel of Jesus Christ, putting words into action. We can accomplish our goal through partnerships with caring people, churches, businesses, foundations, governments, fraternal societies, civic groups, and people in need. Habitat's funding relies on the generosity of individual donors and organizations that look to us as an effective solution and

145

answer to the problems of poverty housing and homelessness.

AN OPEN DOOR

Habitat for Humanity is not a church. It
is a servant of the church, with an open-
door policy—welcoming all, regardless of
race, color or creed.

Because Habitat is a solution, is open
to everyone with a caring heart, and relies on grass-roots support, the work has
drawn volunteers in the hundreds of
thousands worldwide. In fact, one of our
statements of mission acknowledges the
commitment and strength of this open
door to all, stating that we aspire "to enable an expanding number of persons
from all walks of life to participate in this
ministry."

RECORD OF SUCCESS

On paper, the resultant track record is
impressive. Since 1976, when Habitat for
Humanity International was founded in
southwest rural Georgia, Habitat projects
have built and renovated over 18,000 affordable houses (as of early 1992). Two
affiliates—Atlanta, Georgia, and Charlotte, North Carolina—have built more
than 100 houses each. Many international projects put their totals in the hundreds: a few in the thousands.

We've grown from a handful of
locations to more than 800 affiliated projects in North America and Australia, 15
regional offices and more than 100
sponsored projects in 39 nations in Central and South America, India, Africa,
and the Asian Pacific areas. Affiliated projects are responsible for their own
fundraising, staffing, volunteer recruitment, publicity, and daily administration.
Habitat-sponsored projects are in

developing countries for the most part
and Habitat for Humanity International
takes responsibility for funding and
securing Habitat volunteers for the projects. These volunteers, known as International Partners (IPs) are trained at
international headquarters in Americus,
Georgia, and serve three-year terms. As
part of our covenant with affiliates, we
ask a 10 percent tithe for international
work.

Affiliated projects are being added at a
pace of about 12 to 20 per month. Negotiations are proceeding that could take
Habitat's work to Eastern Europe. Somewhere in the world, at this moment, a
Habitat house is being completed, or
dedicated, and turned over to a family in
need. The sun never sets on Habitat
work.

In human relations terms as well as
on paper, the record is even more gratifying. Habitat for Humanity houses, and
the families occupying them, have en-
ergized and improved entire neighborhoods and communities. The pride, dignity, and responsibilities of homeownership have renewed individuals and
families—often transforming them.
Bread line seekers have become bread
earners. Tax dollar receivers, living off
giveaway programs, have become
taxpayers. Kids who once saw only a future of ghetto life and gang mentality
have gone to schools, held productive
employment, and formed strong family
units themselves.

THE NEEDS

Millions of families in the world live in
wretched shacks and conditions because
they can't afford simple, decent shelter.
In the United States, for example, a census study concluded that about half of all

families and two thirds of all nonfamily households are unable to buy a median-priced home using conventional, fixed-rate, 30-year financing with a minimum 5 percent down payment.

This problem is magnified manyfold in Third World countries, where grinding poverty precludes millions of families from even dreaming of a better home. Whatever income they have must go to basic necessities for life, such as food.

How do we approach this challenge? How do we keep Habitat houses affordable? First, as stated above, through our faith and prayer. And, second, we draw on what we have learned is God's guidance in putting our faith into practical solutions. The Habitat for Humanity "formula" is so basic, so simple, that some have called it radical. Others have said Habitat for Humanity is like a bumblebee: it couldn't possibly fly with its down-to-earth structure and principles. Yet it does, and it works.

At our locations in North America, Habitat houses are built using mostly volunteers of varying skills, working under the tutelage of volunteer or donated management expertise. Houses are built or renovated using donated materials. In many cases, the land has been donated as well. This keeps the basic costs down.

NO INTEREST, NO PROFIT

In addition, Habitat follows Biblical principles. We do not charge interest, and we do not make a profit. The no-interest, no-profit policy enables us to keep mortgage payments—and homeowners must pay—to an affordable level during a 20- to 30-year mortgage schedule.

This means we reach people who have some income, but cannot afford houses with conventional financing. Because the houses are built or renovated using volunteer labor and materials, and we charge no interest and make no profit, the homeowners can afford the required monthly payments. They also receive another blessing: hope, a chance to break out of a cycle of substandard, poverty housing, and the dignity and responsibility of homeownership. The mortgage payments are deposited in a "Fund for Humanity" and are recycled to help pay for the building and renovation of other houses.

AVERAGE COSTS

The average cost of a Habitat house is about $31,800 in the United States. Of course, this rate goes up in some of the more expensive areas of the country, such as California—where astronomically high land prices and costly building codes prevail. In some other areas costs are lower. In the Mississippi Delta, for example, Habitat builds houses for as little as $11,000.

BASIC GUIDELINES

While Habitat for Humanity affiliates enjoy a considerable degree of autonomy in their covenant with international headquarters in Americus, Georgia, there are certain basic guidelines we expect to be followed. For example, we stipulate in our basic building guidelines that the living space provided in a Habitat house—not including stairwells and exterior storage—should be 900 square feet for a two-bedroom house, 1050 square feet for a three-bedroom, and 1150 square feet for a four-bedroom house. We further ask that the basic house have only one bathroom. Each house is to have a covered primary entrance and be handicap accessible. Habitat homes should not have air conditioning, carports, or garages.

Overseas, of course, costs and construction methods differ. The average cost of a Habitat for Humanity house at an international project ranges from $1,000 to $3,000. The size of the house varies from country to country, but all are smaller than Habitat houses in North America and Australia. We often forget, with all our blessings here, that our average living room is palatial to an impoverished Third World family. Entire families live, cook, eat, and sleep in single rooms the size of a small American living room. Habitat's overseas house designs emphasize decency, safety, and compatibility with local cultures and climate conditions.

APPROPRIATE TECHNOLOGY

Habitat for Humanity also puts a priority on implementation of the concept of appropriate technology. Wherever possible, we use local materials, local construction techniques, labor, and expertise. Sometimes this dismays observers from the United States who believe solutions lie in importing "high tech" construction equipment and methods. We've found that, while this might seem a quick-fix solution, in the long run it is counter-productive and even disruptive to a culture. For example, what good is the latest pickup truck or equipment when roads are inadequate, at best, and parts wear down and cannot be replaced? What good have we done if we get a local populace addicted to the latest modern equipment and then leave? Without replacement parts? Without in-

struction on maintenance and handling? Have we really helped them to help themselves? Habitat for Humanity thinks not.

Appropriate technology permits us to keep costs down and is true to a basic Habitat for Humanity principle: Grassroots participation and grass-roots solutions are the best. Habitat's efforts are truly fulfilled when we can walk away from a project because it is being maintained, led, administered, and inspired by the people who live there.

GRASS-ROOTS RECEPTIVENESS

This grass-roots orientation has proven to be enormously effective and popular. Habitat for Humanity empowers local people, laypersons—whether in North America or overseas—to participate in solving their own local problems of affordable housing and homelessness. And to see and feel the results of their labor and commitment almost immediately and for years to come! They are not dictated to by some huge faceless government spending program or a faraway headquarters. They use their gifts, their talents, and share their concerns with others in their respective communities. They make the decisions. They build the relationships with people in need.

After studying a Habitat for Humanity growth chart, both in North America and internationally, the instinctive response is to exclaim: "You must send teams of people out into the field in a full-court press to recruit international projects, affiliates, and volunteers! That's the only way Habitat could grow at such a pace."

Not so. Grass-roots people come to us. Habitat for Humanity goes only where it is invited and actively recruited by grass-roots people who see the ministry as a solution—and are willing to work for its success in their area. Individuals, churches, organizations at local levels hear about Habitat for Humanity and apply for affiliation or for international project sponsorship.

Before becoming an official part of Habitat, they must form committees at the grass-roots level and prove not only their seriousness of intent, but their capacity to recruit volunteers and leaders, raise publicity and funds, and to get the job done.

A HAND UP, NOT A HAND OUT

This approach of being certain that local strength is not only present, but willing, is part of Habitat for Humanity's universal message: the ministry is "a hand up, not a hand out." Affiliates realize they are not on the receiving end of a massive giveaway program. And this is a message they must convey to families which they select as recipients of Habitat houses. Families are required to work on their houses and/or the houses of others. They must pay for their houses. They must maintain them.

This aspect of Habitat for Humanity's approach draws strong support and praise. It's refreshing in a world made increasingly cynical by giveaway programs, lavish but empty promises of bold programs and new initiatives that result more in paperwork than sweat work.

SWEAT EQUITY

Families selected to be Habitat homeowners are not warehoused in huge projects that were built without their participation. Instead, they are required to make their houses and projects a reality with their sweat.

We call this sweat equity. In North America, for example, affiliates require Habitat families to work 300 to 700 hours on their house or houses of others (most Habitat projects require 500 hours). Families learn immediately that their houses are not "freebies." Their sweat goes into the houseraising process. This builds pride and a sense of responsibility. It's reflected years later in the good maintenance and care still being given by original homeowners to Habitat houses. Donors sometimes ask us: "How about years later? Are Habitat houses taken care of?" The answer is yes.

For international projects, usually centered in developing nations and impoverished areas, there are modifications. International headquarters provides funding, as it must because of scarcity of local resources. Here, too, however, we are in the initial phases of a development program to raise funds in the nations where we have projects—increasing the commitment of nationals to Habitat's success.

The sweat equity principle applies at international projects, although—again—sometimes modifications are necessary due to cultural and other considerations. In Peru and Mexico, for example, large groups of families, up to a hundred families, work together to build their houses. When all the work is completed, the families decide which houses go to which families.

PARTNERSHIP

Obviously, partnership is a key to Habitat's growth and success. Habitat for

Humanity, to its core, represents partnership. One of the most gratifying aspects of the work is to witness how many giving people and organizations there are, and how fulfilled they become by sharing the love, progress, dreams, hopes, criticism and credit that goes with the work.

Habitat's partners are many, with each bringing certain gifts, talents, and aspirations to our common table of servanthood. We believe that, first and foremost, we are partners with God. We are servants, fulfilling God's admonition that the poor will always be with us, therefore, we are to share with our brothers and sisters in need and reach out to them in love. Our outreach in this partnership is to work with people in need to assure them of their God-given right to decent, safe shelter.

From there the partnership expands. The faith community—churches and synagogues—have been major partners from our beginning in 1976. They have provided virtual armies of volunteers, support from pulpits, cash and material donations and prayers. Local churches have sponsored the construction of entire houses, sent work crews to build them, and volunteers to work with families after they move in. Yet, Habitat for Humanity believes this particular partnership has a long way to go. Its potential has been only barely touched. If every church was to commit to building one or two affordable houses per year, we would not have a problem.

We have hundreds of thousands of volunteer partners throughout the nation and world. They serve on construction crews, site selection committees, family selection committees, boards of directors. They handle public relations. They work on fundraising events. They provide food at construction sites. They represent all ages, avocations, interests, races, and creeds—and they are all welcome.

Habitat for Humanity's volunteer program has drawn wide attention and praise, including being honored by the President of the United States. In 1989, two Habitat volunteers traveled to Washington, D.C., to receive a Volunteer Action award from President George Bush. Habitat was among 18 nonprofits so recognized for volunteer programs.

The ranks, and variety, of volunteers have expanded in recent years as Habitat for Humanity achieves increased recognition as a solution. For example, Habitat now has a Campus Chapter program, which involves university and college, and high school, groups as partners. The Campus Chapters program has become our fastest-growing outreach. Student and faculty partners have helped build homes and have also been a significant factor in fundraising. As of the end of 1992, there were over 1,000 Habitat Campus Chapters and associated groups.

Corporate partners have also stepped forward. Businesses find partnership with Habitat for Humanity especially rewarding. Habitat's policies of no-interest, no-profit, and requiring homeowner recipients to contribute many hours of sweat equity attract corporations seeking practical, non-giveaway programs. A corporation, linking up with a Habitat affiliate or group of affiliates in a region, can give back something to an area where it does business—and see the results of its work. This is a morale-builder for a company's employees. Habitat has a corporate sponsorship program, still in its infancy, that has been responsible for the construction and renovation of many affordable houses.

PRESIDENT JIMMY CARTER

Habitat's most visible volunteers have been former President Jimmy Carter and wife Rosalynn. They've also been among the organization's most active and committed. The Carters linked up with Habitat for Humanity in 1984, and every year have led the annual Jimmy Carter Work Project. For one week in June the Carters lead hundreds of volunteers in a blitz build in a city, or cities. Entire communities have been built or transformed through their efforts. The 1990 Jimmy Carter Work Project, for instance, was held in San Diego, California, and across the border in Tijuana, Mexico. It was our first transnational effort. One hundred houses were built in the Matamoros area of Tijuana, and seven in San Diego in one week.

OTHER ORGANIZATIONS

We consider other organizations, with approaches that differ from Habitat's, to be partners. We salute them, offer to work with them, and pray for their work. Many have inspired us and we believe Habitat's example has spurred many of them on to greater efforts. We include government as a partner. All organizations seeking to battle poverty housing and homelessness need the cooperation and understanding of government at all levels. This covers a wide range—from building inspections and codes, to construction of sidewalks, utility lines and streets, to laws and policies being deliberated at the municipal, legislative, congressional or White House levels. We're all in this effort!

GOVERNMENT FUNDS

Habitat for Humanity's policy is not to accept government funds—tax money— for the building or renovation of houses or for administrative purposes. Habitat does accept grants of money, land, or houses from governmental units which "set the stage" to build. For example, Habitat affiliates gladly accept loans or direct gifts of land, old houses to be renovated, or the construction of streets, sidewalks and utilities as well as direct grants of money designated to purchase land, put in streets, sidewalks, etc. However, we stipulate that there can be no strings attached which violate Habitat principles.

This policy has been vigorously debated within and without the organization. But we feel it has served us well. We are able much more freely to witness to our God-centered mission. Also, we have learned from the sad experiences of other organizations who were formed as the result of massive, seemingly high-budgeted government programs—only to see the programs die or become clogged in a sea of paperwork and bureaucracy. Habitat for Humanity wants to remain a strong, dynamic grass-roots movement—a people-centered, people-driven movement of faith and love in action. We desire partnership with government, but not domination by, or dependence upon, it.

THE FUTURE

"What you're doing is just a drop in the bucket." How many times have we, and other organizations in this crusade, heard that expression! It's not valid. Had we listened and become discouraged, over 18,000 families today now living in decent houses would be confined to substandard shelter and shacks. Thousands more who'll be touched in the future

With hammer and level in hand, Former President Jimmy Carter and Rosalynn Carter volunteer with Habitat for Humanity to build simple, decent and affordable homes with low-income families.

would not have hope. We also believe that Habitat for Humanity's visibility and infectious enthusiasm has helped arouse the national and international conscience to the needs of the ill-housed and the homeless. This has been, and will be, translated into many other organizations, and government, making progress in providing affordable housing and battling homelessness.

We have faith. We have trust. We have commitment. And we have the muscle and sweat and God-fearing love to give. Poverty housing and homelessness—and hopelessness—will be eliminated from the face of the earth.

APPENDIX

The following designs, reprinted from The Habitat for Humanity Planbook, have been selected from the files of house designs collected over a period of years by the Construction Resources Office at Habitat for Humanity International. They have all come from affiliates, many of them are currently being used by Habitat affiliate projects, and each of them meets the Habitat House Design Criteria. They have come from all regions where Habitat is active and, though not every design will be appropriate for any given region or affiliate, the intention is to provide a variety of options to assist prospective homeowners in choosing their new house. Designs fall into three rough categories, each of which is applicable in one or more of the many different situations and locations in which affiliates are building. There are single-story detached, one-and-a-half story detached, and two-story duplex, or multiplex designs which may also serve as in-fill designs. Most of the designs can be built on either slab, crawl space, or full basement foundations. There are also fully accessible variations of several of the designs useful in the case of an affiliate building with a homeowner with a disability.

The designs are presented here in a schematic form "readable" by Construction Committee members, Family Selection Committee members and—most importantly—by prospective homeowners. They are not meant to be used as working drawings. The Intention is for a representative of the affiliate to work with prospective homeowners in choosing their new house. Though it is recognized that many affiliates build from a single predetermined design, it is hoped that this collection of plans will be used to enrich Habitat's partnership with homeowners and increase their sense of home-ownership. After a family has been selected and has chosen a design, working drawings can be ordered from the Construction Resources Office using the form at the back of the planbook.

Each design is identified by a four-digit code which should be used when ordering working drawings. Each set of working drawings will include schematic floor plans for the homeowner to keep, dimensioned and noted plans and elevations for the construction crew, and a wiring diagram for the electrician. Foundation plans, technical details, and wall sections will not be included because it is impossible to design those details to meet the various local building codes in effect in the different areas that Habitat affiliates are building. It is the responsibility of each affiliate to ensure that their building meets the applicable local codes, and this may require consulting with local officials or professionals.

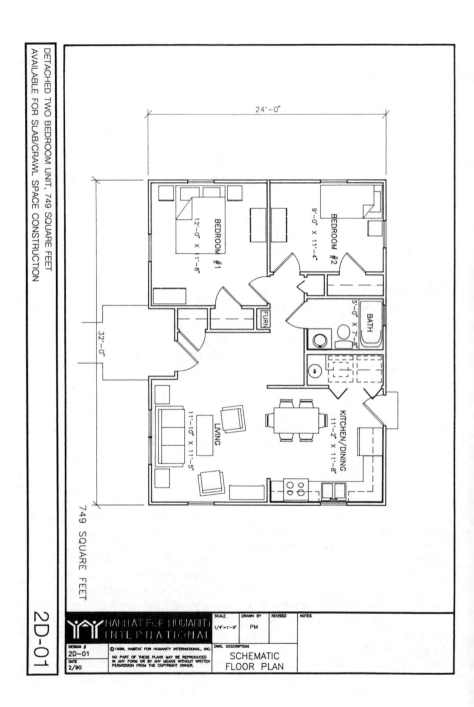

24'-0"

32'-0"

BEDROOM #1
12'-0" X 11'-8"

BEDROOM #2
9'-0" X 11'-4"

FURN.

BATH
5'-0" X 7'-5"

KITCHEN/DINING
11'-2" X 11'-8"

LIVING
11'-10" X 11'-5"

749 SQUARE FEET

2D-01

| SCALE 1/4"=1'-0" | DRAWN BY PM | REVISED | NOTES |

DESIGN #
2D-01
DATE
2/90

DWG. DESCRIPTION
SCHEMATIC
FLOOR PLAN

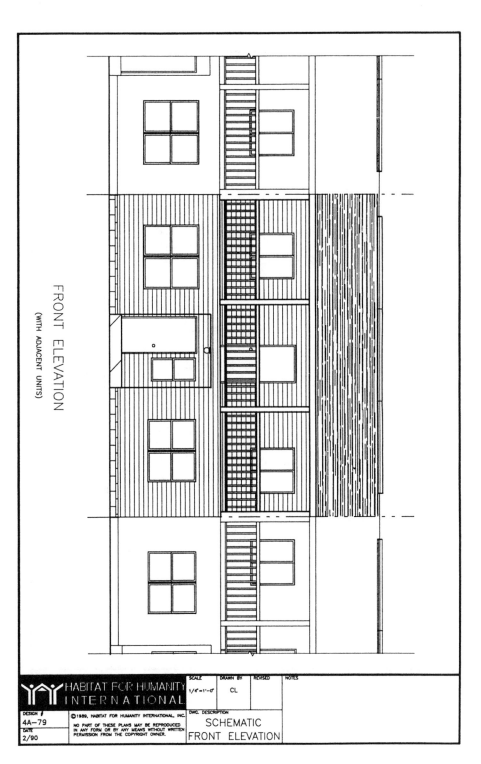

FRONT ELEVATION
(WITH ADJACENT UNITS)

SCALE	DRAWN BY.	REVISED	NOTES
1/4"=1'-0"	CL		

DESIGN #
4A-79
DATE
2/90

DWG. DESCRIPTION
SCHEMATIC
FRONT ELEVATION

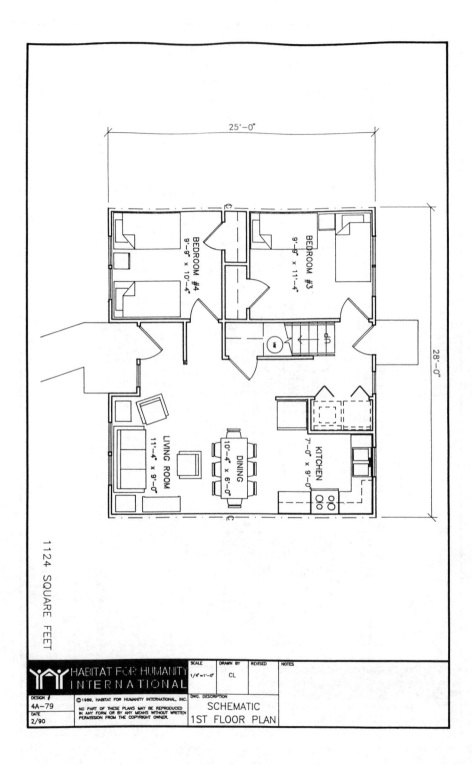

25'-0"

28'-0"

BEDROOM #4
9'-9" x 10'-4"

BEDROOM #3
9'-9" x 11'-4"

UP

LIVING ROOM
11'-4" x 9'-0"

DINING
10'-4" x 6'-0"

KITCHEN
7'-0" x 9'-0"

1124 SQUARE FEET

SCALE	DRAWN BY	REVISED	NOTES
1/4"=1'-0"	CL		

DESIGN
4A-79
DATE
2/90

DWG. DESCRIPTION
SCHEMATIC
1ST FLOOR PLAN

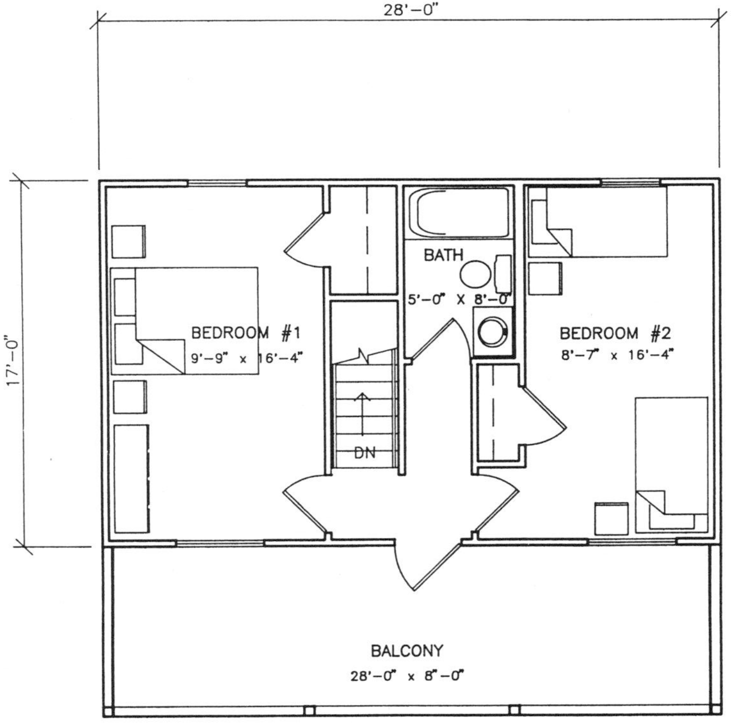

17'-0"

28'-0"

BEDROOM #1
9'-9" x 16'-4"

BALCONY
28'-0" x 8'-0"

DN

BATH
5'-0" X 8'-0"

BEDROOM #2
8'-7" x 16'-4"

HABITAT FOR HUMANITY
INTERNATIONAL

SCALE	DRAWN BY	REVISED	NOTES
1/4"=1'-0"	CL		

DESIGN #
4A-79
DATE
2/90

©1988, HABITAT FOR HUMANITY INTERNATIONAL, INC.
NO PART OF THESE PLANS MAY BE REPRODUCED
IN ANY FORM OR BY ANY MEANS WITHOUT WRITTEN
PERMISSION FROM THE COPYRIGHT OWNER.

DWG. DESCRIPTION
SCHEMATIC
2ND FLOOR PLAN

Chapter 13

Future Directions for Housing Urban America

Bertrand Goldberg
Bertrand Goldberg Associates, Inc.

"Housing" is an American word which back in 1920 simply included family, children, holidays, and in general what the Germans call *gemütlichkeit*. During the 1930s "functionalism" entered into our concepts of "housing": designs of square feet, of closets, of equipment, playgrounds, of safety and of service were added to "housing" from 1930 onward.

By 1950, concepts of housing had become more complex in response to the vast changes in our cities. The role of the city as a home for American manufacturing disappeared; the role of the city as a home for the American middle class disappeared. A sudden polarity of urban rich and urban poor was among the results of these changes and we added this to our program for "housing" in our cities.

Since 1930 construction of urban housing has produced profits for developers, but it has not produced solutions to deal with the urban "housing problem."

The problems of housing urban America resemble the problems of governing America—nothing we have done to correct these problems has worked. Nothing we planned for housing includes the fundamental changes made in urban life during the last half of this century—changes in **technology, society,** and **politics.**

But while we radically changed our lives, we have made no changes in the cities where we live. Our cities remain as they were designed in the nineteenth century: divided into separate zones for housing, work, and recreation which defy our need for community, communication, and security. Zoned American cities would have suited the regimented urban organization of Karl Marx's social planning, but zoning today

159

blocks the development of new mixed-use communities that form our neighborhoods.

"Housing" is a word we use when we mean "living in the city." It has broadened its meaning to include much more than "shelter." A menu for new housing in the twenty-first century must broaden its scope even more.

TECHNOLOGICAL CHANGES

Technological upgrading of housing has become a necessity through advantages and economies revealed by our research and development related to housing:

1. To conserve energy is a major concern in our national planning. Some countries see housing as a wasteful consumer of energy, including both fossil fuels and electricity. Sweden now requires six inches of insulation in all new structures. America can conserve electricity as well as fossil fuel in our housing by the intelligent use of new materials to reduce energy consumption.

2. Mass transportation properly related to our housing centers will replace the use of the automobile. Accessibility of transportation, rider acceptance and proper location of new work centers will bring lower-cost transportation to the plans for our housing. The proper location of housing closer to distribution centers of consumer goods can reduce transportation mileage.

3. Random transportation today is the automobile. New technology permits replacing the auto for random movement with special new mass-transportation devices. Future development of new housing centers will combine them with mass-transportation centers and reduce our dependency on the automobile.

4. New communication devices have expanded the use of the home into a business center and enlarged the concept of education for adults and children.

5. Environmental protection in minor ways is sought by all new housing development; but new developments to protect our environment will require major new engineering of traffic routes, energy usage, and distribution of open land.

6. Health protection is a recognized requirement in public facilities; new technology makes it possible to design our future housing to protect our health at home.

7. Distribution systems to deliver consumer goods are determined by our population patterns. The cost of distribution must be reduced. Concentration of housing is one way to reduce this cost of distribution.

8. Infrastructure of utilities and streets originally was laid out by patterns for marketing land. Today the technology of utility distribution and traffic movement enables us to plan more effective and economical patterns. Our infrastructure will be changed in the next century to reduce the cost of delivering and maintaining our utilities.

SOCIAL CHANGES

Social changes which affect our future housing have been created largely by economic development. Such changes affect the structure of family and community, which in turn require new concepts of housing:

1. **The change in family structure.** Fewer than 25 percent of American families with children have two parents. The work force of urban America is more than 50 percent women. The role of seniors is unidentified: there are more of them, with less available work, and fewer family connections to absorb their time.

2. **The change in education.** Education for both kids and adults twists in the wind: there are more solutions than problems. We don't know what to learn or how to teach. Most distressing of all is the family willingness to give their kids to some super-authority to learn their value standards.

3. **The change in demography.** Specialized groups in the city continue to increase their numbers. Both rich and poor have increased their population in the city.

The poor came to the city for jobs and remained to raise their increasing families while claiming entitlements. One of the new entitlements has become access to jobs for the lower-middle-income group unable to match the needs of high-tech employers in the private economy: city government in the new city-state has become a well-paid industry that provides employment for "unemployables."

The educated and rich have found well-paid urban jobs in the related fields of money, law, and communication.

The middle class has fled to the suburbs. The polarity of poor and rich diminishes the breadth of our urban planning to the detriment of our housing.

4. **The change in the streetscape.** The face of the city is gap-toothed. The city streets no longer are lined with a network of next-door buildings. There are no next-door neighbors. City lots are empty and city factories are empty. Urban manufacturing (the substantial reason for the existence of the twentieth century American city) has gone away forever and left holes in the face of the city which we don't know how to fill. Urban community needs physical revival for reasons of security and identity.

5. **The change in neighborhoods.** For those neighborhoods which remain, the social glue is gone. No churches, no neighborhood manufacturing, no ethnic identity, no homeownership, no candy stores, and no saloons to keep us together. People no longer touch each other. Urban humanism needs rejuvenation to remind us of our social values and responsibilities.

POLITICAL CHANGES

Political changes require new responses in the design of housing: the city has become a city-state with the increased responsibility which comes from increased power. The role of the city no longer is limited to the basic services of security and education: the role of the city encompasses financial planning, cultural development, health and welfare, communication—a vast assortment of responsibilities which we have gradually delegated to our urban governments.

1. Every power formerly reserved for the federal government, except those of declaring war and coining money, now has been delegated to the city.

2. One man, one vote, has given the governance of the city a new political system with new values for planning our environment.

3. The city has assumed responsibilities as it has added to its political power: the city has promised to provide to its greater numbers of dependent voters more services at greater cost.

4. The city has assumed economic responsibility: its political system must drive an economy which finances both public service and the well-being of its private business sector.

HOW LARGE WILL THE CITY BE?

Plato said that 25,000 people could form a city. Plato's number today is only adequate to form an urban neighborhood. The city needs many neighborhoods to form the critical mass which can support its systems of transportation, communication, cultural development, education, economic activity and the infrastructure of utilities. Rex Tugwell (who remembers that name from FDR's days?) once said: "The nature of the city is to be dense—it is the architect's job to make it livable."

The numbers involved in development of housing also must match the numbers we watch in growth of population and economics: our new scale of billions and trillions. This economy of new numbers must be supported by more people living pleasantly in a denser plan. Public transportation, garbage collection, education, streets, sewers, and water cannot fit our taxation budgets unless we distribute their cost among a larger group of taxpayers.

The costs of urban living are directly reduced for each taxpayer by the increased scale. An industrialized economy of larger numbers can provide a reduced cost of housing and living for each family: reduced cost of construction, of energy, of taxes, of distribution of goods, of transportation.

The cost of housing construction, like the cost of city services, can be reduced by increasing the scale of production. Construction of housing in an industrialized economy must be industrialized. A dwelling in a building with 750 units can cost half as much as a dwelling in a building with 75 units.

Large-scale housing provides indirect economies in many ways. Two hundred gallons of oil per family unit per year can be saved in a major housing development when compared to the consumption for the single-family house. Recycling of water and heat are further steps in a search toward rent reduction.

A shift to the private sector in providing educational, recreational and security services could reduce the tax burden now automatically assessed against new developments. We are accustomed to providing the swimming pool with new housing: why not include the planning for new education as well as a broad range of municipal services? Paid directly by a concentrated tenant group, such services probably will cost less than if provided by the city in a political environment.

Cost of utilities can be reduced by concentration of users. Should a large centralized neighborhood development with automated meter billing for electricity pay the same rate that includes monthly visits to the last homeowner's meter at the end of an urban sprawl?

Distribution of goods costs less if consumption is concentrated. One supermarket requires the volume produced by the consumption of about 2,500 families. Why not provide several supermarkets within walking distance of a high-density neighborhood? The cost of distribution for all family supplies can be diminished by a concentration of buying power.

Costs of transportation are a large budget item in urban living because walk-to-work jobs have disappeared from our cities. Jobs have been excluded from our urban housing by reason of our nineteenth-century zoning concepts. In American cities we separated jobs, recreation, education and living from each other. With our new resources in the technology of communication, it is appropriate that we bring all of our living and working activities back together: the cities of Europe began with high densities of mixed use, and this continues in European planning to this day. Walk to work! It's time-saving and dollar-saving.

Congressman Henry Reuss (Wis.) described the future of policy goals 20 years ago in a congressional study on the future of urbanism in America:

> "The role of the city as the Great Conservator of land, energy and resources can be enhanced by city planning to encourage homes within walking, bicycling or short commuting distances of work places, shopping and recreation ... by population shifts to bring ... middle class people back to the city in which they work: by a zoning reform making for a mix of homes, jobs and shops."

In summation, the housing for urban America should be planned for three objectives:

a. Increase (restore) the city's taxpaying middle-income population; bring the people back from the suburbs.

b. Reduce the ratio of cost of living (housing) to income in urban centers;

c. Provide a mixed-use housing and neighborhood environment for new family types.

Together these three targets must be enhanced with a magic we call humanism.

WHAT WILL THE NEW HOUSING LOOK LIKE?

The emphasis on the economics of concentrated urban communities should not divert us from the importance of the visual and environmental humanism of our future housing.

A new urbanism cannot be produced by today's developers. Our current definition of the housing developer is a salesman with an option to buy a piece of land and a loan to build on it. The developer we need for the future is one who can build new neighborhoods for an urbanism of the new century. Neighborhoods can provide extensive mixed use and make identity of the individual possible within a community environment. A combination of jobs, culture, education, security, recreation, visual pleasure must be the responsibility of a neighborhood developer.

Architecture reflects our society. A man from Mars who viewed our architecture for the first time could properly guess that our housing of the past was the environment for a highly regulated people. But the social changes of the past fifty years have been aimed at increasing the identity and the "freedom" of the individual.

The visual message of our urban neighborhoods can assure our humanism. Building must communicate friendship, a promise of touching, comfort, and an option for the privacy which urbanism can offer. Open spaces of streetscapes, access to outdoor views from balconies, can restore the ego and the scale of the human body.

If the architecture for our new society is to reflect it, then our spaces, our private environments, our working environments will be designed to make our self-awareness possible. The box may not be adequate for our ego. The technology exists to supply new structural forms and new spaces with both the economy and spirit which a new urban housing requires.

Technology of building construction has made it possible to build whatever we can creatively propose in the shapes of our rooms and our structures. No longer is it necessary to design boxes in which to store our families and our future. There can be a new architecture without the regimentation of the right angle and without the silly ornamental glitz that we have used for the past 20 years as a substitute for creativity under the name of post-modernism.

Across the entire spectrum of architecture in the Western Hemisphere, the past 20 years has produced few examples of thoughtful housing design. But the operative fact in this statement is that examples do exist of logical, socially directed, and frequently beautiful housing.

If our developers, our real estate financiers will insist that the architectural world provides concern for the issues of our society, then the technology, the politics, the housing will follow. A new architecture for housing does not need a new style—it needs responsibility. Our architecture will answer to our changes and demonstrate it has performed with awareness. Developers and bankers will be our ombudsmen.

The issue of housing the homeless, generally thought of as "public housing," is not included in this vision of housing America. Public housing programs begun before World War II have merely emphasized the identity of an underclass. For 60 years we have trapped four generations of poverty in identifiable ghettos. Surely this problem of economics cannot be solved by the housing plans which daily separate the poor from the remainder of our urban living. Our American search for causes of social maladjustments has mistakenly shifted the emphasis of this search to housing.

Mies van der Rohe once suggested that affordable housing could be provided by raising wages of the tenants. More affordable housing also can be provided by some of the planning and industrialized procedures suggested earlier in this proposal. But the economic disparities which produce homeless families are not related to the cost of housing. There is no acceptable architectural or urban planning solution for the homeless which is free of government subsidy.

Housing follows our changes—it does not create them. We should think how we want a humanistic urban environment to perform. The architects can design whatever we think.

Section III

Federal, State, and Local Government Programs

Chapter 14

The Department of Housing and Urban Development under Jack Kemp

Judith Serrin
Director of Admissions, Placement and Special Programs
Columbia University School of Business

President Theodore Roosevelt first raised the idea of federal involvement in housing policy and in 1908, his presidential commission studying slum conditions in the District of Columbia recommended: "A little government aid extended to these unfortunates in the form of a loan to build them habitable dwellings would tend immensely toward their uplifting and improvement."

Four decades later, in the Housing Act of 1949, the federal government, reflecting housing programs spawned by the Depression and the post-World War II era, committed itself to "the goal of a decent home and a suitable living environment for every American family."

And four decades after that, President George Bush stated the housing policy of his new administration: "Helping low-income families find affordable, decent housing . . . helping more of the 80 million Americans who don't own a home join the ranks of homeowners . . . These are aims well within our reach."

The constancy of the statements over eight decades illustrates the difficulty, through changing economic and political times, of dealing with the problem of providing the nation's citizens with what has come to be seen as a right—a safe, affordable home of their own. Upon that possession, said the congressional act establishing the Department of Housing and Urban Development (HUD) in 1966, depends the general welfare and security of the nation.

"Homeownership has always been a

chief pathway to the American Dream," said Jack Kemp, who became HUD secretary in 1989 after 18 years in the House of Representatives.

"I've always thought . . . anything HUD and the government could do to get people into that first home would really help to expand opportunity in America and improve social welfare."

To reach these goals, Kemp had as his resources a department with 13,000 employees in 1991 and, in the 1991 fiscal year, an annual budget of $24.3 billion.

Bush and Kemp came into office after eight years of sharp cuts in federal housing efforts during President Ronald Reagan's administration. Reagan shifted money from construction of public housing to a voucher program to enable recipients of housing aid to receive help with their rents wherever they lived. The number of federally subsidized units being built dropped from 175,000 in fiscal year 1982 to fewer than 35,000 in fiscal year 1988. According to *Congressional Quarterly*, "Spending, which had peaked at $30.1 billion in the last year of the Carter administration, totaled barely more than that—$33.2 billion— for Reagan's entire second term."

THE HOPE PROGRAM

There was a mood in Congress for a change. "We have been going now for years and years and years without an adequate response to the housing needs of this country," said one senator.

Working well with congressional forces, Secretary Kemp helped fashion the National Affordable Housing Act, which was signed into law in November 1990. The law was also known as the Cranston-Gonzalez Act, in recognition of the efforts of Sen. Alan Cranston (D-Calif.) and Rep. Henry Gonzalez.

The legislation was the first major overhaul of federal housing policy since 1974.

As a result of the act, U.S. housing policy for the 1990s is focused on a program called HOPE—Homeownership and Opportunity for People Everywhere. HOPE included seven new initiatives calling for $3.1 billion in additional resources in its first two years:

• HOPE grants will help public and Indian housing residents to purchase their homes and to help tenants in multi-family housing restore and purchase their homes.

• For the homeless, the act includes a provision for Shelter Plus Care, linking housing with supportive services for those homeless most difficult to serve, the seriously mentally ill and substance abusers.

• For the elderly, a demonstration program for elderly independence to help fund services to enable the elderly to live independently, including in their own homes.

• Family self-sufficiency programs will combine housing assistance with services such as job training, child care and transportation.

• Owners of federally assisted rental housing will be encouraged to maintain the property as affordable rental housing, even though they are eligible to prepay their mortgages and remove the housing from low-income status.

• Operation Bootstrap would provide job training, child care and help with transportation for families receiving housing assistance.

- A program to help first-time buyers with their down payments and mortgage rates by enabling them to withdraw funds from tax-deferred individual retirement accounts without penalty.

THE AFFORDABILITY CRISIS

The housing situation facing the country in the 1990s is a combination of old woes and new dismal wrinkles.

Homeownership rates fell in the 1980s for the first time in four decades, said Kent W. Colton, executive vice president of the National Association of Home Builders (NAHB). In 1980, according to Editorial Research Reports, homeownership peaked at 65.8 percent of U.S. households, up from about half in the late 1940s. "Had the rate held constant at its 1980 peak," said Colton, "an additional two million households would own their homes today."

Young people looking for their first homes were increasingly thwarted by high costs, with the result that the proportion of first-time buyers among home purchasers dropped to as low as one-eighth in the 1980s, compared to one-third in the 1970s. Housing affordability is a particular problem in California and the Northeast, according to the NAHB's Housing Opportunity Index in September 1991. The Midwest and the South were the most affordable areas.

Farther down the economic scale, old problems remain.

"Low-income people face an unprecedented housing crisis," Barry Zigas, president of the National Low-Income Housing Coalition of Washington, D.C., told a congressional hearing. "High rents, overcrowding, homelessness and displacement plague low-income households throughout our cities and towns. Severe cutbacks in federal housing assistance funds have spelled disaster for millions of renters and owners."

A 1989 report by the Joint Center for Housing Studies of Harvard University, "The State of the Nation's Housing," reported that the proportion of poor people spending more than 50 percent of their income on rent was up from 57 percent in 1974 to 70 percent in 1985. The Low-Income Housing Information Service reported that 45 percent of all poor renters in 1985 were spending more than 70 percent of their income on housing.

Three million families live in public housing, and, although the living conditions in many public housing buildings are deplorable, large cities such as New York have years-long waiting lists of families willing to move in. Richard Y. Nelson, Jr., executive director of the National Association for Housing and Redevelopment Officials, said that 800,000 to one million families are on waiting lists for public housing across the nation and one million are waiting for federal vouchers for rent subsidies.

The number of families in public housing "doubling-up" with relatives is also rising, housing administrators say. Although such a practice is technically against public housing rules, many project managers look the other way rather than add more people to the homeless statistics, a number that varies greatly from 250,000 to two million.

The demand for safe, affordable housing is thus well-documented. But on the supply side, HUD faced unusual problems at the start of the 1990s.

The sluggish economy and past overbuilding made many builders reluctant to start new construction. Changes in the Tax Reform Act in 1986 brought a major drop in multifamily construction and slowed urban gentrification. Development around many cities is so sprawling that land prices have been bid up and affordable new houses are built miles outside of the cities or suburbs.

Instability and failures in the savings and loan industry, and the financial reforms enacted in response, caused a number of thrift institutions, a major source of lending for home buyers, to cut back or call in their construction loans. And sloppy practices at the Federal Housing Administration and scandals in HUD allocations meant that Secretary Kemp had to devote much of his early attention to damage control and repair rather than new initiatives.

"We found more than 40 material weaknesses in HUD's operations when I came on board," Kemp said in the spring of 1990, "which is almost incomprehensible when you consider that, if HUD were a private company, it would be third in the Fortune 500."

FHA, for example, had never had an outside audit before Kemp's arrival. When that audit was released in May 1989, it showed serious weaknesses in the agency's accounting system and financial records. FHA regulations were tightened so that buyers had to pay more of the housing closing costs and annual insurance fees. Standards were allowed to vary across the country to accommodate local economic conditions and credit risks.

Kemp instituted other financial reforms that included bringing in a chief financial officer for HUD and comptrollers for FHA and other programs.

"We will have people who can help restore the integrity of HUD's business practices, which fell so far into disrepair and disrepute in the 1980s," Kemp said. "We intend to make HUD a model of federal government accountability."

RESIDENT MANAGEMENT AND THE USE OF VOUCHERS

The two keynotes of the Bush-Kemp housing policy were an emphasis on resident management and purchase of public housing and a shift from federal housing construction to use of vouchers for low-income housing.

"We are trying to aim all of our programs toward giving the residents some empowerment and a homeownership opportunity," said Kemp. "However, we don't look down on the renter ... But the homeownership opportunity is where I would most like to take HUD in the 1990s."

Under this initiative, HUD provides training in resident management to enable public housing residents to purchase their units, and an Office of Resident Initiatives was established to encourage resident participation and management. Families will not be required to pay more than 30 percent of their adjusted income to purchase a residence; if tenants do not want to become owners, they will be allowed to remain as renters or receive certificates or vouchers to move to private housing. At the start of the administration, 13 resident management programs existed; with full funding, the administration said, the number could be 250 programs, involving 62,000 new homeowners.

The administration said it was pleased

with the results. An accountant's study of the sale of the Kenilworth/Parkside project in Washington, D.C., estimated taxpayer savings of $6 million in 10 years and $11 million after 15 years. Resident management was said to reduce operating costs by 45 percent.

Tenant groups in FHA-insured housing also were to be helped to purchase projects if owners seek to prepay mortgages and eliminate low-income use of the property. Between now and 2005, owners of about 334,000 units of such housing are qualified to prepay their mortgages. In that case, Kemp said, tenants have the first right to purchase the project, with federal assistance equal to the value of 10 years of housing vouchers.

As for renters, almost all new budget requests were for vouchers. Supporters of vouchers traditionally argue that the housing problem is not a lack of housing but of renters' money. Kemp argued that public housing has more than 100,000 vacant units. "There is housing nationally," said Alfred A. DelliBovi, HUD undersecretary. "If you look across the nation, there's about 105 million housing units with 500 million rooms, and that's about a bedroom for every person in the United States." DelliBovi also argued to Congress that vouchers enable people to choose where to live and "to reject the building where there's no heat in the winter and where the elevator is not consistently repaired." Administration officials also calculated that a voucher can be provided to a family at about half the cost of new construction subsidies.

Critics saw supply as more of a problem, and note, for example, that the number of vacant housing units in the nation's small towns and rural areas is of little help to an inner-city resident with a voucher in hand. Final congressional action under the Home Ownership Made Easy Partnership called for 10 percent of the money appropriated to cities and states the first year and 15 percent the second year to be set aside for construction of affordable housing.

NOT IN MY BACKYARD

To bring attention to what the administration saw as overregulation, Bush appointed an Advisory Commission on Regulatory Barriers to Affordable Housing. The commission produced a "Not in My Backyard" report in July 1991. The title came from a reaction that residents often have to housing proposals that would bring a different kind of citizen, often of lower income, into their neighborhood. These residents often organize to bring political pressure on local officials, thus producing what the commission called the "NIMTOO" effect— "Not in My Term of Office."

Thomas H. Kean, president of Drew University in New Jersey and former governor of that state, was the commission chairman. He concluded: "The cost of housing is being driven up by an increasingly expensive and time-consuming permit-approval process, by exclusionary zoning, and by well-intentioned laws aimed at protecting the environment and other features of modern-day life. The result is that fewer and fewer young families can afford to buy or rent the home they want."

"Exclusionary, discriminatory, and unnecessary regulations," the commission said, raised housing costs by 20 to 35 percent in some communities.

The commission pointed out that increased housing costs were often unintentional results of other government policies. Historic preservation laws, for example, may be so stringent that they prevent modern insulation from being used in historic homes, thus driving up the energy costs and making the homes unaffordable to some. Environmental protection regulations can increase the cost of timber, the commission said, and that adds to the cost of houses.

Rent control, designed to hold down the cost of housing, can end up benefiting the wealthy more than the poor. "The slow turnover at the high end of the rental market adversely affects renters in less comfortable circumstances," the commission found. Communities in six states and the District of Columbia have such ordinances.

Barriers to affordable housing are most severe, the commission said, in suburban areas of rapid growth. Suburban areas in the path of rapid expansion often impose growth controls because residents are afraid that an influx of newcomers will change their quality of life. Land may be "downzoned" to increase lot size. A cap may be placed on the number of building permits to be issued. Tracts of land may be zoned for agricultural use, thus limiting development. Development may be tied to the growth of infrastructure to support it. Developers may be required to meet "gold-plated standards" for construction that did not apply to previous homes and that increase the price. Local governments, the custodians of building regulations, may skew requirements to favor businesses that bring in a larger tax base, but keep out housing. Layers of delay add to increased cost.

In Orange County, California, the commission said, a cumbersome approval process adds $20,000 to the cost of a single-family unit. In Mercer County, New Jersey, a subdivision got 11 different reviews, seven of them dealing with storm water drainage. In King County, Washington, the rapidly growing area that includes Seattle, the zoning of more than 1,500 square miles allows only one house per five acres.

When communities adopt such development strategies, the commission said, "they simply shift congestion and other tangible burdens of development onto their neighbors." The commission suggests that state governments work to increase affordable housing by developing model zoning and land-planning codes to remove such barriers to affordability. Legislation could, for example, set time limits on building approvals and reviews. If the local governing body did not act within that time, approval would be automatic.

The commission lamented what could be called an old-fashioned mind-set among officials who control housing policies in some communities. Such officials remain biased in favor of single-family housing units, even though multi-family units are more affordable. The commission urged, for example, removal of local ordinances that restrict accessory apartments in single-family homes or on single-family lots. Such apartments, the commission said, typically rent at one-third the cost of conventional rentals and can provide valuable income to current residents.

Modern building techniques have also advanced beyond many building codes, the commission said, but housing officials have not adapted. The report urged increased acceptance of manufactured housing—previously called "mobile homes." Many communities ban the homes or limit them to mobile home parks; two-thirds of manufactured housing goes to rural areas. But the commission noted that manufactured housing is much larger and sturdier than it was decades ago. And, with the average price for the largest multisectional home about $35,000, the homes are more affordable than most new construction.

Similar restrictions unduly limit the use of modular units in construction, which can save about 15 percent on costs in urban areas, the commission said. Other restrictions on new building technology, such as plastic plumbing pipes and plastic conduits for electrical wiring, add to both materials and labor costs.

In all, the commission made 31 recommendations for federal, state, local and private action that it said would remove barriers to housing affordability.

The report has drawn criticism, however, because it relies on deregulation to solve the problem, with no mention of increasing federal aid to housing.

Gale Cincotta, a long-time housing advocate from Chicago, said the ommission was deliberate. "We were told that we could not make recommendations for money," she said.

Among the recommendations were these:

• Federal agencies should have to provide a Housing Impact Analysis for any new rule or regulation.

• HUD assistance to state and local governments should be contingent upon those governments' working to remove barriers to housing affordabilities.

• Reinvestment in older urban communities should be encouraged and federal policy should protect the communities from discrimination in lending.

• States should consolidate their regulatory activities on housing.

• States should set time limits on building and zoning permits and appeals.

• States should pass statewide land-developments legislation or develop model codes for local use.

• Local governments should initiate barrier-removal strategies.

• Employers and local groups concerned about the need for affordable housing should try to bring pressure on local officials to reduce the "NIMBY" syndrome.

The commission noted that 10 other major federal studies of housing affordability had been conducted since 1967. Yet, the report said, "The fact that the problem remains today should not deter continued efforts to resolve it."

LOOKING TO THE FUTURE

For all the talk about vouchers, mortgages and housing construction, however—and Secretary Kemp drew considerable support for his housing ideas and for the energy he expended supporting them—the Bush administration professed to have a larger agenda.

Bush and Kemp described the HOPE program as "the first stage of a new and successful war against poverty, deploying the forces of private-sector entrepreneurship and economic incentive to create opportunity, jobs, and"—not an afterthought, but not first either—"affordable housing."

The HOPE program addresses this issue most sharply through its call for federal enterprise zones, depressed areas in which the capital gains tax would be eliminated to encourage the starting of new businesses and creation of new jobs. Secretary Kemp said the change would "greenline inner-city neighborhoods" and lure in investment money. In addition, an income tax credit would go to workers in a zone with wages below $20,000. President Bush called for 50 of such federal zones to be created.

"An enterprise zone makes the reward for working greater than the reward for not working," Kemp said. "It makes the reward for investing in a minority enterprise or an inner-city enterprise marginally greater than investing in municipal tax-free bonds. We want to remove the disincentives and expand the incentives."

Operation Bootstrap combines jobs and housing in another way. Under the provisions of this program, at least 10 percent of housing vouchers, public housing allotments and certificates will be combined with child care, job training and education. The goal was for more than 30,000 families to be participating in the program by the end of 1992.

Secretary Kemp liked to use two analogies when talking about this overall effort. One is the example of Abraham Lincoln and the Homestead Act of 1862, which Kemp said "transferred government lands to the poor and became the most successful anti-poverty program in American history." The other is the example of Eastern European economies with their absence of economic incentives and rewards. These economies, Kemp said, resemble the economies of poverty pockets in the United States.

"If we are to present the example of democratic capitalism and the rule of law to the rest of the world, we've got to make it work for the low-income people and distressed neighborhoods and communities right here in our own country."

He said such economic goals are inseparable from housing goals.

"You cannot talk about housing," Kemp said, "and not talk about jobs that give people enough income to afford to buy or rent."

Chapter 15

The Resolution Trust Corporation: Creating Affordable Housing Opportunities from the Savings and Loan Cleanup

Muriel T. Watkins
Program Coordinator
The Resolution Trust Corporation

When Congress passed landmark legislation in 1989 to resolve the savings and loan crisis, one mandate was made clear. Families with low and moderate incomes—who were to share the taxpayers' burden of financing the massive cleanup effort—would benefit from the sale of residential properties sold from failed S&Ls.

The Financial Institutions Reform, Recovery, and Enforcement Act of 1989 (FIRREA) created the Resolution Trust Corporation (RTC) as the agency charged with managing the disposition of properties acquired from the resolution of failed S&Ls. As a part of this mission the RTC was given a special mandate to "maximize the preservation of the availability and affordability of residential property for low- and moderate-income individuals." This duty was included under Sec. 21A(b) (3) (C) and given equal weight with the requirements under that section to maximize the net present value return on the sale or other disposition of assets and the requirement to minimize the impact of such transactions on local real estate markets. Through the implementation of the RTC's Affordable Housing Disposition Program, these seemingly conflicting goals have been brought into balance.

The publication of the Final Rule on August 31, 1990, transformed the RTC's affordable housing effort from a mere demonstration into a full-blown marketing venture. A previous sales restriction offering only 100 single-family properties was lifted, allowing a potential inventory of 18,000 single-family and multifamily properties to be marketed and sold.

STATUTORY INGREDIENTS TO A SUCCESSFUL DISPOSITION PROGRAM

The success of the RTC's marketing can be tied to the statutory provisions and enhancements to the mandate, as outlined in the program regulation and implemented across RTC regional offices.

Rules Governing Qualified Buyers Help the RTC Capture Affordable Single-Family Market

FIRREA requires the RTC to market affordable-housing properties for the first 90 days to qualified low- and moderate-income purchasers. This provision, in effect, creates an exclusive right-of-first-refusal option on the sale of single-family property valued at $67,500 or less. As implemented, the RTC can respond on a first-come, first-served basis to any offer made by a qualifying purchaser during the 90-day marketing period. The RTC aggressively pursues all avenues to identify and encourage qualified buyers to make an offer on a property.

The law clearly stipulates that the RTC is to sell to families whose incomes do not exceed 115 percent of area median income and to actively market properties to families whose incomes do not exceed 80 percent of area median. The income limit of 115 percent of median income, in locations where the RTC holds a large inventory, is $47,350 in Houston; $46,100 in Peoria, Illinois; $40,850 in Phoenix, Arizona; $41,500 in Baton Rouge; and $54,650 in Boston.

An analysis of the annual income requirement for properties in the program indicates that a property valued at $67,500 is affordable to a family of four whose income is equal to $30,000, based on 95 percent loan to value (LTV) conventional 10 percent financing with a 30-year term. Using credit-enhanced FHA-insured financing, at 2.5 percent below conventional rates, as provided through mortgage revenue bond programs, a house valued at $67,500 is affordable to a family with an income of $26,000.

The typical purchaser of a single-family property sold under the affordable-housing program is a family with an average income of $22,136, which is equivalent to 58 percent of area median income. The average purchase price is $32,297. Thus through targeted marketing the RTC has captured the market for single-family affordable housing and, in so doing, exceeded the goals contemplated by Congress.

Involvement of Nonprofit Organizations and Public Agencies Expands Market and Sales Potential

To ensure that the RTC meets the statutory goals for affordable housing, FIRREA outlines a disposition process which is to involve public agencies and nonprofit organizations serving as clearinghouses to disseminate property information to eligible purchasers. As contemplated, the RTC would benefit from public agencies and nonprofit organizations who have established information networks involving moderate- and low-income families.

The RTC has taken the law's mandate a step further by defining a broader role for nonprofit organizations and public agencies, to benefit from their expertise and long-term involvement in providing specialized assistance in helping low- and low-moderate-income families purchase property. The role of the technical assistance advisor (TAA) was included to involve the public and nonprofit sector in identifying qualified buyers, assisting with the prescreening and prequalification of purchasers, and assistance in arranging financing.

Within 10 months of program operation the RTC had established clearinghouse agreements with 35 state housing finance agencies where there is an inventory of property, all 12 Federal Home Loan District Banks, and one national nonprofit organization. Eleven state housing finance agencies also serve an expanded role of providing technical assistance to potential buyers. Thirty-nine community-based organizations serve as local TAAs and the RTC has established TAA agreements with four national nonprofit organizations. As envisioned, the combined involvement of clearinghouses and technical assistance advisors has expanded marketing and outreach and enhanced the RTC's ability to sell its inventory of affordable properties to families who are to benefit.

IMPLEMENTATION OF PROGRAM FOR VOLUME DISPOSITION HELPS THE RTC BALANCE COMPETING GOALS

Marketing events intended to showcase and sell a large number of properties over the course of a weekend have been found to be the most effective sales method for selling a large volume of properties and bringing into balance other goals related to timely disposition and minimizing taxpayer loss.

On September 8, 1990, the RTC launched a series of successful marketing fairs showcasing affordable-housing properties. On that date an Affordable Home Fair was held in Phoenix, Arizona, featuring 100 area homes open for viewing, with additional properties included in the marketing brochure prepared for the event. Three hundred twenty-nine families responded to advertisements encouraging qualified families to register to attend. Forty-one offers were received and accepted on the spot and the RTC received additional offers within two weeks of the weekend home fair to bring the total sales figure to 100. On average, buyers responded with offers approximating the RTC's list price, resulting in sales at 95 percent of market value.

The Arizona Home Fair was followed by several more marketing events, each capturing the interest of a significant number of prospective home buyers. A home fair was held in New Orleans on October 28; and in November "Home for the Holidays" fairs were held in Colorado Springs and in three cities in Texas.

In response to an announced sales goal for 1991 to sell 30,000 properties valued under $100,000, 94 special sales events were held between March and June 30 to sell 8,500 properties valued at $305 million. To meet this very aggressive sales goal, the RTC hosted the first affordable-housing auction in Atlanta, Georgia, on March 28. The auction of affordable properties requires that bidders are prequalified with respect to income eligibility as a precondition to attend the event and bid on property. Most of the auctions are held on weekends or during other hours convenient to the schedule of working families. Marketing of the event typically involves a buyer awareness session to familiarize potential purchasers with the process, sometimes including a mock auction, and open house previews over the course of several weekends. One benefit of the auction derives from a buyer's ability to bid on a home, present a contract, and complete the mortgage application all at one site and within a two- to three-hour time frame.

Auction marketing has proven to be the most effective process for reaching qualified purchasers and selling 100 percent of the properties included in a sales event. The effectiveness of auctions and other special marketing events has been heightened by the authority granted by the RTC Refunding Act of 1991 (March 23, 1991), which allows the RTC to sell affordable conservatorship and receivership properties absolute, without regard to a minimum reserve price. As a result of the use of auction marketing the RTC increased monthly sales figures far in excess of 1,000 properties per month. More important, absolute auctions have enabled the RTC to create homeownership opportunities for families whose incomes are well below 80 percent of median income and who never dreamed of having the ability to own a home.

INVOLVEMENT OF A BROAD RANGE OF RESOURCES

Real Estate Brokers Play a Key Role

Although not required under FIRREA's affordable-housing provisions, the RTC's use of real estate brokers is consistent with the law's intent to employ private sector contractors. Local real estate communities are integral to marketing affordable housing successfully. Realtors are key in assisting the RTC to meet the requirement of providing access for inspection of properties available for sale. Additionally, the affordable-housing program also benefits from the expanded marketing through the local multiple-listing service.

During the RTC's affordable-housing fairs and auctions, real estate brokers have played other key roles. They have helped conduct open houses and worked with buyers to make contract offers and assist with closings. As authorized under the program, compensation arrangements for real estate agents have often included an incentive of approximately 1 percent above the customary level of compensation for sales to qualified families participating in a home fair or sealed-bid marketing event. The success of the special marketing events depends on the involvement of a sufficient number of real estate brokers to assist families with sales offers.

Availability of Financing

Given the projected life of the RTC (which is mandated to close by December 31, 1996), the agency has involved the private sector in underwriting mortgage loans for affordable-housing properties. Although FIRREA contains provisions allowing the RTC to provide a direct loan to expedite property sales, several of the law's provisions encourage the assistance by HUD, Farmers Home Administration, and the secondary mortgage market. According to the law, the RTC should attempt to exhaust private resources first, using RTC financing on a more limited basis. This objective was furthered by the authority granted by the Oversight Board to purchase mortgage revenue bond commitments.

The RTC has entered into negotiations with state and local housing agencies to secure commitments of low-interest bond money to provide financing to low- and moderate-income buyers of RTC affordable-housing properties. With the availability of mortgage revenue bond financing, low- and moderate-income purchasers can benefit from below-market-rate financing at 2 to 2.5 points below conventional mortgage rates. For example, in late July 1990, the Texas Housing Agency pledged $140 million to finance the purchase of RTC properties. Within three months, the RTC had received offers on 600 single-family homes resulting from the announced availability of low-cost financing. For the September 1990 Phoenix home fair, which featured 100 area homes, the RTC used $10 million in mortgage bond financing along with mortgage subsidy funds and closing-cost assistance from local housing agencies. With the financing commitment, families with incomes under 80 percent of area median ($27,350 for a family of four) were eligible for mortgage subsidies and down-payment assistance. Additionally, the subsidies further reduced mortgage interest rates from 8.39 percent to 6.39 percent. Sales at all RTC home fairs, sealed-bid and auction events are supported by mortgage revenue bond financing or RTC seller financing where appropriate.

The presence of lenders to provide financing material and to perform preliminary applicant screening for underwriting purposes has also been key to the success of RTC-sponsored affordable-housing sales events. Their involvement represents a unique opportunity to expand the institution's service area and community lending program while benefiting the RTC. For the RTC an on-the-spot credit review or loan commitment helps guarantee that a potential buyer will be able to close on the sale.

A LOOK TO THE FUTURE

Multifamily Property Marketing

With the enactment of the affordable-housing program, the RTC gained expanded authority to expedite the sale of multifamily residential properties meeting the value limits under the program. Qualified multifamily purchasers include nonprofit organizations, public agencies or profit-motivated sponsors who commit to maintaining the affordability of 35 percent of the units purchased.

As with single-family property, multifamily property has attracted considerable interest by nonprofit and for-profit sponsors interested in individual multifamily properties and bulk acquisition of multiple properties. This interest was demonstrated by the response to the initial marketing of over 250 properties in Florida, Texas, and Colorado.

Sales have been driven primarily by interest in markets that are experiencing an economic recovery. In Texas, for example, multifamily housing development ceased after the building boom of the mid-1980s as occupancy rates dropped below 75 percent. Now that occupancy rates are 90 percent or higher, interest in the affordable-property inventory is considerable, and often centers around multiproperty acquisitions. Because of the projected potential market rents, profit-motivated investors appear undeterred by the required 35 percent occupancy requirements governing the sale of the affordable multifamily property. Nonprofit sponsors view the multifamily property as a unique opportunity to preserve units in attractive projects as affordable housing for years to come and at a cost about one-third of the cost of construction.

Nonprofit Organizations and Public Agencies as Acquirers

In addition to selling directly to households, FIRREA also defined nonprofit organizations and public agencies as qualified purchasers with the proviso that such sponsors would make the property available for occupancy by lower-income families, either through a resale or rental. The RTC had established a Memorandum of Agreement with HUD which provides for the acquisition of properties by Local Urban Homesteading Agencies (LURA). Under this agreement local urban homesteading agencies are able to purchase properties which need $10,000 to $15,000 or more in repairs and then make these properties available to low-income families at nominal cost. Nonprofit organizations and public agencies are provided information on properties available for sale and have also been invited to participate and bid at auction for properties. The Northwest Georgia Services, a Community Action Agency, purchased eight single-family detached houses in Chatooga County, Georgia, to rehabilitate for low-cost housing. Providing housing is an extension of the other family support services offered by the agency.

On a larger scale, the Colorado Housing and Finance Authority (CHFA) purchased 10 multifamily properties in the Denver area, comprising 433 units. CHFA purchased the properties with the intent to resell to local nonprofit organizations. Four properties were resold immediately. CHFA is working with

other state agencies to assist local nonprofit organizations to acquire, rehabilitate, and manage the other properties as affordable multifamily housing.

In addition to purchasing properties, the RTC has established a no-cost conveyance program. Properties with considerable holding costs or otherwise deemed to have little or no reasonable recovery value are made available to nonprofit organizations and public agencies for use as housing for lower-income families (including the homeless), day-care centers for children of low- and moderate-income families, or other such public purposes designated by the Secretary of Housing and Urban Development. The United Methodist Centers Inc. of Tampa was an early beneficiary of this authority when it purchased five houses and had a sixth house conveyed at no cost. Plans called for rehabilitating the five houses and demolishing the sixth and building a new house. The six houses are to be resold to first-time home buyers.

The RTC has conveyed approximately 600 properties to nonprofit organizations and public agencies for public use. Examples of how nonprofit organizations have used the program include the conveyance of 177 houses to the San Antonio Housing Finance Corporation for rehabilitation for low-income rental housing; a house and two lots in Austin were conveyed to the Mary Lee Foundation for transitional housing for multi-handicapped individuals; 14 houses in the Polytechnic Heights neighborhood of Fort Worth, Texas, were conveyed to the Liberation Community for rehabilitation and resale; and four historic (1904) houses on Rainbow Row in Galveston, Texas, were conveyed to the Galveston Historical Foundation for rehabilitation and sale to low- and moderate-income families. Other plans for conveyed RTC property include use as a shelter for battered women; a shelter for families at risk of becoming homeless; and two houses in Texas which are scheduled for demolition for construction of a Head Start center.

CONCLUSION

The RTC's Affordable Housing Disposition Program has already achieved great success in home sales to families who are to benefit from the affordable-housing provisions of FIRREA. These accomplishments have been the result of implementing a program which has involved targeted outreach and marketing through the participation of nonprofit organizations, the provision of low-cost financing, and the involvement of a range of other resources to assist buyers. Through both the sales and conveyance of properties the RTC has expanded homeownership opportunities for famil-

ies through the disposition of foreclosed S&L assets. By following the affordable-housing mandates of FIRREA, other RTC disposition goals have also been realized. Such success has enabled the RTC to expedite the disposition of problem assets and limit holding costs. Turning vacant properties to owner-occupied housing not only has a positive impact on local real estate markets but also enhances the local tax base.

The timely disposition of affordable properties has drawn the attention of other agencies with foreclosed assets. Within a week of the RTC's Boston affordable-housing auction, Freddie Mac and FDIC announced plans to conduct similar auctions and reached out to involve some of the same nonprofit organizations that provided assistance to buyers as technical assistance advisors. The best news is that the program could foster a network of support that lives on after the limited life span of the RTC and the S&L cleanup.

Chapter 16

The Role of State Housing Finance Agencies and the Need for a National Housing Policy

F. Lynn Luallen
President
The Housing Partnership, Inc.

Twenty years ago, in an effort to find solutions to the problem of housing affordability, states began to form state housing finance agencies to assist low- and moderate-income home buyers. These agencies joined together as the Council of State Housing Agencies, conceived and organized by people like Chuck Edson in Washington, John Burnett of New York, and Bill Johnston of New Jersey.

In the mid-1970s, Tom White, now an executive with the Federal National Mortgage Association (FNMA), became the first executive vice president of the Council of State Housing Agencies, followed by Carl Riedy, presently the vice president for affordable housing for the Federal Home Loan Mortgage Corporation (Freddie Mac). It was during Carl's tenure that the organization added "National" to its name and began to gain more stature in the housing industry and the halls of Congress. The National Council of State Housing Agencies has continued to play a prominent role under the guidance of John McEvoy and the professionals on its staff.

Over the past 25 years, state housing agencies have, through the use of mortgage revenue bonds (MRBs) and low-income housing tax credits (LIHTCs), provided millions of Americans with affordable housing, including both rentals and homeownership. The following statistics, which are based on MRB loans made by the Kentucky Housing Corporation during the first six months of 1990, give a good indication of the niche that MRBs fill in the market:

Average Purchase Price: $41,676

Average Down Payment: $1,341

Average Borrower Age: 29 years

Average Gross Income: $22,009

Average Interest Rate: 8.50%

The LIHTC is a credit or reduction in tax liability each year for 10 years for the owners of low-income rental housing that is based on the costs of development and the number of qualified low-income units. A project must have a minimum of either 20 percent of its units occupied by low-income households with incomes under 50 percent of area median income, or 40 percent of its units occupied by low-income households with incomes under 60 percent of area median income.

Unfortunately, both MRBs and LIHTCs must be sanctioned by Congress, and have repeatedly come under threat of extinction (indeed, this threat, which is referred to as "sunset," is once again present as of this writing). If tax bills are not passed to extend these two provisions, hundreds of thousands of families will be without affordable housing in the years to come. Over the years numerous stalemates have occurred in Congress over this issue, and in at least once instance a hiatus between congressional sessions developed where state housing finance agencies could not issue tax-exempt MRB debt. This lack of a national housing policy and program direction is self-defeating for both providers and seekers of housing. Because of a lack of continuity and direction in these tax matters, false markets for housing bonds have been created when several agencies have issued bonds at the same time, glutting the bond market. This has typic-

ally occurred because of an impending sunset, which forces the issue of bonds, rather than the neutral forces of supply and demand.

Collectively, state housing finance agencies represent millions of low-, moderate-, and middle-income families and have provided housing opportunities in every state to home buyers and renters. They have devised innovative solutions for special-needs groups, such as the elderly, disabled, female-headed households, and the homeless. They are in place and working, and would be the natural entity for placement of new federal housing funds to initiative innovative, state-based housing programs tailored to local needs and circumstances.

State housing finance agencies are a part of the great success story of housing in the United States. They have created joint partnerships with the private sector, the federal government, and localities. They did it with the goal of providing decent, affordable housing for all those they serve. The agencies have used all the available tools: tax-exempt financing, federal mortgage insurance, rent subsidies, entitlement, and action grant programs.

Unfortunately, the goal of providing affordable housing for all remains elusive. Economic, political, and social hurdles keep that goal well out in front of us. The deficit, erosion of personal income, the trade imbalance, and a slowly growing economy have increased the number of families requiring housing assistance. Social changes have added to the number of households living in poverty and to the longer waiting lists for assisted housing. Some political forces are still trying to dismantle the framework that has for decades made us one of the best housed nations in the world. The sunset of the tax-exempt housing tax credits, the continuing restrictions of this type of financing, the efforts to privatize the federal housing initiatives, and the funding cutbacks of housing programs illustrate the extent to which the administration in the 1980s and early 1990s has been willing to go to eliminate housing from the federal vocabulary. The federal government during this period has grossly underestimated the value of public purpose programs. It knows the cost, but not the value, of housing people decently.

Government at all levels does have to care about the standard of living of those we serve. Without hope for a better standard we will create a large underclass that will end up being a drain on society—a drain which will show itself in many forms: drugs, prison, crime, welfare.

Housing has to be a main focus of government in this country; states and local jurisdictions need to agree on that focus. We need a *national housing policy* that will lay out the roles of government and of the private sector, one that will consider new technology and new ways to make decisions about our land use.

The *federal role* needs to be continuous and responsible to the marketplace for lower-income families. It must continue to be the source of inexpensive mortgage insurance and of tax incentives that allow states and localities to fulfill their responsibilities. Tax-exempt financing is still one of the most efficient methods of serving lower-income home buyers.

States must be willing investors in housing programs. They must creatively use their state housing finance agencies to educate, finance, design, and facilitate the development of housing for lower-income families and for special-needs groups.

Localities must establish the standard for housing in their communities. They must be in the frontline of defense against unsafe, overcrowded, or substandard housing. And they must provide support services to housing—fire, police, utilities, streets, etc. And localities must work to ensure that planning and zoning and other regulations do not unduly burden the lower-income family.

Together we can forge a strong partnership of housing activism rather than silent demise. We must cooperate, share ideas, and create programs. The need is at our doorstep and a new generation is already coming to see if it, too, can share in our American Dream.

CREATIVE HOUSING PROGRAMS OFFERED BY STATE HOUSING FINANCE AGENCIES

Florida:

Affordable Housing Demonstration Program: $1.6 million trust fund for permanent and construction loans to sponsors or developers of single-family or multifamily housing (state appropriated).

Georgia:

Rental Rehabilitation Program: To assist in the rehab of rental projects by providing a "forgivable loan" of up to $5,000 to owners of rental property. Funded at $2.5 million by HUD and Georgia Residential Finance Authority (GRFA).

Residential Energy Savings Program: Grants and interest-free loans for energy conservation measures. Over $2 million funding by GRFA and various federal agencies.

Housemate Match: Matches persons over 60 and a younger housemate.

Kentucky:

Homeownership: Provides fixed-rate, low-interest loans for low- and moderate-income citizens of Kentucky.

Grants to the Elderly for Energy Repairs (GEER): Utilizes matching funds to weather homes of low-income, elderly homeowners.

Training for Affordable Construction (TAC): Program assists unemployed Vietnam veterans in receiving on-the-job training in the construction industry. Reduced housing costs result in more-affordable housing for lower- and moderate-income Kentuckians.

Housing Trust Fund: Funded solely by income derived from investments of the Kentucky Housing Corporation, it is available to home buyers with special housing needs. Loans have been made to families with incomes as low as $8,000.

Cluster Loan Program: Provides low-interest financing for newly constructed homes located in distressed city neighborhoods.

Small City In-Fill Construction: Program generates affordable housing while revitalizing deteriorating neighborhoods in smaller cities.

Single Parent/Head of Household: Program provides housing, counseling services, and on-site day care to single parents while they obtain educational and vocational training. Lexington (15 units)—Louisville (34 units).

Disabled: Group homes furnish housing for fewer than four developmentally disabled adults while they are being trained to become independent, contributing members of their communities.

OCS/Elderly/Low Income/Plumbing Program: Matching grant with Health and Human Services, this program was implemented to provide plumbing facilities where they are lacking and front-line energy repairs for rural elderly residents on fixed incomes.

Senior Homeownership Program: Provides lower interest rates on mortgage loans to home buyers aged 62 and over. Interest rate depends on individual's ability to pay.

Rental: Provides construction and below-market interest rate permanent financing for apartment units; administers Section 8 subsidy programs for U.S. Department of Housing & Urban Development for individuals whose incomes are below 50 percent of the area median incomes established by HUD.

Maryland:

Home Maintenance and Repair Program: Grants to local entities to provide minor repairs to properties occupied by low-income elderly and handicapped.

Construction Loan Program: Two-year loans to nonprofits and local governments for rehab, acquisition, or construction of single-family and multifamily housing for low-income households. Funded with $2 million from agency reserves.

Homeowners' Emergency Meeting Assistance: Loans to unemployed homeowners to make delinquent mortgage payments.

Homeownership Incentive Programs: Commitments made to local governments and nonprofits for funding below-market mortgage loans for households with annual incomes under $20,000.

Group Home Financing Program: Financing to acquire and modify existing housing for use as group homes and shelters.

Low-Income Rental Housing Production: Low-interest loans to developers to construct or substantially rehab rental housing for households with incomes below $20,000.

Elderly Rental Housing Program: Financing for rental housing production for elderly citizens with incomes between $4,000 and $10,000 per year.

Renters Tax Credit Program: Property tax credits for renters aged 60 and over.

Missouri:

Blended-Rate Financing: Bond proceeds and commission reserves are used to provide blended-rate financing to stimulate production of housing for low- and moderate-income families and individuals.

Arkansas:

Home Energy Loan Programs: Low-interest loans for energy saving repairs and/or equipment. Funded at $3.25 million from MRBs and a one-time $315,000 grant to the Arkansas Development Finance Authority (ADFA) from the state energy office.

Home-Equity Living Plan (home-equity conversion): Frees up the equity in older people's homes so they have needed cash for living expenses. Elderly homeowners sell the remainder of interest in their homes to ADFA, in exchange for a life estate, a monthly sum for life, as well as real estate taxes, hazard insurance, and maintenance costs paid for by ADFA. Funded at $5 million.

"Housing in Arkansas: Current Conditions and Policy Options" (1985): Study which looks at shortage of adequate housing in the state and presents a framework for policy alternatives to address the problem.

Delaware:

Delaware Assisted Loan Program: One percent buydown of the interest rate of a 1985 MRB issue to 8¾ percent. Funded at $5 million from bond authority set-aside. Loans made to households that are first-time home buyers earning less than $21,600.

Housing Rehabilitation Loan Program (pilot program): Three percent loans to renters and/or investors who rent to low- and moderate-income families. Purpose is to bring properties up to local building or housing codes and handicapped accessibility standards. Funded at $2 million through a fund created by state appropriations.

Housing Development Fund: Trust fund to provide no- and low-interest loans for seed and interim construction costs to nonprofit and limited-profit housing sponsors. Fund also makes grants. Funded at $11 million, initially through state appropriations. As of July 1986, a $3 surcharge on documents filed with the Recorder of Deeds will flow into the fund.

North Carolina:

Governor's North Carolina Housing Finance Agency/Farmer's Home

Elderly Subsidy Program: Provides rental subsidy of up to $100 per month in order to get rents below the floor of Farmers Home Administration (FmHA) 515 program.

Homeownership Assistance Program: Cash contribution of up to $135 to families earning below $20,000 to assist with mortgage payment.

Tennessee:

Congregate Home Program: Provides construction and permanent financing to community-based nonprofits to build group homes with 8 to 12 bedrooms for retarded adults.

Technical Assistance Program: Provides technical assistance to public and private sponsors of low- and moderate-income housing that propose to participate in Tennessee Housing Development Authority programs.

Virginia:

Rural Homesteading Program: Virginia Housing Development Authority purchases and resells FmHA foreclosed, vacant properties for $1.00, and then provides construction loan for necessary rehab work.

Virginia Housing Fund: $45 million fund to finance housing for lower-income people, especially the elderly, handicapped, and homeless.

Oklahoma:

Housing Director for Older Oklahomans: Directory which lists facilities throughout the state providing homes for older people.

West Virginia:

Flood Recovery Plan: $98 million to assist families, developers, and small businesses with construction and rehab loans to address flood recovery needs that will not be met through federal assistance.

New Small Development Program: Provide construction and/or permanent financing for the rehab of commercial and multifamily housing units in downtown areas.

Louisiana:

Homestead Exemption: Homesteads belonging to persons 65 and over, veterans and their surviving spouse or minor children are exempt from state, parish, and special taxes to the extent of $3,000 of assessed valuation.

Mississippi:

Shared Living for the Elderly: Renovation of a house for a shared-living residence.

Texas:

Elderly limits in multifamily housing developments: At least 5 percent of the units in a multifamily housing development must be occupied by low-income older people or low- or moderate-income families in which an older person is the household head.

For more information on the creative programs of state housing finance agencies, contact John McEvoy, executive director, National Council of State Housing Agencies, 444 North Capitol Street, N.W., Suite 412, Washington, DC 20001. (202) 624-7710.

Chapter 17

Maine State Housing Authority Finds a Way

Dwight A. Sewell
Director
Maine State Housing Authority

INTRODUCTION

Mary was going to school to become a nurse and working part time at the local hospital. She was tired of paying rent, and ending with nothing to show for it. But how could she afford to buy a home with current bank interest rates and the high cost of homes?

The Maine State Housing Authority found a way to help Mary. Our home ownership program is not intended to help very-low-income people, but the use of a state housing trust fund to provide extraordinarily low interest rates (compared with conventional loans) has made it possible for hundreds of people like Mary, who could not afford a bank mortgage, to become homeowners.

She applied for and received a low-interest-rate mortgage through our home ownership program, and that enabled her to buy the older home of her dreams.

She later used our home improvement loan program to finance needed changes.

"I was paying rent for 10 or 11 years," Mary said. "I started thinking about that . . . and what that amount was. Instead of paying rent, I wanted to pay rent into a mortgage, into a home, that would be my own.

"I really love this house. It's great. It's really old and has a lot of character, but there were some things that were wrong with it, that needed to be improved to make it that much better.

"I think the programs of the Maine State Housing Authority are great, both the home improvement and the home purchase. I wouldn't be sitting here in my own home if it weren't for them."

Our programs obviously made a big difference in Mary's life, even if in the big housing picture her story is but one statistic.

A study of our housing programs and how they have made a difference in people's lives, such as Mary's, could be called "Some Small Stories." That is often what we see today as states in general, and state housing finance agencies in particular, take more responsibility for providing decent housing. This was a role the federal government played less than 10 years ago.

Small stories. Small victories. They all add up. We help a working family buy its first home and reach the American dream of homeownership. We help a lower-income family make the necessary repairs to allow them to remain in their home. Targeted programs make it possible for persons with physical or mental disabilities to secure decent housing, including sometimes their own home or apartment, suitably equipped. A homeless family is provided a long-term lease for an apartment and given appropriate services to help it break the vicious cycle of homelessness. A run-down trailer park is purchased and rehabilitated by a nonprofit housing agency, and the tenants given the opportunity to buy their mobile homes. Daily we work with other nonprofit organizations as well as private developers to promote more affordable housing.

These are examples of housing assistance we provide today—a far different type of assistance than state housing finance agencies once provided.

THE CHANGING ROLE OF STATE HOUSING FINANCE AGENCIES

State housing finance agencies once offered only a few broad programs to make housing more affordable for low- or moderate-income people. There is a rea-son for this. For many years state housing finance agencies, including the Maine State Housing Authority (MHSA), functioned solely with their resources. They sold tax-exempt bonds to raise revenues, passing on the interest rate savings the tax exemption provides to borrowers who used that money for mortgages.

The bonds also provided revenue to operate the agency. MHSA and other housing finance agencies received no state money for their operations or to subsidize their housing programs.

The result was shallow subsidy programs, or programs that worked with large federal housing programs. The federal Section 8 New Construction program, for example, provided long-term rental assistance for lower-income tenants in new, privately owned apartments. MSHA would provide the mortgage financing for these new buildings from the sale of tax-exempt bonds.

MSHA and many other state housing finance agencies also offered reduced-interest-rate mortgage loans for lower income home buyers. Again, the financing came from the sale of tax-exempt bonds, and again the programs offered a shallow subsidy. Usually, mortgage loans were one to two points below market mortgage rates.

Rigid federal requirements and lack of resources to provide other sorts of deep subsidy assistance led to inflexible programs that failed to meet special housing needs or unusual housing requirements. People who didn't qualify for a program for one reason or another simply were not helped.

State housing finance agencies lacked the financial resources to craft their programs to help those who needed a deeper subsidy to make their housing affordable.

The federal government's decision to substantially cut back housing aid in the early 1980s made the housing situation for low- and moderate-income people much worse. State housing finance agency programs that helped the lowest-income people were eliminated or sharply reduced.

Also in the early 1980s interest rates increased sharply. Home mortgage rates rose to 17 percent or 18 percent. The shallow subsidy we could provide proved insufficient to make home ownership affordable.

THE HOME FUND

Maine's solution to this dual problem was to create a state housing trust fund, the Housing Opportunities for Maine (HOME) Fund. It provides us a flexible source of money to combine with tax-exempt bonds resources, to leverage other financial assistance, or to use by itself to finance housing.

An appropriation initially approved by the Maine Legislature in 1982 financed the HOME Fund. In 1985 the legislature made the Fund a continuing program by dedicating a portion (45 percent) of the state's Real Estate Transfer Tax to the Fund. The money is reserved for housing programs—none is used to support the operation of MSHA.

The Fund, with revenues of about $5 million annually, has proven itself by doing all supporters thought it would, and much more.

For example, we became one of the first state housing finance agencies in the country to offer aid to the homeless. The HOME Fund provided grants or 1 per-

cent, 30-year loans to finance emergency shelters for the homeless as early as 1983.

More recently the HOME Fund financed alternative homeless housing, such as transitional housing. Transitional housing gives homeless families long-term apartment housing while they receive social services, such as education and job training.

A unique Housing Preservation Loan Program (HPLP) provides nonprofit housing developers with HOME Funds to establish a revolving loan fund to repair homes of very low income Maine people. We estimate there are 35,000 Maine homeowners with annual incomes of $10,000 or less who cannot afford to repair or improve their home using conventional loans. HPLP, which won a national housing award, specifically calls for the nonprofit sponsors to develop creative loan repayment methods to enable the low-income homeowners to access HPLP capital.

Among other things, HOME funds have financed accessibility improvement to homes and apartments of persons with physical disabilities; have encouraged involvement of nonprofit organizations in low-income housing and financed some of their proposals; have leveraged tax-exempt bonds to provide lower-interest-rate housing loans for group homes for developmentally disabled adults and children, and others.

The HOME Fund has accomplished its primary goal of financing affordable homes and apartments for lower-income Maine people.

By combining the HOME Fund and our tax exempt bonds we have created two or more homeownership programs targeted toward different groups. The shallow subsidy program, which uses little HOME Fund support, helps working families with moderate incomes. Often these families earn too much to qualify for deeply subsidized federal housing programs, but cannot afford to buy a home with a conventional mortgage.

MSHA's program, by providing a mortgage interest rate lower than the rate from a conventional lender, by lowering down-payment requirements to 5 percent or less, and by offering a long repayment term, makes it possible for these families to buy their first homes. For example, the program may offer loans at the rate of 7.75 percent while most conventional loans carry a rate of 9.5 percent.

We use more HOME Funds in the Targeted Home Start program, which may offer loans at interest rates as low as 5 percent. This program helps first-time home buyers with incomes below—usually significantly below—the state's median income.

Combined, the two programs generally provide from $50 million to $100 million worth of mortgage loans annually. Over the past five years they have helped more than 5,000 Maine families become homeowners for the first time.

The HOME Fund also successfully helped finance new or rehabilitated rental housing for low-income tenants. In the Rental Housing Loan program we combine our tax-exempt bonds with HOME money to lower the interest rate on the borrowed funds. Developers who use the program must reserve a portion of the units (generally 20 percent to 40 percent) for low- or very-low-income renters. Sometimes nonprofit developers have reserved all the units for lower-income tenants. The program has financed

about 1,500 new or rehabilitated apartments since the mid-1980s.

We have used the HOME Fund in other ways to develop affordable apartments, too. We committed HOME money to provide rental assistance in several federally financed Farmers Home Administration (FmHA) developments. This assistance allowed Maine's FmHA office to attract bonus federal mortgage funds and finance an additional 200 low-income apartments in the state.

We have allocated other HOME money to nonprofit developers to finance start-up costs associated with the federal Housing and Urban Development 202 program. The 202 program provides a deep rental subsidy for new housing for low-income elderly persons, or persons with disabilities. The program is complex and the predevelopment costs prevent nonprofits from taking advantage of it. MSHA's HOME Fund provides the needed "bridge" financing to make the program work.

When I became Director of MSHA in 1990 I was determined to make the most of these programs to help the neediest Maine people. My task was to foster a "can do" attitude at the agency. To the greatest extent possible I wanted to rid programs of bureaucratic red tape that often slowed or delayed desperately needed housing assistance. Our new slogan,—"Let's Find A Way,"—reflects our new attitude.

Frequently overlooked in the success of various housing programs are the people that have been helped. Everyone, it seems, has heard of welfare "cheats" and the problems with urban public housing projects. Too few know of the successes, and what having a decent home can mean to a family. Security, self-worth, a sense of belonging and a sense of community are only a few of the benefits decent housing brings.

MSHA programs have provided this sense of dignity, belonging, and safety to thousands of Maine low- and moderate-income families, to the elderly, to the homeless, to those with disabilities and special housing needs. The programs have kept the dream of homeownership alive for thousands of working families who, without MSHA, would not have been able to buy their first home. The programs have provided decent, affordable rental housing to lower-income tenants who otherwise would have lived in substandard housing. The programs have provided shelter to the homeless and housing for persons with physical or mental disabilities.

CASE STUDIES

Roger and Linda and their two sons are typical of what MSHA programs have meant to many Maine people. Like thousands of others in the state, the family lived for years in a substandard rural home. Though both parents worked and tried to improve their home, they did not earn enough to make the necessary repairs.

But they didn't give up hope and continued to struggle, even when it seemed they would fall back two steps for each step forward.

Help finally arrived in the form of the Rural Community Action Ministries (RCAM), a nonprofit group involved in housing, and our agency, which had been working with RCAM to improve rural housing in their region.

Linda poignantly described the family's plight and rescue in a letter.

"We spent 13 years in a home—unsafe, no bathroom plumbing, buried between four walls with the cold winter winds whistling through the cracks, the roof caving in inch by inch, year after year, the chimney tile collecting piece by piece at the bottom of the clean out; taking baths out of buckets preheated on the stove. The only water we had running to the kitchen sink froze every winter, and dried up in the summer. I remember melting snow many times to do my laundry . . . thank goodness for cold water detergent.

"I could go on and on describing the little dilemmas of everyday survival, asking myself . . . where is the sun? Where is the light at the end of the tunnel? Forget about the pot of gold—where is the rainbow?"

Little things kept the family's faith that someday, somehow, their living conditions would improve.

"And then one day I would come home from work and find a box of groceries on my doorstep. I remember Santa Claus coming to our house to put presents under our barren tree for our two children," Linda wrote. "These are the things that kept us going. The Thanksgiving food baskets, the Christmas dinners given to us by caring people—one more thread to hang on to, reaching deeper inside ourselves to gather more strength, and hanging on to a dream, to a day when we could be self-sufficient."

But Linda realized it took more than dreaming to make the family's hopes a reality. She wrote that "The reality of a dream takes hard work, careful planning, and the power of the people. There is a program for every cause. Draw from these resources. Ask questions. Get involved. Begin today in making your dream come true. Don't wait 13 years like we did. Swallow your pride and know someday, somewhere, somehow, you will be able to return the favor."

The dream did come true—after much hard work by Roger, Linda, and RCAM, volunteers, and our financing.

"Our small one-and-a-half-story Cape was built by my husband, a carpenter, from RCAM, and volunteers from college students, a local carpenter's union, to a "friend of a friend." Church groups became involved, as well as the major supermarket Shop-N-Save, to feed our volunteers. This barn raising experience was put together by three organizations—Maine State Housing Authority, RCAM, and the Enterprise Foundation.

"We started planning for our new home in March of 1987. It took eight months for planning and preparation, and eight months to build to completion. My husband and I worked 40-plus hours a week at our regular jobs, but together we spent hour upon hour (on our home), squeezing in an estimate here and a price check there."

How has owning a decent home affected the family? Linda writes:

"Our living conditions have improved 100 percent, to say nothing of our self-esteem, but it's still a struggle to stay above the fine line between poverty and holding our own ... I spent so many years seeing no further than the end of my nose. The world passed me by unseen. Now, as I sit at my desk, I count my blessings as well as struggle with my mortgage payments. I realize I *am* like everyone else, and it all started with the burning desire to succeed."

Linda knows that her family's good fortune results from a helping hand by other people "from large organizations to the one person who decided to lend a helping hand out of love for his fellow man. All these people hold a special place in our hearts."

The program that helped the family evolved to become our Housing Preservation Loan Program. Generally, the program finances repairs to homes of very low income, but occasionally it helps finance a new home. This happens when the existing home is too dilapidated to make repairs cost-effective.

A life of poverty is a life of chaos, and when it rains it pours misery. Such was the case with Ed and Betty and their three children. Ed held a minimum-wage job at a sawmill in another community up the road from the family's ramshackle, rapidly deteriorating rural home. His income barely kept the family in food and clothing, leaving nothing for necessary home repairs.

Inevitably the home's condition worsened. The 50-year-old shack lacked a foundation and septic system. As the electrical system failed, it was shut down line by line. The chimney tilted and filled with creosote. The wood stove used for heat began showing holes at the seams. The home looked as if a strong gust could topple it.

The final blow was contamination of their well by road salt.

Community officials, particularly the town's code enforcement officer, became concerned about the family's welfare. The officer could have condemned the home as unsafe, but he went a step beyond that easy answer. He called the local CAP agency and us, and helped forge a community effort to aid the family, including volunteers, donations from area businesses, and MSHA and CAP financing.

Our staff, though used to seeing poor housing conditions, was shocked. The house was a death trap. Rules were stretched, and extra hours willingly worked, to push through the paperwork and pave the way to begin building a new home before the dead of winter arrived. The goal was to build a three-bedroom ranch, using whatever could be donated, for about $21,000.

The work began in earnest three weeks before Christmas. Backhoes and bulldozers arrived; within two weeks there was a septic system and a 26-foot by 40-foot concrete slab. Several older buildings were razed and burned.

Many area firms contributed materials free or at steeply discounted costs. The material and volunteers arrived a week before Christmas. In less than a week the new home was framed and enclosed. Christmas 1990 was different from any other Christmas for the children.

The family occupied the new three-bedroom ranch just after New Year's Day 1991. The old house was demolished. For the first time, the children were living in a safe, modern home. A letter of thanks from the family to the workers illustrates this:

"Roger and men: Thank you *all* so much. The nice hot bath felt so good and soothing for us. All so much appreciated for so much hard work well done."

Real poverty seems characterized by one blow after another to a family, a series of assaults on their physical and mental well-being. The details vary from one family to another, but the effect is the same. Living in poverty is living under a siege.

Frank and Judy and their two children were a family that "fell through the cracks" of the state and federal welfare system. Frank required medication to continue working, while one son had to be transported twice weekly to a special school. Yet the family earned too much to qualify for federal low-income housing programs, until Judy was laid off when a local manufacturer closed its doors. Unfortunately, no federal funds were available.

We didn't give up, and neither did the local CAP agency. We extended the CAP another $10,000 in special loan money. Local contractors tightened their estimates, and within two months the house had a new septic system, reconstructed well, new bathroom, two new bedrooms, and a new second story. The roof was new, and electricians upgraded the electrical system to eliminate more than 30 hazardous situations.

The elderly as well as young families are not immune to poverty. Mike and Sarah were in their seventies when disaster struck—a fire leveled their old farmhouse. The couple, with nowhere to turn, moved to an 8-foot by 10-foot travel trailer on the property. There was no well or septic. Community officials knew the couple could not survive there during the long cold winter that approached.

There was no time to build a home. The local CAP director and I approached the town's largest mobile home dealer. Could he donate a used mobile home? When we left, we weren't sure. But the next day the dealer said yes, and in addition agreed to supply the gravel to set the home up on a pad.

Within a week the home was on the site and the well and septic hooked up. In a race against the coming cold, a local contractor hired by the CAP, with help from church volunteers, replaced the interior finish, skirted the home, and built and installed two sets of stairs. An area appliance dealer supplied a new refrigerator and range.

Within a week the elderly couple was warm and safe in their new affordable housing. Long-range plans call for them to sell some acreage they own (I hope for an affordable-housing development) and use the money to construct a new home on their property.

We have helped provide housing for many persons with physical or mental disabilities—we have programs specifically for both populations—but the most remarkable case involved Bob. Bob had been a small contractor when he moved to Maine and began building his unusual home, which involved a geodesic dome and enclosed greenhouse. Six years ago, with the home 75 percent complete, Bob began having physical problems. A visit to the doctor confirmed the worst; he had multiple sclerosis.

The strength in his legs disappeared rapidly and he soon needed crutches to get around. His hands and heart were strong, though, and he remained determined to finish the home he started. When the local CAP agency visited him, he was trying to tape drywall seams, install plumbing, and finish the glazing on the dome.

"I drove up one day and couldn't believe what I saw," the CAP construction supervisor told me. "There he was, near the peak of the dome, holding on with one arm and a knee, trying to fit in glazing panels. Bob has to be the most determined person I've ever met."

The CAP was just as determined to help and found resources to complete the glazing. That left plumbing, taping, and some wiring to do, and we provided money to have that done. Now Bob lives

comfortably in his unique home. Under the large dome, on the second level, is the greenhouse, which can grow enough food to support eight people.

"Now all I need is another seven people to feed," Bob remarked. Given his determination, I wouldn't be surprised if he found them.

HOUSING FOR THE HOMELESS

Of all the different types of housing problems we deal with, perhaps none are more serious and difficult than the homeless. We have been involved in homeless housing for nearly a decade now, and our work includes studies of the problem as well as financing shelters and other types of housing.

Sometimes our efforts are rewarded not by individuals we have helped, but by an entire organization. More nonprofit organizations in Maine have become involved in helping the homeless as more is known about the extent of the problem. One of the most successful has been an organization that decided to do something about homelessness in the coastal region of central Maine.

The acquisition and rehab of an old farmhouse, in which we provided the financing, capped a year-long effort by the organization to find a place to provide shelter. Initially the group offered services from the basement of a local church.

Among other things, the shelter provides temporary housing for wives and family who are visiting people at the nearby state prison. The home also has provided housing for people who are working but "living on the margin," as one of the organization's workers said.

In addition to the emergency housing,

in which stays are limited to two nights except in unusual circumstances, a wing of the rambling farmhouse offers housing to some foster parents. This couple helps care for foster children, young pregnant women, and single mothers with children.

The house now helps up to 10 people a day, and it gets plenty of referrals from area churches, town officials, and social service agencies. We are proud to have helped this group and its shelters achieve success, and they have acknowledged our assistance. A recent letter from them says "We appreciate your attention to detail and your encouragement to finishing touches. We've enjoyed working with you . . ."

Short-term emergency housing is one of the critical housing needs to deal with the homelessness problem, but it is not the total solution. Our long involvement with the homeless led us to conclude that emergency homeless housing is not always the best solution to that population's housing needs either.

During the latter part of the 1980s our statistics reflected an increasing number of homeless families (rather than individuals) for whom shelters were a poor substitute for decent housing.

We reasoned that if homeless families could be provided longer-term housing than the shelters provided, and if the housing could be linked with social services such as education and job training, the family eventually could become self-sufficient and break the cycle of shelter housing. This was the origin of our Transitional Housing program.

One family benefiting from the program was Tom and Diane and their two children. The family moved from a large apartment that cost $350 a month (plus $200 a month utilities) to a small one bedroom apartment at $195 a month for rent and utilities. The family hoped to save enough money through the move to get out on their own, but the new apartment proved hopeless. Diane writes:

"I became very depressed . . . In the 18 months we were living there the shower floor let go as I was stepping out of the shower. Then, a couple of weeks later, my two-year-old son fell through the bathroom floor and thanks to the good Lord . . . he did not lose his grip on the old rotten boards. Had he lost his grip, he would have landed in approximately six inches of sewer that ran under the house. A couple of months later my same son was sitting in a high chair eating lunch and fell through the kitchen floor."

Disgusted with the apartment's condition, the family called the community code enforcement officer, and organized other tenants to complain. The landlord had a few days to correct major problems, but did nothing.

Meanwhile Tom discovered that the local CAP agency, the Mid-Coast Human Resources Council, offered a Transitional Housing program with MSHA financial support. The family accepted the two-bedroom apartment offered, just as the city condemned their old apartment.

"Since we have moved here we have been able to set some very large goals and follow through with them," Diane writes. "Our largest goal was to apply for a Farmers Home Administration (FmHA) loan. We did and are very pleased to say we have been approved.

"We also have been able to pay off several small bills and purchase a pair of eyeglasses for me so I can work on getting a driver's license.

"The project has done wonders for us as a family. Because of good folks like you . . . we have just one big step left to take and that is just going out and finding a house of our own; without you we just could not have done it."

The Transitional Housing Program also helped people like Nora, a young single mother who arrived in Maine during a winter snowstorm. For three weeks she and her young son lived in the car, which had broken down. Local welfare officials finally discovered her predicament and delivered an ultimatum—find housing or have her son taken away.

Nora did find housing because of the Transitional Housing program. She eventually found her own two-bedroom apartment.

"Today I'm living in a nice two-bedroom apartment, and I have a full-time job," she said. "My son goes to a school he likes. Everything is going good for me for a change and actually looking up."

Mary, Roger and Linda, Ed and Betty, Frank and Judy, Mike and Sarah, Bob, Tom and Diane, Nora, the nonprofit group that now houses up to 10 homeless people a night—all are small stories, small victories in the battle to make decent housing available to all Maine people.

The housing in these cases has given a new life to these people. Small cases individually, but collectively they and thousands more like them spell an incremental improvement in the housing for Maine people. And we'll continue to find new, innovative ways to finance housing to make it affordable to all who need our help.

Chapter 18

The New York City Capital Program for Affordable Housing

Felice Michetti
Commissioner
New York City Department of Housing Preservation and Development

INTRODUCTION

The 1980s presented America's cities with a host of new challenges; from increasing crime rates to important environmental concerns such as waste disposal and recycling of reusable resources. One issue, which had long been a concern but which grew in importance during the latter half of the '80s, was the need to provide decent affordable housing for low- and moderate-income households, particularly for those families and individuals who were without a home of any kind.

While the nation's economy was generally expanding throughout the last decade, the skyrocketing cost of obtaining suitable housing in many areas far outpaced the more modest increases in household incomes. As a result, most low- and moderate-income families were forced to cut back on what had heretofore been considered "basic" expenses just to maintain their homes. Worse yet, those families who were already at the margin and simply could not afford to pay any more for housing were literally left out in the cold. In fact, a number of national studies have concluded that the number of homeless people in this country is now greater than at any time since the Great Depression.

The tremendous increase in the number of homeless Americans, especially homeless families, has certainly been the most dramatic representation of the nation's growing housing crisis. At the same time however, there continue to be many other indications of this crisis. First, housing—even modest housing—has become increasingly expensive in relation to what Americans can afford. By 1989, most families were spending a greater percentage of their income for

199

housing than they had been at the start of the decade. This upward swing in housing expenditures was so pervasive that it prompted the decision makers in Washington to increase the long-recognized standard of housing affordability from 25 percent to 30 percent of income. Notwithstanding this shift, the 1987 New York City Housing and Vacancy Survey showed that approximately 44 percent of all renters in New York were paying in excess of the new standard.

In some areas housing was not only too expensive for low- and moderate-income families, it was often not available at all. In New York City, the vacancy rate for available housing hovered around 2 percent, or less than half of what had been considered the minimum rate for a healthy market. Not surprisingly, the supply of vacant low-cost units (i.e., those renting for less than $300 a month) was virtually nonexistent, with a rate of less than 1 percent. At the same time, tens of thousands of families were forced to live "doubled up" in shared apartments while the waiting lists for units in New York City's Public Housing projects had swelled to more than 200,000. Finally, much of the low-cost housing which was available was badly deteriorated and substandard in quality.

In New York City, the municipal government continued to face the daunting task of maintaining the vast number of residential properties—both occupied and vacant—to which it had taken ownership in the '60s, '70s, and early '80s due to nonpayment of real estate taxes. These properties had suffered from years of disinvestment prior to their being vested by the city. Consequently, most of the buildings acquired in this manner were in deplorable condition by the time they arrived in city ownership. Strapped for funds, the city was left with the responsibility of caring for these projects and ensuring that basic services were provided.

To compound these problems, the federal government, which had traditionally played a major role in generating housing production initiatives to assist low- and moderate-income families, instead chose to distance itself from America's worsening housing dilemma, dismantling nearly all of the existing programs that assisted in the creation and/or rehabilitation of affordable housing. In fact, in the course of six short years—from 1981 to 1987—the federal budget for assisted housing plummeted from more than $30 billion to less than $8 billion, barely one quarter of its former size. In New York City, this precipitous drop in federal spending translated into a loss of approximately $16 billion in federal support which would otherwise have been received over the decade had the funding remained at the 1981 levels.

The loss of these dollars meant more to the nation's cities than numbers in a ledger column. It meant that desperately needed units would go unbuilt, that badly deteriorating occupied housing would be left unrehabilitated and that tenants in need of rental assistance would have to go without. As a result of these cuts, America's cities had to reassess their housing assistance needs and begin to develop alternative mechanisms to produce and upgrade low- and moderate-income housing on their own. Over the last several years, New York City has responded to this new challenge with a singularly impressive financial commitment and a multitude of creative new housing initiatives designed to put that commitment into action.

NEW YORK CITY'S PROGRAM FOR AFFORDABLE HOUSING: AN OVERVIEW

While New York City has always been in the forefront of the effort to provide decent affordable housing, in 1986 the city redefined and greatly expanded its role with the introduction of its initial Ten Year Plan for Housing. This ambitious program, which eventually proposed a commitment of more than $5 billion of the city's own capital funds to be spent over a 10-year period, marked the beginning of an exciting new era in the field of assisted housing. The stated goals of this program were: to increase the supply of affordable housing; to upgrade those existing affordable units in need of rehabilitation; to expand the provision of permanent housing and support services for the homeless, HIV-affected persons, and others with special needs; and finally to create new homeownership opportunities for first-time home purchasers. Specifically, the Plan called for the following four activities:

• The gut reconstruction of all city-owned vacant buildings suitable for rehabilitation in order to provide new housing for the homeless and other low- and moderate-income residents;

• The moderate rehabilitation of all city-owned occupied buildings in order to preserve this resource and improve the quality of life for the occupants;

• The continued provision of below-market-rate loans to encourage private owners of low- and moderate-income housing to renovate their buildings; and

• The construction of housing units, primarily in the form of new homes for owner-occupants.

Now entering its sixth year, the program has enjoyed great success. More than $2.5 billion has been committed to produce and preserve 98,000 units of affordable housing, representing the largest locally funded housing program in the history of the country. In fact, a survey conducted by the New School of Social Research found that New York City's housing budget alone exceeds the combined budgets of the next 50 largest cities in the nation by a factor of more than three and a half times.

While the major themes of the original plan have remained consistent throughout the first five years, the program was recently modified in several important ways by Mayor David N. Dinkins to reflect the changing needs of the city's residents. Under the leadership of Mayor Dinkins, the city has not only reaffirmed its commitment to affordable housing, it has sharpened the focus of this commitment to ensure that the program is able to serve those who are most in need. For example, additional funds were devoted to the city's substantial rehabilitation projects in order to target these units to families with even lower incomes.

Moreover, in addition to making the basic housing programs more "inclusionary," the new administration has placed a greater focus on economic integration or the development of mixed-income living environments. Thus, while the city's programs now serve greater numbers of homeless families and other households with extremely low incomes, these families are being placed in projects which also house the working poor and moderate-income families, rather than being isolated in large projects devoted solely to public assistance recipients. The development of mixed-income projects not only prevents very-low-income tenants from feeling segregated and stigmatized, it allows the working families to serve as role models to the homeless and other families with limited resources. This approach also benefits the surrounding community by mitigating the perception that the community is being concentrated with so-called "problem families." In fact, in many instances these mixed-income projects are preferred and welcomed since the low- and moderate-income units provide housing opportunities for existing community residents.

Finally, the Dinkins administration has attempted to employ a more comprehensive approach to housing production and community development planning. Thus, the city is not only concerned with selecting appropriate sites for individual housing projects, but also with developing projects that complement and support the other city resources in the neighborhood. As part of this effort, HPD is coordinating its housing initiatives with various other city agencies who are collectively responsible for the provision of social services, police and fire protection, education, public transportation, commercial development, and parks and other recreational facilities. This comprehensive neighborhood approach is designed to ensure the best possible qual-

ity of life for residents of city-assisted housing projects.

THE CITY'S HOUSING PROGRAM: INDIVIDUAL PROGRAM DESCRIPTIONS

The city employs an array of individual housing programs which together make up the overall Housing Program. Following is a detailed discussion of those programs, grouped according to the four major categories of activities. A brief description of HPD's housing incentive programs follows the capital program descriptions.

1. Substantial Rehabilitation Programs

Perhaps the single most important element of the city's Housing Plan is the substantial rehabilitation or reconstruction of vacant abandoned building shells. This effort serves the dual purpose of creating much needed affordable housing while simultaneously eradicating dangerous and unsightly blighting influences on struggling low- and moderate-income communities.

As noted earlier, the vast majority of the vacant abandoned buildings in New York are owned by the city itself, having been acquired through real estate tax foreclosure. As also noted, the Housing Program commits the city to reconstructing every single vacant property in city ownership which is structurally sound and suitable for rehabilitation.

It is virtually impossible to overstate the significance of this tremendous commitment. At the time the original Ten Year Capital Program was announced,

HPD owned approximately 5,000 vacant buildings accounting for about 50,000 units of abandoned housing. Today, 42,000 of these units have either already been rebuilt, are currently undergoing rehabilitation, or are in the preconstruction development stage. When this effort is complete, it will be possible for the first time in several decades to walk through the low- and moderate-income neighborhoods of the South Bronx, Harlem, or Central Brooklyn and not come upon a vacant burned-out building.

While all of the City's substantial rehabilitation programs involve the transformation of vacant uninhabitable structures into decent, safe, and affordable housing, a wide variety of methods are used to accomplish this transformation. The following is a brief description of the major substantial or "gut" rehabilitation programs currently operated by the New York City Department of Housing Preservation and Development (HPD).

The LISC/Enterprise Program uses equity raised through the Federal Low Income Housing Tax Credit along with direct loans from the city to fund the gut rehabilitation of vacant in rem buildings. After rehabilitation, these buildings serve as long-term low-income housing, with 30 percent of the units set aside for the homeless. This program is a collaborative effort between the City of New York and two nationally prominent nonprofit community development organizations: the Enterprise Foundation and the Local Initiatives Support Corporation (LISC).

For its part, the city provides a vacant building at a nominal price—$500 per unit—and a direct loan for approxi-

mately 70 percent of the rehabilitation costs. This loan is structured as a 1 percent, interest-only note, with a balloon due in 30 years. In turn, LISC and Enterprise raise a pool of equity contributions from private corporations in order to fund the remaining 30 percent of the development cost not covered by the city's loan. These contributions are raised through a syndication of the tax credits generated by the project. The non-profit sponsor (generally a locally based community development corporation) who will eventually own and manage the project is trained and selected by LISC/Enterprise and approved by the city. To date, the LISC/Enterprise Program has produced more than 3,000 new units of low-income housing.

The Vacant Building Program uses a competitive process to select qualified private and not-for-profit developers to buy vacant city-owned buildings and rehabilitate them pursuant to city-established standards. The housing which is created is reserved for low- and moderate-income households, with a minimum set aside of 20 percent of the units for the homeless and other low-income households. Projects which exceed this minimum are awarded extra points in the competitive selection process.

Through this program, the city sells the buildings for $500 per dwelling unit and provides partial financing of the rehabilitation through a combination of a low-interest loan for the low- and moderate-income portion of the project and a special grant for the portion of the building devoted to the homeless. The private developer is required to raise the remainder of the development funds (generally 15-25 percent) through a combination of a bank loan and their equity contribution. Once the units are rehabilitated, they are rented at pre-established rent levels. While these projects contain a sizable percentage of very-low-income households, some of the units (i.e., the moderate-income units) are rented at higher levels than the rents found in a LISC/Enterprise project. These rents are necessary to amortize the private debt on the project.

The Special Initiatives Program (SIP) was created specifically to design and reconstruct vacant city-owned buildings in order to provide permanent housing for the homeless. In recent years the projects have been integrated to provide units for other low- and moderate-income families. SIP utilizes city architects and engineers to develop, design and oversee construction. After rehabilitation is complete, the buildings are conveyed to not-for-profit community sponsors for one dollar. The sponsors are chosen through a competitive process based on their management track record as well as their social service program. The buildings can be maintained as a long-term resource of low-income housing with these enhanced social services for three reasons. First, the city subsidizes the entire reconstruction cost, and consequently there is no mortgage on the building. Second, property taxes are fully abated. Finally, Section 8 Rental Assistance is provided for income-eligible homeless families, thereby increasing the rental income for the project. SIP buildings now house 60 percent homeless and 40 percent other low- and moderate-income families. As with all HPD programs, 30 percent of the nonhomeless units are targeted for families living in the neighborhood in which the project is located.

The Construction Management and Vacant Cluster Programs were designed as a means of transforming areas with large concentrations of vacant burned-out buildings into vital, fully occupied communities. In the process, the city took advantage of the economies of scale associated with larger-scale rehabilitation and created hundreds of new apartments for low- and moderate-income families, including the homeless. Through these programs, the city contracted with established for-profit construction managers to oversee the rehabilitation of the site. The finished buildings were then sold for a nominal amount to a preselected not-for-profit agency who would own and manage the buildings. Rents in these projects were set so as to be affordable to a mix of low- and moderate-income tenants. Forty-five percent of the units were targeted for low-income residents, 25 percent for moderate-income households, and 30 percent for the homeless. These programs formed a key element in the early years of the city's overall housing plan. Together they successfully rehabilitated six large clusters of abandoned buildings with a total of more than 1,500 apartments and helped to transform what were badly deteriorated areas into active working communities.

The SRO Loan Program was established to preserve and rehabilitate existing Single Room Occupancy (SRO) housing as well as create new affordable SRO units. Through this program, the city provides direct loans to qualified nonprofit organizations to either renovate the properties they own, or to acquire and rehabilitate SRO buildings currently owned by for-profit owners. In general, these properties have suffered from disinvestment and are in need of a relatively significant amount of rehabilitation. In some cases, however, the properties are in relatively good condition. In these instances the focus of the program is to obtain the units for use as affordable housing. Consequently, the bulk of the loan is for acquisition. Loans are provided at zero percent to 3 percent interest for terms up to 30 years. Not-for-profit owners whose projects will provide permanent homeless housing resources may be eligible to have all or part of the loan forgiven after successful completion of the project. Buildings providing homeless housing placements have rents set at the current shelter allowances but may be supplemented with available Section 8 rent subsidies. In some cases, the city also augments its own development funds with assistance through the McKinney Section 8 Moderate Rehabilitation for SROs Program.

The Small Home Rehabilitation and Sale Program is designed to develop small city-owned buildings (1-16 units) as affordable-ownership housing. Under the Program, HPD combines small buildings into sites generally containing a minimum of 10 units, and then offers them to developers through a competitive Request for Proposals (RFP) process. The city provides the developer with a zero-interest construction loan which equals the difference, if any, between the total projected development cost (including developer and contractor fees) and the target sales price, which is set at a level that is at or below the market price for the area and which is affordable to moderate-income families. Generally, the actual sales price is roughly $25,000 to $30,000 per unit less than the total development-cost figure. Upon sale, the city's subsidy becomes a permanent loan to the purchaser. The subsidy thus enables moderate- and middle-income families to afford these new homes.

The Mutual Housing Association of New York (MHANY) Program is designed to provide homeownership opportunities for low- and moderate-income families by renovating vacant in rem buildings. Through this program, selected city-owned properties are sold to the Mutual Housing Association of New York for a nominal price. Full rehabilitation financing is available through city capital loans. Although the program generally does not involve private permanent financing, the size of the city loan is reduced by the fact that the occupants have pledged to contribute their sweat equity to do the finishing work. As in the other city efforts aimed at the very-low-income population, the city financing is in the form of a 30-year, 1 percent nonamortizing loan, so that income generated by the project can be used to cover the cost of maintaining and operating the building. In order to ensure that projects remain affordable and continue to serve low- and moderate-income households, the Mutual Housing Association retains land titles to each site, only transferring building titles to the individual MHANY homesteader-owner (in the case of the smaller buildings) or to the cooperative in the relatively larger buildings.

2. Moderate Rehabilitation of Occupied City-Owned Housing

In addition to the array of programs designed to bring about the renovation of its vacant inventory, the city also operates a number of programs aimed at rehabilitating the occupied housing it owns. As noted earlier, HPD is currently the owner of some 44,000 occupied housing units, most of which were obtained through tax foreclosure procedures. As a result, the city is responsible for ensuring that the more than 100,000 tenants in these buildings receive adequate shelter and the basic services they need. In light of the deteriorating condition in which most of these buildings entered city ownership, this is not an easy task. However, above and beyond this important and immediate responsibility, HPD, through its Division of Alternative Management Programs (DAMP), is also striving to foster the full-scale renovation and subsequent disposition of this housing out of city ownership.

Unlike the substantial rehabilitation programs described above, the majority of the city's in rem moderate rehabilitation programs were designed in the 1970s and early 1980s, and were already in operation prior to the initial announcement of the city's Ten-Year Housing Plan. However, in recent years these programs have been expanded and modified in the process of being integrated into the larger framework of the city's overall Housing Program.

In general, the DAMP programs pursue two main goals: to rehabilitate existing city-owned projects to a minimum standard as decent, safe, and sanitary housing; and to sell the transfer ownership of the rehabilitated buildings to the tenants themselves or to a qualified nonprofit or for-profit organization. These efforts serve not only to improve living conditions for the current tenants, but also to preserve these buildings as a long-term affordable-housing resource. In all cases, the city structures the project's finances so that the post-sale rents or carrying costs will be sufficient to cover all project expenses while remaining afford-

able to the original low-income tenants. In addition, the buildings are sold with resale restrictions designed to keep these apartments permanently affordable.

The following is a brief description of the major DAMP programs.

The Tenant Interim Lease (TIL) Program offers organized tenant associations in city-owned buildings the opportunity to obtain control of their own buildings. The goal of the program is to develop economically self-sufficient, low-income, tenant-owned cooperatives. Buildings are sold to the tenants at a nominal cost of $250 per unit. However, before ownership is actually transferred, HPD invests a significant amount of city funds in upgrading the properties in order to ensure that the basic systems are sound and functioning properly. This work is done during the period of city ownership and the funds flow as a grant. Thus, the buildings can be sold debt-free. As the building is being renovated, HPD works with an experienced not-for-profit organization to train the tenant association in building management, maintenance and record-keeping so that tenants have the skills necessary to enable them to manage their building properly. During this period, HPD and the tenants jointly establish the initial co-op carrying costs which will be implemented after sale. Again, these charges are set in such a way as to be affordable to the residents while allowing sufficient income to operate the building. The city also assists eligible tenants to obtain Section 8 rent subsidies to cover the difference between the rent and 30 percent of their monthly income.

The Community Management Program (CMP) provides buildings and rehabilitation funds to locally based not-for-profit community housing organizations to manage and oversee the rehabilitation of occupied city-owned buildings. Upon completion of the rehabilitation, these buildings are sold for a nominal amount either to the community group itself or to the tenants in the form of a low-income cooperative. Prior to the sale of the building, rents are restructured to cover operating costs after sale. As in the case of TIL, the rehabilitation work is performed with a grant from the city and consequently the buildings are sold debt-free. Again, as in TIL, HPD assists income-eligible tenants to obtain Section 8 rental assistance.

The Private Ownership and Management Program (POMP) provides private real estate firms with an opportunity to manage, repair and eventually purchase occupied city-owned buildings. Prior to being accepted into the program, the applicant firm is carefully screened with respect to its qualifications and management track record. If the applicant firm receives a positive evaluation, DAMP staff and the firm jointly select appropriate city-owned buildings for a management contract. Community Development Block Grant (CDBG) and city capital funds are allocated to cover major repairs and the difference between operating costs and rent collections for the first six months of the contract. Thereafter, the firm is expected to run the building from the rents collected. The firm is given one year to demonstrate its ability to manage the project. If successful, the firm is eligible to buy the project at a prescribed price of $2,500 per unit. To date, 234 buildings, consisting of over 8,700 units, have been sold to private firms through POMP.

The Neighborhood Ownership Program (NOP) was recently created in an effort to expand the number of in rem

units which can be assisted through the Division of Alternative Management Programs and to create new opportunities for innovative ownership options such as mutual housing associations. The program also serves to offer experienced private management and construction management firms the opportunity to renovate and manage occupied city-owned buildings. Again, the City funds the renovation with a grant. Once the private firms complete the renovation, the buildings will be sold either to the tenants as low-income cooperatives, to neighborhood not-for-profit groups, or to mutual housing entities. The city's capital contribution will be set at approximately $32,000 per unit and the program will focus on neighborhoods where there are no locally based organizations that qualify under the Community Management Program.

3. Moderate Rehabilitation of Privately Owned Buildings

While the bulk of the city's Housing Program involves the renovation of the city-owned housing stock, the city also operates an unrivaled local program to rehabilitate and preserve the existing supply of privately owned affordable housing. While it is clear that the rehabilitation of the in rem stock is absolutely essential if the city is to meet its housing needs, it is also true that the city must preserve the decent affordable housing which is currently available in the private market. Not only is there a tremendous need to improve the qualify of life for the residents of this housing, it is critical that the buildings themselves are maintained and improved so that they do not fall into disrepair and become abandoned. In the simplest terms, each unit that is lost to abandonment is one that must be replaced in some way in order to maintain the overall supply. Conversely, each unit which is preserved lessens the need for the city to create new units. With this in mind, the city has for a number of years operated a range of programs to promote and support the rehabilitation of privately owned housing which is affordable to low- and moderate-income residents. Although there are different formats, these programs generally involve the provision of a low-interest rehabilitation loan and the use of federal Section 8 certificates and vouchers in order to protect low-income tenants from any rent increases attributable to the rehabilitation.

The Participation Loan Program is aimed at predominantly occupied multiple dwellings and provides low-interest loans to private landlords to rehabilitate their buildings by replacing two or more building systems and modernizing building interiors. One percent interest city loans are combined with market-rate private financing to produce a blended, below-market-rate development loan. Upon completion of the project, rents are restructured to help ensure sound operation of the building. In general, the post-rehabilitation rents are significantly lower than the rents which would have resulted had the project been renovated with private funds. In addition, income-eligible tenants are offered Section 8 rental subsidies to ensure continued affordability.

The Article 8A Loan Program provides direct rehabilitation loans to owners of multiple dwellings to replace or upgrade major building systems such as boiler/burners, plumbing, wiring,

windows, etc. and/or correct substandard or unsanitary conditions in the properties. Loans are generally provided at 3 percent interest for terms of up to 20 years. No private financing is involved although the owners are required to make an in-kind equity contribution by paying for and completing specific work items named by the city. Again, the city sets the post-rehabilitation rent adjustments based upon the cost of debt service and income-eligible tenants may receive Section 8 rental subsidies.

The 7A Financial Assistance Program is designed to provide court-appointed building administrators, known as "7A" administrators, with the funds necessary to make major repairs in their buildings (replacement of heating, plumbing, or electrical systems, roofs, etc.). Administrators are appointed to manage buildings where owners have either neglected the buildings or have abandoned them entirely.

Finally, the city also operates a number of home-improvement initiatives designed to assist low-, moderate-, and middle-income homeowners in the repair or moderate rehabilitation of their homes. Two of these programs, the **Senior Citizen Revolving Loan Fund** and the **Senior Homeowner Emergency Loan Program**, are specifically designed to help elderly homeowners who need repairs or who have accrued liens on their property. The **Home Improvement Program (HIP)** and the **Neighborhood Housing Services (NHS)** programs use a combination of city and bank funds in order to provide low-interest loans to eligible homeowners in targeted neighborhoods. These programs predate the creation of the original Ten Year Plan and are similar in structure to other home improvement programs throughout the nation.

4. New Construction of Affordable Homes

Although the majority of the city's funds to date have been devoted to expanding or preserving affordable rental housing, it is also important to create opportunities for moderate- and middle-income families who wish to own their own homes. While many New Yorkers wish to purchase their own homes, the prohibitive costs involved put homeownership out of the reach of most residents. The city's Housing Program provides modest subsidies to help residents realize the dream of homeownership. In addition, these programs increase the overall supply of housing in New York City and consequently serve to free up the rental units which are vacated by the new home purchasers so that others may take advantage of them.

The **Partnership New Homes Program** is designed to increase homeownership opportunities for moderate- to middle-income New Yorkers by producing new homes at prices well below what would be charged for comparable privately built units. HPD works with the New York City Partnership, a not-for-profit organization, as well as private developers and banks to build these homes all over the city. Each project varies enormously in number of units, square footage, and design. The Partnership New Homes Program includes single-family and two-family homes, as well as low- and high-rise condominiums and cooperatives. Through this program, the

city provides a subsidy of $10,000 per unit (most projects also receive a grant from New York State) and also defers payment of the taxes on the property. Provisions to recapture the subsidies are contained in the documents used to effectuate the sale.

The **Nehemiah Program** has won national recognition for its innovative approach to low-cost housing development. The Program relies upon an extremely simple method of construction and uniform home design to keep homes affordable to its target moderate-income population, mostly families who earn less than $25,000 per year. Homes are generally two-story brick rowhouses with two or three bedrooms and are sold for $57,500. The Program builds the homes in large clusters to ensure neighborhood stability as well as to take advantage of economies of scale. Large tracts of city-owned land are sold for $1 per home and each home receives a $10,000 city subsidy (which reverts back to the city upon sale of the property), and property tax abatements.

The **Limited Equity Co-op Program** was recently developed in response to the city's need to expand opportunities for homeownership to low- and moderate-income families. This innovative program provides below-market-rate, tax-exempt financing for the construction of limited-equity cooperatives. The city's Housing Development Corporation inaugurated this program with the issuance of approximately $7 million of revenue bonds in March 1990. The new limited-equity co-op model uses mortgage revenue bonds (MRBs) to finance the underlying or "blanket" permanent mortgage loan for limited-equity co-op housing development. Such bonds have traditionally provided mortgage loans to individual purchasers of one- to four-family homes. This innovative approach marks the first time in the nation that MRBs have been used in this fashion. Since the blanket mortgage will cover 90 percent of the nonsubsidized cost of the projects, individual purchasers will be required only to provide the 10 percent down payment and will not have to qualify for individual mortgages to purchase their units. As a result, the purchasers will not have to pay closing costs such as lender commitment fees, legal, appraisal, title insurance, and mortgage recording taxes, which can increase the cost of a condominium or cooperative single-family residence by an additional 5 to 6 percent, the costs that usually place the dream of homeownership beyond the reach of low-income families.

Incentive Programs

In recognition of the necessity to encourage the participation of the private sector in affordable-housing development, the city also offers several tax-incentive programs. These programs serve to reduce the total development costs and maximize the number of units produced and assisted without actually involving direct expenditures.

The J-51 Tax Incentive Program provides partial tax abatements and/or exemptions to private property owners who agree to rehabilitate their property. This program is often used in conjunction with the various city rehabilitation programs described above. The program provides enhanced benefits to certain projects which were vacant, city-owned

buildings being rehabilitated in a program for affordable housing using substantial governmental assistance and/or involve direct city assistance.

The 421a and 421b Tax Incentive Programs provide partial real estate tax exemptions to owners who build new residential buildings on underdeveloped sites. These programs are "as of right" to developers who build within the established zones. Enhanced benefits are provided to projects which are located in nonmarket areas and/or involve direct city assistance. The 421b program gives a benefit to one- and two-family houses, while the 421a program is designated for multiple dwellings containing three or more units.

The 421a/Low-Income Housing Program is designed to encourage private developers to participate in the production of low- and moderate-income housing without the use of direct city subsidies. Under this special program, developers are allowed to receive tax exemption for market-rate residential construction projects located in specific geographic areas which would otherwise be ineligible "regular" the 421a benefits. To receive the benefits in these areas, the developer must set aside 20 percent of the apartments in a market-rate development as low-income housing or must create low-income units off-site through new construction or substantial rehabilitation.

The Inclusionary Housing Program also provides an incentive for developers providing low- and moderate-income housing. In exchange for providing affordable housing, developers are awarded up to a 20 percent increase in allowable floor area for their market-rate residential projects. Builders have the following options: (1) dedicate a specific number of lower-income units in the market-rate development; (2) build new units; (3) rehabilitate vacant buildings for low- and moderate-income tenants; or (4) make moderate repairs on occupied low-income buildings, including SRO hotels. Off-site housing must be either in the same Community District as the market-rate development or within a half mile radius. The low-income units must be maintained and leased to low-income residents for the life of the increased floor space in the compensated development.

Both programs contain a transfer mechanism, so that a market-rate developer may purchase the benefit from a developer of the low-income units.

PROGRESS TO DATE AND PROJECTIONS FOR THE FUTURE

While New York's housing needs are so great that it is sometimes difficult to actually recognize improvements or accomplishments, the vast array of programs outlined in the preceding pages are in fact making a significant difference in the quality and quantity of affordable housing which is available in New York City. These programs will continue to bring about positive changes as they are expanded in the coming years.

To date, roughly 100,000 units have been assisted since the start of the city's Housing Program in 1987. More than 35,000 units of this total represent new units which have been, or are now in the process of being, created through new construction or substantial rehabilitation programs. When all of these new units

are completed, the city will have produced enough housing to serve the entire population of the city of Trenton, New Jersey.

In the process, the face of New York City is changing dramatically. Already in Harlem and the South Bronx, neighborhoods in which as many as three out of four buildings were vacant and abandoned have been completely rebuilt and repopulated and are now, for the first time in close to 20 years, thriving. At the same time, large tracts of vacant land in East New York which were once occupied by rubble and broken glass have been transformed into whole communities of low- and moderate-income families enjoying the privilege of owning their own home and working hard to improve the community around them.

While the benefits of moderate rehabilitation and preservation efforts are perhaps not as noticeable as those associated with housing production programs, they are nonetheless every bit as important. In fact, in New York City some 63,000 families are now living in improved conditions due to the city's various moderate rehabilitation programs. While their homes may look the same from the outside, they are quite different on the inside. Many families have benefited from a new boiler, a new roof, new plumbing throughout, or other important improvements including repairs to individual apartments. Moreover, these improvements go hand in hand with the city's efforts to renovate vacant shells, most of which are located in the very same neighborhoods where the city is working to renovate the occupied stock as well.

Finally, a significant number of the

new units which have been created, as well as thousands of units which have been renovated in the city's occupied in rem stock, have been set aside to house the homeless. Since 1984 the city has provided permanent homes for over 27,000 homeless households. For many of these families, the move from the shelter system to a newly refurbished apartment in a decent, safe residential building represents an opportunity they may have never thought possible.

Despite these accomplishments, the city's housing needs remain. The supply of vacant affordable units is still far too small to meet the demand, and the number of homeless families has remained steady despite the thousands of units which have been created. At the same time, many New Yorkers who do have adequate homes continue to be hard-pressed to afford them.

In response to this continuing need, the City of New York has renewed its commitment to affordable housing. Despite its current financial problems, the city's most recent ten-year spending plan calls for an additional $4.9 billion to be spent for housing over the next ten years, building on the $2.5 billion committed over the first five years of the program. While this effort will continue to bring positive results for the city, the experience of the last five years only serves to highlight the fact that no matter how much one locality does on its own, it cannot and will not solve its housing problems without the full support of the federal government.

While years of repeated federal funding cuts and program terminations have left housing advocates with little reason to be optimistic, recent events had restored the hope that the federal government would once again assume its leadership role in the field of assisted housing. First, in October of 1990 Congress passed the Cranston-Gonzales National Affordable Housing Act. This landmark legislation created several new important housing initiatives. Far and away the most significant of these was the HOME program, a new housing block grant initiative which promised to transfer both greater resources and increased control of those resources to state and local governments. Moreover, for the first time in years, the federal government acknowledged the need to assist localities in the creation of new units as well as the provision of rental assistance and moderate rehabilitation assistance.

In addition, the law created a new program to assist the development of housing for people with AIDS and established the HOPE program, the administration's attempt to foster homeownership opportunities through the sale of governmentally owned buildings. The law also authorized billions of dollars in expenditures to extend expiring Section 8 contracts and preserve existing federal projects in jeopardy of converting to market-rate uses. Just as importantly, the bill stressed the importance of maintaining support for ongoing efforts such as the Public Housing Program and the Community Development Block Grant (CDBG) program. In short, this legislation sent a clear message that the old programs were not to be traded off for the new.

While there has been some uncertainty over the last year as to whether the Appropriations Committees would in fact hear this message, the recently passed Housing and Veterans Administration Appropriations Bill offered a resounding affirmation of the need to provide increased funds for assisted housing. This act allocated a total of $1.5 billion for the new HOME program while increasing the CDBG budget and the total amount of new funds for public housing.

The creation of these important new programs and the appropriation of the funds to undertake them are indeed welcome. Yet, this represents just one step in what must be a continuing process toward a renewed federal commitment to housing. Even with the additions included in the recent spending bill, the federal government's budget for new assisted housing units is still only slightly more than a third of what it was in 1981.

Nevertheless, for the first time in nearly a decade, the necessary programs have been authorized and the tools are in place to launch a major federally assisted housing initiative. The challenge for Congress as we move through the '90s will be to see if it can once again devote the funds necessary to support these programs. Of course, the challenge for localities will be to apply these new funds to effective and efficient local housing strategies. With dozens of successful programs currently in operation, and with a long history of building, rehabilitating, and preserving housing, the City of New York is uniquely ready and able to accept that challenge.

Section IV

Neighborhood Development Organizations

Chapter 19

Neighborhood Reinvestment Corporation: How Residents, Lenders and Local Government Officials Are Working Together to Create Affordable Housing

George Knight
Executive Director
Neighborhood Reinvestment Corporation

The dream of owning a home, or even the more modest dream of living in an apartment that is safe, well-maintained, and affordable, is a dream often deferred because of a complex array of circumstances.

In high-priced real estate markets there is often an affordability gap between the earnings of low- to moderate-income people and the cost of homes on the market. In economically depressed communities, homes may be affordable but jobs may be nonexistent, and families may not qualify for mortgages under conventional underwriting criteria. In communities all across Amer-

ica, housing stock is aging, but loans for repairs are unavailable; as these homes deteriorate, entire communities become unstable, morale sinks, and businesses and families pull out.

How can this cycle of disinvestment and discouragement be broken? What does it take to reinvigorate a community—to get real estate values back up, and to make a neighborhood one of choice, rather than one of last resort? How can this come about without encouraging gentrification and displacing current residents?

These and many other issues have been tackled for the last 20 years by locally based organizations whose successes rely on a single, simple premise: that local residents, local lenders, and local government officials—working together—can amass the resources they need to build housing, rehabilitate housing and finance housing for low- to moderate-income families.

This partnership model has been replicated in over 300 neighborhoods representing every conceivable housing scenario (in inner-city, urban neighborhoods, in small to mid-sized towns, in rural communities, and in real estate markets both hot and cold) and for every conceivable type of housing (single-family homes of all shapes and sizes, small multifamily buildings and large apartment complexes).

Under the stewardship of the Neighborhood Reinvestment Corporation, this network—known as the national NeighborWorks^{SM} network[1]—of locally based programs has grown into the largest neighborhood revitalization system in the country. As such, it has set a national standard for training, technical assistance, and support.

Neighborhood Reinvestment, a public, nonprofit organization funded primarily by a congressional appropriation, was established by Act of Congress in 1978 (Public Law 95-557) "to revitalize older urban neighborhoods by mobilizing public, private and community resources at the neighborhood level."

Neighborhood Reinvestment is assisted in this effort by its sister organization, Neighborhood Housing Services of America (see Chapter 6), which operates the only secondary market for below-market loans for low-income families.

Members of the board of directors of the Corporation, as established by the Neighborhood Reinvestment Act of 1978, are: the secretary of Housing and Urban Development (HUD); the Comptroller of the Currency; the director of the Office of Thrift Supervision; and a member of each of the boards of the Federal Reserve System, the Federal Deposit Insurance Corporation, and the National Credit Union Administration.

In Anchorage, Alaska; Gainesville, Florida; West Rutland, Vermont; Pittsburgh, Pennsylvania; San Antonio, Texas; and more than 160 other, diverse locations, Neighborhood Reinvestment field staff and headquarters staff work diligently to bring all possible resources to bear on the housing and development needs of particular communities.

THE MISSION OF NEIGHBORHOOD REINVESTMENT

The mission of Neighborhood Reinvestment is not only to change the buildings in which people live, but to give residents the power to change the way they live and tools by which they can make the changes they decide are necessary.

To carry out its mission, Neighborhood Reinvestment creates new organizations and helps them expand. It preserves neighborhoods by encouraging investment and instilling pride. It continually trains staff and volunteers and reviews local programs to help the network find ways to leverage resources to finance established and innovative programs. To enhance effectiveness, the Corporation administers its services through district field offices.

THE CREATION OF VITAL NEIGHBORHOODS

Neighborhood Reinvestment's mission is

to create stable neighborhoods characterized by healthy real estate markets, sound housing, positive community images, and cores of neighbors able to manage the continuing health of their neighborhoods. The process begins with strong partnerships of residents, local business and government leaders.

After a neighborhood group, city agency, business or financial institution requests help, Neighborhood Reinvestment staff assess local resources and then begin six months of planning and development assistance.

Instead of recommending a set formula, the Corporation's field staff begins by asking the community representatives, "What is the real problem here? And what will it take to do what needs to be done?"

All of the developmental work is accomplished by committees representing the prospective partners. They define a part of a community (the target neighborhood) and set goals. A series of workshops is held that brings together representatives from all of the partnership groups. Often, this is the first time lenders and local government officials have ever sat down together with community-based development organizations and local residents to discuss working together for positive change.

As members of the various partnership groups become convinced that the partnership model can work, an autonomous, state-chartered, tax-exempt nonprofit organization is created. A board of directors is elected, staff is hired, and the difficult yet challenging work of neighborhood revitalization begins.

Each organization's board of directors is made up of all three sectors of the partnership, with residents in the major-

ity. The local board of directors guides the organization as it sets about accomplishing its goals.

In order to stabilize neighborhoods and reverse decline, local organizations typically offer:

- Access to low-interest loans for housing rehabilitation and homeownership, supported by a revolving loan fund whose loans are sold to Neighborhood Housing Services of America (NHSA), which packages them for the secondary market;

- Monitoring services as rehabilitation is undertaken or as new construction occurs;

- Counseling services for first-time home buyers; and

- Management assistance for multifamily properties.

An average NeighborWorks[SM] neighborhood has about 9,000 residents and a median household income that is 67 percent of the national median. About 2.7 million people live in more than 300 targeted neighborhoods. Most of the residents are minorities.

SUPPORTING NETWORK ORGANIZATIONS

The goal of most NeighborWorks[SM] organizations is to return a neighborhood to economic health with stability, a relatively sound real estate market and local leadership that can maintain the restored status.

Neighborhood Reinvestment helps local organizations expand into new service areas or increase the capacity and scope of strategies in an existing target neighborhood. Sometimes this means tackling problems like drugs, crime, a lack of confidence in the value of property, or unemployment that may undermine housing efforts.

With 12 years of experience, Neighborhood Reinvestment's field and training staff are expert at solving problems, presenting the neighborhood revitalization strategy concept to new potential partners, helping local organizations strengthen their financial management systems, and helping organizations develop the capacity to handle new programs. Sometimes this means learning to rehab and then manage multifamily housing projects, develop commercial districts, or create foreclosure prevention strategies.

At least twice a year, the Corporation sponsors training institutes attended by as many as 400 network staff, board members and volunteers, as well as staff and volunteers from other nonprofits. Practitioners with at least five years of hands-on experience teach courses from plumbing to effective administration. Neighborhood Reinvestment also provides regular training for new executive directors and workshops for resident leaders in subjects ranging from computerized accounting systems to leadership development.

Some of the most important transfers of knowledge take place informally when network members from across the country get together to exchange information. Their similar problems and values underlie the importance of such interaction.

Through its eight district offices, the Corporation focuses on assistance for skills and knowledge needed by local network organizations: staff recruitment, nonprofit management practices, contract compliance, construction policies and processing, community relations, marketing and neighborhood strategy development.

Program Reviews

Pioneered by Neighborhood Reinvestment, program reviews are tremendously powerful tools that measure the health of a local organization. More than an audit, more than technical advice, they are designed to help local boards assess their efforts and set future goals. Program reviews are a tool for local organizations to identify their successes, vulnerabilities and challenges for future development.

Each review is tailored to meet the needs and issues of a specific organization, but they all include a review of loan procedures, accounting systems and rehabilitation sites.

To augment training and program reviews, the Corporation's field staff provide assistance that is equivalent to specialized consulting in the private sector. Field services officers help local organizations work through hard times, increase capacity, or add program initiatives.

Financial Assistance

To expand loan and capital availability, Neighborhood Reinvestment and NHSA provide a variety of resources, including technical assistance to help network organizations develop local lender pools or acquire low-cost financing, direct financial assistance for predevelopment costs, "gap" financing and start-up grants for revolving loan funds.

Local organizations are responsible for their basic operating, administrative and revolving loan fund costs. However, Neighborhood Reinvestment gives grants for such activities as: start-up money for revolving loan funds, expanding into new areas, researching and developing innovative strategies, developing affordable housing, training and consultation.

Revolving loan funds are designed so that low-income people can repay their loans over several years, and therefore the funds revolve slowly. Since 1976, NHSA has operated a unique secondary market to purchase these loans, infusing the local funds with new capital. NHSA sells the notes backed by the loans to institutional investors, who agree to receive a below-market rate of return on their "social investment."

The largest group of revolving loan fund borrowers are the poorest. Nearly 51 percent of revolving loan fund borrowers have incomes below 50 percent of the local area median. More than 80 percent have incomes below 80 percent of the median. Revolving loan funds assist older residents, with one third of all loans made to people who are at least 55 years old. Half of the primary borrowers are female.

To help the NeighborWorks^{SM} network accomplish its mission, a group of CEOs in the banking, thrift and insurance industries initiated a "Social Compact" in January 1990. The agreement formalizes and increases a long-standing dedication on their part to the NeighborWorks^{SM} network by committing billions of dollars in conventional and below-market-rate loans to network neighborhoods during the 1990s.

The Social Compact includes such sponsors as Allstate Insurance, BankAmerica Corporation, Carteret Savings Bank, Citicorp, and WSGP Financial Management Company.

ASSISTING THE PRESERVATION OF AFFORDABLE HOUSING

Realizing that one of the greatest resources of older neighborhoods is the existing housing, Neighborhood Reinvestment helps NeighborWorks^{SM} organizations preserve housing by increasing homeownership and expanding the number of affordable rental units.

To increase homeownership, Neighborhood Reinvestment staff provides training and assistance in pre-purchase counseling, housing rehab, financing options and marketing.

To address distressed multifamily and rental properties, Neighborhood Reinvestment assists local organizations with strategies involving financial techniques, reimbursable acquisitions and equity grants for rehabilitation.

Neighborhood Reinvestment also promotes particular models that have been studied and tested for their applicability to the network's needs. One of these is the concept of a mutual housing association, which is a private, nonprofit partnership organization that develops, owns and manages affordable housing. A step up from rental housing but not as costly as home-ownership, its resident members have security of tenure, long-term affordability and control over the operation of their housing. The Corporation provides ongoing, sophisticated technical assistance for development, construction, financing and management of mutual housing associations, and may also provide grant assistance for pre-development acquisition and equity needs that are not met locally. Mutual housing associations are being established all across the country, from the Lower East Side of New York to Austin and to Anchorage.

Neighborhood Reinvestment keeps on top of current financial and industry trends and conditions and attempts to develop programs that take advantage of them for the benefit of local programs. For example, Neighborhood Reinvestment is one of four national nonprofit organizations to be under contract with the Resolution Trust Corporation for disposition of its assets.

Cumulatively through 1989, the NeighborWorks[SM] network rehabilitated 95,500 housing units, constructed 910 new units, and directly assisted more than 5,300 tenants to become homeowners. In 1990 alone, the direct reinvestment efforts of NeighborWorks[SM] organizations amounted to $161.3 million. For every dollar of revolving loan reinvestment an additional $6 was leveraged from public or private sources.

AFFORDABLE HOMEOWNERSHIP: Techniques for Making It Attainable

Over the last decade, homeownership opportunities for working-income families have varied widely from region to region and have been characterized by price instability. Prices dropped in Detroit, Davenport, and Denver while affordable home purchase seemed impossible in Boston, Los Angeles, and San Francisco. Homeownership—a bedrock of so much of the U.S. economy—appeared to decline as a solid investment while at the same time becoming more exclusive.

Fortunately, through the work of Neighborhood Reinvestment, we found these observations were not applicable to many cities throughout the country. Indeed, it has been our experience that working-income families earning roughly 80 percent of median income can buy houses in hundreds of communities. Moreover, these families can purchase homes using largely market-rate capital.

Neighborhood Reinvestment Corporation has helped to establish and continues to work with more than 163 nonprofit neighborhood development and affordable-housing corporations located in 141 cities in 42 states plus the District of Columbia and Puerto Rico. Through working with these nonprofits we have practical knowledge of the housing markets in more than 200 neighborhoods. In more than half of these neighborhoods a three-bedroom, one-bath, single-family house in good condition can be bought for $35,000 or less, sometimes much less. Moreover, for an additional $5,000 to $15,000, families can repair a house to a quality condition. This means that depending on the amount of rehab, the local taxes, and prevailing rates for 30-year financing, monthly mortgage payments can often be kept below $400. Therefore, families with only modest monthly debts ($50-80) and incomes in the high teens to low twenties can meet the debt-to-income ratios required of borrowers.

To learn more about the nature of purchases in working-income neighborhoods, we looked at data from seven affordable home-purchase programs from six states. We focused on the 168 most typical purchases. The evidence was clear. Given flexibility and assistance in the purchase process, home buyers with family incomes of $23,000 could purchase and repair sound, attractive homes on solid blocks for $34,000 on average, with a typical monthly payment of $370 (principal, interest, taxes and insurance). (See Table 19.1.)

Moreover, these opportunities are not limited to a few neighborhoods. If we examine recent sales data from the National Association of Realtors, we see a widespread pattern. In December of 1990, 15.3 percent of all single-family properties in the United States sold for less than $50,000. Nearly 9 percent sold for less than $40,000. In certain parts of the country, these patterns are even more noticeable. In the South 16.9 percent of all single-family houses were sold for less than $50,000 and nearly 10 percent were under $40,000. In the Midwest, 24.5 percent were purchased for less than $50,000 and nearly 15 percent were under $40,000. In Saginaw, Michigan, the median price for all houses sold in 1990 was $48,100, with places like Peoria and Oklahoma City only slightly more expensive.

If such properties exist in so many places, what then inhibits purchases from happening? Is there no demand? Are buyers too wary of the unsettled home-purchase marketplace? Are there problems in the purchasing process that undermine sales?

It is our belief that the problem is not fundamentally consumer resistance or a lack of demand, but ineffective sales and financing mechanisms. Yet, both sales and financing are an integral part of the American economic system. They're done by real estate and financial industries that need to show profitability, which is particularly difficult in these instances.

What we have found is that the normal education and marketing function of the real estate industry can't afford to be invested in these low-return properties.

Further, for a variety of competitive and market reasons, the lending industry can't afford to service very-low-down-payment buyers who often have imperfect or nonexistent credit histories. Lenders usually cannot recapture the higher costs of loaning rehab money as part of the purchase or of loaning funds even minimally ahead of current appraised values. These realities are not lost on prospective buyers who, therefore, drop out of the market or purchase elsewhere at higher prices. This, of course, reinforces the market distortions.

To understand these issues more completely, we chose to study affordable home-purchase programs in 12 cities from a list of 44 projects. These programs, in one form or another, looked at and addressed the same four issues.

Essentially, lower-income buyers asked:

- How can we get the information and assistance to make locating, evaluating, and buying a house possible?

- How can we buy with little or no down payment and/or an imperfect or nonexisting credit history?

- How can we buy a home in good repair or get the financing to bring the house to a level we can be proud of?

- How can we be sure that this house is a sound investment—that the neighborhood will be stable?

I. CAN WE MAKE THE MARKETING PROCESS WORK EFFECTIVELY IN OUR NEIGHBORHOOD?

In contemporary America, education and marketing are closely entwined. This particularly applies to the purchase of

Table 19.1 Sample of Single Family Sales, 1989–1991

City	# of Sales	Average Purchase Price	Average Rehab Amount	Average Rehab + Purchase	Average Income of Buyer	Average PITI
Burton, Michigan	14	$19,696	$14,753	$34,449	$14,191	$334
Great Falls	16	44,515	None	44,515	18,828	N.A.
Kalamazoo, Michigan						
Round 1	33	28,857	5,233	34,090	26,484	433
Round 2	29	25,357	6,927	32,284	24,040	N.A.
Kankakee, Illinois	21	21,400	3,340	24,740	24,057	N.A.
Lincoln, Nebraska	8	24,695	10,723	35,418	15,743	271
Toledo, Ohio	26	21,850	4,350	26,200	24,714	292
West Palm Beach, Florida	21	42,357	11,309	53,666	19,824	417
Total	168	$28,559	$5,529	$34,088	$22,387	$368*

*PITI figure based on 102 sales

housing. The bulk of this education is handled by the real estate industry, which advertises available units and shows the houses while educating the potential buyers about the intricacies of the home-purchase process. However, if the listing price is low, if the property is in poor repair, or if buyers are inexperienced, many realtors feel that it is not good business to be extensively involved in the sale. As a result, lower-priced older houses, which have underwriting problems and which often attract unsophisticated buyers, are seldom served well by the traditional market system. Therefore, if a neighborhood wants to influence how properties are sold in its community, it often must develop its own education and marketing strategies.

Some programs that have done a good job in marketing older homes and educating potential buyers can be found in Great Falls, Montana; Davenport, Iowa; and Toledo, Ohio.

Great Falls

Neighborhood Issue:

Great Falls had a boom/bust economy. During boom times, there was a great deal of construction and expansion into the suburbs. The downtown areas were neglected in favor of newer housing and shopping areas. As a result, the older downtown neighborhoods were no longer "neighborhoods of choice" for new home buyers. Existing homeowners were moving out if possible, often selling their homes to investors as rental units.

Challenge:

The NHS had the dual challenge of trying to attract buyers to the "old" part of town and to "old" houses. To accomplish this, they needed to market the neighborhood as well as the homes.

Strategy:

The NHS employed a variety of strategies to market the neighborhood and to make it competitive for homeowners vis-a-vis other city neighborhoods. First, they concentrated on getting rid of neighborhood eyesores including deteriorated buildings, many of which had been originally built with no foundations. With the cooperation of the city, the NHS cleaned vacant lots and demolished dilapidated buildings. Buildings that were salvageable were rehabbed. Six years ago when the NHS entered the neighborhood, there were close to 300 boarded-up buildings. Now there are less than 60.

The NHS spreads the good news about the changes in the neighborhood through a newsletter that comes out five times a year. This is distributed to everyone the NHS works with, including residents in the neighborhood, businesses, and social service agencies. The NHS also spends considerable time educating realtors about their neighborhood and the improvements being made in it.

A particularly successful tool for marketing the neighborhood has been the offering of favorable financing terms to persons purchasing homes in the target area.

Over the last four years, the Montana Board of Housing has allocated low-interest money for mortgage loans in the NHS target area. In addition, Neighborhood Reinvestment granted $10,000 to the NHS to be used to assist families buying new houses in the target area with down-payment and closing costs. The families were paid to do interior work (painting, etc.) and exterior work such as landscaping on other homes, which provided the buyers with cash for part of the down-payment and closing costs.

The NHS will soon have a new tool to promote homeownership. The NHS will receive $50,000 through the Affordable Housing Program of the Federal Home Loan Bank, which it will use for down-payment and closing-costs grants of $2,500 for 20 families. The NHS will provide homeownership counseling to these families.

Results:

The average income of 41 buyers granted NHS 6⅞ percent loans by the Montana Board of Housing was $19,166. Incomes ranged from $12,000 to $29,000 for FHA-approved homes. Under unusual circumstances, NHS has been able to help people of even lower income into homeownership.

Davenport

Neighborhood Issue:

The neighborhoods served by the Davenport NHS include a number of older houses dating to the founding of the city and houses built as recently as the 1950s. Due to the downturn in the manufacturing and agricultural economies, there is a very soft housing market, slow housing sales, and widespread vacancy and abandonment.

Challenge:

The NHS board knew that the overall economy was a problem. Moreover, the real estate industry had largely written off the neighborhood and the key lenders had chosen to make no loans for less than $30,000, effectively disallowing mortgages on almost all the single-family houses. And there remained a strong market bias against the NHS neighborhoods, which are both older and racially mixed.

Strategy:

The board decided to market the desirability of living in these neighborhoods through promotional events and to do direct outreach to families by matching them to available houses.

In conjunction with General Electric Mortgage Insurance Companies (GEMICO), the NHS developed a $2.4 million first-mortgage program. The program, which utilizes a pool created by all seven local lenders, offers loans to first-time home buyers at 9.9 percent interest for 30 years.

Buyers are required to put down 5 percent. An additional 5 percent will come from deferred zero-percent loans from the City of Davenport. Buyers from the NHS target will also be eligible for 6 percent rehab loans from the NHS. State funding is pending for rehab loans outside the NHS target area. An important aspect of the program is that there is no minimum mortgage amount. In the past, conventional lending for mortgages under $30,000 has not been readily available.

Potential buyers are required to attend training sessions covering topics such as how to buy a house, closing costs and escrow, credit analysis, and budget planning. After purchase, buyers must attend classes on maintenance and foreclosure prevention. These sessions are held in community settings throughout the neighborhoods and are lead by 30 volunteers and residents who have received special training.

Results:

In the first eight weeks of the program, the NHS closed on four houses and twelve additional purchase offers were made. Sales prices have ranged from $27,900 to $36,000. The income of the buyers has ranged from $13,000 to $25,000.

The NHS has been focusing its earliest efforts on houses that do not require significant rehab work since they are waiting for state funding for rehab loans outside their immediate target area. In the future, the NHS expects more interest on homes selling for $25,000 or less that require rehab work.

The NHS forecasts between 90 and 100 mortgages through this program over the next two years. This level of production will be closely tracked as part of the evaluation of the Mentor Project and as a way to identify models for replication elsewhere.

Toledo

Neighborhood Issue:

The NHS target neighborhoods had numerous vacant, vandalized properties as well as many "for sale" properties. A Mentor Project market analysis showed there was a good market for properties in Toledo at or below $30,000 to $35,000. The NHS wanted to find a way to encourage families looking in this price range to buy into the target neighborhoods.

Challenge:

The NHS objective was to make it easier or more attractive for potential buyers to choose to buy in these neighborhoods as opposed to other nearby areas. The goal was to attract the most stable buyers who are committed and able to improve both the houses and the neighborhoods.

Strategy:

The NHS developed a 100 percent financing program for their target neighborhoods, using a Lender Participation Program. Since down payment is a major hurdle for many first-time buyers, the availability of 100 percent financing in certain neighborhoods gives those neighborhoods areas of competitive advantage vis-a-vis other communities. It was reasoned that this competitive advantage would bring the real estate community more effectively into the process.

Here's how it works:

NHS makes a 100 percent mortgage to the buyer who is only required to provide a $100 application fee and a paid property insurance policy at closing. The financing includes both acquisition and rehab costs and the remaining closing costs.

The NHS uses strict underwriting criteria. Except for the down payment requirement, the buyers would most likely qualify for conventional financing. The NHS, in fact, made a point of not using CDBG funds to fund the mortgages, so the loans would not have to comply with any special income requirements.

The NHS sells a 90 percent participation in the loan to a local lender. The NHS can then use that money to make additional loans. The NHS of Toledo currently has seven lenders who have pledged to buy a total of $900,000 in participation. The banks have recourse through the NHS's loan fund. If a participation loan goes bad, they can exchange it for a performing loan from the NHS's loan pool.

Most of the marketing for this program was done through realtors who were extremely enthusiastic about this extra tool to sell homes in an otherwise flat neighborhood marketplace. The realtors were brought fully into the process through direct outreach by the Mentor.

Results:

Since January 1990, the NHS has closed sixteen loans through this program. Ten more properties are currently in the pipeline. The average loans were for around $27,000-$28,000. The NHS expects to be able to close 30-35 loans a year through this program. This high volume of sales for the neighborhood has invigorated a stagnant sales market and prompted real estate agents to market the neighborhood more aggressively. This, in turn, is leading to more and stronger buyers and to fewer long-term for-sale signs.

II. CAN WE EXPAND THE NUMBERS OF FAMILIES QUALIFYING FOR FINANCING?

The obstacles to families buying houses are common throughout the country. First-time buyers usually lack substantial savings and often have had past credit problems. While the lack of savings is not a new problem, perhaps no generation of Americans have been so seduced by easy credit availability. Unfortunately, this has occurred during a time of tremendous volatility in lower-income employment. This dangerous pattern, coupled with higher rates of divorce, soaring medical costs, and other family stresses leaves us with few families that have unblemished credit records. On the opposite extreme, there are many families who have never joined the credit-using majority and may not even use checking accounts. As a result many first-time buyers have either no credit history or an imperfect record.

Fortunately, these obstacles can be resolved through hard work by the families and through creative effort by the nonprofits and the lending communities. Rent records can substitute for nonexistent credit records. Counseling can be used to resolve credit problems and to establish new spending and savings patterns. Rent-to-buy options can be used to demonstrate stability. The issue is the commitment of both the families and programs to make purchase possible. And the pay-off is tremendous. We not only get new homeowners; we also get new human resources in the neighborhood.

A large number of programs have developed innovative strategies which take chances on such people while minimizing risks. Examples of strategies have been used in Burton, Michigan; Kalamazoo, Michigan; and Kankakee, Illinois.

Burton

Neighborhood Issue:

There are a significant number of foreclosed houses in the neighborhood—especially HUD-foreclosed houses. These houses are becoming increasingly run-down and are negatively affecting nearby homes. Investors have been buying some of properties, doing only minimal repairs, and renting them as low-quality units.

Challenge:

The NHS wants homeowners to buy these houses, rather than investors. However, the families interested in buying homes in their neighborhood often cannot get conventional financing to purchase because they lack money for a down payment and/or have a poor credit history or do not have the standard two-year job history. In addition, the NHS wants the properties, many of which have fallen into disrepair, to be brought up to a level that sets a high community standard.

Strategy:

The NHS, through a specially negotiated agreement with HUD, can purchase HUD-reacquired homes in the neighborhood at 10 percent off list price (20 percent off list price if the NHS can show that rehab would bring the property to above market value). Today NHS, using CDBG funds, is buying selected HUD-foreclosed properties, rehabbing them, and selling them, through a variety of programs, to low- and moderate-income families who would, in most cases, not qualify for conventional financing due to job or credit history or the lack of down-payment funds.

NHS, through its outreach efforts and word-of-mouth, has a pool of families interested in buying a home in Bendel, their target neighborhood. In all cases, NHS buys the property and then determines which financing plan and secondary market they should use, based on client affordability. The NHS utilizes a variety of financing plans to meet the needs of the individual families but always includes rehab in the financing package to assure quality properties.

One technique is the Fannie Mae Lease-Option Program. The Burton plan was partially developed by the W. Alton Jones Mentor but was innovatively tailored to local needs by the NHS staff. Under this plan, the NHS buys and rehabs the property, using a conventional bank mortgage. The NHS then offers to land contract the homes to a family through a mechanism similar to a lease-purchase agreement. The family pays directly to the NHS which, in turn, places a portion of their monthly rental payment against the first mortgage, a portion into escrow for taxes and insurance, and a portion to pay down the NHS's equity in the property. Over three to five years, depending on the family, contract buyers are able to accumulate enough equity and/or clean up their credit history to a point where they can assume the first mortgage which had been held by the NHS. Fannie Mae has committed to purchase $500,000 of first mortgages made to the NHS and assumable by the lease-purchasing families.

The NHS uses a variety of other methods to help families buy. This includes helping buyers to meet down-payment costs or to lower their monthly payments. In some cases the NHS will accept sweat equity as a way of earning part of the down payment or will use State of Michigan or Neighborhood Reinvestment funds to help families with down-payment costs. In addition, the NHS makes its own first or second mortgages at reduced interest rates to increase affordability. The NHS is able to resell some of their loans at 9½ percent to Neighborhood Housing Services of America to revolve their limited funds. They are developing other secondary markets for their loans.

Results:

Over the last two years, the NHS has sold nineteen single-family homes. Seventeen of these were HUD-reacquired houses. The family income of the buyers ranged from $6,000 to

$32,000, with the majority being under $20,000. The NHS is very flexible in its lending practices and tries to arrange financing so that the buyers' PITI is $350 or lower, the average rent for a house in the neighborhood.

Kankakee

Neighborhood Issue:

Due to a downturn in the local economy caused by factory closings, the real estate market in Kankakee was severely depressed in the early 1980s. There was an excess of housing for sale and property values were dropping. By 1985, the local economy started to improve, but most families had exhausted their savings during the previous periods of unemployment, so they didn't have enough savings for the 20 percent down payment required by conventional lenders for mortgage financing.

Challenge:

The challenge for the NHS was to find a way to bring new homeowners into the neighborhood, knowing that most first-time buyers in the area had little or no savings.

Strategy:

The NHS set up a program geared to assist first-time home buyers to save enough money for a down payment on a conventional mortgage loan. This is a "rapid equity growth" strategy.

First, the NHS negotiated with the Illinois Housing Development Authority to receive a $200,000 loan at 2 percent interest for two years. The NHS then used this money to make nine-month, zero-percent-interest loans to first-time

home buyers who did not have adequate savings for a down payment on a conventional mortgage loan but would otherwise qualify. The program is targeted to families who have good credit histories, stable job histories, and sufficient income to meet the monthly mortgage payments.

The program works as follows:

1. An interested family comes to NHS and NHS determines what the family can afford to buy. Sometimes the buyers have a particular house in mind, but many times the family is only beginning the process.

2. Once the particular house is chosen, NHS works up a financing package which includes acquisition and rehab costs.

3. NHS determines what the 20 percent down payment and closing costs will total and, in turn, sets a monthly payment for nine months. The buyers pay this amount each month for nine months into an escrow account.

4. The NHS gets an advanced commitment from a private lender to provide the 80 percent take-out financing for the mortgage at the end of the nine-month period. The lenders are not asked to make underwriting exceptions for these clients though often they will agree to overlook certain credit problems as long as they are resolved within the nine-month period. NHS provides budget and credit counseling to these buyers.

5. The NHS buys the house using the money from IHDA. The potential buyers sign a contract with NHS (similar to a land contract) which says

they will pay a certain amount each month into the escrow account for nine months. Their monthly payment is used to cover taxes and insurance and the rest is put aside to pay for a down payment and closing costs.

6. At the end of the nine-month period, if the potential buyers have met their payments, they sign for a conventional mortgage with the bank. The escrow account is used to cover down-payment and closing costs. NHS receives the purchase money from the bank and repays IHDA at the end of the two-year period.

Results:

Over the last two years, the NHS has completed seventeen home purchases under this program. The income of the buyers ranges from $15,600 to $35,000, with the average income being $24,204. The average sales price is $20,824 and the typical rehab costs run about $3,300. The average monthly savings escrow deposit on these sales was $503, which is 25 percent of the average income.

Kalamazoo

Neighborhood Issue:

The majority of the units of housing in the NHS target neighborhoods is rental and some of it is poorly maintained. Since the rent on many of these homes is equivalent to what a monthly mortgage payment would be, the NHS wanted to find a way to help low- and moderate-income families buy the homes.

Challenge:

Although many families in the area could afford the monthly payments on the homes, which sell for around $35,000, they do not have enough savings to meet the down-payment requirements for conventional loans. The challenge was how to find a way to help these families buy homes and also to make sure the homes were brought up to code or better.

Strategy:

The NHS put together a loan pool from seven local lenders totalling $1 million. This money is used to provide financing for the acquisition and rehab of houses in the two NHS target areas. Buyers receive a seven-year adjustable-rate first mortgage covering 90 percent of the appraised value of the property after rehab. The rate for the first three years is 8¾ percent. The remaining costs are met by a 7 percent second mortgage from NHS up to 120 percent of appraised value. The term of the NHS second mortgage varies based on client affordability.

Applicants are required to pay a $50 application fee and a minimum $500 down payment to cover a portion of the closing costs. Applicants must have a good rental history, good credit, and a stable employment record. Applicants must be at or below 60 percent of median income unless the property receives $3,000 of rehab work. In that case, there are no income limitations.

Results:

Thirty-seven properties were sold through the program between June 1989 and April 1990, when the program had depleted all loan revenues. A second round is just beginning using a new loan pool of $1 million from eight lenders. The local project is now one of a nearly a dozen that have agreed to train other programs around the country in the development of affordable-homeownership initiatives.

III. CAN WE ASSURE THE APPROPRIATE LEVEL OF PROPERTY REHABILITATION?

Most Americans buy a house at the top of their "affordability." They try to qualify for as much house as their finances allow. As a result, for the first few years of ownership there is usually little flexibility in the budget for making improvements. Even if the owner qualifies for a home improvement loan, the higher interest rates and shorter payment schedules make such loans unattractive compared to mortgage loans.

Therefore, if programs wish to assure good-quality properties, they must plan for it at time of the home purchase or as part of the mortgage. The techniques for doing this vary widely. Some programs build new houses to assure a quality product; others arrange for "gut rehab" before sale. Still others sell houses with a predesigned rehab package and loan. Others place simultaneous purchase and rehab loans. Moreover, some intentionally design products which require purchaser hands-on efforts in order to assure that the buyers learn some basic skills and achieve a greater sense of personal ownership. The range of answers is obviously extensive.

The important recognition is that this doesn't happen by accident but is part of a conscious plan that not only assures that the particular house is high-quality but that the house becomes a model for the rest of the neighborhood. Some of the cities which have programs that have

attempted to influence these issues include Chicago, Illinois; Lincoln, Nebraska; and Washington, D.C.

Chicago

Neighborhood Issue:

There were a large number of vacant, abandoned properties in the target areas at the same time there was a great need for affordable housing. These vacants had reached a percentage on certain blocks that they were beginning to dominate not only the sales market but the extent of current homeowner repair activity.

Challenge:

The challenge for the NHS neighborhood programs was to attract interested buyers and to make possible affordable rehabilitation of the vacant, derelict buildings. This would involve extensive marketing as well as the provision of flexible financing options.

Strategy:

NHS targets HUD and FSLIC properties available for redevelopment. NHS acquires them and in some cases undertakes emergency repairs and exterior rehab. NHS markets these homes to neighborhood families interested in becoming homeowners. NHS helps buyers assemble financing, utilizing conventional sources and low-interest loans from its revolving loan fund and other low-interest loan resources. It provides technical rehab assistance, including contractor referral and building supply sources.

A typical sale would be one where the NHS buys the property using money from the MacArthur Foundation, which provides a $50,000 line of credit at 8 percent. The ultimate buyer gets conventional financing from a local bank. NHS packages a city rehab loan to go along with the purchase financing and monitors the rehab. Although this is the most typical type of sale, there are many scenarios including one in which the NHS makes the entire purchase and rehab financing out of its own revolving loan fund. The key is flexibility and a close relationship between the buyer and the NHS program.

Results:

Thirty-one homes in five target neighborhoods were sold by NHS from the HUD and FSLIC inventories of foreclosed properties between February 1989 and May 1990. All were derelict and boarded when acquired. The average sales cost to end buyers was between $35,000 and $42,000. The NHS's goal is to sell 60 properties this year.

Lincoln

Neighborhood Issue:

Lincoln has many of the features of a university town, with some neighborhoods facing a high demand for rental units. In fact, the demand is so high that landlords are able to easily rent units that are in poor condition. This large number of poorly maintained rental units discourages current homeowners from further investing in their properties and diverts potential home buyers from purchasing in the neighborhood.

In addition, potential home buyers interested in the neighborhood often have problems obtaining financing. Many houses in these neighborhoods are priced at less than $30,000 and the minimum loan amount required by many lending institutions in the area ranges from $25,000 to $35,000. Large investors with high lines of credit at the banks do not encounter this problem since they put additional properties on a master note.

Challenge:

The challenge for the NHS was to make homeownership attractive and possible to low- and moderate-income families while at the same time improving the housing stock in the neighborhood to reinforce the current homeowners.

Strategy:

The NHS initiated the H.O.M.E. (Home Ownership Made Easy) program which offered qualified low-income home buyers 97 percent financing as well as needed rehab loans. Buyers must not exceed certain income guidelines (approximately $26,000 for a family of four) and the properties must require rehab work values at least 17 percent of the sales price.

The program worked as follows:

1. The buyer provides a 3 percent down payment.

2. The NHS offers a 17 percent downpayment loan at the appropriate interest rate needed to make the deal work.

3. Participating lenders provide an 80 percent mortgage based on the sales price of on the property. Each of the participating banks offer some special deal to the buyer such as a lower interest rate, no appraisal fee, or less points. This varies from bank to bank.

4. The NHS provides a rehab loan also at whatever interest rate is needed to

make the financing work. The rehab loan is made at closing although the actual work is done after closing. The lenders like this arrangement since their position on the loan will improve once the property is reassessed after rehab.

5. The NHS receives 2 percent of the purchase price at settlement as an operating contribution.

Results:

The NHS has closed 14 loans under this program. Five of these loans were for duplexes, one was for a triplex, and the rest were for single-family homes.

The income of the buyers ranged from $7,200 to $21,060. Most of the buyers have incomes in the mid- to high teens. Monthly mortgage payments range from $184 to $424 (duplex).

Rehab costs ranged from $3,345 to $35,000, with most houses requiring $12,000-$13,000 of rehab.

Washington, D.C.

Neighborhood Issue:

The Anacostia neighborhood in Washington, D.C., has a number of abandoned, foreclosed properties as well as numerous vacant lots. At the same time, there is a need for affordable homeownership opportunities in the neighborhood. Current neighborhood residents who are interested in becoming homeowners can not find suitable affordable houses for sale in Anacostia. "For sale" homes are either in terrible condition or are very expensive. As a result, families often save their money until they can afford to move to the nearby suburbs.

Many people choose to live in the District for a variety of reasons. District government employees, for example, are required to live within the city limits. Washington is a very high-cost market and the high cost of "for sale" housing often makes it very difficult for such employees to become homeowners despite their stable employment histories.

Challenge:

The challenge to the neighborhood was developing attractive affordable housing within Anacostia as well as finding a way to deal with the abandoned, foreclosed properties and the vacant lots.

Strategy:

The NHS established a separate development corporation with an initial focus on developing homeownership opportunities in Anacostia. Over time, the development group plans to expand to other parts of the city.

Neighborhood Housing Development Corporation's (NHDC) first project was to build three infill townhouses on vacant lots in the neighborhood. These units were the first new residential construction in the neighborhood in over 50 years. Using favorable financing from local banks as well as city homeownership and rehab programs, the NHDC was able to offer the properties at $75,000-$88,000. Moreover, lenders agreed to make mortgages for 95 percent or more of the value of the property. They looked at each loan on a case-by-case basis, looking more at job history than at savings.

The NHDC also has a rehab and resale model. In this program, the NHDC purchases properties through a variety of sources: auctions, HUD/VA foreclosures, private sales, and lender contacts. NHDC then performs selective rehabilitation to correct code deficiencies and offers the properties at prices slightly below market. The buyers are prequalified by a city down-payment assistance program. A second city program provides NHDC with a $7,500 developer's fee for each property. The NHDC received an initial capitalization of $150,000 from the NHS and has a credit line of $500,000 from local lenders. Sales prices on the rehabbed houses range from $59,000 to $89,000.

Results:

The NHDC has sold three new townhouses and seven rehabbed houses through the program. They are holding nine more properties in their inventory for sale. Seven of these properties have contracts for sale and are awaiting financing.

The income of buyers ranged from $16,000 to $52,000. The median income of buyers was $23,000. All of the buyers are African-Americans and 80 percent are female heads of household. Approximately half of the buyers have children.

IV. CAN WE MAKE HOMEOWNERSHIP AFFORDABLE TO OUR TARGET POPULATION WITHOUT UNDERMINING THE LONG-TERM STABILITY OF THE NEIGHBORHOOD?

Making homeownership affordable to low- and moderate-income families while at the same time reinforcing the future housing market in a neighborhood is a critical challenge.

Direct cash subsidies are risky. They create the image that people are living in the neighborhood only because they were "bought" into the area. Also unless there is an unusually high amount of subsidy dollars, the neighborhood risks being viewed as a subsidy site and then not having enough subsidy to get any real improvement.

There are very few neighborhoods that achieve stability with only very-low-income home buyers. Yet, often this is what neighborhoods are asked to do. National policies limit the use of the bulk of certain federal dollars to families at no more than 80 percent of median income, or, in certain cases, no more than 50 percent of median income. An example of how these policies hurt neighborhoods could be found in one northern city where the many neighborhoods have large, eight- to nine-room, frame houses that are extremely costly to maintain and heat. At the same time, the median incomes in the area are fairly low. A family of four must earn less than 80 percent of median ($23,300 annually) to qualify for most programs that offer assistance in either buying or rehabbing homes. As a result, few families that qualify for assistance are willing to take loans and most make only minimal repairs. Grants become the major means of neighborhood assistance and, therefore, the demand for loans dwindles even further. Families earning over 80 percent of the median income have increasingly less incentive to invest in their properties or to stay in the neighborhoods.

The trick is to balance the low-income focus with strong emphasis on high-quality improvements and sustained commitments by the new buyers. Examples of this can be found in Barberton, Ohio; Kenosha, Wisconsin; and Aberdeen, Washington.

Barberton

Neighborhood Issue:

The neighborhood had a large amount of vacant land (close to 30 percent of the neighborhood) and had a large elderly population. The community association wanted to attract young families to the area to help stabilize the neighborhood.

Challenge:

The challenge for the neighborhood was to find a way to attract young families who would become truly committed to the area. The housing needed to be attractive enough to entice these families, while at the same time be affordable to buyers with little or no savings and the ability to pay only about $350 a month in mortgage payments.

Strategy:

The local community association determined that new construction would be the best way to attract young families to the neighborhood. However, they had to find a way to make the new construction affordable to families with incomes in the high teens to low twenties.

The Neighborhood Conservation Services of Barberton, working in conjunction with Neighborhood Reinvestment, HUD, the City of Barberton, the State of Ohio, and local lenders were able to build eighteen single-family houses for sale to low- and moderate-income families.

The city donated the land for the project and five lenders agreed to make first mortgages on the houses at 1 percent below market rate. Working with the city, the NCS was able to receive $145,000 in a special grant from HUD

and $50,000 from the state of Ohio. Neighborhood Reinvestment provided a $74,000 grant.

To make the homes affordable, the projects had sweat equity built into the purchasing. Buyers agreed to invest 380 hours in "sweat equity" in their new homes and those of their neighbors before settlement. In exchange, buyers are able to purchase the new homes with a deposit of $500 and monthly payment of approximately $320.

Results:

The houses were bought by families with an income between $13,000 and $24,000, most of whom had never conceived of homeownership as a real option. Today, they see themselves as a permanent part of the community. Moreover, for the first time in years there has been new construction, which means fewer vacant lots and more well-maintained houses and yards.

Kenosha

Neighborhood Issue:

The overall housing market was soft and houses seemed to sell slowly. Some properties were undergoing foreclosure and in many cases abandonment. Over the past years, many substandard eyesore properties had been demolished in the NHS target area. As a result, there were a large number of vacant lots. Many of these lots were owned by the Public Housing Authority, which was reviewing what to do with them. Since they constituted such a significant part of the neighborhood, the NHS wanted to be in a position to determine what would happen.

Challenge:

Through the work of the Mentor Project, the NHS saw a dual challenge: (1) the development of the vacant lots in the neighborhood in such a way to best market and promote the neighborhood, and (2) the need to sell nearby vacant or foreclosed properties or houses long on the for-sale market.

Strategy:

The NHS decided that the most effective overall way to revitalize the neighborhood would be to increase homeownership. Moreover, the city leaders and the state had established rehabilitation loan programs and the NHS Board felt it did not need to concentrate as much effort on providing rehabilitation services. The NHS's Homeownership Promotion Program had four main aspects:

1. Construction of new single-family homes on the vacant lots,

2. Sales facilitation of existing properties,

3. Moderate rehab and sale of vacant or abandoned properties, and

4. Foreclosure intervention/resolution.

Results:

The program has already built and sold six new houses and is being pressed to construct more. An additional six houses that were on the market have been sold to first-time buyers and five moderate rehabs and sales of troubled properties are completed. In addition, the program has helped three families buy foreclosed houses which were likely to become neighborhood problems.

Aberdeen

Neighborhood Issue:

A downswing in the local economy resulted in a decline in property values and an increasing amount of cheap "for sale" housing. At the same time rents remained stable. Investors who had bought their properties in better, more expensive times could often not afford to lower their rents. As a result, many low-income people were paying rents that were as high as a monthly mortgage payment would be on a newly purchased house.

In addition, due to the reduced sales values investors were reluctant to put much money into maintaining their properties, so the rental units were becoming increasingly low-quality.

Challenge:

The challenge for the NHS was to devise a program that would allow low- and moderate-income families to buy and rehab the houses with affordable monthly payments but require a little savings for down-payment and closing costs.

Strategy:

The NHS devised a 100 percent financing program that would include down-payment and closing costs as well as necessary rehab work. To raise the money for such a program, the NHS set up a lender participation program whereby local lenders buy participations in NHS-originated purchase/rehab loans.

Here's how it works. The NHS makes the entire loan, including purchase, rehab, down-payment and closing costs. The buyers are encouraged but not required to put down some money. The NHS then sells a portion of the loans to one of the participating banks.

The lender sends NHS a check for its portion of the loan. The NHS then has that amount available to lend again.

The mortgagee pays the entire monthly mortgage payment to NHS, with the NHS sending the appropriate portion of the payment to the bank. Since the participating lenders require 9½ percent interest on their loans, the amount of a loan sold to a lender varies depending on what the buyer can afford.

Results:

Over the first two years of the program, the NHS closed on 17 loans. The family income of most of the buyers was in the low to mid-teens. In most cases, the families' PITI was roughly equal to their previous rents.

The NHS learned the hard way that homeownership was not a feasible option for every family. At the beginning of their program, they tried to work with every family that was interested, regardless of income. They discovered that when the primary income of a family was from eligibility programs such as public assistance, there was often too much economic instability to meet the demands of homeownership. As a result, the NHS had to foreclose on early loans. The NHS is now looking more carefully at stability of income. The NHS, however, continues to work with low-income families whose income is not dependent on entitlement programs which are subject to significant change.

The NHS was particularly pleased that many of the new homeowners are young families in an area that was losing its young population. In addition, several of the buyers have become active community volunteers.

OBSERVATIONS

Whether we are looking at these 12 case studies or in more than five dozen neighborhoods, it is clear that affordable homeownership is a powerful tool for helping families and for stabilizing neighborhoods. The strategies employed are unique, based on each neighborhood and the differences in family needs. What has become clear is that lending resources, underwriting, appraisals, credit issues, and down payments are not insurmountable obstacles; indeed, information—marketing, counselling, rehab advice—is probably able to meet any obstacle for many families.

As new opportunities arise—AHP, Fannie Mae and Freddie Mac initiative, and new nonprofit secondary-market resources—this sales facilitation capacity issue will rise again and again. And as homeownership gives real stability and confidence to families, it also does the same for neighborhoods. Further, as neighborhoods stabilize, the potential for retaining long-term affordable housing becomes more realistic. In other words, this is a dream that can be real and attainable.

ASSESSING IMPACT

The impact of Neighborhood Reinvestment's work cannot be conveyed by statistics only. Rather, stories of individual successes, of lives transformed, convey the true worth of our efforts.

Such stories as that of Cheryl Allen, a thirty-three-year-old mother of two who moved in with her grandmother in hopes of saving a nest egg with which to purchase a home. Although her wages as a typist for an insurance company seemed meager, she was among the fortunate to have a job at all in Shreveport, Louisiana, a city with nearly 9 percent unemployment. When a friend told Allen about the Shreveport Neighborhood Housing Services' Urban Homesteading Program, she became one of eleven people to eventually purchase a repossessed HUD home. The result: a home of her own—rehabbed with new carpeting, a new roof, and central air and heat—and a payment almost $100 less than what she had been paying for rent.

Or the story of Ever B. Williams, who lived in an apartment building for 40 years and suffered through its continuing deterioration. Renewal came via the Beloit, Wisconsin, NHS's rental rehab program, which enabled the owner of the building to replace drywall, windows and carpeting and install new furnaces and appliances.

Or the story of Robert and Kathy Stevens (not their real names) who were saved from having to put their child into foster care when they were rescued from homelessness by the Boise, Idaho, NHS. Homeward Bound, the NHS's model program, provided the Stevenses with housing and social services like child care and job training until they could find permanent housing.

Having an impact in individual communities so that local people can help local families is the goal of Neighborhood Reinvestment. We are proud to have

been able to replicate a model that is as strong and adaptable as the resident private sector-public sector model has proven to be.

ENDNOTE

[1] "NeighborWorks" is a service mark for the neighborhood revitalization services and educational programs offered by Neighborhood Reinvestment, its sister organization Neighborhood Housing Services of America (NHSA), and a national network of public-private partnerships, including Neighborhood Housing Services (NHSs), Apartment Improvement Programs (AIPs) and Mutual Housing Associations. Neighborhood Housing Services of America (NHSA) is a private, nonprofit, tax-exempt corporation that administers a secondary market for local NeighborWorks organization revolving loan funds. An NHS is an independent, nonprofit organization directed by a resident-led partnership with local business and government leaders and dedicated to the revitalization of a specific, declining neighborhood. An AIP joins city officials, financial institutions, property owners, tenants and neighborhood organizations in a partnership to upgrade multifamily buildings without displacing current residents. A Mutual Housing Association offers its residents life occupancy and a quality home at an affordable cost.

Chapter 20

The Enterprise Foundation: How a National Intermediary Assists Nonprofit Community Development

Rick Cohen
Vice President
The Enterprise Foundation

INTRODUCTION

In the wake of federal funding cutbacks in the early 1980s, private foundations, religious organizations, and other charitable groups dramatically increased their assistance and support to nonprofit developers of low-income housing. A particularly significant initiative in response to the federal withdrawal has been the creation of nonprofit intermediary organizations which "stand between local nonprofits and other players in the development process such as lenders, investors, etc."[1] Addressing the disappearance of most HUD resources for low-income housing at the neighborhood level, "intermediary organizations . . . have sought to fill some of the gaps left by federal neglect."[2]

The range of intermediary interests and emphases is broad. For example, the Institute for Community Economics works with local community land trusts (CLTs) and community loan funds (CLFs). In rural areas, the National Rural Development and Finance Corporation deals with a variety of development projects. In urban areas, emphasizing affordable housing is The Community Builders (TCB), the national successor to Greater Boston Community Development (GBCD). A quasi-governmental national intermediary, the National Reinvestment Corporation (NRC) works primarily with local Neighborhood Housing Services (NHS) groups to foster neighborhood redevelopment through attracting private capital and governmental funding to support the housing rehabilitation efforts of homeowners and small investors (for rentals) in moderate-income neighborhoods. Emphasizing the linkage of jobs, housing, and services by partnerships of hospitals, universities, and community-based developers is the Structured Employment/Economic Development Corporation (SEEDCO). In addition to distinctions by function, intermediaries operate in disparate geographic terrains, some national, others regional, statewide, or citywide (for example, the Wisconsin Housing Partnership, the Boston Housing Partnership, California's SAMCO).

The two best-known national intermediaries dedicated largely to affordable housing are the Enterprise Foundation and the Local Initiatives Support Corporation (LISC), termed by one observer as "creatures of the Reagan era,"[3] established in 1982 and 1980, respectively. The recency of the phenomenon of intermediaries makes them relatively unknown, enigmatic, and occasionally controversial to many observers. In comparison to this nation's grossly deficient commitment to community-based housing development, the major intermediaries have amassed what appear to be substantial low-income housing resources and have assisted the development of tens of thousands of affordable dwelling units.

Despite the productive track records, intermediaries provoke lively discussion among community-based development organizations, governmental agencies, and foundations. During the past two years, the National Congress for Community Economic Development (NCCED), itself an intermediary of sorts between community-based organizations and the national housing intermediaries, has raised manifold issues about the roles and relationships of intermediaries and community-based nonprofit development corporations:[4]

- How intermediaries increase the availability of capital for community-based nonprofits

- Whether intermediaries place unrealistic expectations on the productive capacities of local nonprofits

- How intermediaries' accountability is defined and measured

- How intermediaries (and their funders) can serve groups and areas that see themselves as underserved

- How intermediaries make decisions about programs and projects

- What are the appropriate means of building the development capacity of community-based nonprofit developers

Given the multiplicity of intermediaries, not merely by function but by geographic area, these questions defy simple answers. The beliefs, values, history, and functions of the Enterprise Foundation underscore the complexity of the advent of community development intermediaries. By examining the history, programs, and impacts of the Enterprise Foundation, this article addresses how intermediaries operate and what types of communities and organizations are served by intermediaries.

CONCEIVING ENTERPRISE

The Enterprise Foundation's goal is straightforward: to provide decent and affordable housing for the poor of this country and to assist people out of the cycle of poverty. Enterprise is the outgrowth of the lifetime commitment of

Jim and Patty Rouse to affordable housing for the poor. Among the nation's
leading real estate developers, the Rouses
had long been committed to the support
of Jubilee Housing, a church-based nonprofit in Washington's Adams-Morgan
neighborhood. In 1982, at Jim Rouse's
invitation, community activists from
Washington, Baltimore, Denver, Pittsburgh, Oakland, and Lynchburg met at
Washington's Church of the Saviour to
chart a mission for the Enterprise
Foundation:

- Financial assistance for nonprofit housing developers, including seed money,
  revolving loan funds, etc.

- Technical assistance and training for
  nonprofits to reduce the capital costs
  of rehabilitation and new construction

- Mechanisms for nonprofit developers
  to exchange information and share experiences about their low-income
  housing development activities

- The design of an evaluation model to
  assess the productivity and accomplishments of nonprofit developers

- The articulation and strengthening of a
  vision to make all housing fit and
  affordable for low-income persons.

Galvanizing the participants in
Enterprise's initial working group was
the example of Jubilee, which between
1973 and 1979 acquired six buildings
and rehabilitated 213 dwelling units, assisted by a "private-sector support group
. . . to provide technical assistance and
advice" as well as "grants, low-interest
loans, and in-kind services"[5] organized
by Rouse. The "Jubilee Model," combining grass-roots activism, private sector involvement, and public subsidies, con-
stitutes the essence of Enterprise's origi-

nal identity. Other "Jubilees," from Baltimore to Oakland, were formed to replicate the model in Washington.

In practice, the Enterprise model,
beginning with Washington's Jubilee
Housing and over the years continuing in
new and diverse forms such as
Chattanooga Neighborhood Enterprise,
Philadelphia Neighborhood Enterprise,
Enterprise New York, and others,
illustrates the concept of public-private
partnerships. The term's overuse and
abuse have robbed it of most meaning,
but it accurately characterizes successful,
persevering community-based low-income developers.

Intermediaries are themselves partnerships, albeit not community-based. Like
Enterprise, most obtain geographic funds
from foundations, corporations, and
philanthropically minded inddividuals.
They raise loans and grants for nonprofit
housing developers, including equity
capital invested through federal Low Income Housing Tax Credits. They lobby
at all governmental levels to secure the
deep public subsidies necessary to make
housing truly affordable to very-low-income households. At the local level,
partnerships are vital instruments to spur
nonprofit development.

In many cities, Enterprise creates locally controlled public-private partnerships
which seed and sustain nonprofit affordable-housing growth. Where the Jubilee
model worked through one nonprofit
concentrating on a specific neighborhood
such as Adams-Morgan, the recent
generation of Enterprise city programs assists dozens of nonprofits in each program site through citywide nonprofit
partnerships. Enterprise's New York City
program supports more than 30 nonprofit housing developers with a combination of corporate equity raised from

tax-credit syndications and public funding from city and state sources. By the end of 1990, 1,537 units had been developed in the first four years of Enterprise New York, with another 600 contemplated in 1991. In other Enterprise citywide program locations such as Cleveland, York, Philadelphia, and Miami, Enterprise staff have packaged tax credits, predevelopment financing, training and technical assistance, and public policy advocacy to build nonprofit development capacity and bring development projects to fruition. Enterprise-assisted production through Enterprise city programs and Enterprise Network organizations topped 16,000 low-income dwelling units early in 1991.

THE ENTERPRISE PROGRAM

From its roots with Jubilee, Enterprise has responded to the call of dozens of cities requesting Enterprise's assistance. The legitimacy of an outside intermediary organization in any locality is critical. While Enterprise can and does assist individual organizations, it cannot attempt to create broad-based, citywide partnerships in the absence of convincing, authentic local interest and sponsors. It takes all sectors—local and state government, foundations, corporations, religious institutions, banks and S&Ls, corporations, private builders, and especially the community-based nonprofit sector—to produce low-income housing.

Enterprise's city programs do not merely assist nonprofits to build housing. To create long-term nonprofit development capacity, the system for producing housing needs to be reconsidered and redesigned. Fundamentally, working in partnership with the nonprofit, public, and private sectors, Enterprise's city programs change the "way cities do business" to get low-income housing done. That task definitely requires partnership efforts.

In response to requests for assistance, Enterprise initiates assessments of low-income housing needs, conditions, production, resources, and public-private partnership opportunities, followed by cooperative ventures with municipal governments, local foundations, and community-based nonprofits to fashion workable public-private partnerships devoted to low-income housing. The assessments ensure that Enterprise responds to local needs and fits its resources and problems to the uniqueness of each community. An unfortunate tendency on the part of national organizations, if they permit themselves to be too removed from local perspectives, is to homogenize the potential constituents for and consumers of their programs, ending up with inflexible national program models. By closely assessing the low-income housing and development capacity needs of each locality, Enterprise ensures that its program repertoire is tailored to the city rather than forcing the city to fit a generic program model.

Enterprise's assistance in cities involves:

- Facilitating the preparation of *strategic plans* for redesigning and redirecting the programs and resources available for low-income housing production

- Providing *on-site capacity building assistance* for nonprofit staff, public-private partnership board and staff, and municipal officials

- Offering *regional and national training programs* for partnership participants in housing finance, housing construction, loan processing, housing counseling, and low-income nonprofit development

- Delivering *on-site technical and financial packaging assistance* to low-income housing developments emerging from the community-based nonprofits and public-private partnerships supported by Enterprise staff

- Using *equity and bridge loans* through state, local, and national equity funds managed by the Enterprise Social Investment Corporation (ESIC) and

capitalized by corporate partners including Fannie Mae and Freddie Mac

Depending on the specific needs of each community, Enterprise program staff assemble the expertise and models that are responsive and appropriate to community needs. Enterprise has field-tested its working models throughout the U.S. during nine years of concentrated technical assistance and financing. (See Table 20.1.)

Some of these program models are

Table 20.1   Enterprise Foundation Program Models

Rehab Work Group	Technical expertise in cost-cutting through innovative rehab techniques, substitute materials, selective rehab, use of modular or manufactured housing
City Homes	Bulk purchasing and management of privately owned rental properties, maintained as low- rent apartments through nonprofit management, selective rehab, and tenant mobilization and participation, currently operating in Baltimore and Dallas and planned for Greensboro, NC
Lender consortia	Joining private lenders to pool resources and perform joint underwriting and lending for affordable rehab and new construction financing
Public-private partnerships	Multisector, citywide organizations created to assist nonprofit low-income housing developers by generating public and private sector funding commitments, packaging financial resources, and training potential developers
Neighborhood Transformation	Metamorphosis of specific neighborhoods through comprehensive restructuring and redirection of physical, social, and organizational resources devoted to neighborhood revitalization
Equity syndication	Use of federal Low Income Housing Tax Credits, with investors assembled by the Enterprise Social Investment Corporation, a wholly owned subsidiary of the Enterprise Foundation, to subsidize low-income rental housing

Table continues

Table 20.1   Continued

Bridge financing	Short-term loans for nonprofit sponsors of tax-credit projects, repaid by syndication proceeds, and loans made during the lease period of single-family lease-purchase programs
Predevelopment financing	Use of program-related investments (PRIs) and other resources to provide short-term financial assistance to nonprofit housing developers for predevelopment costs such as architectural and engineering, property acquisition, other up-front development costs
Supportive Housing Management Services	Model effort to integrate human services and residential property management, targeted to special needs and other vulnerable population groups
Benevolent loan funds	Resources loaned by individuals and private corporations to nonprofit loan funds to be reloaned to low-income housing developers at terms significantly below conventional financing
Housing production training	Instruction for staff of community-based nonprofit organizations and public sector agencies to expedite the process of rehabilitating or constructing low-income housing, including automating the function of writing construction specs
Strategic planning for low-income housing	Assisting public-private partnerships, cities, and states with redesigning and restructuring resources to expand low-income housing production
Model low-income production programs	Providing nonprofits and communities with implementable models for low-income production, including single-family rehab and new construction, multifamily rehab, special needs housing (including SROs), acquisition and rehabilitation of HUD and RTC properties, intervention and acquisition of HUD-subsidized properties facing prepayment/opt-out situations; also advising cities on financing resources for low-income housing, including dedicated local revenue sources for housing, such as general obligation bonds, real estate transfer fees, and housing linkage programs
Acquisition of distressed properties	Cornerstone Housing, Inc., a supporting nonprofit of Enterprise, to acquire Resolution Trust Corporation (RTC) multifamily stock to increase opportunities for affordable housing

strongly associated with the Enterprise Foundation and reflect the fulfillment of one of the original missions spawned at the initial Enterprise Network meeting at the Church of the Saviour—to reduce the capital costs of rehab and new construction. The City Homes model, piloted in Baltimore and replicated in Dallas, is distinctive. It is a nonprofit group that acquires deteriorated rental housing in bulk, repairs it to frugal standards, and maintains it as decent rental housing. The City Homes rehabilitation makes the units "clean, safe, durable, painted and comfortable," yet through selective instead of gut rehab has succeeded in Baltimore at keeping total acquisition, rehab, and soft costs at an average of $22,500 per unit, approximately $40,000 less than the cost of substantial rehab.[6]

In fact, Enterprise's Rehab Work Group (RWG) has taken the lead in devising many innovations in reducing the cost of low-income housing. Launched in 1983, RWG started with a national competition to solicit cost-cutting ideas, documented the most workable techniques in widely distributed manuals[7], and has been recognized by the Ford Foundation for achieving cost savings of 37 to 50 percent in specific projects in Cleveland, Chattanooga, and Philadelphia.[8]

The concept of selective rehabilitation is not without controversy. Perceived in some communities as an excessive lowering of rehabilitation standards, the modest rehab of a City Homes-type program does not lend itself to the kind of ribbon-cutting publicity associated with large, substantial rehabilitation projects. But the low per-unit subsidies of selective rehab enable nonprofits to take on many more units and maintain them in

the affordable inventory. In Baltimore, after two-and-one-half years of operation, City Homes had acquired and rehabilitated more than 170 rental rowhouses, maintained at rents averaging $250 a month plus utilities.[9] The techniques of selective rehab, bulk buying of rental properties, and nonprofit management, blended in the City Homes model, help retain low-cost rentals that are otherwise being removed from the affordable inventory due to housing disinvestment, abandonment, and upward filtration.[10]

On-Site Enterprise Program Operations

Enterprise programs vary from city to city. As of 1991, Enterprise maintains a full-time on-site staff presence in eight locations assisting community-based nonprofit housing developers with identifying, securing, and packaging resources for low-income housing development. In addition, program staff assist some of the cities with the *development of strategic plans* (including the preparation of CHAS documents and facilitating local CHAS processes) for low-income housing (e.g., Dallas, Chattanooga) and *create new citywide institutional actors* for elevating low-income housing development (e.g., a lenders consortium in Dallas, equity funds in New York City, benevolent loan funds in Baltimore):

- Dallas: The Dallas Affordable Housing Partnership announced its formal beginning in 1991. Organized by Enterprise, the lender consortium, with total commitments of $57 million, includes eleven banks and S&Ls, plus Exxon, Fannie Mae, the City of Dallas, and Enterprise. Fannie Mae has agreed to purchase all of the Partnership's single-family loans. In addition, Enterprise was awarded $250,000 from the Federal Home Loan Bank for subsidized single-family loans to low-income buyers.

- Philadelphia: Philadelphia Neighborhood Enterprise (PNE) acquires, rehabs, and sells FHA and other houses to low-income families and provides technical assistance to numerous community-based nonprofit housing development organizations. PNE assists the Philadelphia Housing Authority with the implementation of its homeownership program and received Affordable Housing Program funds from the Office of Thrift Supervision for use as 7 percent, 30-year loans.

- York: Enterprise works with the Housing Initiatives Program of the United Way of York County to produce housing in partnership with neighborhood groups, businesses, private lenders, and the local government.

NCDI PROGRAM LOCATIONs

Seven national foundations plus Prudential Life Insurance and Freddie Mac have created a $67.5 million pool of funds for a number of communities served by LISC and the Enterprise Foundation. The effort is called the National Community Development Initiative (NCDI). In nine cities, Enterprise is devoting grant and loan funds totalling approximately $1,300,000 to $1,500,000 per city over a three-year period to build community-based nonprofit capacity and raise low-income housing production to significantly higher levels through the linkage of nonprofit developers to neighborhood or city-wide public-private "umbrella partner-

ships." These NCDI cities reflect a mix of longstanding Enterprise program sites and new expansion communities, in an effort to extend Enterprise technical and financial assistance outside the locations routinely served by national intermediaries. Examples include:

- Washington: An established Enterprise location, but a major new initiative through Jubilee Enterprise of Greater Washington for acquiring, rehabilitating, managing, and preserving as low-income rental housing HUD-subsidized multifamily properties facing prepayments of opt-outs or troubled properties already taken into the HUD inventory;

- Atlanta: A new Enterprise program location, working with the recently created Atlanta Neighborhood Development Partnership to build capacity among Atlanta nonprofits to create affordable housing;

- Baltimore: Through NCDI, supporting the first of three "neighborhood transformation" demonstration projects nationwide: in Baltimore's Sandtown/Winchester neighborhood, Enterprise has initiated work in partnership with neighborhood leaders to address all public and private support systems—including housing, education, human services, health care, employment, public safety, and recreation—to empower neighborhood residents to achieve their highest capabilities and well-being;

- New York City: Helping community-based organizations to create community life centers to provide child development and other human services to low-income residents of non-profit-sponsored housing development;

- Cleveland: Providing housing development incentives through Neighborhood Progress Inc. to spur housing production by 18 community-based nonprofit housing developers;

- Columbus: Launching three new nonprofit community-based housing developers capable of acquiring, developing, and managing low-income housing.

Strategic Programming Assistance

In 35 cities, Enterprise provides program assistance, ranging from strategic planning and nonprofit/partnership training to financial packaging, tax credit equity, and predevelopment loans. This effort is supported by a cooperative agreement with the U.S. Department of Housing and Urban Development. Additional similar program sites are supported by Fannie Mae in St. Louis, Springfield, Memphis, and elsewhere by funds provided by municipal governments and other local funders. Both the HUD and Fannie Mae programs reflect conscious strategies to link public and private sector institutions to create more low-income housing production capacity. Examples include:

- Fort Worth/Tarrant Co.: Enterprise is facilitating the formation of a housing partnership of public sector governmental agencies, corporate leaders, bankers, and philanthropic organizations, in response to an initiative convened by the United Way;

- Jackson: Enterprise is facilitating this Mississippi city's CHAS process, providing technical advice and helping moderate meetings of CHAS participants;

- Greensboro: Enterprise has guided Greensboro in the formation of the Greensboro Community Homes Program, a multibank lending consortium, tied to both an agreement with Freddie Mac to purchase the consortium's loans and a relationship with Triad Minority Development for a citywide housing counseling program.

Enterprise Network Program

Enterprise maintains close working relationships with more than 100 community-based and citywide nonprofit housing development organizations, providing direct assistance ranging from technical assistance to predevelopment financing to Enterprise Network groups. Production is the byword of the Network, and for calendar year 1991, Enterprise Network groups had outstanding commitments for 1,022 units, 886 units under construction, and 1,417 placed in service. From 1982 through May 1991, Network groups were responsible for the production of 9,653 low-income units, 60 percent of Enterprise's total production of 16,068, the remainder being tax-credit syndication deals and other projects through the Enterprise Social Investment Corporation. The Network is more than a gathering of housing producers. Network members constitute a national movement of low-income housing advocates, prepared to mobilize and advocate at local, state, and federal levels for the retention and expansion of housing programs for poverty-stricken families.

Enterprise Social Investment Corporation

The Enterprise Social Investment Corporation (ESIC), Enterprise's wholly owned subsidiary, has three national equity fund initiatives (Enterprise Housing Partners, Housing Outreach Fund, and Corporate Housing Initiatives) and several local and state equity funds that provide equity assistance to community-based low-income developers. Depending on investor conditions on its equity funds, ESIC considers syndication of projects proposed by Network organizations, by community-based organizations in Enterprise program locations, and by other nonprofit organizations in areas targeted by ESIC investors. The unusual aspects of ESIC's funds encompass the small-project emphasis of the Housing Outreach Fund and the dedication to homeless and special-needs housing in Corporate Housing Initiatives. Since the initiation of the federal Low Income Housing Tax Credits in 1986, ESIC has raised more than $205 million in equity, invested in 124 projects yielding 7,186 low-income units.

In addition to structuring syndications and creating and managing equity funds, ESIC develops low-income housing through its subsidiary, the Enterprise Construction Company (ECC). With more than 400 units already completed in Howard County and Baltimore, ECC is working on the financing and construction of another 790 units in Baltimore, Prince Georges County, and Montgomery County. All of ECC's projects to date have been in Maryland. Two of the ECC projects are federally

assisted Nehemiah projects, including the nation's largest single Nehemiah grant.

WHOM DOES ENTERPRISE SERVE?

The difficulty some observers have with intermediary organizations such as Enterprise is the comparison with governmental funders. With government, particularly since the advent of the Community Development Block Grant (CDBG) program in 1974, and repeated in the structure of the HOME program in the National Affordable Housing Act of 1990 (see Chapter 18), governmental moneys for low-income housing and community revitalization are frequently distributed by formula. With the "privatization" of low-income housing development since the Reagan administration, decision making on the distribution of scarce housing dollars depends in some measure on the priorities of philanthropic funders, corporate investors in tax credits, and the intermediaries themselves.

In many communities around the U.S., low-income housing problems are burgeoning, and few cities are equipped to handle the onslaught. The availability of the technical and financial resources of an entity like Enterprise has tremendous import for mid-sized communities, such as Chattanooga, York, and Portland, Oregon, as well as cities of the Southeast and Southwest, many of which are relative newcomers to the challenges of community-based low-income housing development, such as Atlanta, Dallas, Jackson, and San Antonio. While trying to guard against overtaxing its limited staff and financial resources, Enterprise has consciously reached out and responded to cities and regions normally underserved by national community development intermediaries, maintaining various levels of programs and assistance in 32 states.

A more fundamental issue of reaching out to underserved areas is the identification of an intermediary's customers. Enterprise draws a wide definition of the kinds of organizations and ventures that could qualify as community-based nonprofit housing developers. Rather than pigeonholing organizations into a narrowly delineated definition of community development corporations, Enterprise is committed to working with housing efforts that start at the neighborhood level and are directed by and responsible to neighborhood residents. Within those parameters, several types of low-income developers become eligible for Enterprise technical and financial assistance:

- Traditional *community development corporations* (CDCs) which are community-based nonprofit housing producers;

- Social service providers, many of which have grown from operating emergency or transitional housing to building and managing transitional and permanent housing facilities;

- Housing services organizations, which offer counseling, loan packaging, and construction services in addition to developing owner-occupied and rental housing;

- Religious organizations, including groups founded by or associated with specific religious denominations as well as others such as Habitat for Humanity;

- Tenant organizations, including *tenant cooperatives*, which rehabilitate, own,

and manage apartment buildings to ensure long-term affordability and security for the residents;

- Land trusts, *community loan funds* (CLFs), and *housing partnerships*, which often take on housing development roles in addition to assembling moneys for construction and permanent financing, usually functioning on behalf of or in conjunction with local organizations;

- *Settlement houses and other special-needs housing providers* which focus on housing development benefiting population groups such as persons with physical or developmental disabilities;

- *Mutual housing associations* (MHAs) and other untraditional housing developers, implementing innovative nonprofit development schemes to produce housing for low-income neighborhoods.

With this nation's astounding and increasing affordable-housing need, Enterprise does not see a need to place nonprofit developers into a particular mold. The key is that the housing is truly affordable to very-low-income households and that the affordability is protected through deed restrictions and other affordability controls.

An example of such flexibility is Enterprise's work with the Columbus Housing Partnership in Ohio. In the Hilltop neighborhood of Columbus, CHP has worked with Catholic Social Services to rehabilitate 62 single-family homes and duplexes. Throughout the city, CHP acquires and rehabilitates houses for homeless families associated with the Phoenix Alliance, a multichurch effort which provides the families with job training, parenting, day care, and other assistance. While engaging in acquisition and rehabilitation efforts with neighborhood and church groups, CHP is also spawning traditional CDCs such as the Homes on the Hill Community Development Corporation, the Northside Community Development Corporation, and the Eastside Christian Community Development Corporation. In 1990 alone, working with these disparate models of community-based development, CHP began development of 428 housing units, including homes for first-time home buyers as well as rental housing.

As Enterprise generates loans and equity for nonprofit development projects, it also seeks to strengthen the entire low-income housing delivery system. Enterprise has taken a prominent role in public policy advocacy at all levels of government. At the federal level, Jim Rouse co-chaired the National Housing Task Force in 1987 that was the basis for the National Affordable Housing Act in 1990.

Continuing Enterprise federal public policy initiatives to strengthen the nonprofit low-income development process target:

- Appropriations for the HOME program (flexible, targeted federal financing to states and localities), giving nonprofits a preferential role (a 15 percent set-aside) in the National Affordable Housing Act;

- Permanent extension of the Low Income Housing Tax Credit, through which a minimum of 10 percent of the nation's $3 billion tax-credit allocation is set aside for nonprofits, with actual 1990 nonprofit usage in excess of 15 percent;

- Protecting and strengthening the Community Reinvestment Act (CRA) of 1977, which community groups have used to secure more than $7.5 billion in commitments from banks and S&Ls for investment in targeted low-income communities;

- Appropriations and realistic standards for the abatement of lead-based-paint hazards, one of the greatest challenges facing nonprofit developers of older housing in inner-city neighborhoods.

Like the advocacy work at the federal level, at state and local levels Enterprise staff work in partnership with community organizations and governmental officials to devise and lobby for new systems for the production of low-income housing.[11]

CONCLUSION

Community development intermediaries are an integral part of the nonprofit affordable-housing terrain. According to NCCED, they provide assistance to community-based nonprofit developers including: "new and increased sources of capital for projects, programs, and operating expenses; a means to coordinate resources and groups; information exchange and networking; organizational and skills training; advanced technical assistance; brokering and financial packaging for large, complex developments; program and policy advocacy; greater credibility and visibility; (and) access to centers of influence, both public and private.[12]

Organizations like Enterprise also add value beyond funding: a national network of nonprofits committed and mobilized to advocate for low-income development; innovative housing program models that can be adapted to specific community needs; and technical training and support by a field team of TA providers to build nonprofit capacity and package low-income housing developments.

Enterprise combines aspects of three kinds of intermediary functions—*financial brokering* for projects through assembling and leveraging funds from a variety of sources including lenders and investors; *technical assistance* through an in-depth program repertoire of capacity-building training programs; and *information sharing and networking* through a diverse group of members and affiliates cooperating on development, public policy advocacy, and program modelling. Like other intermediaries, Enterprise represents a new way of doing business to help community-based nonprofit developers achieve new levels of low-income housing production.

ENDNOTES

1 Phillip L. Clay, *Mainstreaming the Community Builders: The Challenge of Expanding the Capacity of Nonprofit Housing Development Organizations* (Cambridge, MA: Massachusetts Institute of Technology, 1990), fn. p. 98.

2 David C. Schwartz, Richard C. Ferlauto, and Daniel N. Hoffman, *A New Housing Policy for America: Recapturing the American Dream* (Philadelphia: Temple University Press, 1988), p. 172.

3 Doug Turetsky, "The Go-Betweens," *City Limits* (June/July 1991), p. 8.

4 National Congress for Community Economic Development, "Working Paper on Community Development Intermediaries" (Draft report prepared for the Intermediary Task Force Meeting, April 25, 1991, at the NCCED Annual Meeting in Milwaukee, Wisconsin).

5 Rachel G. Bratt, *Rebuilding a Low-Income Housing Policy* (Philadelphia: Temple University Press, 1989), p. 333.

6 Peter Werwath and Nadine Post, "City Homes: Unique Rehab Effort Stems Loss of Marginal Rental Housing," *Lessons of Enterprise* (Columbia, MD: No. 2, 1990), p. 2.

7 Robert M. Santucci, Brooke C. Stoddard, and Peter Werwath, *A Consumer's Guide to Home Improvement, Renovation & Repair*; Robert M. Santucci, Jon Thomas, Cecilia Cassidy, and Peter Werwath, *The Cost Cuts Manual: Nailing Down Saving for Least-Cost Housing*; and the three-volume housing production manuals edited by Robert M. Santucci, Peter Werwath, and Cecilia Cassidy, *Multifamily Selective Rehabilitation, Single Family Selective Rehabilitation,* and *Substantial Rehabilitation/New Construction.*

8 The Ford Foundation, *Affordable Housing: The Years Ahead* (New York: August 1989), p. 17.

9 Werwath and Post, p. 2.

10 William C. Apgar, "Preservation of Existing Housing: A Key Element in a Revitalized National Housing Policy," *Housing Policy Debate* (Vol. 2, No. 2, 1991, pp. 207-208); calling for a mix of demand- and supply-side approaches to preserving low-cost rental housing, Apgar concludes: "In other

instances, modest rehabilitation efforts targeted to private landlords make sense. In some areas, a cost-effective approach may be to underwrite the transfer of existing units at risk of loss from private owners to community-based groups interested in

and capable of preserving low-cost housing."

[11] Cf. Rick Cohen, "Actions Cities and States Can Take to Support Low-Income Housing," in *Cost Cuts* (Vol. 8, No. 3, May/June, 1991), pp. 6-7.

[12] NCCED, *op. cit.*, p. 1.

Chapter 21

Louisville, Kentucky: The Housing Partnership, Inc.

F. Lynn Luallen
President
The Housing Partnerships, Inc.

Housing Partnerships are beginning to make their mark on housing in the United States. There are several organizations, such as those in Boston, Chicago, and Cleveland which have been around for a long time. But there are many, including our own in Louisville, Kentucky, which have had their genesis only in the past five to ten years.

In Louisville, Mayor Jerry Abramson appointed a task force of civic leaders to study housing and give him proposals that would lead to more production of housing and increased opportunity for low- and moderate-income individuals and families. The task force recommended the creation of the Louisville Housing Development Corporation (LHDC), which began working in November 1988 with housing developers, the city Department of Housing and Urban Development, and not-for-profits as well as advocates to produce multifamily housing using low-income housing tax credits and low-interest local bank loans. LHDC served as program initiator and program administrator for the City of Louisville Single-Family Homeownership program targeted to first-time home buyers. Following a year-and-one-half study effort, coupled with the existence of LHDC and Mayor Abramson's and County Judge/Executive David Armstrong's commitment, The Housing Partnership, Inc., was formed from the old LHDC.

The Housing Partnership, Inc., is an inclusive, community-wide organizations with nearly 200 members representing corporations, not-for-profits and individuals. Four standing membership committees—finance, support services, government funding, and housing providers—have been formed and have established mission statements and goals and objectives. The Partnership is chaired by Michael N. Harreld, president of Citizens Fidelity Bank and Trust Company. I have been asked to serve as its first president and we presently have a staff of seven full-time employees.

It is our public purpose to provide housing opportunities to:

• The first-time home buyer with problems of affordability;

• The low-income elderly, many of whom must choose to "heat or eat";

• Low-income female-headed households and the resulting number of children living in poverty and substandard housing;

• The homeless, including the growing numbers of homeless families and homeless working poor;

• The one in eight children under 12 who live in poverty and do not have enough to eat.

Additionally, our purpose is to plan for:

• The preservation of our existing low-income housing inventory in light of the limited tax credit and the reduction in Community Development Block Grant and Urban Development Action Grant programs;

• The potential loss of hundreds of thousands of low-income units when their Section 8 contracts start expiring over the next decade.

We work closely with the investment community and look for new financing tools. We work with the home builders, realtors, mortgage bankers, savings and loans, commercial banks, developers, nonprofit entities, and coalitions.

We have many partners. As a community we are gifted because of these partnerships. City and county governments, state housing officials, advocates, providers, support groups, and individuals work to meet our collective housing goals.

The following is the Program of Work adopted by The Housing Partnership Board in April of 1991 for our next fiscal year. It will give the reader insight into the thinking and inner working of housing partnerships.

THE HOUSING PARTNERSHIP, INC.

PROGRAM OF WORK

APRIL-JUNE, 1991

FISCAL YEAR 1991-92

Program of Work

I. Specific program initiatives which are continuations from the Louisville Housing Development Corporation program of work expanded to meet growth in geographic area of responsibility of The Housing Partnership, Inc., and including Kentucky Housing Corporation (KHC) initiatives toward long-range joint ventures.

A. Single-Family Mortgage Loan Program

Purpose

Create new monies for the financing of new construction and existing housing in the service area of The Housing Partnership, Inc., for those whose incomes do not exceed 115 percent of area median. Target groups are first-time home buyers, single-parent heads of household, working homeless, those ready to leave public housing, to name a few.

1. *Targeted Homeownership Marketing*—KHC will allocate $5 million of its Recoveries of Principal funds to The Housing Partnership to be used in initiating a targeted marketing program in specific neighborhoods within the service area of The Housing Partnership. As consideration for undertaking this marketing effort, KHC will compensate The Partnership 50 basis points (0.5 percent) for each loan closed under this program. If the initial allocation of $5 million is fully utilized prior to June 30, 1992, an additional allocation of funds will be made. **This special allocation is in addition to funds which will be allocated to lenders for use in Jefferson County.** By June 1, 1991, the City of Louisville and Jefferson County shall designate those neighborhoods to be targeted for receiving funds under this special allocation.

2. *Construction Loan Line of Credit*—KHC will establish a construction loan line of credit of $750,000 for use by The Housing Partnership to stimulate single-family home construction in the targeted neighborhoods designated above. These funds will be available at interest rates at or below prime rate. This commitment will run through June 30, 1992, and may be extended based on actual performance levels.

Since over 45 percent of KHC mortgage revenue bond proceeds come to the present service area of The Housing Partnership, Inc., these funds would be an additional funding source for targeted areas as determined by governmental policy makers and other policy contributors.

If, after further study, there appears to be a need for additional mortgage revenue bond funds, The Partnership Board should open discussions with KHC to determine the appropriate route to take in keeping with the necessity of non-competition in the bond marketplace as well as in the lending arena.

B. Multifamily Mortgage Loan Program

Purpose

Create new monies for new construction and rehabilitation of existing multifamily properties within The Housing Partnership's service area for those whose incomes do not exceed 115 percent of area median. When the Low-Income Housing Tax Credit is used, this will not exceed 60 percent of area median for 40 percent of the units of the project.

Continue financial advisory role to not-for-profit and for-profit developers of multifamily housing utilizing the Low-Income Housing Tax Credit.

1. *Low-Income Housing Tax Credit Compliance Monitoring*—Effective January 1, 1992, KHC will have responsibility to establish a monitoring program for all projects receiving tax credit commitments since January 1, 1987. KHC proposes to contract with The Housing Partnership to accomplish this monitoring requirement in Jefferson, Oldham, Bullitt, and Shelby counties. It is expected that The Partnership will be compensated at a rate currently estimated at $12/unit/year.

2. *Multifamily Project Development*—The Partnership will work with local builders to identify potential multifamily projects which would qualify for construction and permanent financing by KHC. It is expected that The Partnership will generate revenues from the packaging of individual project proposals for financing and/or allocation of tax credits.

3. *Preservation of Existing Multifamily Housing Stock*—The Partnership, in conjunction with KHC, should initiate a long-range plan for the preservation of existing multifamily developments in Jefferson County. This plan would reflect appropriate roles for the private sector, nonprofit organizations, Jefferson County government, the City of Louisville and KHC. Development of a coordinated strategy will ensure that limited resources are applied to those developments which reflect the agreed-upon priorities of all interested parties.

C. Three specific special-needs programs which would replicate statewide efforts by KHC. These would be advanced only on a pilot basis after ascertaining need and demand.

1. Prepare requests for funding to submit to foundations for a *Training for Affordable Construction* program. This program would provide funding for not-for-profit agencies to hire unemployed persons at minimum wage plus benefits and provide training in housing construction. If a for-profit builder participates in the program, the amount funded would be 75 percent. The training would last up to 50 weeks per worker. This program has a twofold purpose: train the unemployed in a marketable skill and at the same time lower construction costs by using trainees.

2. Develop a plan of action to help elderly homeowners on fixed incomes (in income range of our objectives) to maintain their homes to provide safe, decent, sanitary housing. This would include a financial mechanism to finance needed repairs and maintenance. Under a *Grants to the Elderly for Energy Repair (GEER) Program*, owner/occupants 60 years of age or older

with an annual income of less than 50 percent of the area median income would be eligible for grants of up to $3,000 to make their homes weathertight and energy efficient. This would provide a more comfortable environment, protecting a lifelong investment and ensuring continued homeownership.

3. *Rehabilitation Loan Program*—There is a growing need to augment the existing rehabilitation loan program to allow homeowners to make improvements to their homes. U.S. HUD has expressed an interest in working with KHC and other interested organizations to structure a program which would be eligible for HUD insurance. The Housing Partnership would work with KHC in designing a proposal for presentation to HUD. It is expected that The Partnership would be able to administer such a program in the service area of The Housing Partnership, Inc., once HUD approval is obtained.

D. In early 1990 the Louisville Housing Development Corporation sponsored a seminar on the subject of Employer-Assisted Housing. We (The Housing Partnership, Inc.) have continued a steady dialogue with Mr. David Schwartz of Rutgers University and the American Affordable Housing Institute. Several local companies and organizations have also been in touch with Mr. Schwartz and are pursuing some possible program initiatives.

The following is a partial list of potential employer-assisted housing providers:

City and County Government
National Corporate
Regional Corporate
Law Firms
Hospitals
Financial Institutions

Frankly, anyone who has a payroll to make can have an employer-assisted housing program. These programs take many forms; some are cash-intensive, many are not. Here are some examples:

1. Group mortgage origination discount plans;

2. Mortgage interest-rate buydown plans;

3. Down payment loan plans;

4. Mortgage guarantee and insurance plans;

5. Housing sites;

6. Construction financing assistance.

The role The Housing Partnership should play is to educate potential sponsors of an employer-assisted housing program and aid them in setting up whichever plan they are comfortable with for their employees once they determine the desirability to offer such a plan to their employees.

II. Public Information and Education Programs and Initiatives

A. General Activities

1. In concert with Metropolitan Housing Coalition, develop an education program for general public of housing needs, existing programs, housing providers, and support service activities within the service area of The Housing Partnership, Inc.

2. In concert with the local school system (both high school and university level), develop an education program of testing and counseling which will lead to job placement for certain target groups, i.e., single-parent heads of household. Initially this would be targeted to those projects where The Housing Partnership, Inc., acted as financial advisor.

3. Aid, support, and interact with the Enterprise Foundation housing needs analysis and strategic plan for Louisville and Jefferson County. This effort will extend over a two-year period.

B. Specific activities which have been approved by the Board of Directors on March 25, 1991.

1. In concert with Channel 15-WKPC public television, develop a series of videotape presentations for lenders and first-time home buyers. These tapes will be used in school systems within the service area of The Housing Partnership, Inc., as well as being made available to housing providers, support groups, and distributed nationally.

2. Develop and fund a housing information system bringing together seekers with housing providers. Request for proposal to be completed April 30, 1991, for submission to a foundation for funding start-up; purchase of computers and phone system; accessing housing provider information and placing in computer system; preparing housing seeker profile questionnaire; training staff operators.

III. Governmental and Non-Governmental Housing Organizations and The Housing Partnership Relations

A. One of the most significant activities of The Housing Partnership from its previous life as Louisville Housing Development Corporation to the present has been the goodwill and cooperative relationship with the federal, state and local government housing entities. These cooperative efforts have added to our program of work as well as aided them in the production of affordable housing to meet their program goals and objectives.

These entities are, to name a few, the City of Louisville HUD office, Louisville Housing Authority, Jefferson County Housing Authority, U.S. HUD District office, office of the Mayor, office of the County Judge/Executive, Kentucky Housing Corporation.

B. Some of the non-governmental housing entities which we interface with are: Metropolitan Housing Coalition, Neighborhood Housing Services, Neighborhood

Development Corporation, Urban League, New Directions Housing Corporation, Habitat for Humanity, Coalition for the Homeless, Volunteers of America.

C. Expand the service area of The Housing Partnership, Inc., beyond Jefferson County to include Kentucky counties of Oldham, Shelby, and Bullitt and Indiana counties of Floyd, Clark, and Harrison.

Fundraising

The following is a description of the types of funds necessary for this community to develop an appropriate response to the needs of housing seekers for affordable housing and the needs of builders-developers, both for-profit and not-for-profit, to be able to participate as providers of safe, decent, sanitary, affordable shelter. From a historical perspective, every task force, every not-for-profit (including LHDC) and every housing needs analysis for the past 15 years has indicated funding shortfalls, particularly since 1980 when the federal government began its retreat from funding housing.

The funds discussed here are in addition to what presently is available through state and local government funding as well as the continually dwindling federal commitment. These funds are also in addition to what is presently being achieved through the local financial institutions' Community Reinvestment Act activities.

I. Develop and fund three funds from local financial, corporate, and government members:

Mortgage Pool (single-family and multifamily)—A pool of conventional-loan funds will be developed in which financial institutions participate to develop affordable interest rates for both rental units and homeownership. The Housing Partnership, Inc., will assist financial institutions in implementing such programs.

Equity Fund—A pool of funds from those corporations and financial institutions desiring direct participation in housing projects. Low-Income Housing Tax Credits will be the primary incentive for participation in the fund, which is aimed at the rental-housing market.

Housing Assistance Fund—A pool consisting of contributions, gifts, and outright grants from foundations, individuals, and trusts. This fund will provide gap financing, bridge loans, and guaranteed down payments but will not be limited to those areas, thus giving The Housing Partnership, Inc., a unique capability to creatively address the housing funding problem.

1991 Goals & Objectives
Single-Family Mortgage Pool
$40,000,000
Multifamily Mortgage Pool
$15,000,000
Equity Fund $7.5-$10 million
Housing Assistance Fund
$1,000,000
–Suggested set-aside for not-
for-profits: 20% of all funds

II. There are two most important fund activities which have equal weight to I. (above). These two funds relate primarily to The Housing Partnership, Inc., and our not-for-profit community. While I. is related to financing the much-needed housing, II. is the delivery system by which to produce the housing.

A. Develop fundraising activities not exclusive to financial institutions and government entities (as is now) to fund administration of The Housing Partnership, Inc. These funds would be supplemented by Housing Partnership activities, i.e., program administrator for mortgage revenue bond programs, compliance administrator for Low-Income Housing Tax Credit program, financial advising to not-for-profit and for-profit developers. (See revenue sources list.)

B. In concert with Metropolitan Housing Coalition and the Enterprise Foundation, secure funding for existing not-for-profits for operating as well as programmatic needs and help create new not-for-profits to help answer unmet needs of housing seekers in The Housing Partnership, Inc., service area.

Income from The Housing Partnership, Inc., program activities:

1. Financial Advisor for Low-Income Tax Credit projects.

2. Compliance review of existing Low-Income Tax Credit projects.

3. Program Administrator of 1989-90 City of Louisville mortgage revenue bond issue.

4. Program Administrator for mortgage revenue bond program for single-family activity in The Housing Partnership, Inc., service area.

5. Program Administrator for mortgage revenue bond program for multifamily activity in The Housing Partnership, Inc., service area.

6. Administrative fees from grant programs applied for and approved by foundations.

7. Sale of financial advisory software.

8. Administrator of KHC Joint Venture Programs.

Financial Support from:

1. Mayor Jerry Abramson and Board of Aldermen—City of Louisville

2. County Judge/Executive David Armstrong and Fiscal Court—Jefferson County

3. Citizens Fidelity Bank & Trust Company

4. First National Bank

5. Liberty National Bank & Trust Company

6. Corporate fund drive

7. Other city and county governments in service area of The Housing Partnership, Inc.

As you can see, this is an ambitious set of goals and objectives and will challenge our community of housing providers and funding sources. These goals and objectives will further educate people in our community as to the need of the seekers of affordable housing. We all belong to the community and we are the lesser if we do not look to help those less able to afford housing, for if one is ill-housed, we are all ill-housed. Providing these types of opportunities as spelled out in this work plan is the right thing to do. Positive political will and hard work will determine our success.

Another aspect of housing development which must be considered along with the social aspects is economic development. Aside from the social benefit of providing housing programs for the very-low-, low- and moderate-income individual or family in our community, the economic benefit is staggering. A study by the Illinois Homebuilders in the mid-1980s showed that for every $100 million in new construction and rehab, the community realized over a four-to-one economic boost, or in other words, $400 million was generated in addition to the $100 million for jobs, supplies, and other ancillary items related to the housing industry. Also, an additional 3,000 permanent/part-time jobs are created.

Lisbeth Schorr in her book, *Within Our Reach*, wrote that she was astonished to find out how much we know as Americans, but dismayed by how little we use what we know. The real tragedy of our time is that we have the know-how to solve many of our problems, housing needs being one of them, but we lack the will.

There are five elements required to build a strong and resilient civic infrastructure. (James J. Joseph, "The Genesis of Community—Get Our Own House in Order," *Vital Speeches of the Day*, October 1, 1990, p. 750.) The same is true for a housing program.

1. Civic participation

2. Community leadership

3. Government performance

4. Volunteerism and philanthropy

5. Intergroup relations

Hopefully, we can pull these elements together in our community and you in yours.

To have a city, a county, a state, and a nation that is truly strong, we must provide all our citizens four basic opportunities:

1. Educational excellence—from Head Start to doctoral degrees

2. Meaningful employment

3. Appropriate nutrition

4. Affordable housing

The Housing Partnership is one way to help achieve those ends for our community.

One of the wonderful, fulfilling things about working in this field of endeavor, housing, is that as you sit across from someone who needs your help, and they look at you and see the promise of the American Dream begin to unfold for them. Looking back, you see the dream of a better America for all of us.

If there is one among us who is ill-housed, ill-fed, malnourished, or undereducated, we are all the poorer.

We are the President. We are the Congress. We are the Governors. We are the Legislatures. We are the Mayors. We are the City Council.

We must not forget it is our government. We are the governed, but we also govern.

John F. Kennedy:

"I am certain that after the dust of centuries has passed over our cities, we too will be remembered not for victories or defeats in battle or politics but for our contribution to the human spirit."

Chapter 22

Mount Vernon, New York: The Housing and Neighborhood Development Institute, Inc.

William Jones
Executive Director
The Housing and Neighborhood Development Institute, Inc.

In 1978, in response to the housing crisis, the City of Mount Vernon along with some concerned citizens convened a "Liveable City Housing" Conference.

According to the 1980 census, the City of Mount Vernon ranked ninth in density in the United States. Comprised of 4.24 square miles with a population of roughly 65,000 people, it serves as an example of both urban and suburban America. Often called the "City of Homes," Mt. Vernon lies north of New York City (bordered by the Bronx) nestled in Westchester County, one of the most affluent counties in the country.

The result of the conference was the formation of the Housing and Neighborhood Development Institute, Inc., better known today as HANDI.

HANDI's mission is to address housing problems and neighborhood development requirements by assessing, evaluating, and documenting community needs. This information is then used to develop feasible and reliable resources, coordinate the distribution of services and resources, and institute programs that will enhance the liveability, standards, and quality of life of the residents of the City of Mount Vernon.

Today HANDI operates four major components.

1. NICHE

NICHE is the economic development component which strives to identify and provide minor repair services to households within HANDI's designated target area. Operating in conjunction with another housing group, HANDI strives to assist residential and commercial owners with minor repairs. After extensive research, HANDI realized that there is a gap between what people can do and are willing to do themselves (the DIY market) and what they must call a licensed contractor—electrical, plumbing, or carpentry—to do. HANDI identified that niche and subsequently developed a program to address that market. Hence the name NICHE, which stands for Needed Improvements for Community Household Enterprises. Currently the NICHE program conducts minor repairs like sheetrocking, plastering, painting, replacing washers in leaking faucets, cutting grass, trimming hedges, washing exterior windows, clearing lots, and any other minor types of repairs. We are also engaged in periodic superintendent training programs.

NICHE was initially funded by both the City of Mount Vernon and the National Association of Neighborhoods.

2. Development Programs

In 1978 HANDI acquired a building from the City of Mount Vernon for one dollar. After financing and Urban Initiative funding from the New York State Division of Housing and Community Development, an eight-unit building was completely rehabilitated and now provides the largest, cleanest, and most affordable housing in the City of Mount Vernon.

As of this writing we have successfully assisted 118 other units of housing to become more marketable while retaining their affordability. Chosen by both the federal government and the City of Mount Vernon, we have rehabilitated

drug dens and deteriorated buildings. Through the Speigel Act HANDI is currently a 7A administrator of a building which had been a bane on the City of Mount Vernon for 20 years.

3. Block and Neighborhood Consortium

Due to the need for more and better information about what is going on in the housing field, HANDI developed the Block and Neighborhood Consortium (BANC). BANC provides information through a newsletter and arranges workshops and information sessions for the more than 45 block, neighborhood, and tenant groups in the City of Mount Vernon.

HANDI recognized that many associations have wrestled with problems and found solutions to crime, drugs, and tenant problems. We felt that this information should be shared and applauded. BANC, especially the newsletter, provides the vehicle for dissemination of this information and sharing of resources.

4. Housing Counseling

The Housing Counseling program grew out of a need to assist local residents in securing safe, decent, affordable housing. Initially the program was geared toward helping people find housing. It grew to deal with the social, psychological, economic, and personal issues that people, including homeless people, face.

HANDI's housing counseling program has achieved a great deal despite operating with limited resources. In one year alone, with only one housing counselor, we successfully placed over 200 homeless families. Since the program's inception in 1988 we have provided housing counseling training and acquisition workshops to three homeless shelters and assisted over one thousand people in securing housing. Our program is designed to assist the clients in finding housing, but most important it assists them in keeping that housing and securing housing on their own in the future. Because of the success of this program, and because we have found it to be emulated by so many institutions, we will focus on this program as our model of a detailed specific program that can provide the broadest audience with information and expertise that is both functional and dynamic.

HOUSING COUNSELING COMPONENT

First one must open people's minds to a new set of definitions. Housing counseling as currently defined and utilized by HUD is archaic. It has not caught up with the times. HUD's Housing Counseling Program is really Home Ownership Counseling. It is designed to assist residents in home purchasing and foreclosure counseling. Their certificated counseling program does not address people living in substandard or overcrowded housing. It does not address homeless clients or apartment dwellers who are looking to secure permanent rental housing. Currently the largest market in urban areas is rental housing. There is an enormous need for counseling which addresses this market segment. HANDI's housing program breaks with the HUD paradigm of Home Ownership counseling. It is designed for assisting low- and-moderate income people in securing safe, decent, affordable housing. This housing is primarily apartment rental units.

The process outlined below is summarized by the Housing Counseling Flow Charts. (See Figure 22.1)

Phase I

Step One

The Intake. (See Figure 22.2) The first step in our process is to identify the client.

The significance of this step cannot be overemphasized. The intake process is very important. It identifies the client's needs, motivation, and circumstances. It also helps the intake worker determine the urgency of the situation (i.e., how soon the person must be relocated). Great care must be taken to train the intake worker on this process, because the success or failure in helping someone securing housing could very well depend upon the success of the intake.

Very often, depending upon the client's history, the biggest obstacle to success will be the person's motivation. After living in homeless shelters, shared situations, or any number of alternative housing arrangements, a person can very easily become disillusioned. It is a long uphill battle to help a person who has reached these depths.

Step Two

The Contract. This is done after intake and prior to actually working with the client. It is extremely important that the client realizes that he or she is engaged in a commitment with you. Their commitment is to help themselves. For purposes of follow-up and continuity the contract stipulates that if the client misses a certain number of meetings, appointments, etc., he or she will be removed from the program and will not be able to be admitted again for 90 days.

Figure 22.1   HANDI Housing Counseling Flow Chart

Phase I

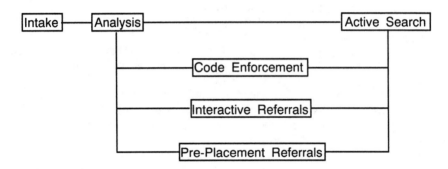

Phase II

This has proven invaluable in identifying and eliminating people who are not serious and are not motivated.

Step Three

Once the intake is done, then an analysis

Figure 22.2   HANDI Housing Counseling Intake Form

Intake Date: _____   Intake Worker: _____

Client Number: _____   Computer Control Number: _____

Date Placed: _____   Date Placed: _____

HOUSING HISTORY

Name: _____

Current Address: _____

Last Permanent Address: _____

Zip: _____

How Long at Last Permanent Address: _____

Rent or Own: _____

Number of Rooms: _____

Type of Residents (Check One):

1-4 Family House: ◯   Public Housing: ◯   Abandoned Building: ◯

6 or More Apartment Building ◯   Boarding House/SRO: ◯

Other (Explain): _____

Reason for Visit (Check One):

Eviction: Non-Payment ◯   Building Sold ◯

No Cert. of Occupancy ◯   No Lease ◯

Dispute with Owner ◯   Change of Ownership ◯

Non-Eviction: Poor Conditions ◯   Sharing/Must Move ◯

Temporary Shelter ◯   Rent Increase ◯

From _____ To _____

Other Reason (Explain): _____

Figure 22.2 Continued

Head of Household - Sex: _____ Age: _____

Family Size: _____

Number of Boys: _____ Ages: _____

Number of Girls: _____ Ages: _____

HOUSING EFFORTS TO DATE

Agencies/Institutions/People You Have Worked With: _____

_____

_____

_____

REHOUSING PLANS

Rent Range: _____ Acceptable Locations: _____

Number of Bedrooms: _____ _____

Number of Children: _____ Number of Senior Citizens: _____

Special Needs:

Disability (Type): _____

Other: _____

Additional Information and Notes on Housing Efforts:

_____

_____

_____

_____

(HC2)

of the client in relationship to the housing market must take place. Although this step does not involve the client, it is very important. It is here that a determination of methodology is made. Determining factors may be:

1. Size of family

2. Educational level

3. Working versus non-working

4. Level of motivation

5. Whether the person is homeless or being evicted or living with someone

6. Prior efforts to find housing

In essence, this step summarizes the reasons that the client came to us in the first place. As the flow chart in Figure 22.1 shows, there are various levels of assistance that a client can receive prior to a determination that we need to help the client locate new housing.

Three primary scenarios are possible.

1. *Code Search.* The apartment that the person currently lives in needs repairs. That is a building code problem. After determination that it is a code problem, communication is set up with the local building department. If the matter can be resolved through the building department, then the case is considered closed. If not, then the client goes to Phase II, Active Search.

2. *Interactive Referrals.* This section is designed to assist clients who need mediation services because of landlord/tenant problems. There are many circumstances where misunderstandings and poor communication contribute to people feeling they need to move. It may

be caused by problems with neighbors. It may be the superintendent. It may be that the tenant never pays the rent on time and the landlord has threatened him with eviction.

In these cases we either set up meetings with the tenant and the landlord or we refer the tenant to another local service company that specializes in mediation. If the problem can be resolved the case is closed; if not, the client then goes to Phase II.

3. *Pre-placement referrals.* In many circumstances the clients have very serious alcohol or drug abuse problems. In those cases we refer them to a local clinic or rehabilitation facility. After a client has attended the facility for a period of time and we have communicated with his or her counselor, we make a determination if the client is ready for active search. In some of these cases the client is able to retain tenancy because the landlord sees an improvement.

This scenario utilizes housing assistance as a carrot for getting the client off drugs and into rehabilitation. It has often been debated whether this is constitutionally correct. However, we have found that this methodology is good for the community, good for the client, and helps us maintain good relationships with our brokers and landlords.

Phase II

The Workshops

Phase II begins with a series of workshops. The workshop series entails a series of classes designed to give the person insight into their circumstances. It helps them to see how they got where they are, what they need to do to get out of this situation, and how not to get in this situation again. Depending upon the clients, a workshop series could be as long as 16 sessions or as short as 8.

The workshops also assist the clients in how to present themselves for apartment hunting. It teaches that finding an apartment is like finding a job. You must present yourself professionally and competently. We emphasize the responsibility the client has once he or she becomes a tenant. This is very important, especially in low-income neighborhoods. The better tenants a counselor is able to place with landlords, the easier it will be in the future to secure housing for his or her clients. The following is a sample workshop outline:

General information and curriculum overview

Goal Setting: How to set goals and measure performance

What you need or want in life

Decision making: How to make and implement decisions based on goals

Setting financial priorities

Planning: How to plan for the short, medium, and long term (includes budgeting)

Positive Attitudes: Self-sufficiency starts with a positive mental attitude. How to develop and nurture it

Positive Reinforcement: How to identify positive motivators and small accomplishments to keep yourself stimulated

Communication:

Appearances

Understanding instructions and forms

Tenant and landlord responsibilities

Case examples of dealing with people in housing search: Brokers, supers, DSS, etc.

Developing a personal operation plan

Setting up a daily plan of action for acquiring an apartment. (i.e., appointments, phone calls, etc.)

The length and number of workshops depends upon the size of the classes, the literacy of the clients, and the workshop's final objectives. In some cases the objective is only to prepare clients for the search. Other situations require that you actually take the client through the search. Finally, some clients only require assistance in the search.

Acquisition

In this phase the client begins training to acquire the apartment. We teach the client telephone skills, budgeting, interviewing techniques, and what to look for in an apartment. Many people are so happy to simply find an affordable apartment that they don't know what they should or should not accept. They must be shown how to check the windows, water pressure, neighborhood, etc. These are all very important items that the client needs to be versed in before even attempting to go looking for an apartment.

By this time we are ready to give the

client a workbook, which allows the client to document everything he or she needs to know. This includes the apartment size that they are eligible for, the location that they would like to live in, how many bedrooms they need, and necessary contact names.

The workbook is also designed so that the client can keep a running record of all appointments and the results of each meeting.

Now the client is ready for the actual search. This entails contacting referrals, identifying brokers and landlords, and tapping resources such as the local church, civic association, and friends.

During this phase the client receives additional training in how the Local Section 8[1] office and Department of Social Services (DSS) offices work. In some cases DSS provides one-time emergency assistance to help the client pay brokers' fees and/or security deposits. Section 8 may have certificates or vouchers available for the client. Some locations have certificates or vouchers for working people as well as those on DSS.

In extreme cases, and depending upon the municipality, we may have the client apply for Section 8 immediately after intake. This is because some Section 8 offices have a long waiting list and by the time the client finally finishes the course the certificate may be available.

The Housing Counselor or Placement Specialist needs to be extremely well versed in the local, county, state, and federal laws governing Section 8 and the Department of Social Services. It would be helpful to know a few case workers and the district administrator at DSS as well as your Section 8 administrator. They can help lead the Counselors

through the paperwork and changes in the laws as they occur.

The interview. This is where the client meets the landlord, broker, or other contact to arrange to see the apartment. The reason this step is listed separately from seeing the apartment is because, in a tight housing market, many brokers and landlords can be choosy. Very often they want to see the clients before they even consider renting them the house or apartment.

At this stage your client needs the most coaching and reinforcement. Often the intimidation of the landlords or brokers wears down much of the confidence that you have helped to instill.

It is also very important to review their plans periodically to determine if they are following through, keeping all their appointments, and meeting other goals.

Invariably, and with perseverance, all your clients will be placed, although not every client will be fully satisfied with their new apartment. In our case roughly 80 percent found that their new quarters were ideal, while 20 percent were unhappy with some aspect of their apartment.

CONCLUSION

HANDI has enjoyed much success in placing people in permanent housing. This is due to having a well-defined program for securing housing and training our clients. A great deal of administrative time is also spent in beginning training and in on-going training of our staff.

In the current housing crisis it is not just enough to build or find permanent housing; we must train our clients to be better tenants, to be better neighbors. We must train our clients and in some cases our staff to be more sensitive to their environments. We must expand the philosophy that we are a community and that every member of the community must be productive. Every member of the community must be receptive to the needs of the entire community. We must all understand that "livability" is the key to the survival of our neighborhood, our community, our cities, our states, and our entire country. Before we can successfully help our neighbor we need to spend some time cleaning up our own backyard. We must first instill the virtues of good tenancy within ourselves.

Housing is a human right. The number of children who are well educated, emotionally stable, and successful who do not have homes are very few.

Our experience has shown us that the housing crisis is not truly a crisis but a mismanagement of resources and a misunderstanding of priorities. Our experience has borne out that the number of units, the money, and the services are all there. The true problem is that local, state, and national government has not invested in the coordination of its resources.

The results of the National Affordable Housing Act of 1991 will be just as shallow as those that followed before if an investment in managerial competence is not made. The government should look to the creativity of the local nonprofits for guidance, and to business for the technical and managerial sophistication it needs to accomplish the task.

If government does not take the initiative and institute the reforms that are necessary, then it is up to the people whom those reforms are for to do something about it. It is up to the people to vote for the representatives who will make a difference. And if they are not sure, then vote for a new representative each election. The politicians will get the message.

ENDNOTE

[1] HUD's Section 8 voucher and certificate program is designed for low- and moderate-income people. The Section 8 program calculates subsidy based on family composition and gross family income. The difference between a Section 8 Voucher and Certificate is that the certificate always pays 30 percent of income. The Voucher works on applicable payment standards and rents will vary.

Chapter 23

Waukegan, Illinois: Lake County Community Action Project

Barbara A. Gordon
Executive Director
Lake County Community Action Project

INTRODUCTION

The Lake County Community Action Project was organized in 1965, through the combined efforts of many local civic groups, such as the Waukegan Area Conference on Religion and Race, the Waukegan-North Chicago Area Project and the Lake County Welfare Association. The original application for a grant for Program Development was submitted in June 1965.

The project was approved by the Office of Economic Opportunity, and on October 7, 1965, the Lake County Community Action Project opened its doors to begin its "War on Poverty."

In the mid-1970s there was an assault on the Office of Economic Opportunity by the Nixon administration, and OEO died and was laid to rest. The spirit of the War on Poverty lived on, trans-migrating to the new body of the Community Services Administration (CSA), with only the letters changed to protect the programs, including the new and important ones of Weatherization and Energy Assistance.

The causes and conditions of poverty in Lake County are little changed from what they were in 1965. Poverty is the condition in which *poor people live.* Poor people are human beings who never have enough money to pay for the minimum necessities of a decent life in the United States of America.

Poor people in Lake County have additional woes because they have the dubious "blessing" of living in one of the wealthiest counties in the country with one of the highest standards of living. This appearance of affluence hides more effectively the urban and rural poor among us, and hides the actual condition of the poor in wealthy Lake County.

Poor people are locked into a situation where only the cash on hand keeps the wolf outside the door. There are no stocks, bonds, depreciation allowances, or tax write-offs. There are no savings accounts drawing interest and not even a small "nest egg" put away for a rainy day. The rainy day is today and every day! The average citizen doesn't seem to mind having his taxes pay for oil depletion allowances or agricultural subsidies for not growing crops, defense skirmishes or wars in the name of National Security, and savings and loan bailouts, but he views the welfare recipient with suspicion and animosity. He is surprisingly willing to extend welfare to the wealthy but begrudges the pittance that proportionately goes to the poor, who have nothing at all to cushion the present, and even less to make any provisions for the future.

The primary goal of the Lake County Community Action Project (LCCAP) is the eradication of the paradox of poverty in the midst of plenty in Lake County. Our efforts are directed toward enabling the poor to become self-sufficient and promoting institutional sensitivity and responsiveness to the needs of the poor. LCCAP provides a range of services and activities that have a measurable and major impact on the causes of poverty in the community.

Lake County Community Action Project's twenty-sixth year marks a literal as well as figurative coming-of-age for the Agency. We have matured from a reactive posture of knee-jerk responses to the *effects* of poverty to a an active stance of formulating and implementing strategies to eliminate the *causes* of poverty through economic development, jobs, self-sufficiency, affordable-housing development, etc.

We have begun to address the longstanding problems of insufficient and inadequate housing for the low-income population. We are actively involved in promoting affordable-housing opportunities for low- and moderate-income residents of Lake County.

Our past involvement in the housing arena includes counseling as a certified HUD agency for homeowners who are delinquent with mortgage payments or pending foreclosure; providing housing relocation assistance to individuals affected by revitalization Community Block Grant activities; providing financial assistance to the homeless and near homeless; mediating landlord/tenant disputes, and applying weatherization services to qualified households.

Affordable-housing plans for the future now include the acquisition of a 150-unit apartment complex in partnership with a respected minority management and development corporation, East Lake Management and Development Corporation. Our immediate attention is directed toward the Community Investment Program of Lake County.

The establishment of the Community Investment Program of Lake County has been an 18-month-long process. During this time we were confronted with frustrations; we perceived them as challenges. We had a few setbacks; we embraced them as opportunities.

Ultimately, through the committed and hardworking financial institution representatives, in cooperation with our dedicated, professional, and compassionate staff, we are happy to share the program described in the following pages. We are certain that the Community Investment Program will significantly contribute to the revitalization of several low-income neighborhoods and their families.

We are grateful to Kenneth Sinclair, Jr., administrative director, for the tremendous effort and energy expended in developing this chapter and to Jennifer Jones, my executive secretary, for her patience in the many drafts before we were sure we said what we wanted to say.

THE COMMUNITY INVESTMENT PROGRAM OF LAKE COUNTY

Steve Butzlaff and Wesley Ley, both vice presidents at the Northern Trust Bank of Lake Forest, Illinois, were charged with developing a plan for the bank to meet some of the Community Reinvestment Act (CRA) goals (see Chapter 1) in targeted areas. Both attacked the new assignment with the same alacrity for which they had become known. Steve's momentum and motivation, however, were more personal than those of most bankers. He had an acquaintance who experienced the systematic discriminatory practices of redlining exercised routinely by banks in "redlined areas" of Chicago. Recalling the incident was intensely displeasing to him. His African-American friend was a good man, an outstanding member of the community, but was denied the opportunity to realize his ambitions. Steve Butzlaff's determination to establish a neighborhood revitalization program with financial-institution involvement became a personal goal.

Together with Wes Ley, Steve attempted to develop a plan that would involve five or six Lake County area banks to form some kind of organization to address the problem of blight in some census tracts of the county.

Butzlaff envisioned better opportunit-

ies for financing through "nontraditional financing methods." Through an organization of financial institutions and a lending pool, the group could be creative in their lending practices and still protect capital investment through safe loans. These objectives would satisfy CRA requirements as well. They knew that a local community would have to be involved to make their plan a reality. They also knew that the local community involvement they needed was not to be found in Lake Forest, Illinois. Lake Forest is one of the most affluent communities on the North Shore, where the prices of homes begin at $200,000. There is not a sizeable population of low-income residents.

Although the border of the Lake Forest/Lake Bluff communities is contiguous with some of the county's most abject poverty, Northern Trust Bank of Lake Forest is not generally thought of in terms of a low-income person's full-service banking facility. To add to this impression, Northern Trust Bank leadership efforts were oftentimes considered a turn-off by many member banks in the "shared" service area, because of their large size, location, and seeming aloofness. Because of this reputation and because of the community involvement that would be required for this revitalization idea to bear fruit, Butzlaff and Ley set out to find the missing ingredient the plan needed for success.

Butzlaff recalls, "it was pure luck and innocence" that they approached Barbara Gordon, the executive director of the Lake County Community Action Project, the county's largest social service agency.

Gordon was well known and well respected in the banking community. She had a seat on the Board of the Bank of Northern Illinois, one of the Lake

County area's largest and oldest banks, which happens to be located on the periphery of the target area. A special quality needed for this job was her ability to bring banks, savings and loan institutions, and municipalities into one cohesive working unit. She could do it. Butzlaff and Ley selected wisely.

Gordon had a warm reception to the Butzlaff/Ley idea and received a green light from the Lake County Community Action Project board of directors.

The board, consisting of 15 members, historically has been very supportive of initiatives coming from their veteran executive director and viewed this new thrust as one more in a list of successful programs designed to realize the agency's mission of "eradicating the paradox of poverty in the midst of plenty."

After some preliminary meetings with Northern Trust and others, Gordon assigned her assistant, Kenneth Robinson, to the task of accumulating data on exactly what each financial institution had done to date relative to their CRA requirements. It was found that most had only analyzed their target markets, and had not developed meaningful CRA programs. After completing this assignment, Robinson turned his attention to introducing each of the participating institutions' management to the concept of combining their collective resources.

Finally, Robinson encouraged the local bankers, about 22 in all, to meet to discuss how they might form a partnership of banks, savings and loans, and municipalities to address the needs of neighborhood revitalization through a reinvestment strategy.

Robinson said that he was very surprised by how quickly that first effort was accomplished. "Within one month, I had met with all the bank representatives, completed my investigation, and established a date for all interested to get together.

"I think everyone felt a need to do something, and the financial institutions knew that something had to be done in order to fulfill their CRA requirements. Initially, there was some mistrust, but eventually all realized that together they could make a difference," Robinson observed.

Regular meetings were scheduled. With each meeting the process of growth and development began to take shape. Strategies of other established housing groups were scrutinized closely by the Lake County consortium of banks, savings and loans, municipalities, and the Lake County Community Action Project, now referred to as the Community Investment Program of Lake County (CIP). Experts like Charlie Rault from the Shoreline Bank-Shoreline Advisory Service and Joan Pougie of the Woodlawn Consulting Firm were solicited to give their input on consortium development. Although the experts' opinions were highly valued, and their many successes considered, the Lake County CIP wanted to develop its own model for affordable-housing revitalization in Lake County.

Paul Gergen, from the Kenosha Savings and Loan (now Advantage Bank) in North Chicago and Kenosha, Wisconsin, introduced the bankers to the Neighborhood Housing Services (see Chapter 6) project in Kenosha. He had good firsthand information about it, by virtue of his serving on its board. When the group toured the Kenosha Housing Services and the designated housing rehab areas, they became truly excited about the prospects of what could be done in Lake County.

Two Kenosha Neighborhood Housing Services neighborhoods were visited during the tour. The group reacted positively to a simple paint program in the Lincoln and Columbus Park neighborhoods. Each householder was given paint to spruce up his or her dwelling. This simple, but economical, act served to make each resident a part of the overall program and had a significant impact on the neighborhood, even though almost no major rehabilitation was required.

In the other neighborhood the NHS program was more advanced, and dilapidated houses had been razed and replaced by new homes.

The director of the Kenosha Neighborhood Housing Services, Dominick Martinelli, was its only director since its inception in 1982. Martinelli was still very excited about the work in the neighborhoods and looked forward to venturing out with similar programs in other areas in Kenosha. His delight was most obvious when he talked about the people whose lives had been enhanced as a result of the Kenosha Neighborhood Housing Service Program.

Nearly a year had passed since the initial meeting between Barbara Gordon, Wes Ley, and Steve Butzlaff. Walter Kroll, president of North Shore Trust and Savings, situated on the North Chicago/Waukegan border, serves as unofficial host for the consortium and its meetings.

Although some posturing between savings and loans and banks and cities was expected, it did not surface. The organization moved toward a real commitment to the community's revitalization needs. It was obvious to most that Northern Trust Bank of Lake Forest had pulled back from their somewhat aggressive earlier stance, perhaps, "to allow a natural leadership to emerge from within the group."

Northern Trust Bank of Lake Forest hosted a press conference that officially announced the Community Investment Program of Lake County, and to introduce to the community the newly hired development director, John Nowell. Marsha Nedland, Neighborhood Reinvestment (see Chapter 19) Representative for the Midwest, was on hand to present and explain the Neighborhood Reinvestment Corporation to which the Community Investment Program (CIP) had applied for membership. The membership in the Community Investment Program of Lake County now approached 20 active financial institutions.

The Lake County Community Action Project, under Barbara Gordon, acted as the umbrella organization, replete with a not-for-profit status with the State of Illinois. LCCAP had the community based organization (CBO) background and through its executive director the ability to speak to all segments of the population. It provided space for the meetings of the various CIP groups and committees. The location is known to all targeted low-income residents.

Comments and thoughts from some of the members of the initial group:

Paul Stahr, senior vice president, First of America Bank, North East Illinois, saw in the consortium an opportunity to combine financial resources to aid depressed communities and to spread the liability among the members. Additionally, he wanted to tap the expertise of the member financial institutions to help create a sound base of information upon which to make critical decisions about the poor and blighted areas. Like the other members, First of America felt the overwhelming need to address the problems of blight in the targeted areas. This would be in addition to individual efforts initiated by the banks or savings and loan institutions. Paul Stahr also talks about an effort by his bank to assist more westerly rural parts of the county with similar efforts.

As for the future of the Community Investment Program, Paul Stahr asserts that "CIP will be a great success because of the way the community has supported its formation. I am optimistic that all envisioned for the program will come true, because all the elements are in place in the partnership to make it work; business, government, and residents."

Frank Mynard, president, Bank of Northern Illinois, N.A. The bank's location is contiguous to the target area. The Bank of Northern Illinois has the reputation of serving the greatest number of residents from the target area in terms of their service needs. Mynard is very sensitive to what exists in the target area.

He knows that the condition of the neighborhood that abuts his facility has some reflection on his bank, although the Bank of Northern Illinois is no more singularly responsible for the blight in the target area than any of the other financial institutions. Mynard sees the CIP as a "positive" for all, and especially for the institutions located in or near the target area.

He believes that the more developed an area becomes, the better the area looks, the better the public perception is

about it, and (for the benefit of the bank) the more opportunity there is to expand other services. Speculation suggests that if residents feel poorly about where they live, their property will reflect their feeling. Further, if their attitude about their condition relates to their values, then they probably won't be dependable jobholders and consequently not good credit risks.

Mynard believes that his bank's investment in the CIP is small compared to the many rewards his institution will realize when the program becomes fully operational. Instead of practically no business from the target area, there is the opportunity to get home or rehab loans, auto loans, school loans, short-term loans, checking accounts, savings accounts, and business loans.

Despite the impact of the CRA legislation, *Walter Kroll, president of North Shore Trust & Savings, believes the need for a "Reinvestment or Improvement" program was always there for the area. The focus just was not there, nor was the idea of pooling resources among financial institutions.*

Walter Kroll was born and raised in the target area. He has worked at and for North Shore Trust & Savings most of his adult life. He has seen the area grow and prosper and he has also seen the area deteriorate.

Kroll believes that something like the Community Investment Program is just what the community needs to restore and revitalize the old neighborhoods.

"I don't think the area will ever get back to where it once was, but I do think it can be a very pleasant place to live and work. Good leadership, both from our representatives and the citizens is a must. The community must be involved for the program to succeed."

Kroll has had a highly visible position in the financial community and has used it to do what he could to prevent the community's deterioration through personal efforts in a variety of areas. In addition to serving with various civic organizations and committees, he served on the North Chicago High School Board of Education during a time of great growth and expansion in the district.

Kroll was at first concerned that the aloofness normally attributed to financial institutions would be very difficult to overcome in the Community Investment Program. "The trust which goes along with it might be a very difficult commodity to achieve, he opined."

Kroll asserts, Barbara Gordon was instrumental in helping the consortium overcome the mistrust he had anticipated between and among banks, savings and loans, and their representatives. Kroll says, "it was imperative that the organization have good, strong, effective leadership that could cut through long-standing differences, real or imagined." He believes Gordon brought all those characteristics to the group.

Additionally, a key to the success of this organization is community involvement. Kroll knew, through past association, that Barbara Gordon could bring this very needed dimension to the Community Investment Program.

Kroll said, "I always believed in the concept of the Community Investment Program, and we, at North Shore Trust & Savings, were eager to make it happen. When the consortium visited and closely observed the Kenosha Housing model, and saw how well it worked, we knew, with a few modifications in the resident involvement component and the staffing pattern (more outreach and support services), it would work in Lake County."

Another important member of that initial core group of six institutions is *Peggy Gupton, president and chief executive officer of the Waukegan Savings and Loan and president of the Association of Savings and Loan Institutions of Lake County.*

Gupton presides over two facilities, and the older of the two is situated on the street that separates the cities of Waukegan and North Chicago. The other is located in the more affluent northside area of Waukegan.

Peggy Gupton observed many times throughout the process that the financial institutions had never come together on anything and considered the current involvement of the banks and savings and loans a miracle. She mentioned that an association of the original thirteen savings and loan institutions has met and operated as an organization for years, but that there was nothing similar for the banks. She didn't believe at first that such a relationship between them would work. She credits Barbara Gordon with that successful merger.

Although Ms. Gupton believes her financial institution and others would have continued to work individually in an attempt to do a little here and a little there, she knows that through the combined efforts of all partners, a more comprehensive approach through total committed involvement works better. "Some of the financial institutions would not be able to do as much in the neighborhoods because of their small size," she said. Also, as we have seen in the Kenosha model, the little things like giving paint away to owners in a target area does so much to help the neighborhood." I just don't think anyone (financial institution) would sponsor that kind of effort by themselves."

Peggy Gupton calls herself one who is affected by "Finishitis," getting something started and finished in a short period of time.

Every original consortium member felt that the Community Investment Program moved into high gear after the introduction to the NHS of Kenosha model. They all felt that the Kenosha model could work in Lake County.

Learning to Work Together

Time has been the most effective device in overcoming whatever mistrust existed among the various factions and groups in the Lake County Community Investment Program. The many twice-monthly meetings helped to dissolve the differences each faction may have had. A weekend retreat conducted by the NHS was particularly effective. Once given the opportunity to take off their ties and dress blues and grays and call each other by first names, the financial institution representatives, staff and residents' image of each other disappeared.

Marsha Nedland, Neighborhood Reinvestment Corporation Representative for the Midwest, also believed from the initial meeting with Barbara Gordon and development director John Nowell that the Lake County model would work. Normally, cities, counties, and neighborhoods are approached *by* the Neighborhood Reinvestment Corporation. She thought that Lake County was somewhat unique in that the Community Investment Program approached the Neighborhood Reinvestment Corporation. "When we look at what CIP was able to bring to the table it was certainly different from the average applicant," stated Marsha.

Normally, there is much jockeying and posturing in an organization such as this. But because the Community Investment Program of Lake County came to the table with interested residents, a development director, operating expenses fully financed by the financial institutions, pledges of continuing support to the project, a Lake County Community Action Project outreach grant, and a revolving loan pool, the Community Investment Program had all the necessary ingredients to operate as a redevelopment organization.

The Neighborhood Reinvestment Corporation, or NeighborWorks as the network of members is known nationally, provides technical expertise to the member groups, training, and even a financial grant. It expects a three- to five-year commitment from the funding source, in this case, the financial institutions. The Neighborhood Reinvestment Corporation, in turn, will grant a community of this size $20,000. Contracts relative to the goals and assessment of operational readiness are also required.

Although each operation is locally administered and operated, the Neighborhood Reinvestment Corporation does help set rates and terms for loans which borrowers can afford. One of the few criterion is that a Neighborhood Reinvestment Corporation lend to people who cannot normally secure a loan from a conventional bank source.

NeighborWorks utilizes a proven formula in their neighborhood partnership organizations, where locally operated and locally funded. Part of the formula consists of a series of workshops and training sessions for the participants, residents, and business or financial resource group and staff.

The Organizational Workshop

The formal development of the Lake County Community Investment Program model began with the weekend organizational workshop. More than 60 persons attended the Friday, Saturday, and Sunday retreat in Lake Bluff, Illinois. CIP development director John Nowell and another staff person used many techniques to get target people involved in CIP. Some residents came to participate as a result of canvassing the area; some in response to news articles, flyers, and radio programs discussing CIP; others came from trusted relationships that had developed through day-to-day contact. Individuals were selected to participate by neighborhood. They also had to possess an ability to work with others. They would become the first committee members in the organization.

Marsha Nedland was elated at how well the weekend worked. The retreat was designed to break down barriers to communication that normally exist between people from diverse backgrounds. She said, "Taking a person out of his usual environment, and having him interact on a continuous basis with people he may never have met is usually a strained process.

"But this group of Whites, Hispanics, African-Americans, rich, poor, skilled and unskilled, dissolved those barriers very quickly and effectively. Everybody is in the same place, twenty-four hours per day. They had an opportunity to work together and socialize together and work on team-building exercises.

"It is a must to take time away from job and home to really focus on this project. I am excited at the outcome of the workshop. What is more exciting, though, is the partnership of people,

financial support, and local government interest," said Nedland.

Since the major intent of the initial meeting was to get people to know each other and to establish the short- and long-term goals, it is not necessary to repeat the weekend long format. Future workshops will be held at a church meeting hall, Lake County Community Action Project, or a bank.

John Nowell spent his first few months on the job persuading influential neighbors to sponsor small get-togethers at their homes, or to encourage their friends, neighbors or relatives to attend the meetings in homes, at the Community Investment office or other community locations.

Because the bankers were amenable to a rapid development of the program in Lake County and because of the Neighborhood Reinvestment Corporation district office's ability to put together the community member training workshop at the weekend retreat, the process progressed much faster than ever anticipated.

If there were to be any factor that hampered growth of the program in the target area, it would have been gaining the trust and confidence of the residents, a process that we expected would take time. "The small group meetings went well. The credible community residents we contacted were very helpful and very sincere in their desire to help, but nothing has worked more effectively in getting the kind of commitment we needed from the residents themselves than the effect of the weekend retreat in developing the working relationship we needed among the residents, financial community, and local government," said Nowell.

If all the factors in a program fell into

place without too many hurdles, a community could expect to have a program under way in about 18 months from beginning to actually being able to make its first loan.

The format in Lake County may eventually follow any one of a number of possibilities, i.e., rehab, new construction, in-fill construction, etc., but the goal is the same. To build a more homogenous neighborhood through citizen interaction and positive group activity.

Revitalizing the Community

The mission of the Community Investment Program of Lake County is simple: "To revitalize the target neighborhood using affordable housing as the tool for redevelopment."

The Community Investment Program of Lake County selected an area which borders south Waukegan and north North Chicago, the oldest and most time-worn portion of the two cities. It was the area first settled. Much of it was built without regard for zoning and construction standards. And, like any other housing development pattern which expands in concentric circles from the original industrial core, the housing in the zone was most often used as transitional housing as immigrants moved up the socio-economic ladder. The natural consequence of the way the area grew is that the neighborhood has suffered from neglect.

One of the ways the CIP hopes to reduce the incidence of neglect in the area is to encourage private homeownership. Along with revitalizing a neighborhood, CIP's mission is to *create opportunities for affordable housing and affordable homeownership.* By increasing the number of private owners in a deteriorating neighborhood, the CIP hopes to create a concerned population in the area—a population that is not only concerned about the condition of neighborhood services. Homeowners know that if garbage pick-up is accomplished in a timely way, and if the neighborhood gets its share of street and sidewalk repairs, the value of their properties will increase.

The Lake County CIP hopes to mirror the Kenosha NHS model. The Kenosha model has worked very well because much of the momentum of the movement came as a result of grass-roots political activity. In fact, the activity in Kenosha became so intense at one period during the development of the neighborhoods that residents themselves eventually elected a person to represent their interests on the Kenosha City Council.

The Lake County (Waukegan/North Chicago model) is not very politically oriented, although aldermen representing the affected part of each of the two cities have been very involved in the activities of the CIP. They have attended organizational meetings and have been active participants. They have used their political clout to get those neighborhoods their just due in city services. The aldermen attended the retreat. A very productive relationship has developed between political and residential interests.

Through the aldermen, CIP has the attention of the political leadership at each of the city halls.

A Case Study

The question may be asked—What does CIP mean to the average resident?

The following story is about one resident. Her name has been changed to protect her privacy.

Diana Lopez, is an attractive thirty-two-year-old Hispanic mother of two from Waukegan. She never dreamed there would be a chance for her to make things better for herself and her family.

She, like so many other young mothers in the Lake County community, is a single, female head of household. Divorced two years ago, Diana is trying to support her family in a lifestyle to which they had become accustomed, but she is finding it increasingly more difficult to stretch her dollars for the mortgage and to keep up with the necessary repairs to her 50-year-old bungalow.

CIP can review her current income, her determination and commitment, and while she may not be eligible for a loan under traditional standards, she may qualify for a low-interest loan through a revolving loan fund established by the LCCAP with a grant from the Department of Commerce and Community Affairs, State of Illinois (DCCA).

Now Diana is excited because she sees a mechanism moving into place in her neighborhood, a mechanism designed for someone like her. She feels confident that the Community Investment Program will benefit her family's home repair needs in the south Waukegan area. Her optimistic plans now call for fixing up her home, and maybe someday selling her home to buy income property to assure security for herself and her family.

"After hearing of the program, I knew it was something I could use," said Diana. But, more than that, I know that this is the kind of program that will help many, many others who would like to rehab their homes or buy in the neighborhood."

Diana Lopez is working on various committees to help ensure that CIP is a success in her neighborhood. Though she has only a little time to devote to organizing, because of her work schedule and demands from her young family, she is one of CIP's most dedicated volunteers. She was instrumental in getting a good turnout of young Hispanic couples for the Retreat.

Diana has become familiar with CIP. She understands that through CIP low-interest money for home improvement or rehabilitation will soon be available for individuals such as herself. Then, she can take steps to avoid watching her house deteriorate before her very eyes. She currently is not in a position to pay her mortgage and at the same time do needed repairs without the benefit of a program like CIP.

Historically, Diana would not be eligible for any type of loan from a financial institution. Her home is located in a blighted area of town and her income is not sufficient to meet the usual loan-approval criteria. She is female, Hispanic, and a single parent. All these factors at one time suggested both geography and the individual were unbankable.

Diana's gross income is slightly more than $20,000 a year. She works a full-time job at a social agency that helps people to develop skills for employment and to find jobs as well. She also works part-time as a department store clerk. Her mother is the primary source for baby-sitting her two youngsters and her mother is paid for this service, which is an even greater drain on her meager resources.

Diana drives a 14-year-old car. She

has about 50 percent equity in a home valued at sixty thousand dollars. She is regular with her mortgage payments. When she attempted to secure a loan to remodel her home, she was told that she would need a co-signer in order to qualify.

How might CIP help Diana? What the Community Investment Program will consider in this case is that Diana is a hardworking single parent. It is for Diana and for the countless others who also dream of improving their lives that programs like the Community Investment Program have been formed.

Editor's note: In October of 1991 the Community Investment Program *became incorporated as a separate, autonomous, non-profit corporation and subsequently changed its name to Neighborhood Housing Services of Lake County. In July of 1992 it opened its business office in the heart of the Lake County target area, where its staff of three runs serves a Board of Directors of 21 volunteers, more than half of whom are local neighborhood residents.*

In September of 1992 NHS of Lake County closed its first mortgage loan and rehabitation loan for a low-income home buyer—and its service to the Lake County community has been expanding rapidly.

B. Gordon

Section V

Housing for the Homeless

Chapter 24

The National Alliance to End Homelessness*

Thomas L. Kenyon
President
and
Nan P. Roman
Vice President for Policy and Programs
The National Alliance to End Homelessness

INTRODUCTION

What would we do if all of the homes in a city the size of Austin were destroyed overnight and its inhabitants were forced to roam the nation's streets, alleys, and campgrounds looking for a place to call home?

What would we do if 100,000 American children—all of the children in Boston, for example—had nowhere to live, no regular place to go to school, no doctor to care for them and no confidence when they went to bed that there would be something to eat in the morning?

What would we do if our hospitals began to fill with people dying of diseases we thought we would never see again—diseases like tuberculosis and polio? What would we do if there was talk of re-opening tuberculosis sanitariums because the hospitals were flooded with the victims of new, not yet understood, epidemics?

What would we do if half of America's single-room occupancy hotels were lost, leaving thousands of our poorest men and women to fend for themselves in doorways, over grates, and on the streets?

What would we do if people's incomes steadily fell until rent took nearly their whole paycheck? What would we do if, progressively unable to afford food, medicine, or clothing, they finally could not even afford a place to live?

---

*This chapter was written in 1991. Program specifics and other information may have changed.

What would we do if 750,000 Americans were homeless tonight?

These "what if's" are the reality of homelessness in America's cities and farmlands today, and it is the mission of the National Alliance to End Homelessness (the Alliance) to answer the question, "what can we do?" The Alliance accomplishes this by working with every sector of American society in an effort to find, and implement, programs and policies that will bring an end to homelessness.

WHO AND WHY?

To know how to solve homelessness in America today, we must first know who the homeless are and why they are homeless.

Homeless people are the poorest of our nation's poor, and as such they reflect the face of poverty in America. They are families, primarily with one parent, but often with two. They are people who work but whose earnings are not enough to pay for housing. They are youngsters who have run away from home or have been thrown out and are forced to live on the streets. And, they are the unemployed—those looking for work and those, young and old, who have never worked.

The number of homeless people has been a subject of some controversy, a controversy which was recently renewed when the Census Bureau released its 1990 "enumeration of segments of the homeless population." While there is no consensus on the numbers, there is universal agreement that they are unacceptably large. The National Alliance to End Homelessness estimates that on any given night some 750,000 Americans are homeless. Over the course of a

year, between 1.3 and 2 million people will experience homelessness. This is the number of people who live on the street, in emergency or transitional shelters, in cars, campgrounds, etc. It does not include the several million people estimated to be doubled-up—staying temporarily with family and friends but with no housing of their own. Nor does it include people housed in prisons, mental hospitals, or in other institutions, but without any independent home. Another six million people are precariously housed, paying such a large percentage of their incomes for rent that any unforeseen medical expense, or temporary job loss could dislodge them. They form the pool from which people will cycle in and out of homelessness.

Most homeless people, probably somewhat over half, are single men. A much smaller percentage, approximately 10 to 15 percent, are single women. Approximately one-third of homeless people are families with children and 3 to 4 percent are unaccompanied youth. The U.S. Conference of Mayors conducts an annual survey of hunger and homelessness in a sample of cities, basing their findings largely on demand for and use of services. In the 1990 survey, they found that two thirds of the homeless were members of minority groups. Forty-six percent were found to be African-American, 15 percent Hispanic, 3 percent Native American, and 1 percent Asian. Thirty-four percent were found to be white. These are national estimates, and the picture may be substantially different in a given state or locality, or in rural areas. For example, the majority of New York City's homeless population is families with children, while by some estimates the percentage of families among Chicago's homeless is less than 15 percent.

The homeless population exhibits a wide variety of characteristics. To those of us whose contact with homeless people takes place exclusively on the streets, it often seems that the vast majority are either mentally ill or have serious alcohol or substance abuse problems. While by no means all homeless people suffer from these conditions, they are over-represented in the homeless population. Between 25 percent and 30 percent of homeless people suffer from chronic mental illness. While many blame deinstitutionalization for precipitating the crisis of homelessness, that is not, strictly speaking, the case. Massive deinstitution-alization took place in the late 1960s and early 1970s. Mentally ill homeless people of today, many of whom have never been institutionalized, are hampered by the failure of community facilities to meet their needs, and by continuing loss of affordable housing. Estimates of the number of homeless people who suffer from alcohol and drug abuse problems range from 25 percent to 40 percent. Whether alcohol and substance abuse problems cause homelessness—or are caused by it—has not been adequately addressed.

There are other important character-istics present in the homeless population. A small but growing percentage have AIDS or are HIV positive. As many as 10 percent are physically handicapped. Many have been involved in the criminal justice system. Others lack the training or skills that can provide a living wage. And many people who are homeless ex-hibit more than one of these characterist-ics, making it even harder for them to find and maintain housing.

These are the characteristics of home-less people and yet these are not the causes of homelessness. Out of more than 30 million poor people in America, why are these one or two million people homeless? They are homeless because of a lack of affordable housing, because of inadequate incomes, and because of the lack of services to help them overcome personal problems. If homelessness is to end, they require two things. First, homeless people must be able to obtain housing. Second, many must have the help necessary to overcome the problems that complicate or interfere with their in-dependent living.

By its very name, we imply that homelessness is a housing problem. And, indeed, the sole common characteristic of homeless people is that they do not have housing. If we are to end homeless-ness in America, we must make more housing available to poor and low-in-come people. One way to do this is to increase the supply of such housing. There is not a housing shortage in Amer-ica today; there is a shortage of afford-able housing. Over the past 20 years, the supply of housing available to low-in-come people has declined. In 1970 there were twice as many low-cost units avail-able as there were low-income house-holds. By 1983 this number had been reversed—there were two households competing for every available unit. This loss of affordable housing units can be attributed largely to abandonment, urban renewal, gentrification, arson, and con-dominium and cooperative conversion. In the past, the gap in the affordable-housing supply was filled by either the federal government or the private sector. However, this is no longer the case. After a budget reduction of some 70 percent in federal housing programs in the 1980s, the HUD budget has begun to rise again, but this increase is not directly focused on increasing the supply of affordable housing. Rather, emphasis is placed on tenant-based subsidies. Also, the tax changes of the late 1980s no longer make it profitable for the private sector to create low-cost housing. As a result, the stock continues to dwindle. One approach to solving the housing side of the homelessness equation, then, is to create enough affordable housing to meet the demand.

A second approach is to raise incomes enough to make more of the available housing accessible to those for whom it is now out of reach. Work is the chief source of income for homeless people, followed by public benefits. Yet, not surprisingly, the incomes of homeless people are very, very low. As has been amply documented, the prosperity of the 1980s only served to drive a wider wedge between the haves and the have-nots. According to the Center on Budget and Policy Priorities, in 1989, the seventh year of the economic recovery, the poverty rate was higher than at any time in the 1970s, including that decade's recession years. Given the forecast for slow economic growth during the 1990s, the poverty picture is unlikely to improve. Again according to the Center on Budget and Policy Priorities, the average hourly wage for a non-supervisory worker is now lower, after adjustment for inflation, than at any time since 1969. The minimum wage, which used to raise a family of three above the poverty line with one adult working, now leaves that family $2,300 below it. Those relying on public benefits do not fare much better. Between 1970 and 1990, for example, the real value of Aid to Families with Dependent Children benefits, the most common support for poor families, declined by 30 percent. Even with other benefits factored in,

there was a substantial real decline. Other public benefits have also failed to keep pace with costs. These reductions, while striking hard at all poor people, become critically important to the poorest of the poor—the homeless. Another approach to ending homelessness by improving access to housing, then, would be to increase the incomes of homeless people. A variety of methods are available to us, including employment training, job development, and increasing public benefits.

But even if there was a ready and abundant supply of affordable housing and all homeless people had incomes that allowed them to obtain that housing, people who are homeless today might still require assistance to overcome the problems that interfere with their independence. They might need residential recovery programs to help them deal with drug and alcohol abuse problems, and follow-up programs to provide long-term assistance. They might need case management to help them develop and then access that support network that most of us can rely upon to help us handle the crises of daily living. They might require treatment and counseling to assist them in managing their mental illness. They might need child care to give them the time and energy to train and apply for a job. They might need legal aid to help them escape from a debilitating domestic situation.

In order for people to escape homelessness and lead stable and independent lives, they must have access to housing and the comprehensive services that will allow them to overcome any personal problems they may have. In order to stem the flow of more and more poor people into homelessness, housing and services must be made available to a wider group of poor and low-income people who cycle regularly in and out of homelessness. Creating this supply of housing and services is a significant undertaking, requiring the cooperation of all sectors of society—the public (including federal, state, and local governments) the private (corporations and foundations) and the nonprofit. This is the mission of the National Alliance to End Homelessness—to bring together all sectors of society and find and implement workable housing and service solutions to homelessness.

HISTORY

The National Alliance to End Homelessness was formed in 1983 under the name of the National Citizens' Committee for Food and Shelter (later changed to the Committee for Food and Shelter). The mission of the group was to access public and private surplus resources (food, buildings, blankets, clothing, etc.) for immediate emergency relief of homeless people. It seemed at that time that homelessness was an anomaly, attributable to the recession and destined to end with the onset of economic recovery. Sadly, this was not to be the case, but the early Committee set the groundwork for many important initiatives that have continued to provide relief for millions of homeless people. These include:

- Establishment of a system whereby un- or under-used federal buildings are made available for use by homeless people

- Establishment of a system in which surplus commissary foodstuffs are made available to homeless people

- Establishment of a network of coopera-

tion among federal agencies that help homeless people

- Implementation of a national Food Stamp Information Campaign through which millions of Americans were informed about food stamp eligibility and hundreds of thousands found their way onto the Food Stamp rolls

In 1987, after forming and working with three national councils on housing, health and public awareness, the Alliance formally recognized that the problems of homelessness were deep-rooted and systemic and that emergency assistance—while critical—was not the answer to homelessness. The board of directors, therefore, voted to revise the mission and goals of the organization (see Figure 24.1) and to change its name to more accurately reflect this new mandate.

In June 1987, the Committee for Food and Shelter became the National Alliance to End Homelessness. A long-range plan was developed to redirect the program focus of the organization toward the new goals and objectives.

ALLIANCE ACTIVITIES

The National Alliance to End Homelessness is a membership organization which works to bring all sectors of society together in an integrated structure of research, advocacy, project implementation, and education. The following are ongoing activities of the Alliance.

MEMBERSHIP

The Alliance has two categories of membership.

General Membership. Nonprofit service providers, public agencies and

Figure 24.1

ALLIANCE MISSION

Our mission is to mobilize all sectors of society in an alliance to end homelessness. No American should have to be homeless. The National Alliance to End Homelessness is a nonprofit membership organization dedicated to solving the problems of homelessness and to preventing its continued growth.

ALLIANCE GOALS

The formation of a national alliance made up of people which will reduce the size of the homeless population.

The implementation of policies and programs which will prevent those at risk from becoming homeless.

ALLIANCE OBJECTIVES

To bring together the public (federal, state and, local governments), private (businesses and individuals), and nonprofit (community development organizations, service agencies, churches) sectors in partnerships which can develop and implement programs and policies that address the long-term systemic problems of homelessness.

To work with Alliance members to implement comprehensive assistance programs for the homeless and those at risk. Such programs address the housing, health, employment, and education needs of homeless people in a coordinated fashion. The Alliance works with policy makers to help design such programs and provides service providers with the technical skills to implement them.

To research and evaluate programs which emphasize comprehensive long-term solutions to homelessness. The Alliance then shares this research with policy makers and service providers in an effort to promote and replicate successful programs.

To educate Americans about the nature and causes of homelessness and encourage the public's participation in its prevention and elimination.

---

officials, national organizations and individuals pay an annual membership fee to become general members of the Alliance. As members, they receive *ALLIANCE*, the monthly newsletter; reduced rates at conferences and on publications; access to the Alliance Resource Bank; eligibility for membership in Alliance Network; and the information and advocacy resources of the Alliance.

Business Advisory Council (BAC). Corporations which contribute funds or goods to the Alliance become members of the Alliance Business Advisory Council. Members receive the newsletter and regular information updates, and meet annually to discuss the corporate role in ending homelessness.

ALLIANCE ROUNDTABLE

The Alliance Roundtable regularly convenes the executive and policy-level staff of national organizations to discuss solutions to the problems of homelessness. The forum brings together civil rights, anti-poverty, housing, social service and other groups which have an interest in the issue. Roundtable speakers including representatives of Congress, the administration, corporations and foundations, raise relevant issues which are then discussed by participants.

ALLIANCE RESOURCE BANK

The Alliance Resource Bank helps businesses to distribute surplus or unused goods by identifying Alliance member organizations that can best utilize them. The Alliance has worked with Gantos, Inc., a national clothing retailer, to distribute over half a million dollars' worth of new women's clothing; with Best Western to distribute furnishings; and with London Fog to collect and distribute coats.

ALLIANCE NETWORKS

Alliance Networks provide specialized information to members with a particular program interest. The Alliance currently has two Networks, the SRO (single room occupancy) Network and the Transitional Programs Network. A third Network on income programs is planned for the fall of 1993.

Network members receive a specialized monthly newsletter, reduced rates at regional training conferences in the relevant specialty area, and access to database directories which contain detailed program information. The Networks are also used to promote the exchange of information with federal officials.

ADVOCACY

The Alliance works on its own and in coalition with other national and local organizations on a variety of issues critical to ending homelessness. These include: design of federal programs to aide the homeless; congressional appropriations; Census Bureau enumeration of segments of the homeless population; the Community Reinvestment Act; the low-income housing tax credit; and a variety of other issues in the areas of housing, employment, health care, education, youth, and more.

ALLIANCE PROGRAMS

In addition to its ongoing activities, the Alliance has the following programs:

Alliance Awards Program

The National Alliance to End Homelessness Awards Program recognizes organizations from the nonprofit sector, the public sector, and the private sector which have made an outstanding achievement in ending homelessness. In addition, the John W. Macy, Jr., Award is presented to an individual who has made a significant contribution to this goal. Nonprofit-sector awards have been presented to the Community of Hope in Washington, D.C., SRO Housing, Inc., in Los Angeles and Chinese Community

Housing Corp., San Francisco, CA. Public-sector awards have been presented to the City of Seattle, to Rep. Henry Gonzalez on behalf of the House Committee on Banking and Urban Affairs, and to the St. Louis Homeless Services Network and Board, St. Louis, MO. Private-sector achievement awards have been presented to the Hartz Group, Inc., Pitney Bowes, Inc. and Chemical Bank, NY. The Macy Award has been presented to James Rouse of the Enterprise Foundation and Cushing Dolbeare. The awards ceremony, which is chaired and hosted by Fannie Mae, is attended by hundreds of concerned individuals, cabinet secretaries, members of Congress, and others.

Publications

Checklist for Success: Programs to Help the Hungry and Homeless, published in 1990, was written for the Emergency Food and Shelter National Board. It examines programs to help hungry and homeless people. It includes an in-depth examination of 17 food and shelter programs, ranging from emergency assistance to programs that deal with long-term needs. The report analyzes what makes these programs successful. Also examined are three cities (Minneapolis, Seattle, and St. Louis) and one state (California) in which organizations work together in a network to provide a continuum of services that can move a homeless person into permanent housing. The report includes a bibliography and resource list.

SRO Handbook, published in 1991, is a compilation of materials presented at the Alliance's first two conferences on single room occupancy housing. This Handbook also reviews some of the major issues raised at these conferences. Materials cover predevelopment (architecture and engineering, building community support, public policy, etc.), development (financing and construction), operations (tenant selection, management, eviction, etc.) and service delivery (case management, primary health care, mental health care, etc.) in SRO projects.

What Corporations Can Do to Help End Homelessness was published in 1990. The Alliance surveyed more than 700 corporations to find out what they are doing to help end homelessness. The results of the survey are contained in this book, which gives concrete suggestions for corporate activity in the areas of volunteerism, philanthropy, collection of contributions, awards programs, in-kind assistance, information sharing, networking, employment, advocacy and housing.

What You Can Do to Help the Homeless was published in 1991 by Simon and Schuster. This simple yet comprehensive publication discusses what individuals and families can do that will make a difference in ending homelessness. Examples range from tutoring homeless children and donating used appliances to resettled families, to organizing your church or club to adopt a homeless family or becoming an advocate. The book contains the names and addresses of many sources of information on the issue.

Housing and Homelessness was published by the Alliance in 1987. Developed with the Alliance Housing Council, this publication describes the demographics of homelessness, nationally, and recommends housing solutions to the problem.

Alliance Conferences

The Alliance focuses national attention on issues about which it has a special concern by holding national conferences. These conferences provide in-depth, concrete program information and explore the policy implications of the issue. They are directed to nonprofit organizations, public officials and administrators, private corporations and foundation representatives, and people who are or were homeless.

SRO Housing Conferences

In November 1989 our first national conference on service-enriched single room/efficiency housing was held in Arlington, Virginia. Forty speakers, including Secretaries Jack Kemp of HUD and Dr. Louis Sullivan of HHS made presentations. The focus of the conference was threefold: predevelopment issues (siting, architecture and engineering), development issues (financing and construction) and operation issues (management and services). The Catholic University of America National School of Social Service co-sponsored the conference.

In June 1990 the Alliance and Single Room Occupancy Housing Corporation of Los Angeles sponsored our second national conference on SROs in Los Angeles. The conference presented case studies of five SRO/efficiency housing projects, each serving a different tenant population, including: chronically mentally ill people, people with AIDS, people

with alcohol and substance-abuse problems, general population, and small families (transitional housing, only).

In April 1991 a third national SRO conference was held in Chicago, Illinois, hosted by Lakefront SRO Corporation and Chicago's Single Room Operators' Association. Secretary Kemp once again addressed the participants, announcing the implementation of a new program of FHA insurance for SROs.

Following these three SRO conferences, and at the request of conference participants, an Alliance SRO Network was formed to maintain contact among those concerned about SRO housing (see Alliance Activities).

Transitional Housing Conferences

Transitional housing is designed to help homeless people make the move from shelter, or the street, to a permanent and stable living environment. Transitional housing is generally enriched with a variety of social services which help people to overcome problems that may have contributed to their homelessness.

In November 1990 the Alliance held its first national conference on transitional housing in Arlington, Virginia. Secretary of Labor Elizabeth Dole was the keynote speaker. Participants examined ways in which transitional programs are developed, managed and enriched with social serves by examining a series of case examples. The primary focus on the conference was transitional housing for families.

In June 1991 the Alliance held its second national conference on transitional housing in St. Louis, Missouri. It was hosted by the St. Louis Salvation Army. James Rouse, Chairman of the Enterprise Foundation, was the keynote speaker. This conference examined transitional housing for families as well as facilities for youth, people with alcohol and substance abuse problems, and single homeless people.

Prevention Conferences

In October and November of 1991 the Alliance held two national conferences on the prevention of homelessness in Washington, D.C., and San Francisco, California.

WHAT IT WILL TAKE TO END HOMELESSNESS

Homelessness is a severe and persistent problem, rooted in poverty and often cyclical in nature. And yet there *are* solutions to homelessness. There are programs that help homeless people to stabilize their lives and to become productive members of society. The Alliance bases its activities on discovering and prompting programs that work. Following are some examples.

SRO Housing. Over the past 20 years, gentrification and abandonment have claimed as much as half of our nation's single room occupancy housing. Traditionally a critical housing resource for very-low-income and poor men and women, the loss of SRO housing has spelled homelessness for thousands who cannot afford a more conventional place to live.

Today, nonprofit organizations around the country are working to save and bring back this housing. In Los Angeles, SRO Housing Corporation now owns and operates some 14 hotels in Skid Row. The hotels contain more than 1,000 housing units. The SRO hotels operated by this innovative organization do not fit the traditional picture of a transient hotel. Each is meticulously renovated with plain, but clean and dignified rooms. Each unit has a sink, but bathrooms and kitchens are shared. The kitchens, in particular, provide an important opportunity for socializing and sharing work. SRO has both general population hotels and ones set aside for special populations such as elderly and chronically mentally ill people. The hotels are rigorously managed and many of the employees are drawn from the resident population. Social services are readily available and access to them is facilitated by the staff. In order to help stabilize the community and maintain a safe and human environment, SRO maintains several neighborhood parks. This includes not only gardening the areas, but supervising them and keeping them secure. SRO provides safe, dignified permanent housing for hundreds who would otherwise be homeless.

In other cities around the country, similar SRO projects are under way. In Shreveport, Louisiana, the McAdoo Hotel serves a general population and under the same management (Nesbitt Management Corporation), the Burkhalter now houses people with alcohol and substance abuse problems. In San Francisco, Chinese Community Housing Corporation operates a variety of SRO-type projects in Chinatown, while the Peter Claver Community is a home for people with AIDS who also have alcohol, substance abuse, neurological and other programs. In New York City, St. Francis Residences provide permanent housing and services for people who are chronically mentally ill. In Chicago, Lakefront SRO has permanent housing and services and is working to preserve the existing SRO housing in the city. Certainly SRO housing is an important solution to homelessness for many Americans.

Services and Housing. Around the country there are many successful programs which provide homeless people with the housing and the services they need to get back on their feet. Some of these are long-term, transitional programs. For example, in Washington, D.C., the Community of Hope helps homeless families to stabilize their lives. It provides housing in which the families can stay while they make use of the facility's extensive services, ranging from education and training to counseling. An on-site clinic helps people with any lingering health problems, and a legal aid office works with them to handle any legal entanglements. An excellent child care program is available so that parents can pursue these opportunities without worrying about the safety of their children. Most of Community of Hope's services are provided on-site, so that families need not waste time and resources getting to and from appointments. And many of these services are also available to the community at large. Community of Hope believes that it is critical for programs such as theirs to be well integrated into the neighboring community. The people that they serve are not, and cannot be, isolated from that community. Community of Hope is also involved in developing permanent housing because Washington, D.C.'s shortage of affordable housing makes it difficult for families to find a place to go when they leave the program. And it has embarked

upon a new "learning center" concept in which it will work to help families not only to find permanent housing, but to become fully self-sufficient.

There are many, many other superior programs around the country which help families or individuals with the services and housing they need to get back on their feet. In Birmingham, Alabama, PATH (Partnership Assistance to the Homeless) provides transitional housing and an intensive array of services, including a cottage industry project. In New York City the Homes for the Homeless program also provides transitional housing with services and has an impressive follow-up program that keeps track of clients after they have left to help prevent a recurrence of homelessness. In D.C., ConServe takes the approach of finding families permanent housing and then providing transitional services, which are reduced as the need diminishes. All of these programs are successful at helping people get back on their feet and stabilized in a permanent home.

Prevention. A key to ending homelessness is to prevent people from becoming homeless. The New Jersey Homelessness Prevention Program, for example, is a statewide effort which provides on-time emergency financial assistance to state residents who are at risk of becoming homeless through eviction or foreclosure. The theory is that an early investment of a few hundred dollars can prevent the later public expenditure of thousands of dollars on emergency and transitional shelter. The Connecticut Rent Bank is a similar effort that also has an extensive mediation program to help landlords and tenants work out an agreement and a payment schedule that will prevent eviction. But even these are crisis intervention strategies. We must develop a prevention infrastructure of adequate jobs, housing, and services that will keep people away from the brink of homelessness and save the terrible human and financial costs of this all-too-preventable problem.

*

The National Alliance to End Homelessness firmly believes that it is possible to end homelessness in America. It believes that no American should have to be homeless. It believes that the root of homelessness lies in three areas:

- Lack of affordable housing

- Inadequate incomes

- Insufficient services to deal with personal problems that complicate independent living

In order to truly solve homelessness, all three of these issues must be addressed at the local and national levels. There are many workable and working solutions to homelessness being implemented around the country today and we must develop policies which support and magnify these efforts. We must work to convince every sector of American society and every individual American that they have a role to play in ending homelessness.

These are the tasks that the National Alliance to End Homelessness sets for itself—to discover what works to end homelessness and to build the support and leadership needed to implement these strategies. Homelessness is not acceptable in our land of abundance. We know how to end it and we are compelled, as human beings and as Americans, to do so. It is to this goal, and accepting none less, that the Alliance is committed.

BIBLIOGRAPHY

Baker, Susan G., "Homelessness in America." *Labor Notes*, National Governors' Association Center for Policy Research, Washington, D.C., June 28, 1991.

Housing and Homelessness: A Report of The National Alliance to End Homelessness, Washington, D.C., June 1988.

Mihaly, Lisa K., *Homeless Families: Failed Policies and Young Victims.* Children's Defense Fund Child, Youth, and Family Futures Clearinghouse, Washington, D.C., 1991.

"Testimony of Robert Greenstein, director, Center on Budget and Policy Priorities, before the House Committee on Ways and Means," Washington, D.C., March 13, 1991.

Wright, James D., and Beth A. Rubin, "Is Homelessness a Housing Problem?" Presented at, "Counting the Homeless: The Methodologies, Policies, and Social Significance Behind the Numbers," sponsored by Fannie Mae, Washington, D.C., May 1991.

Chapter 25

Hope for the Homeless: The United Way of America

Pat Ward
United Way of America

Providing basic emergency services—a bed and a hot meal—to alleviate the suffering of those without permanent shelter is the priority of communities in their responses to homelessness. But homelessness is a complex problem that cannot be solved by providing housing alone. More and more, United Ways are turning their attention to helping resolve the problems that lead people into homelessness and keep them there. This chapter details the efforts of a few of the many United Ways around the country which are facing the crisis of homelessness and responding quickly—and creatively.

THE FIRST STEP: ORGANIZE FOR ACTION

In Reno, Nevada, what had started in the mid-1980s as a trickle of homeless peo-ple—mostly homeless men seen on downtown streets—turned into a flood of homeless two years later. Nonprofit groups working with the homeless could not keep up with the influx—first homeless men, then families, especially those headed by women. In October 1987, United Way of Northern Nevada and the Sierra gathered together some 80 representatives of business, organized labor, state and local government, churches, and social service agencies. These community leaders formed a task force to address the needs of the homeless on a comprehensive basis.

Task force members met with people who were homeless and talked with nonprofit groups serving the homeless. To get an even broader view, United Way commissioned a local survey based on interviews with approximately 600 homeless individuals—one of the few

301

such surveys ever conducted to date in the nation. The task force issued a report citing results of the research, as well as 14 recommendations for action. Organizations designated representatives to serve on a Homeless Coalition, which undertook the challenging job of implementing recommendations of the Task Force.

A similar process took place in Kansas City, Missouri. In 1986, Heart of America United Way and the Greater Kansas City Community Foundation and Affiliated Trusts established the Joint Committee on Homelessness. This committee, composed of a broad-based group of concerned community members, developed a plan to help resolve the homelessness problem, raised money to carry out the plan, and was ready to put the plan in action by the end of the year.

One long-time Kansas City community leader said that he had never seen a group respond so quickly and appropriately. "So often," he said, "people study and talk about a community problem and then nothing happens for years. Fortunately, this was not the case in Kansas City."

PREVENTION

United Ways have learned that the most cost-effective solution to deal with homelessness is to prevent people from losing their homes in the first place. Obviously, this solution is the least disruptive to families as well. One way to help prevent the loss of homes is through emergency financial assistance programs that enable people to pay their rent or mortgage. In Houston, The Houston Campaign for the Homeless, a project of 1,000 Houston congregations and United Way of the Texas Gulf Coast, raised $1.6

million in 1989, part of which was used for this very purpose. More than 1,000 families were given emergency aid to prevent eviction.

Another form of emergency aid helps the "in-transit homeless"—people who get stranded while en route from one community to another. United Way of Northern Nevada and the Sierra discovered through its survey of the homeless that people in this group may have a job, or the promise of one, or a family to go in another community. They have become stranded in Reno because of a vehicle breakdown, financial problems, or the desire to earn more money to continue their journey. Emergency assistance funds, gas vouchers, a day-labor employment bureau, and discounted bus tickets are some of the methods suggested by the Task Force to help people continue their journeys.

Locating low-cost housing is another factor in preventing homelessness. The Homelessness Project, an effort of Heart of America United Way in Kansas City, Missouri, and other concerned groups, established a computerized databank that helped 30 community agencies located affordable housing for their clients. Their Housing Listing Service maintains information about the size, cost, location, and availability of nearly 9,000 reasonably priced rental units.

INTERVENTION

Families or individuals who are homeless often require a variety of services ranging from housing and child-care assistance to job and personal counseling to get them back on their feet. United Way of Southeastern Pennsylvania staff was convinced that there were more productive, less-costly alternatives to housing families in emergency shelters for lengthy periods of time. With money raised from designated contributions, over and above the annual campaign gift, the Homeless Families Initiative was begun. To date, 192 families have entered the program.

Experienced case managers with a small caseload—no more than ten families per caseworker—help families secure such services as life-skills education, job training, job placement, day care, housing, transportation, health care, legal services, and more. The case managers help the families develop a plan to achieve the families' own goals for independence. Weekly home visits by case managers help keep each family on track.

Families ready to move from transitional housing to permanent housing face another obstacle: substantial rent and utility deposits. In Reno, it costs somewhere between $500 and $1,000 for a family to move into permanent accommodations. A fund made up of money from several sources—including the Reno/Sparks Board of Realtors, whose 1,400 members are asked to contribute $12 a year to the fund—enables families to take advantage of no-interest loans to meet one-time costs. Kristina Olson, director of United Way's Homeless Outreach and Mobilization Effort (H.O.M.E.), says that some landlords have been willing to waive the deposits because they knew that the prospective tenants are eligible for an H.O.M.E. loan. Almost 300 families have been helped by this program.

Families participating in United Way of Southeastern Pennsylvania's Homeless Families Initiative are eligible for payments from the Family Assistance Fund, a special pool of funds held in reserve. Monies have been allocated to each family so that security deposits and such basic move-in needs as bedding, linens, furniture, and appliances can be arranged.

Sometimes a temporary refuge where parents can stay together and maintain some semblance of normal homelife is all that a homeless family needs to succeed. The Homeless Project in Kansas City created Open Hearts/Open Homes, an experimental program that matches those needing transitional housing with people willing to share their homes for short periods of time. In the first year of the program, 67 people were matched with "host" families.

In Reno, Nevada, a similar "Adopt-a-Family" program is under way under the auspices of the Reno/Sparks Metro Ministry, a United Way-supported agency. Several local churches are sponsoring families to help them get back on their feet. Church members provide assistance with employment, housing and clothing.

FACING REALITY

As United Ways actively involved in long-term efforts to help the homeless have discovered, the issue of local housing conditions must be addressed. An adequate supply of low-cost, decent housing to accommodate all the people who need it is necessary to prevent homelessness.

NEW START TRANSITIONAL HOUSING: ON THE ROAD TO SELF-SUFFICIENCY

United Way of the Ozarks' New Start housing project, the first of its kind in Springfield, Missouri, moves selected families from area shelters into furnished apartments. The project's goal is for families to become self-sufficient within 18 months. This transitional housing provides a more solid base from which homeless people can venture back to independent living.

United Way of the Ozarks developed the project with the City of Springfield. United Way will see the project through the initial phases, then the Salvation Army and the Ozarks Area Community Action Corporation will jointly assume responsibility. The major contributors to the program include the Junior League of Springfield, the Missouri Housing Development Commission, and the Department of Housing and Urban Development (HUD). Junior League funds were used to purchase furnishing and supplies; the Missouri Housing Development Commission supplied the rental assistance funds; and a five-year HUD grant helped expand the program.

Families are referred to New Start by area shelter and service providers. The case manager makes an initial evaluation of a family's eligibility for the program, then a screening committee made up of agencies' staff makes the final decision. After a family enters the New Start program, the case manager works with family members to develop a plan. A typical plan identifies the family's problem areas, its goals, and action steps required to reach those goals.

The case manager visits the family in its apartment at least twice each week to monitor its progress. The family also meets twice a month with a nutrition expert who helps the family plan nutritious, low-cost meals. Children who live in New Start Housing also meet with the nutrition expert in a group setting to learn about nutrition and life skills.

As the family progresses toward self-sufficiency, the case manager and family work together to locate and secure permanent housing. After the family's graduation from New Start, the case manager will provide follow-up services to each family for one year, helping to ensure that the transition to independent living is smooth and permanent.

The Homelessness Project in Kansas City is committed to raising more than $4 million in seed money to build and rehabilitate 500 low-cost housing units—called "Take Part" units—over the next five years. Construction is under way on the first phase of the project. These Take Part housing units will be offered to low-income working families for $200 to $235 per month.

In Houston, money raised through the Houston Campaign for the Homeless helps fund Habitat for Humanity, which provides volunteer-built housing—or rehabilitated housing—for low-income families.

Perhaps the most promising vehicles for building affordable housing are community development corporations (CDCs), nonprofit organizations dedicated to revitalizing urban neighborhoods and rural areas. United Way of Massachusetts Bay, in Boston, was one of the first United Ways to recognize the mutually beneficial potential of forming a partnership with such organizations.

To encourage other communities to replicate the Boston model, United Way of America, with funding from the Ford Foundation, selected five communities to participate in a national demonstration project. United Ways in the communities selected—Chicago, Illinois; Pontiac, Michigan; Rochester, New York; York County, Pennsylvania; and Houston, Texas—have now formed partnerships with other groups to support the work and expand the scope of CDCs.

The shortage of affordable housing in Houston is particularly acute. Substandard housing, deteriorating neighborhoods, overcrowding, few public housing units, and long waiting lists for both conventional public housing and subsidized housing are a few of the many problems facing Houston. Working with four other partners, United Way of Texas Gulf Coast has established New Foundations. Currently, New Foundations is committed to strengthening three promising CDCs in the hopes of increasing the number of housing units.

MAKING A CASE FOR CASE MANAGEMENT

The United Way of Southeastern Pennsylvania Homeless Families Initiative came about out of the desire to demonstrate that providing support services to homeless families was less costly then providing stopgap emergency services. In Philadelphia, it costs $6,300 to provide the most intensive services needed to help participating families move into permanent homes. The cost of sheltering a family of four for one year is nearly double that amount.

United Way of Southeastern Pennsylvania also set out to prove that the downward spiral of poverty and dysfunction which leads to homelessness can be broken through a comprehensive case-management system. In the process, the data on families in the Initiative program revealed some key facts about the homeless population and uncovered gaps in services in the Philadelphia area.

These are the services that the case managers provided to the families:

- Case managers help parents identify their educational and employment goals, and plan appropriate steps to achieve them.

- Due to frequent moves, many families do not receive benefits to which they are entitled. Case managers help families in receiving public assistance, medical-assistance coverage, and supplemental food from the Women, Infants, and Children (WIC) program.

- Parents and children are encouraged to have complete physical examinations and are connected to a source of ongoing health care. Children are brought up-to-date on their immunizations, thereby ensuring they will be able to start school. Information about family planning and AIDS education is frequently discussed with the parent.

- The long-term effects of poverty and family disruption, combined with the rigors of living in a shelter, mean that parents often lack the skills necessary for parenting. All of the Initiative's case managers have been trained to recognize problem areas and develop ways to intervene with parents when problems are identified.

- Research shows that nearly one-half of the women participating in the Initiative have been battered. Case managers provide counseling regarding abuse and refer the family to specialized services when necessary. Case managers work with the police, Community Legal Services, the court system, and other organizations to protect the families.

- The development of peer support groups for women has helped them gain self-esteem and support from each other. The Initiative sponsored a Thanksgiving dinner to help families get acquainted and it also served as an introduction to the peer-support-group concept.

- Day care has been provided to enable mothers to have time apart from their children to keep appointments, locate housing, participate in vocational and educational programs, and seek employment.

- Case managers have observed that many homeless children do not receive the stimulation required to develop at an age-appropriate level because of the parents' daily struggle to provide for the family's basic needs. In addition, school-age children attend school infrequently or not at all because of the family's frequent moves, the administrative difficulties of enrolling in a new school, or the lack of proper school clothing. Case managers help enroll children in school and provide them with school clothing and supplies. Children with serious behavior problems receive psychological testing and are assigned to special education classes. Another important component of the Initiative is to identify and address homeless children's educational and developmental gaps for their future well-being.

CONCLUSION

United Ways engaged in helping to resolve the "homeless problem" know that this is not a problem to be solved anytime soon. Studies show that a three-step program—one which first moves homeless families and individuals from emergency shelters to transitional housing and then to permanent housing—has been more successful than a program that places people from emergency shelters directly into permanent housing. But groups working with the homeless are concerned due to the number of people who are still unable to remain in permanent housing and return to shelters.

While much remains to be done, United Ways' work with the homeless shows that public, private, nonprofit, and business partnerships are effective in mobilizing the forces to deal with pressing homeless problems.

Chapter 26

Coalition for the Homeless

Mary Brosnahan
Executive Director
Coalition for the Homeless

INTRODUCTION

In the summer of 1980, two young researchers, Ellen Baxter and Kim Hopper, were collecting tales of despair and heroism from New York City streets which would culminate in their groundbreaking study, *Private Lives, Public Spaces.* David Beseda and Kathy Clarkson were earning $5 a week tending to the physical and spiritual ills of homeless women at the Catholic Worker. Bob Hayes was a third-year associate at Sullivan & Cromwell, the bluest of the blue-chip Wall Street law firms. When he wasn't tending to the corporate matters of his biggest clients, Hayes somehow managed to find time to formulate a legal strategy which would win the right to shelter for homeless New Yorkers. This cast, along with a few service providers and homeless persons, had worked alongside one another, always cooperative, occasionally overlapping in efforts. But it was not until the eve of the Democratic Convention of 1980 that a coalition was formed—originally in protest of the sweeps taking place around Madison Square Garden.

Twelve years later, New York was poised for another visit from the Democratic party. The breadth of the sweeps of homeless persons from public spaces has sharply escalated in the last few years as local officials' tolerance for this visible poverty continues to erode. Much has changed too for the coalition. A decade after its incorporation, the Coalition for the Homeless has evolved into a $5 million a year organization, which not only continues to bring class-action lawsuits and advocates for change on a systemic level but also offers direct relief to tens of thousands of homeless people through service programs.

Through a brief look at the early history of the Coalition, major class-action suits (both won and lost), and the evolution of the Coalition's direct service component, this chapter will attempt to delineate the elements of effective advocacy, and at the same time address a growing concern that the problem of homelessness is rapidly being reduced to one of pathology.

EARLY HISTORY

Two weeks before the opening of the 1980 Democratic Convention in New York City, workers at The Dwelling Place (a small shelter and drop-in center for women) tipped off Baxter and Hopper that police were forcibly removing homeless men and women from the plaza surrounding Penn Station and Madison Square Garden. The two approached the brothers at St. Francis of Assisi on West 31st Street to use the church's modest courtyard for those evicted nearby. What they hadn't counted on was the sheer number of homeless people who showed up. Dozens of people spilled out of the small courtyard onto surrounding sidewalks. Sleeping mats, food, drink, and medical care were provided each evening of the vigil, which lasted throughout the convention. Although no press release or media advisory had been issued, *The New York Times* covered what it called this "counter convention," and television reports contrasted shots of delegates with street people who had nowhere else to turn.

In order to hold together this effective group, monthly meetings were initiated. From all accounts the general thrust of the discussion was *emergency* relief for persons on the street—pressing the city for instance, to rescind the mandatory gynecological exams and showers which were prerequisites for admission to a women's shelter, or documenting the

number of persons requesting shelter who were turned away each' night. The early debates were divided along what would become classic positions: the dangers of institutionalizing emergency measures vs. the urgent need for immediate relief. Then, the rallying cries ranged from "Shelters are simply expensive Band-Aids" to "Look, it's November and we can't let folks freeze." But all agree today that homelessness was viewed as a temporary crisis which called for emergency measures. David Beseda recalls, "Someone might show up at one of these meetings with information on a movie theater which had just closed. Why not re-open it and let homeless people sleep in the padded seats? I mean really, that was the attitude then. This is an emergency and we must get people off the streets."

Ellen Baxter cites the opening of the Keener Building on Ward's Island in the winter of 1980 as a turning point for this viewpoint. Although Hayes would be successful in getting the city to sign a consent decree which dictated a right to shelter for any man requesting it (*Callahan* v. *Carey*), the Human Resources Administration chose a former psychiatric hospital building located on an island in the East River for its first expansion shelter. Baxter, Hopper, and Hayes were convinced that men would not travel to Keener, and briefly considered withdrawing from negotiations with the city. But the opening night census of 180 rose to over 600 when the weather turned cold. Baxter: "We thought, if this place is so horrible and hard to access and people are still showing up, this is even worse than any of us expected. We were in for the long haul, and temporary shelter is not where it's at."

From Coalition to Coalition

With growing public awareness focused on the emerging crisis, both Hayes and Hopper realized that some vehicle was needed to utilize the offers of help streaming in from a wide spectrum of people. In March of 1981, the Coalition for the Homeless was incorporated, and Hayes left Wall Street for cramped quarters on 22nd Street and began to advocate full-time. Since the initial quandary between emergency relief and structural change remains unresolved, one can well appreciate that the theory driving the Coalition's early strategy on this debate was ill-formulated.

1. Callahan

In August of 1981, the city and state entered into the formal *Callahan* consent decree. Hopper has since likened the two parties to "signatories on a blank check," as in 1981, the size and composition of the class seeking relief were unknown. During the final round of negotiations, Hayes was willing to limit the mandated relief to a mere 700 beds, but the city argued vehemently that the real need was far less. Hence, the compromise that *any* man seeking assistance would be sheltered. (Subsequent Coalition lawsuits, *Eldredge* v. *Koch* and *McCain* v. *Koch*, expanded this right to shelter to include women and families.) The court further appointed the Coalition employees and volunteers as independent inspectors to the new system, with 24-hour access. Through both the Coalition's role in winning the *Callahan* lawsuit and in its role as monitor, the young Coalition was clearly cast in the role of chief proponent and watchdog over what was assumed by advocates to be a stopgap, temporary system. As we know today, the much-needed second half of the equation—adequate permanent housing and services—never materialized.

During the mid- to late-eighties, a good deal of the blame for the absence of long-term solutions was laid at the feet of advocates connected with the Coalition. After all, queried municipal and state bureaucrats, how can New York develop a practical housing plan when all our time and resources are being squandered on shelter? The Coalition was steadfast in its belief that:

• The costs and inefficiencies of a burgeoning shelter system may provide the needed impetus for more permanent solutions to homelessness, namely construction of subsidized housing units. Thus the manifest irrationalities and hardships of a shelter system that is expanding under the prodding of advocates may be countenanced only because shelter itself is viewed as a transitional expedient.

Keeping the city's feet to the transitional fire was fine in theory, but in reality the institutional makeshifts soon developed an inertial force all their own. In this sense, the signing of the consent decree became the flashpoint for a decade-long cold war, since neither the Coalition or the administration had anticipated the sheer scale of need. The more pressure leveraged by Hayes and company to enforce basic minimal standards of decency, the further then-mayor Ed Koch dug in his heels, seemingly convinced that an abysmal municipal shelter system would force the unhoused indigent to find other sources of assistance. Hopper best captured the frustration of a well-intentioned, but failed strategy:

- As long as shelter is endorsed as the solution to homelessness, the deeper structural issues to which the problem indirectly bears witness will be swept under the spreading carpet of permanent emergency relief. A policy of containment substitutes for a thoroughgoing revamping of the apparatus of public assistance. The complexities of need and the parallel complexities of appropriate public response they call for, are ignored in favor of visible evidence that something is being done.

In essence, by refusing to accept its share of responsibility for mass homelessness in the eighties, and by adopting a posture of permanent crisis management, the city inadvertently invented a new form of public housing for the desperately poor.

2. Early Lawsuits and Reports

A lawyer by training and an advocate by instinct, Bob Hayes proceeded to blaze an impressive trail of legal victories on behalf of New York's homeless population. Although Hayes was bolstered by *Callahan* and the public outrage it galvanized, he quickly realized that the shelter victories would ring hollow were there no permanent housing and supportive services. As litigating a broad right to housing would prove impossible, Hayes set out to establish categories of homeless persons for whom a right to supportive housing was feasible.

The first of these cases, *Klostermann* v. *Cuomo*, was brought in 1983 solely against state officials on behalf of some 6,000 former state psychiatric patients who were rendered homeless upon discharge from state facilities. The case was initially dismissed by the trial court and

the state's intermediate appellate court as being nonjusticiable, but the state's highest court ruled unanimously to the contrary. In effect, it held that the judiciary was the proper forum for seeking to enforce the rights of the homeless mentally ill and that lack of funds is not a defense for the state's failure to meet statutorily defined obligations. The state then renewed its efforts to dismiss the case on the ground it owes no duty to the homeless mentally ill. The court again found that the plaintiffs had stated a legitimate claim against the state.

But this twisted legal history took years to unfold. By the time the path was cleared for *Klostermann* to go to trial, the facts surrounding the plight of mentally ill homeless persons had substantially changed. Although the Coalition had initially brought the action against the state, the city in the intervening years had also begun to discharge psychiatric patients onto the streets or to municipal shelters. Because of these factual changes, the Coalition brought two new suits in 1987, *Heard* v. *Cuomo* and *Koskinas* v. *Boufford*, the former against the state hospital system and the latter against city hospitals. Both went to joint trial, and in March of 1991 Justice Lehner of the state supreme court found that "a discharge to the street, to as congregate public shelter or to a flophouse" was not appropriate for this group of individuals and, further, that the city has the obligation to provide such appropriate housing. Justice Lehner underscored that the failure in fulfilling this obligation "is one of the root causes of the homeless crisis in our city." The city immediately appealed the ruling, which triggered a stay in the delivery of relief. In October of 1991 the Coalition will again return to appellate court to argue the case and ask that the state also share in the burden of relief.

Klostermann typifies not only the theory behind many of the Coalition's subsequent legal cases, but also the limitations inherent in litigating these cases. A brief rundown of the major cases in this sphere includes:

• *Palmer* v. *Cuomo*. This case was brought by a group of young people under the age of 21 who were discharged from foster care onto the streets. The plaintiffs sought care until age 21 as well as the education and training while in foster care needed to live independently. In granting a preliminary injunction to plaintiffs in July 1985, the court held that foster children are entitled to care until age 21 and to "career counselling and training in a marketable skill or trade." New York State has issued new regulations defining this responsibility, and the Coalition continues to monitor implementation of these regulations.

• *Grant* v. *Cuomo*. This case successfully sought to require New York City to provide basic protective and preventive services to needy children. State law mandates that reports of suspected incidents of child abuse or neglect be investigated within 24 hours. Often, that was not done. In addition, children in danger of maltreatment or at risk of being placed in foster care were routinely denied a host of family support services including day care. This action also sought to force city and state officials to provide sufficient protection services to children in need. In May 1986, the Supreme Court ruled that city officials must (1) in-vestigate all allegations of maltreatment of children within 24 hours; and (2) provide preventive services that a caseworker considers useful in avoiding the need to place a child in foster care.

• *Mixon* v. *Grinker*. This class-action case demands that medically appropriate housing—including at a minimum private sleeping accommodations and private sanitary facilities—be provided to all homeless persons in New York City who are seropositive for the virus that causes AIDS. The Coalition contends that conditions in city shelters and the street endanger people whose immune systems are compromised by the Human Immunodeficiency Virus (HIV). In January of 1989, a state supreme court judge issued a preliminary injunction ordering the defendants to provide the named plaintiff with a residential placement that would not be injurious to his health.

With each of these cases, the Coalition sought to tackle the problem of homelessness further upstream, seeking either supportive housing or preventive services rather than mass shelters. The trick was to find an enforceable reason why a particular group should not be allowed to languish in shelters, or to find a trace of government entanglement in the group's past. The major drawback, obviously, is time. Although *Klostermann* was conceived in the early 1980s, no relief has stemmed literally from this or the subsequent *Heard* or *Koskinas* cases. And yet, according to Hayes, the real value of *Klostermann* and clones is the opportunity to turn such litigation into a political issue. It was through Hayes's genius for seizing this dual opportunity that the Coalition flourished. The filing of *Klostermann*, for instance, was reported on the front page of *The New York Times*, and most believe that thousands of the new supportive housing units for mentally ill homeless people in New York sprang largely from the heat of the public debate sparked by this case. Similarly, it may be years before the final argument is heard in the *Mixon* case, yet it continues to drive the effort to expand the city's Scattered Site Housing Program for people with AIDS to include all persons infected with HIV.

3. Direct Services

The Coalition's early forays into directly tending to the needs of the homeless poor were admittedly reactive. As court-appointed monitors of the shelter system, Coalition workers often served as personal advocates for the growing numbers of homeless men, women, and children lining up at the office door each morning. Whether it was someone "coded" out of the system for crossing a city employee the night before, cut from welfare benefits due to an administrative foul-up, or living on the street and in need of a referral letter for warm clothing or a meal, Coalition staffers took turns tackling the most immediate needs of the day. Such interventions kept the Coalition in touch with a variety of emergency nightmares—from the city's attempt to centralize all intake for the shelter system, to the needs of the growing numbers of homeless persons who were HIV-ill—many of which would be litigated in one form or another.

A. Grand Central Food Program

Although the Coalition's early service programs were emotionally driven, they also served to strengthen the advocacy mission of the organization by both informing it of the changing nature of the problem and allowing for the development of working models ready for widespread replication. In the winter of 1984, a thirty-two-year-old woman died of malnutrition in Grand Central Terminal, and the next evening David and Trudy Beseda brought a few cartons of sandwiches into the waiting areas and train platforms. This developed quickly into a full-fledged feeding program, but its infancy coincided with massive sweeps in the Terminal, which began closing its doors from 1:00 to 5:00 a.m.

The Grand Central Food Program serves a simple dinner of a sandwich, fruit, milk, juice, and soup to over 800 people every night of the year. The food is prepared by homeless workers and the program is headed by Cyril Young, himself formerly homeless. A large volunteer corps distributes the meals, an exercise which has an unfailing politicizing effect on its participants. After all, you don't have to hand out many sandwiches to realize that people shouldn't have to stand in soup lines for food. Similarly, it's one thing to recognize that people live in the street, and quite another to realize, on your way home at the end of a long evening on a food line, that those with whom you were just talking haven't one. In addition to serving what for many is their only meal of the day, the Grand Central Food Program breaks down barriers and distance between homeless and domiciled New Yorkers and humanizes the problems so often dismissed with the catchphrase "the homeless." A good number of Coalition employees have come up through the ranks of this program.

B. Camp Homeward Bound

Camp Homeward Bound, a sleepaway camp for homeless children, was the brainchild of the Coalition's first programs director, Tom Styron. Styron persuaded city officials to direct the food allowance money for children in welfare hotels to a camp project also funded by private contributions. Thus the stage was set for a respite of green trees and cool lakes—far from the squalor the campers know as "home." Over 400 children in three sessions experienced both the challenges and tranquility of nature in the summer of 1991. And true to Coalition form, this first camp established for homeless children has been replicated many times over.

C. Rental Assistance Program

Beyond feeding people inexpensive, nutritious meals and giving homeless youngsters a lasting glimpse at a different way of life, the advocacy ramifications of these early programs may not be immediately apparent. But once the Coalition committed itself to creating small, workable models to address a variety of ills, the "payoff" was more easily sold to both City Hall and Albany. For instance, New York's welfare hotels are scandalous not only for their filthy conditions, but because the city willingly pays an average of $2,300 per month to "house" a family of four in a 9-foot by 12-foot room. The city and the state together, however, will pay no more than $312 for an apartment for the same four people. Why not subsidize a family for up to two years at $200 per month to bring their shelter allowance into line with rental rates, get the family out of the hotel, and work with the mother to design a strategic plan for financial independence

two years hence? Hayes worked closely with Stephen Brill of *Manhattan Lawyer* to solicit regular donations from New York's legal community at the rate of $10 per partner, per month. The Rental Assistance Program counts around 40 families in its ranks at any given time and since its inception in 1987, over 80 percent of its graduates have successfully made the transition from welfare to work—a powerful programmatic victory to point to when lobbying for an increase in the shelter allowance.

D. Coalition Houses

In May of 1987 Jay and Stewart Poldolsky and Jack and Philip Roitman were brought to trial on charges of systematically terrorizing the mostly elderly tenants living in three brownstone buildings on West 77th Street. The Poldolskys and Roitmans had rushed to join the ranks of landlords cashing in on soaring rental and co-op prices by emptying the SRO for conversion. As their trial progressed, tenants told of attack dogs, prostitutes and drug dealers given free rein over the buildings as well as constant bodily threats and a physical structure on the verge of collapse. As part of a plea-bargained agreement, the judge awarded the three buildings to the Coalition for the Homeless along with $1 million earmarked for renovation and first-year operating expenses. Today, Coalition Houses are fully renovated and occupied by original tenants and homeless single adults from the surrounding neighborhood. Staffed by a live-in superintendent and a social worker, the building offers a thriving example of humane, affordable housing in one of the world's most brutal real estate markets.

While Lauren Steinfeld, the director

of the Rental Assistance Program, occasionally tangles with her clients'
landlords, RAP families are housed
throughout the city in private
developments. Apartments are located by
the RAP parents and the Coalition is
blissfully separated from the daily
management and upkeep of the housing.
Clearly Coalition Houses is more labor-
intensive as the buildings themselves
were riddled with structural problems
and tenant strife. The final two housing
projects of the Coalition are also split
along similar programmatic/owner-oper-
ator lines.

E. Scatter Site Housing Program

Infection with HIV, and the resulting
illnesses, is fast becoming a primary
cause of homelessness in New York City.
This group is not only subject to
widespread discrimination, but the
recurring illness and episodic hospitaliza-
tion of persons who are HIV-ill often
results in a loss of employment and housing. Once they have lost their homes,
people with AIDS or HIV-related illness
rarely have the resources to fight their
way back into an extremely tight real estate market. If NIMBY is the battle cry
directed at developers of low- and very-
low-income housing, imagine the resistance facing those trying to site housing
for homeless people with AIDS.

One effective end-run around staunch
opposition is the Scatter Site Housing
Program for people with AIDS. Under
contract with the city, the Coalition has
found 40 apartments scattered throughout upper Manhattan, subsidized by the
city for homeless singles and family
members with AIDS. But this program
delivers more than just a room and key.
The Coalition's Scatter Site staff consists
of a project director, mental health coun-

selor, substance abuse specialist, three
caseworkers, a maintenance person (for
physical repairs and moving), and clerical
help. This single 40-unit program costs
the City of New York around $850,000
a year, or $21,250 per client—far less
than the cost of admission to the revolving doors of shelter/street/hospital.

F. 124th Street Bridge Building

In the Fall of 1991, the Coalition opened
the Bridge Building on East 124th Street
in Harlem, providing permanent housing
and support services for homeless,
doubled-up, and working poor families.
In 1989, the city and state each anted up
$85 million, and the Bridge Building will
be the first "85/85" project to come on-
line. An additional $1.5 million in tax-
credit funds will subsidize the programmatic portion of the project, which
includes a full-time project manager/so-
cial worker and a job training program.
The kitchen for the Grand Central Food
Program is now located in the basement
of the building.

4. Future Directions

Ten years after *Callahan* was endorsed,
New York City's municipal shelter system has swollen to include 26 facilities
for approximately 10,000 single adults,
and dozens of welfare hotels, congregate
and Tier II shelters for another 15,000
homeless parents and their children. But
what of the other tens of thousands of
homeless New Yorkers bedding down on
city streets, in public parks and abandoned buildings? The sad fact is that, as
huge as the public shelter system has
grown, the guiding principle of its operation remains—as it has been all along—
one of active deterrence. Massive armories house drill floors with up to a
thousand cots just three feet apart from

one another. Virtually insecurable, un-speakably filthy, and overrun with drugs, crime, and rodents, shelters such as Fort Washington Armory in Manhattan serve not so much to offer decent relief to their residents, but rather to stem the seemingly endless tide of homeless men and women just outside their doors. Ironically, because this *is* what passes for relief and, nightly, tens of thousands *do* accept it, no more potent signifier of the depth of distress of homeless Americans could be devised.

New York City is not alone in its con-viction that municipalities have largely been left holding the bag following an eleven-year retreat by the federal govern-ment from coherent housing policy. In this era of budget cuts, the tensions between emergency-shelter and perman-ent solutions have actually escalated. But what will it take to reverse the current free-fall in housing prospects for very-low-income Americans? The first step requires a radical rethinking of what defines "adequate shelter." Substantial reductions in size of the barracks-style facilities must be coupled with a re-com-mitment to the transitional notion of "shelter." Of course the only way effectively to shift from the status quo of shelter as permanent warehouse to shel-ter as a necessary but temporary evil is to rethink, simultaneously, the question of affordable housing. This means that en-ergies devoted to subsidized, permanent housing must be redoubled. It also means that the time to consider housing as a right is now. Federal legislation is currently being drafted to redefine hous-ing assistance as an entitlement—similar to food stamps or AFDC. As of last year, single, able-bodied adults were added to the ranks of families and disabled adults eligible for the federal government's

limited, but highly effective, Section 8 certificate program. This means that once housing becomes an entitlement, all homeless individuals could benefit from this program, without languishing for years on waiting lists.

Resistance on both levels is substan-tial. One lesson from the past decade is clear: anytime a safe, humane abode is opened, it has never gone wanting for applicants. Certainly the cities must fear the avalanche of people who would clamor for a warm, secure place to rest. But frankly what choice do we have? The quality of life continues to deterior-ate not just for the needy but for every person confronted with this national tragedy. Emergency relief is obviously in-effective and a thorough waste of money, and police actions have proved a crash-ing failure on every conceivable level.

In New York City specifically, the Coalition has shifted its strategy for downsizing shelter away from the courts and toward the City Council. In 1984, the Coalition sought an injunction on behalf of a group of men and women who live in municipal shelters ordering the state to enforce its own regulation prohibiting any single shelter from maintaining a capacity of over 200 per-sons, or from crowding more than 30 beds into a single room (*Wilkins* v. *Per-ales*). (In the spring of 1984, over 1,400 men slept in a single room at one city shelter.) The court held, in early 1985, that the state was free to waive its own regulations limiting the size of shelters. In the fall of 1991, legislation authored by the Coalition was introduced in the City Council outlawing the use of arm-ory shelters by 1993. Although passage is by no means assured, both liberal council members, eager to better the lot of arm-ory residents, and more-conservative legislators who have armories in their districts have rallied around the bill.

On the permanent housing side, major concerns have arisen regarding the restrictive funding streams designated for housing special-needs populations—especially the mentally ill. In New York, particularly, projects are currently coming on line with up to 200 units, all of which are solely reserved for mentally-ill homeless persons as described by the 1990 New York/New York agreement. The danger, of course, is that this strategy will amount to reinstitutionalization on a smaller, more dispersed level. The most successful and stable models one can point to, such as Ellen Baxter's program "The Heights" (located in the Washington Heights area of Manhattan), house an integrated tenancy of formerly homeless working poor, students, elderly *and* mentally ill individuals. Widescale replication of this model of permanent housing with temporary services could also be the first step toward addressing the two thirds of the homeless population who defy compartmentalization into "special needs" categories.

Finally, the battle for bricks and mortar is currently being waged on two ideological fronts: frayed hope and alien definition. Ten years into the modern disgrace of mass homelessness I fear many are on the cusp of losing hope that a working solution is possible. The collective memory is short, and much of the work of the Coalition hinges on reminding Americans that just 10 years ago, we didn't see the thousands upon thousands of homeless poor who wander our streets in search of a safe corner or vestibule to rest. The most potent weapon in the far right's arsenal to undermine a humane solution is the charge that this is not a problem of housing or poverty, but rather, one of pathology. That homeless people are all mentally ill, drug addicts, or in a variety of ways, *fundamentally different* from us, and that it is this difference that accounts for (and, in their eyes, even justifies) their wretched lot, is the subtext of writing from the Heritage Foundation to HUD. The real danger in this trajectory is that there is no better excuse to distance oneself from this human tragedy. If we allow ourselves to confer a sense of "otherness" to the most visibly poor amongst us, surely it is easier to avert our eyes in resignation. But if, in the teeth of this recession, we accept that most of us are a single paycheck or divorce or accident away from the streets, then the essential shift in federal spending priorities cannot be far behind.

Chapter 27

Philadelphia, Pennsylvania: People's Emergency Center

Gloria Guard
Executive Director
People's Emergency Center

This is the story of what happened when our small and dedicated community of volunteers and staff at Pennsylvania's oldest shelter for homeless families was told that we had to move out of our "home"—an old Methodist church in need of repair. It describes the three-year-long process of finding a site, organizing a team, obtaining community support for the move, raising money, designing and building the facility, and finally making and celebrating the move. It also lays out a number of key principles, critical to the success of the deevelopment.

I. HISTORY OF THE ORGANIZATION

Founded in the early 1970s by two young, liberal Methodist ministers, People's Emergency Center (PEC) was originally intended to be a vehicle for community work by active college students enrolled at the University of Pennsylvania and Drexel University. Reverends Jim Hallum and Bob Edgar (later Congressman Edgar) decided to put community space on the first floor of a large, century-old church building to better use and harness the energies of the college kids on both nearby campuses. They started the nonsectarian, nonprofit PEC, Pennsylvania's very first shelter for homeless families in 1972, when homelessness was considered an isolated incident in the lives of stranded travelers or fire victims.

For our first eight years, PEC was open only on weekends, with all-volunteer help. On Monday mornings the students would resume classes and homeless families would be referred to the mainstream service system, which had been closed for the weekend. But by 1980, the lack of a local comprehensive

317

service system, combined with the recognition of domestic violence as an intolerable social problem, brought a growing demand for family shelter. So the PEC Board decided to raise funds to pay staff, who would be supplemented by college volunteers so that the Center could stay open 365 days a year. The Board members wanted to create a model full-service program that could be easily replicated.

By 1983, when I joined PEC, Reagan administration cutbacks were taking their toll, pushing more families out of their homes and bringing the nightly census at PEC up to 35, three times greater than a decade earlier. By 1987, the census had doubled again, the staff and budget had tripled, and the Board had initiated a wide range of comprehensive social and educational support programs that went considerably beyond emergency care. The demand for help had grown each year, while the availability of low-income housing had decreased. Further, while the Center had increased its capacity and its programs, families were staying longer and longer waiting for permanent housing. In 1987, operating at full capacity every night, we were forced to turn away at least 50 families every week.

That was the year we found out that our home, the Asbury Methodist Church, was slated for development by the Methodist Church hierarchy and that PEC would have to move. We were stunned. All of us—the Board, staff, and volunteers—had always identified ourselves with that specific physical structure. That was where we had started and no one had ever expected that we would have to move. The church edifice had protected staff and residents alike from gun-toting battering

husbands and violent boyfriends. Rising in the midst of two college campuses, it had been a symbol of sanctuary and social justice. Though it was hot in the summer, cold in the winter, and almost impossible to keep clean and rodent-free, the Asbury Church had been our home for fifteen years. It was unnerving for us to have to grapple with moving away. And, the church wanted us to move in a year's time.

II. THE PROCESS
A. Putting Together the Team

Once the news had sunk in, one of the very first steps the PEC Board took was to appoint a Relocation Committee, headed by then treasurer David Dayton, who had recently retired as vice president of ARA Services. Members of the Committee included Board president Helen Bigham, recently retired from her post as president of the School Food Service Workers Union, and other Board members including a corporate vice president, whose day-to-day job involved financing large developments, the then-current Methodist minister of the Asbury Church, who acted as go-between with PEC's landlords, and me. This Committee was critical to the success of PEC's future. Its members, along with Mark Schwartz, our attorney, became the repository of all the hundreds of facts that had to be analyzed before any decision could be made. All major decisions, legal and otherwise, were made by the full PEC Board after thorough presentations and discussion. In every case, the Relocation Committee brought already thought-through recommendations to the full Board.

On a parallel track, I kept the staff informed and elicited feedback on selected decisions every few months. PEC's contributors (individuals and organizational funders) were also kept informed with personal calls, letters, and the PEC Newsletter. Early on, I consulted with key groups, such as the United Way, government officials, and political leaders, and kept them informed at every critical turn of events.

Principle #1—Keep everyone fully informed and ask for their help and advice.

Asking for help and advice and keeping everyone informed as much as possible was critical to our overall success. Although this process required many more meetings and steps than some might consider necessary, we did it because we knew how important it was. This principle reflected the way that PEC operated, and continues to operate, all of its programs, and is key to the success of all our undertakings. Our relocation process was so inclusive that, in the end, everyone on PEC's team—Board, staff, volunteers, contributors, elected officials, and neighborhood groups—had ownership of the final product. PEC's success was their success. And when we finally celebrated our move, the hundreds of people who attended genuinely felt that they could take pride in the outcome.

B. Deciding to Own Our Own Site and Site Selection

We were given the option of moving temporarily, for two or three years, while the church was developed by Church trustees with space reserved for the shelter. However, a combination of facts led the PEC Board to decide against this choice. It was very difficult to find a temporary space to rent that was outfitted

for a shelter, and no foundation or government source was willing to make grants for capital improvements to a site that would be used for only a few years. The idea of moving twice was also quite unattractive. But the most important factor was that no one on the Board wanted to be a renter. We didn't want PEC to be vulnerable again and risk having to move. We also wanted to help create a financially secure future for PEC by building or remodeling a piece of our own real estate.

Having made that decision, we began our search for a neighborhood and a site. We wanted to stay in the same general neighborhood for a number of reasons. First, we were known in the area and many of our clients come from nearby. Our affiliation with the two universities had been fruitful, and we still had a number of volunteer college students. The West Philadelphia/University City area is racially and culturally mixed, with a history of being liberal, and we needed understanding neighbors who would accept our primarily African-American young families and young children. We had long-standing relationships with the local schools, hospitals and special children's facilities, and since it was a university community, these facilities were and are easily some of the best if not the best in the city. These factors, along with the close proximity to Center City (Philadelphia's downtown business district), made University City the best choice. The same factors led to the area having become very expensive and somewhat gentrified over the previous two decades. Nevertheless, we set about contacting realtors, following leads, and inspecting potential properties.

Jason Stump, in the city's Office of Housing and Community Development, found us a 30,000-square-foot abandoned factory building at 3902-14 Spring Garden Street, that had been taken over as a result of tax delinquency. The price was right—free, and the location was ideal—in University City next door to the Sixteenth Police District Headquarters and on the edge of the gentrification. But the size was a real problem. We had been living in a 6,000-square-foot space, and we were very crowded, but we never thought that we needed five times the space we had. The building was immense and the Relocation Committee was overwhelmed by the size. I knew about potential state funding for low-income homeless housing and suggested that the third floor of the building be turned over to permanent housing with these funds, while PEC used only the first two floors for its current emergency and for the planned expansion of its transitional operations. But the Committee was daunted and asked me to call Stump and turn down the offer of that building. Stump was disappointed since the abandoned building, which ran a block long, may have ended up standing vacant another 25 years. He suggested that PEC team up with a private, for-profit developer, that could relieve the PEC Board of the responsibility of the nuts and bolts of development. A private housing developer could be given part ownership in the project.

Principle #2—Don't be overwhelmed by the challenge of looking for your ideal situation.

The nature and purpose of our operation had a real bearing on whether or not we should seek development help from the outside or build the capacity internally. By 1987, PEC was operating a comprehensive, year-round program that went well beyond shelter. Our 70 beds were filled each night with people who received not only the basics of food and shelter, but who also participated in every possible kind of social and emotional support programming along with a full array of educational workshops. Often, we would turn away the offer of free legal clinics or employment workshops, telling volunteers that either we already had the help that they were offering or that there just wasn't a free hour between 9 a.m. and 9 p.m. in which to schedule another service. Pediatricians, drug counselors, free lawyers, parenting experts, nurses, literacy and job skills teachers, Girl Scout leaders, and many more professionals and volunteers came in weekly to PEC to work with the residents, in addition to our core staff of over twenty. We had become what the early Board had wanted: a model program that other shelters emulated. Many of Philadelphia's newest initiatives were test run at PEC.

Board and staff were unwilling to deviate from PEC's basic mission, which was to provide direct services in order to become a community development agency. We were very good at what we did and wanted to continue. Our foray into the community development world was motivated by the need to find a new home, not by a change in our mission. That is why we decided to seek out development expertise as opposed to building the capacity in our own staff. We were also financially unable to afford bringing on a consultant or developer that we would have to pay. Although we had set aside some funding for the new site, we wanted to reserve that for the actual bricks and mortar and try to find the help we needed for free. For us, the best answer was to seek out a for-profit developer that we could work with without an outlay of funds. In return for their help we would offer them a solid relationship with a nonprofit with the benefits we would bring.

The prospect of working with a developer partner also opened up the opportunity for the PEC Board to do what we had always dreamed of—provide a physical structure of the best kind to house the programs that we knew would work. We could also provide permanent housing—a critical part of the "real solution to homelessness"—in addition to the emergency and transitional housing that we had operated in the past. With thousands of square feet at our disposal, we could have several spacious rooms for the kids, including separate rooms for different age groups. We would have a secure space for a children's library, a long-time vision of our Education Program Director. Our homeless teens, who came to PEC unaccompanied by parents, could have their own space, away from the adults and the little kids. Moms and their little ones could have rooms that were furnished with real furniture (not lockers) and they could lock up their rooms so that all their possessions weren't constantly at risk of theft from other residents. All the barriers of everyday living in cramped quarters, never designed for housing the homeless, would simply disappear overnight if we had a blank slate and lots of room—and that's exactly what happened.

C. Findin a Developer Partner

By this time, the PEC Board had engaged an attorney, Mark Schwartz, executive director of the Regional Housing Legal Services (RHLS), a nonprofit organization that provides legal and technical assist-ance to other nonprofits to enable them to increase the quantity and quality of housing and economic opportunities available to low-income people. RHLS is part of the Pennsylvania's Legal Services system, so PEC was represented at no cost. Six months previous to this, Schwartz had suggested using a private developer, but the right match of developer and building site had not been available. The Committee reconsidered a partnership when the concept was raised again. Relocation Committee members were visited by John Rosenthal and Rich Barnhart of Pennrose Properties at the suggestion of Jason Stump. The Pennrose owners were different from other developers that PEC had met in that they were very well informed about and experienced in government funding for low-income housing. They had a long history of building and managing elderly and family low-income housing, had worked with other nonprofits, and were familiar with the myriad of regulations and funding streams. They were also knowledgeable about future funding sources and were aware of state financing for homeless housing, so they were in the market for a homeless organization with whom they could work to draw down homeless funds. They were more than willing to be flexible and patient while PEC's Committee considered all the angles.

At first proceeding cautiously, and only after checking with a number of independent sources, we decided to go forward with Pennrose and with the building at 39th and Spring Garden Streets. With the participation of Mark Schwartz, we met with Rosenthal and Barnhart a number of times to come up with a mutually agreed-on description of the nature of our relationship. Although the details would be worked out as the development and funding took shape, here are the general principles of our partnership with Pennrose:

1. PEC, as a nonprofit, would get the property from the City for free;

2. PEC and Pennrose would both have legal ownership of the property, and, after fifteen years, Pennrose would turn over its ownership share to PEC;

3. PEC would operate the shelter, transitional housing, and all social programs on the first and second floors, and Pennrose would operate permanent housing on the third floor as low-income rental housing for a minimum of fifteen years;

4. Both PEC and Pennrose would raise money for their respective parts of the development (2/3 :: 1/3);

5. PEC would be in charge of the social work part of the project, would manage all of the programs operated on-site and would be in charge of referring all potential residents to the permanent housing component;

6. Pennrose would serve the function of the developer—taking responsibility for the design, construction, paperwork, any government regulations and all financial accountability (subject to PEC approval);

7. After the building was completed, Pennrose would manage PEC's portions of the building without a management fee.

The full PEC Board approved an agreement which spelled out the above points, as did Pennrose. At settlement, these issues were spelled out in legal language and agreed to by all the parties.

Principle #3—Get the best partners you can; experience is crucial.

D. Zoning and Neighborhood Relations

Immediately after settling on the site, PEC staff set about the task of educating the people who would become our new neighbors. The neighborhoods in the University City area are highly organized, each with its own organization, officers, and dues-paying membership. The building sits at the apex of four distinct separate communities. The City Planning Commission staff helped us to identify the key community groups as well as the individuals who were active in the area.

We met personally with the president of each of the four critical organizations, went to organizational meetings and made presentations. And we went to the meeting of the West Philadelphia Coalition of Neighborhoods, the umbrella group. We also went door-to-door in a two-block radius of the building, talked to neighbors and left a brochure and explanation of what we planned for the then-abandoned building. The neighbors were very excited about the vacant building being put to good use.

We were able to get endorsements of support from three of the four neighborhoods (the fourth remained silent) and from the umbrella organization, as well as a written agreement with the neighborhood in which we resided that detailed their requests and our willingness to meet their needs. None of their requests were unanticipated or unreasonable. For example, one issue was our assuring that trash would be stored internally in the building and that we would have daily private trash-removal service. That agreement became part of the zoning board decision.

We secured a lease for the property from the city in order to gain site control—thereby meeting one of the federal funding application requirements. With that lease, we requested a zoning hearing. When we went to our hearing, we had letters of support from the neighborhood groups as well as support from the City Planning Commission.

More than two years later, right before we moved into the building, we leafleted all the neighbors within a three-block radius and sent a mailing out to all the organizational leaders telling them exactly when we were moving in, inviting them to our open-house celebration, and asking if they wanted to be on our mailing list. Many of our neighbors came to the open house, and a number are on the newsletter mailing list and receive quarterly mailings.

In addition, we asked the president of the umbrella organization to sit on our Board, where he became an active member. We also use our new facility to host meetings of both the umbrella organization and of the Saunders Park Neighbors Association (our immediate community group).

We had enjoyed a long relationship with our city councilman, Lucien Blackwell, who had been referring constituents to PEC for emergency help consistently over the past fifteen years. Relocation Committee members paid him a visit to explain our plans and to ask for his support. We were greeted with support and a very firm promise of help, based on his appreciation of PEC's work and history.

The councilman wrote us a letter of support for the zoning hearing, and he sponsored the legislation needed to authorize the transfer of city property to PEC through the local Vacant Property Review Committee process. In fact, every time we needed his help and support, all we had to do was ask. He wrote letters and made phone calls whenever we asked. We never had to ask him for city council funds; the local revenues that we needed came through the administration. He was an enormous help in "greasing the wheels" of the bureaucracy and in making it clear to all that our project was one that had his backing.

In addition to our City Councilman, our Mayor, W. Wilson Goode, was completely supportive of the project from its outset. He signed support letters, approved funding, and spoke earnestly our behalf whenever we asked.

Principle #4—Get community and political support as early as possible, and keep them informed throughout the process.

E. Designing the Space

Our developer partners, Pennrose Properties, wanted to use an architect that they had worked with before, and we agreed. Rich Kline was the architect partner in charge from Goldner, Goldfarb and Kline (GGK), the firm selected. In our planning meetings, I represented the Relocation Committee and brought the staff perspective to the table, since our perspective, as the primary users of the building, was critical to the design. We presented security, durability (i.e., commercial-grade hardware), cleanliness, comfort, and ease of use as the elements that were the most important to us, in that order. Rich Barnhart from Pennrose represented our developer partner's interest in the specific design of the apartments, and in the overall design of the building, especially as it related to the management of the property over time.

Funding requirements and building codes had to be included in the design. But we went beyond these requirements in some cases. For example, we asked for help from the Housing Consortium for Disabled Individuals, whose executive director consulted with us and the architects on the design. She pointed out ways to make the building more accessible and more easily used by the disabled without costing more money. Bringing that kind of help in at the design stage assured a building that really can be handicapped-accessible and not just meet government requirements. As of 1993, PEC remains the only truly accessible homeless-family center in the area and we currently house two wheelchair-using adult women.

Working with a triangular-shaped building presented the designer with a challenge, made tougher by the fact that it was formerly two different buildings with a 17-inch difference in floor levels on the second and third floors. Sleeping rooms had to be on the periphery of the building because of the available air and light. Staff wanted the children's educational program rooms also to have natural light. Offices, the huge dining room and kitchen, and storage closets ended up in the windowless area.

Each of the three stories is 10,000

square feet with a separate programmatic purpose and different clientele. The first floor is the emergency shelter and intake and is also where the general public has access. Seven dorms (sheltering up to 16 teenagers and more than a dozen Moms with their 25 babies and toddlers) are on this floor along with a huge ladies' room with baby bathtub and adult bath and showers. The fully equipped restaurant-style kitchen is right next to the dining room, which ends up being the central spot for any parties and celebrations, since all of PEC's residents, staff, and volunteers can fit there at once.

The second floor comprises the transitional housing portion, where 11 private rooms with private baths were planned (one per family). On this floor are the children's program area (three large sunny rooms with all the accouterments of the best learning centers), two conference rooms, resident lounges, and offices.

The third floor was to be permanent apartments, and under usual circumstances would have been able to accommodate 10 to 12 units. Because of the unusual shape of the building, much of the square footage was wasted in triangular corners, so that only nine apartments could fit. The end result is nine spacious and very attractive apartments, some with sunken living rooms and others with lots of extra closet space.

There was a need for a relatively high level of security throughout the building—to protect residents and staff from the outside, to protect residents' and PEC's belongings from one floor to the next, and to protect residents in first-floor dorms from visitors who come into the lobby. A complex system of locks, cameras, alarms, and access had to be designed that would be easy to use and protect. We even had to plan to make it difficult for residents to climb out of windows or get in and out of the building without being seen, since some of our teenage residents are adept at sneaking out late at night or sneaking undesirable guests in.

A building that would be easy to keep clean and that would not require constant repairs was of particular importance to PEC staff and budget. We had spent thousands of dollars and much effort over the years trying to keep up with our first unusual building. Our old home, in the church, although divided over the years into separate program space, was almost impossible to keep clean with its original soft pine floors and wooden cabinets. Although it had been "renovated" over the years, most of the changes were in the form of partitions and work done by volunteers using materials typical of those used in a home. Rehanging doors and repairing the front door locks were a weekly occurrence that we did not want to repeat. We also requested some "comfort" in the form of air-conditioning for Philadelphia's humid and hot summers and a pleasant color scheme.

The architects spent time with us at our then-current home to get a feel for how we ran our operation. They brought in a special restaurant kitchen designer to help set up the design of the kitchen, since we cook and serve in excess of 100,000 meals a year and needed to plan for the most efficient use of space. Whenever appropriate, PEC staff met with the architects to talk about the details of our needs—for the children's areas, custodial storage, trash disposal, office equipment, and other special needs.

The architect took charge of bidding out the job, and we then sat down with the selected contractor to go through the design and whittle down costs. We took a proposed rooftop playground out of the design altogether, saving $250,000, decided on a cheaper HVAC system with fewer local controls, and cut the number of ceiling lights and security cameras back, in addition to numerous small changes. We tried our best to end up with everything that we needed and some things that we wanted, within a tight budget.

The end result is a building that is very livable and secure, easily cleanable with the help of two custodians, and in excellent condition after two years. We have had a few isolated problems that others could avoid if they learned from our experience. First, we had two separate "surprises" in the midst of the actual construction when the city inspectors told us that we did not have the proper fire prevention system. We had to add sprinklers throughout the building, after having been told that they were not necessary, and later added sprinklers at certain windows. These two changes ate up our entire contingency fund, leaving us little room to put back items that we hadn't wanted to eliminate. Second, if I had to do it again, I would insist on a locksmith subcontractor who would work with staff from the outset to organize a key system that was easy to work and extremely secure. Our contractor wanted the hardware subcontractor to supply the locks and key system, and that supplier did not install the locks. The combination of a carpenter installer and a non-security expert being the supplier resulted in our having to replace much of the system with the help of a locksmith. This latter situation was also the result of using an architect and contractor who were more used to housing developments than institutions where security (internal and external) is a live issue twenty-four hours a day.

Principle #5—Always keep in mind what elements are essential when you make cost-based decisions.

F. Financing

From the first day that we learned that we had to move, the Relocation Committee and I were concerned with raising the money needed not only to renovate the building but also to pay for the moving vans, new phone system, beds and lockers, dining room tables, cribs, playpens and all other special equipment and furnishings. We also projected a cost exceeding $2 million for the construction alone.

I had worked with other advocates in the Pennsylvania Low-Income Housing Coalition to urge the state housing finance agency to make low-interest loans available for the development of permanent housing for the homeless. Those funds were perfect for the third-floor apartments, and Pennrose pursued them immediately. Pennrose had committed to securing financing for one third of the project (which ended up totaling over $2.5 million). These state funds comprised half of their financing and were supplemented by their own private equity and some state Department of Community Affairs funding.

Congress had discovered homelessness by 1987 and passed the Stuart McKinney Act, providing capital and operating funds for emergency shelter and for transitional housing, on a competitive basis. As soon as we had settled on the Spring Garden Street site, I started to put together funding proposals for McKinney Act money, limited to $200,000 for transitional housing renovations. Though our first proposal didn't meet minimum criteria (we hadn't had our zoning hearing), the second proposal was successful and came with the bonus of five years of operating funds. A McKinney Act proposal for capital funds for the renovation of the emergency shelter portion of the building was also successful and was granted through the local homeless authority.

We needed much more money to add to the federal contribution to make the project work. We were able to get the interest of W. W. Smith Charitable Trust, a local foundation that had supported PEC in the past and that made capital grants. They made a challenge grant of $200,000 over two years. Their contribution interested other foundations and gave the project an enormous amount of credibility. Two other foundations and two banks made small grants, and a number of individuals and churches made contributions as well.

We made an application for federal Rental Rehabilitation funding for the eleven rental units on the second floor in the transitional housing area. At a unit maximum of $7,000 per unit, we were able to draw down another $77,000 from this source.

We had started discussions with the Philadelphia Office of Housing early on in the process and had secured the commitment of then Housing Director Ed Schwartz for his support. He ended up being the key to putting together the complete financing package, because he controlled the city's Community Development Block Grant (CDBG) funds, which are relatively flexible. He also had a record of helping projects bring in federal, state, and local dollars so that the city was among the participants in any project and not the sole contributor. Ed Schwartz had made some headway in initiating and supporting homeless-housing projects so that the PEC project was well within his vision of the kind of developments that the City of Philadelphia needed to support.

Having the purse strings of the CDBG dollars also allowed Ed Schwartz to take advantage of some pretty innovative funding practices, one of which was used in our project. Since private developers like Pennrose often made a healthy profit by syndicating the proceeds of the tax credits in a low-income housing development, Pennrose offered to contribute a portion of those profits to front-load low-income housing developments trying to get off the ground. Pennrose was willing and able to make a large contribution to the PEC project. We needed that contribution to make ends meet as well as to meet the challenge presented by the W. W. Smith Charitable Trust. In turn, Pennrose took the charitable contribution write-off. In addition, Ed Schwartz was able to contribute CDBG dollars to a project that he knew had an infusion of private dollars, thereby decreasing the need for limited local funds.

PEC needed additional government funding, our own equity of about $100,000, and private financing to close the gap. We had been in conversation with two local banks for several months, having been introduced by our lawyer to the key low-income-housing lenders in Philadelphia. We ended up working with CoreStates/PNB/First Pennsylvania, Philadelphia's most community-minded and largest locally owned bank. CoreStates had a team of experts on staff who helped with the whole project. Not only

did they loan us $315,000 at a fixed rate of only one-half point over their then-prime rate, but they also referred us to their charitable contributions staff, who helped us get a small grant for the duration of the three years of the development. Their lawyer and their lending staff worked closely with us and helped us frame the best possible solutions to our financing challenges. They also protected their investment, and PEC in turn, from potential problems with the different funding sources and partnership arrangements.

Somewhere in the process of hunting for money, a private foundation raised a serious question about making a donation to a project which had a for-profit developer as a partner. Foundations must protect their tax status and cannot be viewed as making a contribution toward an effort, like low-income housing, which would then turn a profit for a private developer in the form of tax syndication. We were very concerned about this issue and turned to our lawyer for help. He suggested legally dividing up the property into two separate pieces of property, like a condominium, so that foundations and others could make a charitable contribution to the nonprofit that owned one of the two condominiums. And, at the end of fifteen years, as covered in our agreement with Pennrose, the third-floor property, consisting of nine apartments, would be given over to PEC by Pennrose.

Although we never succeeded in getting funding from the foundation that raised the issue, we did go forward with dividing up the property, since it made everything clearer and easier to explain, as well as making this project a better recipient of charitable dollars. However, this necessitated bringing in even more lawyers (and having more meetings), which added to the legal costs of the project.

By the time we went to settlement, 17 separate sources of funds had been brought to the table and seven different lawyers were there to represent all the parties to the project. It was a memorable all-day affair. We took up three meeting rooms in one of Philadelphia's prestigious law firms. PEC had two staff members, three Relocation Committee members and our lawyer present all day. Our Board president opened the settlement by asking everyone to join hands for a prayer—shocking some of the more jaded members of the bar and the urbane and sophisticated developers. When she was through with her brief but meaningful prayer, we had all been reminded that we were about to embark on a crucial effort to help the homeless, those much less fortunate than ourselves, whom we had a duty, a responsibility, and an opportunity to serve. And, we were reminded that we needed some divine intervention and support, and that we should set aside our egos and our petty differences to make sure that we completed the settlement successfully. We were blessed with a lot of help not only on that day but throughout our endeavors as well.

Principle #6—Leverage the money and connections you have to bring in financial, community, and political supports.

G. Construction

The contractor we chose, DOMUS, Inc., is run by a man who had built the headquarters for one of Philadelphia's oldest and most well respected African-American community programs—the House of Umoja. Like PEC, his work had its roots in the early seventies when social justice community work was respected and funded. He had been suggested, among other contractors, by our lawyer as a person whose company built solid, responsive buildings and was easy to work with. The PEC Relocation Committee felt good about the choice from the beginning, and our feelings were borne out as accurate over the course of the project.

Construction started very soon after settlement, with the architect responsible for convening job meetings every two weeks on site. PEC was always represented by at least one if not two Board members along with myself. Sometimes we would bring other Board or staff members as the project progressed and when we wanted to talk about specific items. Pennrose was always at the meetings, with at least one of their partners (usually both) and their administrative staff, who was in charge of the arduous and complex billing and change-order paperwork. Government inspectors were also there, state and city inspectors showing up regularly and federal representatives coming less frequently.

These meetings were very educational for me and for the nondevelopers present and informative for everyone involved. We were kept up-to-date on the details of the project and any and all problems, especially ones that might cost money. We had to change some of our original assumptions and plans, but there was nothing that couldn't be overcome with the combination of experts and enough money in the contingency budget. There was always a willingness to work through any differences of opinion and, when in doubt, to go forward with the best-quality solution (not the cheapest).

Because of the nature of our operation, it turned out to be critical that PEC was represented at every meeting. Had we not been there, the architect, developer, or contractor would have made decisions based on assumptions from other buildings. No matter how good anyone is at their job, the people who actually have to live with the facility must take part every time decisions are made that affect the outcome. Toward the end of the project, Pennrose Management staff joined us and provided input about building management issues and decisions.

The construction took 14 months, two months longer than anticipated. The Methodist Church officials were extraordinarily patient with PEC and our inability to move out of their church on schedule. Their minister on the PEC Relocation Committee kept them informed about our progress and, as the building started to rise, like a phoenix out of ashes, she was able to convince them that the end was near and that they would actually have their building by the winter of 1990.

Principle #7—Choose a contractor who shares your values and attends every single job meeting.

H. Moving in and Celebrating

Methodist Church officials were not the only people who were happy that our new home was ready and we were going to move. PEC staff had suffered through another summer, trying to work with stressed-out homeless mothers, kids, and teenagers in an exceedingly overcrowded facility with record-breaking heat and humidity! The dream of a spacious air-conditioned center, custom-made just for us, kept staff from losing their minds.

The move was scheduled for late October, with a celebration and ribbon cutting slated for the second week in November. The movers were hired and staff had started the previous spring to plan for a smooth transition of the residents and the programs and all the furniture and equipment. All staff vacations were scheduled so that the key people would be around through the critical periods.

The actual move had to be put off for a few weeks, awaiting last-minute plumbing alterations. It took two full days, three huge moving vans, and lots and lots of moving men. We were able to completely move without stopping our core services. The shelter residents stayed at PEC and moved with us when we moved. We had temporarily ceased our weekend food cupboard and soup kitchen services and reinstated them within a month of the move.

Even after we moved, the gas couldn't be turned on for several days, leaving us without heat or hot water in the building. We heated baby bottles in the microwave and made the best of the situation. Eight days later, the heat was on and we had several hundred guests at our grand opening.

The ribbon-cutting ceremony had been planned months before, with invitations printed and mailed before we knew we would have heat problems. Nevertheless, we were ready for our guests and had planned an event that we hoped would include all of our supporters and friends.

In concert with our Pennrose partners, we had already presented key politicians and funders with a photo and personalized note, "in appreciation . . ." The morning of the ribbon cutting, we had a full program with speakers from every major funding source, which automatically included elected and appointed officials.

The morning was extremely brisk and we had decided on setting up the dais outside with refreshments and tours inside. The most moving part of the program was a brief presentation made by a PEC "graduate," a mother who had come to PEC for help and who had "made it" out of the grips of poverty and homelessness to stability, employment and to her own home. She cried as she told her story and the audience was visibly moved.

Everyone came in from the cold weather to enjoy the food and take tours led by PEC staff and residents. Literally hundreds of neighbors, sister agency workers, politicians, congregational representatives, press, and curiosity seekers went through that day, and delighted with us in a building that physically stood for the real answer to homelessness.

We tried our best that day to publicly acknowledge everyone who had helped. Some were on the program, some were mentioned from the podium, others saw their names on giant hand-drawn posters, like blow-up thank you cards, posted in appropriate spots (like the poster in the dining room that said "Thank you to the Soroptimists of Philadelphia for donating the dining room tables!" which was decorated with pictures of little tables). And, of course, after the event all the people who had made the building possible were thanked again, with a personal letter from Pennrose Properties and me.

Throughout the three years it took to put the development together, I had kept a computer listing of everyone who had helped, in any way, and that list made it easy not to forget the "little guys." Writing to them, talking to them, and mentioning their names at the opening made them feel like they weren't forgotten and that their work was valued.

Principle #8—Remember everyone who helped, acknowledge their help, and give them credit.

Of course, the story doesn't end with the ribbon cutting—it's just the beginning of our new life in an environment that is conducive to creativity and healing, and to building a community of people who are committed to helping themselves and their sisters and brothers.

Our next challenge is to build a playground, since there is no outdoor space at PEC where children can play. We've already started to work with our now long-time friends and neighbors to develop the People's Emergency Center Community Playground on six vacant, tax-delinquent lots around the corner. And this time we have the benefit of our experience with the building and all the wonderful people we met along the way.

Section VI

Critical Issues in Affordable Housing

Chapter 28

Housing for the Elderly*

Keith Rolland
SeniorCommunity Affairs Specialist
Federal Reserve Bank of Philadelphia

Older people constitute a fast-growing sector in the United States. The population over 65 is projected to grow by 120 percent between 1989 and 2040—and the population over 75 is expected to more than double.[1]

This chapter seeks to provide an overview of some key trends and issues on the vast subject of affordable housing for older people. It will discuss the relationship of health factors to housing; different types of housing alternatives; reverse mortgages for "house rich, cash poor" owners; home repair programs; and the work of nonprofit housing developers.

HOUSING NEEDS OF THE ELDERLY

Most older people live in homes in their communities just like other age groups, while an estimated 10 percent of older people live in age-segregated housing. About 72 percent of older people own their houses, and about 84 percent have paid off their mortgages.

Many older people remain in their own homes and communities, and "age in place." They often have strong emotional attachments to their homes; a lifetime of experiences may be bound up there. And it is familiar territory amidst growing limitations. Nearly half of older Americans have lived in their current residence for more than 20 years, according to a survey by AARP. Although older people move far less than younger people, housing moves may occur in later years. Some move as a result of increased frailty and the need for care; others who are younger and financially able move to areas which have warm climates and recreational amenities.

Older people are very diverse and prefer different housing arrangements. As Eleanor Cain, director of the Delaware Division of Aging, explained: "Older people want choices. Generally, they want to continue to live in their own communities but, as they age, some may need to move in and out of a continuum of care." Older people range from inde-

---

*The views expressed here by the author are his own and are not necessarily those of the Federal Reserve Bank of Philadelphia or the Federal Reserve System.

pendence to dependence—many are in the middle—and as needed should be able to enter the theoretical continuum, ranging from institutional care to in-dependent living at home, with a myriad of housing and supportive services in the middle.

Today, experts believe that the vast majority of households over 65 are ad-equately housed.[2] Housing conditions of older people have improved as income levels have risen, aided in part by social security coverage. Income per capita is approximately the same for older people (over 65) as for people under 65. However, there is persistent poverty among older African-Americans and Hispanics, and poverty is more prevalent among women and the "older old." In fact, the prevalence of poverty among older homeowners is surprisingly high, and more than 40 percent of older homeowners have persistently high hous-ing-cost burdens. Many older homeown-ers in rural housing live in substandard housing.

The biggest increase in the older pop-ulation and household formation by 2000 will be concentrated among those 85 and older, and secondly among those between 75 and 84—age groups which have special housing needs, according to analysis by Sandra J. Newman, associate director for research in the Institute for Policy Studies at Johns Hopkins Univers-ity.[3] She points out that the proportion of women living alone is likely to increase steadily and notes the uneven geographic distribution of the elderly.

Housing and health usually are in-extricably linked for older people. Gerontologists Harold M. Katsura, Raymond J. Struyk, and Sandra J. New-man wrote: "The housing issue has two major dimensions: affordability and gene-ral housing quality on the one hand and suitability for elderly with impairments on the other."[4] Suitability depends on one's functional ability and the housing environment.

Life expectancy has lengthened dramatically in this century but, as one ages, there is a greater probability of some impairment in one's ability to func-tion. The likelihood of having one or more chronic diseases or impairments such as arthritis and hypertensive dis-eases increases with advancing age. The likelihood of a person needing assistance in daily living approximately doubles in each five-year period after 65, according to the National Center for Health Statist-ics.

Older people are assisted in activities of daily living primarily through an infor-mal network of relatives and friends. About 80 percent of all supportive servi-ces delivered in the home are provided on an informal basis; the remainder con-sists of formal or professional services. In addition, there are supportive service programs, which normally require that an older person need assistance in one or more activities of daily living (bathing, dressing, eating, mobility and transfer) or instrumental activities of daily living (such as food shopping, housework, laundry and meal preparation). Suppor-tive services can enhance activity, health and independence. But oftentimes supportive services, health and housing programs are unproductively separate and fragmented.

An older person's physical and mental capacities determine his or her housing needs. And there is a matching process between the capability of residents and the demands of the housing environment. Modifications such as grab bars and extended faucet handles can compensate for physical limitations.

Larry McNickle, director for housing policy at the American Association of Homes for the Aging, commented: "There is an emerging awareness that housing is more than a roof over one's head. Other living needs must be addressed; for the elderly, these include supportive services such as meals, shopping, housekeeping and transportation. This is particularly critical for a frail and vulnerable population. Without effective intervention in the housing setting, people may have limited options and be prematurely forced into a nursing home. Housing needs to be seen as an integral part of our nation's long-term-care strategy."

In recent years, just as the need for comprehensive services such as jobs, day care and social services has been acknowledged in low-income housing development, the need for supportive services to complement the housing of older people is being widely recommended by gerontologists.

The need for supportive services also has become evident in public housing, where many residents have aged in place and now require supportive services. Increasingly, housing managers must choose between providing new kinds of supportive services or evicting functionally dependent or health-impaired tenants and thereby forcing their premature institutionalization, according to research funded by The Robert Wood Johnson Foundation.[5]

Under the foundation's Supportive Services Program in Senior Housing, ten state housing finance agencies (HFAs) have integrated housing and services programs for older people in more than 240 federally assisted housing developments. More than 170 developments coordinate services; some offer housekeeping and heavy chore services, transportation, shopping assistance, or meals. Services are developed based on market surveys of residents and are financed by the HFAs, housing sponsors and residents.

In another development, the National Affordable Housing Bill of 1990 took several actions to link supportive services with housing for older people and other special populations. It authorized the HOPE for Elderly Independence demonstration program, added supportive service planning requirements to the HUD Section 202 program, revised the Congregate Services Housing Program, expanded a reverse mortgage insurance program, authorized a new ECHO Housing Demonstration Program, and provided incentives to prevent for-profit owners of Section 236 and Section 221 (d)(3) housing from prepaying mortgages. (About 25 percent of the units at risk are occupied by older people.)

HOUSING ALTERNATIVES

There is a growing diversity of housing arrangements that older people can choose from. The more prominent ones include:

- Congregate-housing residents— residents have their own apartments, come together for meals and recreation, and may receive additional services;

- Assisted-Living Developments—similar to congregate housing, they also include 24-hour supervision, protective oversight and personal care services (assistance with activities of daily living, such as eating, bathing and grooming);

- Board and Care Homes—the forerunner of congregate housing and assisted living, they provide food, shelter, some protective oversight and oftentimes personal care;

- Continuing-Care Retirement Communities—provide a continuum of care from independent housing to congregate housing, assisted living and nursing care; residents are older but well when joining and pay a sizable entrance fee and monthly fee;

- Accessory Apartments—self-contained living units created within existing single-family houses; has own kitchen, bath, living area, sleeping area and separate entrance;

- ECHO (Elder Cottage Housing Opportunity) Housing—self-contained, temporary, factory-built units placed on the same lot as an existing house; typically occupied by parent or in-law; and

- Shared Housing—Residence housing at least two unrelated people, at least one of whom is 60 years or older, and in which common living spaces are shared.

Congregate housing is a middle ground between independent and institutional living. Residents generally have or anticipate functional impairments. Personal care and housekeeping services are among the services sometimes offered.

Accessory apartments and ECHO units both enable closeness and support between children and parents or older relatives, while also providing privacy and independence. Zoning restrictions, and fears of homeowners that they will result in lower property values, have limited their use.

Accessory apartments typically can be installed for $16,500 to $25,000, according to Patrick H. Hare Planning and Design in Washington, D.C. Communities in which they are found include Greenwich, Connecticut, and Boulder, Colorado. A 1990 report from the U.S. Department of Housing and Urban Development said that accessory apartments were "an easily attainable and relatively inexpensive" strategy for increasing the supply of affordable housing.

ECHO units—which originated as "granny flats" in Australia—are being developed in the U.S. by Coastal Colony Corporation in Manheim, Pennsylvania. Ed Guion, president of Coastal Colony, said about the movable, energy-efficient, fully equipped homes: "I patterned them after guest cottages or garden cottages, matching the siding and roofing, even the roof pitch. I designed them to be so unobtrusive that if you drove by you wouldn't even notice them." A single-bedroom unit with 528 square feet costs $24,425, while a two-bedroom unit with 720 square feet costs $27,250; in addition, there are installation charges of up to $5,000.

The majority of an estimated 100 occupied ECHO units in the U.S. are in Pennsylvania, followed by New Jersey, New York, and Connecticut, Guion said. Most are single units near a main home but private developers have created Swatara Village, which has 20 units and is approved for 184 units, in Pine Grove, Pennsylvania. Meanwhile, the State of New Jersey has provided a grant for the purchase of ECHO units by several county housing authorities, which lease the units to older residents.

REVERSE MORTGAGES

Many older homeowners have found themselves "house rich but cash poor" as they need funds for health or long-term-care expenses, home repairs and other costs. Reverse mortgages have been a way to turn that equity into cash for some owners, and some recent legislation has the potential to significantly increase the availability of these mortgages.

Ken Scholen, a strong advocate of reverse mortgages during the past decade, described the typical borrower. "They're above government subsistence levels, but they're struggling to make ends meet. They wonder if they should sell but the tie to homeownership is very strong and they want to stay where they are." Is the reverse mortgage a kind of affordable housing? "It's making their economic situation more affordable," Scholen replied.

A reverse mortgage, in essence, is a loan made against home equity that provides owners with cash advances and requires no repayment while either of the co-borrowers live in the home. Loan advances plus interest are repaid by the borrowers or their estate upon death, sale of the house, or a permanent relocation. Funds generated from this "rising debt, falling equity" type of loan can be used for any purpose.

About 9,000 reverse mortgages had been made by financial institutions and mortgage companies between 1961 and mid-August, 1991, according to Scholen, who is director of the National Center for Home Equity Conversion. Most of the 9,000 have been made since 1983. In addition, some states and municipalit-ies have operated reverse-mortgage programs.

HUD, which had a demonstration program to insure up to 2,500 loans made by lenders, has expanded the maximum limit to 25,000 until 1995. Under HUD's Home Equity Conversion Mortgage (HECM) Insurance Program, borrowers must be 62 and receive counseling from a HUD-approved counseling agency. Eligible houses must be existing one-unit properties. The program is geared to owners who own their houses clear or have very low balances; existing mortgages must be paid off at settlement.

The maximum amount of equity that can be converted into income is HUD's 203 (b)(2) limit, which ranges from $67,500 in some rural areas to $124,875 in many urban areas (limits in Alaska and Hawaii are higher). There are no income limits. Borrowers may choose any combination of advances (lump sum, monthly advances and lines of credit) and may change the loan advance plan in the future. Any FHA-approved lender can make FHA-insured HECM mortgages; the lender sets the interest rate. However, HECM mortgages are available in some geographic areas but not in others.

Who can benefit most from the HECM? The older you are, the lower the interest rate, and the higher the value of your house and HUD's insurance limit, the larger the amount you may borrow, according to HUD. Also, it seems clear that a substantial house value is a key ingredient for this mortgage to be a substantial cash generator. If the house does not grow in value, the rising loan balance will more quickly reach the house value as well as the maximum amount that can be borrowed. In Philadelphia, HECM borrowers have tended to have house values of approximately $80,000 to $125,000 (the maximum mortgage amount).

Besides HECMs, lender-insured reverse mortgages and uninsured private lender mortgages are available in some states.

Could reverse mortgages be entering an entirely new stage of growth? In 1991, Fannie Mae agreed to purchase two types of HECM mortgages made by lenders. Scholen said that wider availability of reverse-mortgage instruments— and the new development of automated servicing and of the ability to securitize reverse mortgages and sell them on a secondary market—"will start to make a difference."

HOUSING REHABILITATION, MODIFICATIONS, AND CHORE AND MAINTENANCE SERVICES

Older people want to remain in their houses and many are homeowners. In order that housing remain in safe and sound condition, repairs to major roofing, heating and plumbing systems must be done in a timely way. Weatherization and energy repairs are important as well.

However, older homeowners who most need these repairs cannot afford them. Elder-headed households constitute the biggest percentage of all households in owned homes with below-poverty incomes. Of this group of elder-headed households, there is a high proportion of older people who live alone, particularly women. The need for this group would have to be met with government grant or deferred loan programs.

Another need is for modifications, such as grab bars, hand rails and ramps,

to make it easier and safer for older people who have lost some capability in bathing, using stairs and cooking. For frail elderly, these modifications can be important to their safety, functioning and independence.

A related need is for chore and maintenance services. Services such as shopping, shoveling snow, and cutting grass can be valuable to frail elderly. They also have job-creating potential.

The suburbs, with an aging population living largely in single-family houses, have a substantial need for minor repair, chore and maintenance programs.

A directory of housing rehabilitation and modification programs published recently by the Long Term Care National Resource Center at UCLA/USC describes nearly 300 housing rehabilitation, modification and chore and maintenance programs. Programs are sponsored by aging, social service and housing agencies and are funded primarily by Community Development Block Grants, the Older Americans Act and the U.S. Department of Energy. Most programs make modifications and minor repairs using their own staff, supplemented by subcontractors who carry out major repairs.

In Iowa, the Des Moines public schools serve 1,200 older or disabled persons a year and provide work experience for high-risk youths to learn minor home repair skills (plumbing, heating and cooling systems, locks and windows, and extermination). In St. Petersburg, Florida, the Pinellas Opportunity Council provides chore services (cleaning and yardwork) to 2,232 persons annually and employs 29 people full-time. The program is funded from federal, state, city and client payments.

A security program in Jackson, Mississippi, installs deadbolts, alarm systems and door viewers. A program in Riverside, California, fixes plumbing and heating problems, and installs ramps. Brother Redevelopment, Inc., in Denver, Colorado, uses 1,800 volunteers a year to provide 750 older or disabled homeowners with plumbing, carpentry, painting and ramp repairs.

The need for these programs does not always translate into actual consumer demand. Older homeowners may be reluctant to incur any debt or to deal with government. Also, satisfaction with one's housing tends to increase with age, according to research by M. Powell Lawton, Ph.D., director of behavioral research at the Philadelphia Geriatric Center. Therefore, programs should be easy-to-use, attractive and affordable.

NONPROFIT HOUSING DEVELOPERS

Nonprofit housing developers have been sponsors of Section 202 housing and have developed other projects for older people. In one dramatic example of adaptive re-use, the nonprofit Hawthorne Community Council in Philadelphia converted a vacant school into 55 senior housing units. In other examples of nonprofit development, the Chinese Community Housing Corporation in San Francisco developed the Swiss American hotel into 65 units and constructed 31 rental housing units for seniors and handicapped. Meanwhile, the nonprofit Consumer Farmer Foundation in New York City makes deferred-payment, 20-year loans of up to $10,000 to senior homeowners for repairs and mortgage or tax arrears. In 1990, the nonprofit made more than 60 loans to senior households.

Some nonprofits have begun to respond to health as well as housing needs of older people in their communities. The New Community Corporation in Newark, New Jersey, which manages about 1,000 units of senior housing, operates a home health care program, 180-bed skilled nursing home, congregate services nutritional program, adult medical day care center, home chore program, health care center and pharmacy. It also provides transportation and recreational programs.

Meanwhile, in Chicago, Bethel New Life, which has constructed or rehabilitated 800 units, provides chore and homemaker services to 1,000 seniors weekly, operates adult day centers, and is one of ten national demonstration programs on comprehensive community-based care for frail older people. This nonprofit has purchased a hospital and is seeking to convert it to a "campus of care," including a skilled nursing facility, 114 beds of assisted living, and 183 independent living units.

CONCLUSION

Sandra Newman, of Johns Hopkins University, has described the possible future need for government assistance programs, based on income or health status, to older homeowners. Another challenge, she said, will be to determine how housing units can be adapted to allow for the provision of long-term care services.

Meanwhile, Larry McNickle, of the American Association of Homes for the Aging, said that there is a need for further study of effective funding and supportive service delivery models. For example, comprehensive senior centers located in or adjacent to senior housing facilities could provide services to facility and other community residents.

McNickle favors programs that promote independent living while making available timely supportive services and believes that a mixed-income facility, including subsidized, moderate-income, and market-rate units, can stimulate informal support services and attract necessary community resources for supportive services.

ENDNOTES

[1] "Projections of the Population of the United States, by Age, Sex, and Race: 1988 to 2080," Current Population Reports, Series P-25, No. 1018, January 1989, U.S. Department of Commerce Bureau of the Census. "U.S. Population Estimates by Age, Sex, Race, and Hispanic Origin 1989." Current Population Reports, Series P-25, No. 1057, March 1990, U.S. Department of Commerce.

[2] Turner, Lloyd, "Public Policies and Individual Housing Choices." In *Housing an Aging Society: Issues, Alternatives, and Policy,* edited by Robert J. Newcomer, M. Powell Lawton, and Thomas O. Byerts. New York: Van Nostrand Reinhold Company, 1986, p. 51.

[3] Newman, Sandra J., "Demographic Influences on the Future Housing Demand of the Elderly." In *Housing an Aging Society: Issues, Alternatives, and Policy,* pp. 21-32.

[4] Katsura, Struyk, and Newman, *Housing for the Elderly in 2010: Projections and Policy Options,* 1989, p. 4.

[5] *ADVANCES,* national newsletter of The Robert Wood Johnson Foundation, Winter 1989, p. 5.

PUBLICATIONS

Community Housing Choices for Older Americans, edited by M. Powell Lawton, Ph.D., and Sally L. Hoover, M.A. New York: Springer Publishing Company, 1981.

Creating an Accessory Apartment, by Patrick Hare and Jolene N. Ostler. New York: McGraw Hill, 1987.

Deferred Payment Loans: A Program Development and Operations Handbook, by William Perkins. Marshall, Minn.: National Center for Home Equity Conversion.

Home-Made Money: Consumer's Guide to Home Equity Conversion, American Association of Retired Persons. July 1991. (AARP has a similar book for lenders.)

Housing an Aging Society: Issues, Alternatives, and Policy, edited by Robert J. Newcomer, Ph.D., M. Powell Lawton, Ph.D., and Thomas O. Byerts, AIA. New York: Van Nostrand Reinhold Company, 1986.

Retirement Income on the House: Cashing In on Your Home With a "Reverse" Mortgage, by Ken Scholen. Marshall, Minn.: National Center for Home Equity Conversion, 1991.

ORGANIZATIONS

American Association of Homes for the Aging; 1050 17th Street N.W.; Washington, D.C. 20036; (202) 296-5960.

American Association of Retired Persons; 601 E Street, N.W.; Washington, D.C. 20049; (202) 434-6030. Katrinka Smith Sloan, Manager, Consumer Affairs. (AARP also has a Home Equity Information Center.)

National Center for Home Equity Conversion; 1210 East College, Suite 300; Marshall, Minnesota 56258; (507) 532-3230; Ken Scholen, Director.

An Echo Development

An Echo Unit

Chapter 29

Employer-Assisted Housing

Richard D. Koller
President
RDK, Inc.

The aging of baby boomers and the subsequent baby bust of the 1970s are beginning to affect the labor and housing markets. The combination of fewer workers and high-cost housing is leading many companies to re-examine their employee benefit plans and institute employer-assisted housing programs to help current employees buy homes and attract new employees. Many view housing assistance as critical to their recruitment efforts in an increasingly competitive job market. Homeownership continues to be cited as Americans' highest goal and, as always, those employers who help employees achieve their goals will attract and retain a happy and productive work force and, at the same time, minimize costly personnel turnover.

Public and private employers and labor unions have begun to establish "employer-assisted housing" programs, primarily in urban centers where high housing costs discourage workers from affiliating with a firm or living within reasonable proximity to work. Employer-assisted housing programs are perceived as a "wave of the future" and could become a major tool in combating the high cost of housing in America.

Employer-assisted housing programs (EAHPs) can be run by individual companies or groups of employers and can concentrate on either the absorption of existing housing stock or production of new homes. Like most affordable-housing programs, EAHPs tend to drive down costs associated with buying a home and making monthly payments. This chapter describes many of the programs that have been developed to date.

343

CONSUMPTION-ORIENTED PROGRAMS

Group Mortgage Origination Plans are volume discount programs to reduce closing and application costs on mortgage loans.

Group Mortgage Guarantee and Mortgage Insurance Programs substitute employer or third-party mortgage guarantees for normal private or public guarantees at no cost to the employee. The employee can then eliminate the cost of mortgage insurance from his costs both at origination and over the life of the loan. A 100 percent guarantee program can eliminate the need for any down payment.

Mortgage insurance can be underwritten directly or indirectly. Employers who do it directly must be able to carry the value of the mortgage guarantees as a contingent liability on their balance sheets. The indirect approach uses a third-party mortgage insurance policy to cover the potential liability. The trade off is liabilities and perhaps an increased cost of funds for the organization versus insurance premiums. Hybrid co-insurance programs have spun off of this idea.

The most successful and well-known of the insurance programs is the University of Pennsylvania program in Philadelphia, which guarantees, free to the employee, 100 percent of his or her mortgage. The 100 percent guarantee also eliminates the need for a down payment. The result has been neighborhood stabilization, increasing property values, additional economic development and redevelopment in the surrounding area, and only one default in over 2,000 loans insured since 1965.

Mortgage Buydowns (grants) are payments made by an employer to a lender that are applied toward the employee's mortgage. They can be used to reduce the cost of housing or add to the employee's buying power. Buydowns are often paid in a lump sum up-front, creating a tax liability for the employee and a deductible expense for the employer in the year made. Buydowns can also be disadvantageous to employers who do not protect themselves against an employee's premature departure.

Cost-of-Living Allowances (COLAs) are similar to buydowns except that payments are made periodically over a period of time—eliminating the potential exposure of buydowns. COLAs are phased out after the employee's salary reaches a level where the mortgage is affordable on his or her current earnings.

In addition, some companies have provided **income tax assistance** to defray the tax liability these programs can create for employees, **group legal insurance** to cover attorneys' fees at closing, either in part or in whole, and **shared equity** loans in which the employer is a co-owner of the home until the loan is repaid.

PRODUCTION-ORIENTED PROGRAMS

To date, production programs have primarily been limited to corporations, either individually or in groups, making **cash, land,** and **interest reduction** contributions to philanthropic organizations and nonprofit developers to produce affordable housing.

Cash Subsidies made to nonprofit

developers reduce the price of housing that is ultimately marketed, though not necessarily exclusively, to employees of the participating corporation(s).

Land Acquisition Grants, in the form of outright donations or below-market sales or leases, enhance affordability by eliminating or reducing the cost of land on which project and individual homes are built. Land is usually the most expensive component in housing production.

Interest Rate Substitutions reduce the overall interest cost of a project when a contributing corporation uses its short-term cost-of-funds advantage over the developer for the construction loan. In return, the contributing corporation would receive a portion of the reduced-cost housing for its employees. It would seem possible to adapt this concept to permanent mortgages by, for example, buying down the interest rate or associated costs of the permanent loan in return for units.

Master Lease Agreements on apartments reduce the cost of individual units to employees through volume leasing.

FEDERAL GOVERNMENT ROLE

In the 1970s, Congress decided Americans should have greater ownership in the companies for which they work and created the Employee Stock Ownership Plan to help finance employee stock purchases. Through ESOPs, companies use company-owned (treasury) stock as collateral for loans to employees to purchase outstanding shares. As an incentive, the corporations get a 50 percent tax write-off on the interest expense related to ESOPs.

A model exists to adapt Employee Stock Ownership Plans to fund employee housing programs. It suggests a 10 percent investment of ESOP assets into real estate, which could be in the form of employee mortgages or affordable-housing development projects. Authority for such an investment would be derived from the same "prudent man" rule that applies to ESOPs and pension funds.

Another step toward employer-assisted housing programs could be taken with an amendment to the Internal Revenue Service (IRS) definition of "accepted business expenses." By adding mortgage assistance to employees to the code-specified list of acceptable business expenses, employer housing benefits could become tax-free to both parties and provide an impetus for employers to explore housing benefits for their employees.

FEDERAL NATIONAL MORTGAGE ASSOCIATION "MAGNET" PROGRAM

In the spring of 1991, the Federal National Mortgage Association (Fannie Mae) launched a $1 billion employer-assisted housing program, called *Magnet*, as pat of its larger three-year, $10 billion commitment to low- and moderate-income housing.

The *Magnet* program is comprised of two basic products, the *Magnet 5* and *Magnet 3/2,* which can be custom-designed to meet particular needs. The *Magnet 5* product is a conventional mortgage market product, but the *Mag-*

net 3/2 is an affordable-housing/low-
and moderate-income program modeled
from the Fannie Mae *Community Home
Buyers Program 3/2.*

MAGNET 3/2

The *Magnet 3/2* product is available
only to employees whose annual
household income is below 115 percent
of the area median, according to U.S.
Department of Housing and Urban
Development statistics. It uses the
standard 3/2 program ratios of 33/38
percent, i.e., the sum of the borrower's
mortgage payments, including principal,
interest, taxes, and insurance, cannot exceed 33 percent of monthly income;
similarly, the borrower's total monthly
debt payments cannot exceed 38 percent
of income, including all loan support
from employers. The 5 percent down
payment is split between the employee,
who must invest 3 percent, and the
employer, who provides the remaining 2
percent. The employer's 2 percent must
be in the form of an unsecured loan. The
employer's portion must be repaid or
fully forgiven within five years. The maximum LTV of all secured loans is 95 percent.

Employers can provide support above
and beyond 2 percent of the down payment. Grants, unsecured and/or
deferred loans, or loan guarantees can be
used to increase the down payment or
for closing costs. Supplemental loan rates
cannot exceed the rate on the first mortgage, and employee must have the right
to prepay without penalty. Supplemental
loans must not be due in less than five
years (so they do not interfere with the
payback of the employer down payment)

and may not be negatively amortizing
(i.e., deferred interest cannot be added to
the principal balance). Deferred loans
can only be used to increase down
payments beyond 5 percent.

Home buyer education is recommended with the implementation and
operation of the Magnet and any other
low- and moderate-income housing
Fannie Mae program.

THE UNIVERSITY OF PENNSYLVANIA MORTGAGE PROGRAMS

The University of Pennsylvania runs
three mortgage programs for its
employees. The first, and most well
known, is the mortgage insurance program, which has been in operation for
nearly 30 years during which time it has
incurred only two defaults (one of which
was cured) on approximately 2,000 loans
insured. The second program reduces
closing costs, and the third is a new program that links buyers with tax-exempt
bond financing. Each is discrete and cannot be combined with either of the
others.

The mortgage insurance program,
known as the *University Mortgage Program*, is limited to single-family homes
within set boundaries around the university. The administrator is Meritor
Mortgage, a local mortgage company
affiliated with PSFS, a large local bank
with which the university does substantial business. Applicants must meet all
eligibility/qualification criteria set forth
by Meritor, which has ultimate authority
to accept or reject applications. Meritor
generally uses 28/36 ratios to preserve

its ability to sell University loans into the secondary market.

The University's employee eligibility requirements for the insurance program are divided between upper- and lower-level staff. Senior staff is eligible to apply for the program immediately upon hire. Lower-level staff may apply after three years of service to the university.

The second program is with Mellon Bank. It combines an origination fee discount of one point and a waiver of application fees for a total discount of up to $1,925 for university-employed borrowers. Eligibility for this program, in addition to the standard eligibility requirements, requires an annual income of at least $50,000.

The third program, operated in conjunction with the Pennsylvania Housing Finance Agency (PHFA), is a new employer-assisted pilot program for first-time buyers. University employees with at least six months of service can access tax-exempt bond funding at 8.35 percent, 30-year, fixed-rate mortgages if they qualify under PHFA's guidelines. Prices are capped at $109,000 for existing homes and $120,000 for new construction; multifamily properties are not eligible. Buyer income cannot exceed $36,500 for one- and two-person households and $41,000 for larger households. The maximum LTV is 95 percent and the maximum mortgage amount is $114,000. Penn has also expanded its geographic boundaries for the Penn/PHFA program.

The entire unpaid balance of insured loans becomes due when the employee leaves the university, ceases to occupy the property as a principal residence, or when the property is sold. There is no prepayment penalty.

Employees are responsible for the costs of appraisals, credit checks and closing costs, which average 7 percent of the purchase price, in all programs.

OTHER PROGRAMS NATIONWIDE

Colgate-Palmolive pays all points and closing costs on mortgages up to $187,600 and two points and most closing costs on loans above that amount.

Aetna Life and Casualty operates a straightforward kind of program across the country designed to help regular employees—but no officer employees—buy homes. It will make up to 90 percent loans at generally 1 percent below market, with no cap on house prices.

SINA, the Southside Institutions Neighborhood Alliance (a coalition of Hartford Hospital, The Institute of Living, and Trinity College) has a cooperative employer-assisted program for their employees.

SINA's program blends funds from four sources to achieve an interest rate generally 1 percent below market.

1. A commercial bank makes an 80 percent LTV first mortgage at a below-market interest rate.

2. Connecticut Housing Investment Fund (CHIF) makes a 15 percent LTV second mortgage at 8 percent interest.

3. Down payment—the employee makes a minimum of $5,000 down payment under all circumstances.

4. Employer no-interest loan—if the house price is less than $200,000, the

employer contribution is the difference between the employee's $5,000
and 5 percent of the purchase price. If
the price is greater than $200,000,
the employer and employee each contribute 2.5 percent.

SINA borrowers need approximately
$8,000 total for down payment and clos-
ing costs in a metropolitan market with a
median existing single-family home price
in excess of $153,000.

A chart containing sample program
characteristics can be found at the end of
the chapter.

LEGAL AND TAX IMPLICATIONS

Tax and legal implications will likely vary
by state and municipality for both the
employer and employee. At the federal
taxation level, however, if the loan
amount exceeds $10,000, the value of
the subsidized interest rate is usually taxable. Below $10,000, there would likely
be no tax liability on the value of the

subsidy. Also, as with home-equity loans,
interest on loans secured by the home is
tax deductible.

Employers and employees should be
certain the agreement relating to these
loans and advances is clear to both parties and that the agreement is in writing.
First mortgages in all instances have pre-
cedence over any other lien on the property. Employer guarantees are generally
considered contingent liabilities of the
employer. Fannie Mae has specific legal
requirements for each type of assistance
offered.

CONCLUSION

There are some 50 employer-assisted
housing programs in operation across the
country. Each is designed to meet the
needs of particular firms, cities and
regions. Employer-assisted housing programs are in their infancy and present
opportunity for innovation limited only
by the creativity of those developing
them.

Figure 29.1   Comparative Characteristics of Employer-Assisted Housing Programs

	Fannie Mae Magnet 3/2	SINA, Hartford, CT	U of P Mortgage Insurance Program
Eligibility	Maximum income 115% of local median	F/T employees only	F/T employees only; 21 years or older with U.S. citizenship or immigrant visa
Maximum Mortgage	95% of purchase price or appraised value, whichever is less	None	Limited by purchasing ability
Down payment	Minimum 5%; 3% from buyer, 2% from employer	$5,000 if price < $200,000 2.5% if price > $200,000	None required (100% of purchase price insured)
Ratios	33/38	28/36	28/36
MI	LTV greater than 80%	None required	None required
Interest Rate	Prevailing rate	Fixed; lender 1st below market (80%), CHIP 2nd at 8% (15%), employer 3rd no-interest, employee (2.5%). Result: about 1% below market	Fixed or adjustable; prevailing rates
Escrows	Waived	Taxes & insurance	Taxes & insurance

Table continues

Figure 29.1 Continued

	Fannie Mae Magnet 3/2	SINA, Hartford, CT	U of P Mortgage Insurance Program
Maximum Term	30 years	30 years	30 years
Points/Origination Fee	Prevailing/Prevailing	None/1% to CHIF	Prevailing/Prevailing
Closing Costs/Application Fee	Normal pro-rata costs prevailing fee	Normal pro-rata costs $30-$60	Normal pro-rata costs; about $250
Prepayment Penalty	None	None	None
Assumable	No	No	No
Occupancy	Principal residence only	Principal residence only	Principal residence only
Location	Can be designated	Neighborhood	Neighborhood
Eligibility Properties	Single-family (incl. condos)	1–4 family and condos; no conversions	Single-family (incl. condos)
Inspections	Lender requirements	Engineer and exterminator	Lender requirements
Approval Time	Standard approval time	Approximately 30 days	4-8 weeks

Chapter 30

Housing the Rural Poor

Judith A. Calogero
Executive Director
and
Sarah Minier
Communications and Training Coordinator
New York State Rural Housing Coalition

INTRODUCTION: RURAL VS. URBAN ECONOMIES

When people think of New York, chances are they envision one of the largest cities in the world. Look beyond New York City, however, and the state more closely resembles any other, with its mixture of small towns and cities, farmland and major urban areas.

Of the 62 counties in New York State, 44 are defined as rural, with populations of 200,000 or less. As of 1990, the populations of those rural counties totalled 3.2 million.

For all the attention and revenue New York City generates, it also places a unique burden on the rest of the state. Tax monies are needed to fund the myriad of services required by a city of over seven million people. Water and energy are transported to the city from upstate regions. And a staggering amount of garbage is generated by inhabitants of the metropolitan region—28,000 to 30,000 tons of solid waste per day, much of which must be buried in upstate landfills.

Like several other states, New York has converted its rural areas into dumpsites for many of its massive urban problems. Rural areas offer an amenity beyond price to overcrowded urban areas: space. That which we cannot contain in the city, we ship to the country.

One example is the residue of New York City's high crime rate. Between 1985 and 1991, 22 new correctional facilities were built in rural New York to house primarily urban inmates—over 10,900 of them, according to the New

York State Department of Correctional Services.

Yet urban dwellers also turn to the mountains, forests and lakes of rural New York for recreation. The economic circle connecting urban and rural areas becomes complete with the tourism trade: As businesses flee the state in search of fewer restrictions and a lower tax rate, tourism has become a major industry in many rural areas. Rural economies once based in manufacturing and agriculture—particularly dairy farming—are now based in services for the urban population. Like landfills, prisons and other urban-generated industries, tourism is welcomed because there's little else left for the rural worker to do. In the struggle to find jobs, rural populations will accept the unacceptable: a maximum-security prison in exchange for 200 jobs. A trash incineration plant in exchange for a financial boost to the local economy.

Water supply and sewage disposal also create problems in rural areas. Rural counties are less likely than urban areas to have a complete public infrastructure: only 46.9 percent of year-round housing in rural counties is connected to a sewer system, as opposed to 85.4 percent of houses in nonrural counties. Only 58.7 percent of homes in rural counties has access to a public or private water system, versus 95.7 percent of their nonrural counterparts.

DYNAMICS OF RURAL POVERTY

People in both rural and urban areas may become impoverished for the same reasons: loss of a job, serious illness, rise in single-parent families, overwhelming bills, and bankruptcy. In some rural areas, the seasonal economic base of the tourism industry translates into only three to four months of steady employment each year for many workers.

Throughout the 1980s, rural poverty—already deeply imbedded—was taking a turn for the worse.

• During the first half of the 1980s, the number of rural New Yorkers with incomes below the federal poverty level rose by almost 90 percent.

• By 1986, the rural poverty rate had exceeded the urban rate.

• In 1989, 11 rural counties had unemployment rates in excess of 10 percent—nearly double the state and national rates.

At present, one in four rural children live at or below the poverty level. Yet, in the majority of impoverished rural families, at least one person works. In comparisons between rural and urban poverty, it's notable that rural low-income people are less likely to qualify for government assistance then people in urban areas *because* they work. Additionally, the rural median income is 26 percent less than the income in urban areas. Extensive periods of poverty are far more likely for rural families (60 percent) than urban. And rural areas frequently lack the services taken for granted in urban areas, such as transportation, health and human services, and housing.

It is difficult to gauge homelessness in rural New York, due to a lack of homeless shelters and public places. The rural homeless remain hidden, living in chicken coops and broken-down buses, staying with friends and relatives. One of the most striking things about rural poverty is its invisibility. In urban settings, transportation routes generally run through impoverished areas, making a trip through the ghetto a daily part of commuting to work. Major transportation routes in rural areas, however, tend to be surrounded by lush greenery or commercial areas. The pockets of poverty are hidden down dirt roads, on pathways without street signs, far removed from the thoroughfares.

Rental housing issues also differ. Tenants in urban areas have greater access to code enforcement officials and the housing courts when their homes become uninhabitable. Rural tenants are generally on their own, fending for themselves and often making their own repairs to improve habitability.

The proliferation of mobile homes as low-income rural housing may adversely affect the safety people have in their own homes. Older units may have substandard plumbing and installation. The reputation as "matchstick housing" that clings—fairly or not—to older mobile homes is often tragically realized in units with makeshift heating systems or wiring that is dangerous or inadequate. Too often, these conditions have resulted in fires that cause loss of life, or loss of the housing unit.

All these factors led to the formation of an organization that would focus attention on the plight of the rural poor.

COALITION HISTORY

The New York State Rural Housing Coalition was originally formed in 1979 to carry on a program of education, organization and action designed to provide safe, sanitary and affordable housing for low- to moderate-income rural New Yorkers.

The Coalition grew from a grass-roots effort by local rural housing sponsors who saw the need to develop a "power base" to serve the state's rural poor and their housing needs. Part of its goal was to create a network of Rural Preservation Companies (RPCs) that would spearhead the development of affordable housing at the local level. The Coalition would then provide information, technical assistance, networking and research services to the RPCs.

The Coalition's mission statement as of July 1981 stated that the organization would develop and preserve small-town and rural housing, and encourage community development, by:

• Providing a central information point where experience and data relating to low-income housing can be collected, evaluated, and made available to individuals and organizations;

• Taking the lead to develop and encourage new and creative techniques and programs to provide decent homes for low-income people;

• Assisting low-income rural housing groups in obtaining the necessary financial, technical and related assistance;

• Continuing a program of research, education, information and organization, focused on low-income rural housing and directed toward (1) persons of low and moderate incomes who want to improve their housing conditions, (2) the general public, and (3) institutions, including government foundations and financial institutions.

A companion organization, the New York State Rural Advocates, grew from the Coalition in the early 1980s to serve as a forum, lobbyist, and conscience for impoverished rural people in need of adequate affordable housing.

ADVOCACY

The New York State Rural Advocates works to bring the "bigger picture" into focus by bringing the problems of the rural homeless, difficult to house, and impoverished to the attention of policy makers, funders, and state agencies. The Coalition assists these efforts by providing resources, which helps members at the community level to do something about these problems.

The Rural Advocates, formed in 1981, lobbied to create the state Rural Preservation Program and to fund its expansion from 14 groups in 1981 to more than 80 a decade later.

Over the years, the Rural Advocates have:

- Lobbied for establishing the Rural Rental Assistance Program, which has made over 3,500 rental housing units available for very-low-income families and individuals;

- Secured the enactment of the Rural Area Revitalization Program to fund hard-to-finance housing and community development projects in rural areas, and

- Pressured the Farmers Home Administration (FmHA) to maximize the use of federal rural housing funds available to the state, more than doubling the utilization in one year and fully utilizing the funds in New York State for the first time ever in 1988.

Rural Advocates has also been involved in making the state's Homeless Housing Assistance Program, the Low Income Housing Trust Fund, and the Affordable Home Ownership Development Program more workable in rural areas. In addition, the group has worked to make utilities, agencies, and financial institutions responsive to the needs of low-income rural people.

Still, the need to provide a strong, clear voice for the state's rural poor remains as vital as ever, particularly in the face of government funding cutbacks.

COALITION MEMBERSHIP DIVERSIFIES

By the mid-1980s, the Rural Housing Coalition realized a need to extend its assistance to groups other than Rural Preservation Companies. Efforts began to actively diversify the membership base to encompass not only RPCs, but for-profit developers, financial institutions, planners, architects, attorneys, health and human services organizations, and government agencies (including state, county and local).

This diversity enabled a more comprehensive network to evolve by providing a common meeting ground for all professionals who deal with some aspect of affordable housing. While the diversity creates some problems—for example, training programs must be organized around the extremely differing needs of the member base—it ultimately provides the organization's strength by allowing collaborative action. However, it also required careful defining of the Coalition's mission and stated objectives. This diverse membership, with such differing organizational objectives and modes of operation, meets on the common ground of a higher quality of life for its residents. They gelled into a cohesive group through recognizing the goals they share—as defined by the Coalition's mission statement and membership materials—and realizing that each component is vital to reaching the larger objective.

It is also mandatory that the Coalition provide the framework for a symbiotic relationship among all its members—for-profit, nonprofit, and public entities. For example, an individual branch of a bank can only be as strong as the community it serves; by strengthening the community, the bank strengthens its business in the long run. Affordable-housing projects, while strengthening the community backbone, also bring banks a modest profit and help them meet Community Reinvestment Act (CRA) requirements.

As member banks take a second look at loan opportunities that have been traditionally ignored, nonprofit housing agencies find themselves with more lending agents who are willing to back potential projects—frequently, at favorable lending terms. Bank financing can complement government grants, spreading these limited funds further than they would otherwise go.

Cases such as these also increase recognition that the government cannot produce affordable housing alone: financial institutions are an integral part of a housing project team, as are the RPCs, developers, builders, and others at the community level.

Affordable housing also meets the profit motive of other members—such as private developers, attorneys and architects—by bringing about new business opportunities and strengthening rural economies.

THREE PROJECTS

The following sections highlight three Coalition projects, each unique, and each filling a different need for a highly needy population. These include the network of RPC programs developed by the Coalition (and part of the reason for its incep-tion); a demonstration program administered by the Coalition, and a photographic exhibit developed to graphically illustrate the need for affordable housing in rural New York.

RURAL PRESERVATION NETWORK

The state Rural Preservation Program was established in 1980 by the state Private Housing Finance Law, which authorized a state agency to contract with rural nonprofit organizations for housing preservation and community renewal services. The Rural Preservation Program funds the network of rural community-based nonprofit organizations that provide housing services to low-income residents. These nonprofits, in turn, leverage other public and private capital and administrative funds.

In 1989, 44 Rural Preservation Companies documented their tremendous economic impact by:

- Constructing or rehabilitating 1,366 units of housing, worth $40.5 million;

- Completing 3,111 units of moderate rehabilitation and home repair, worth nearly $13.5 million;

- Providing direct client services worth nearly $25.7 million, including mortgage packaging, client counseling, energy and weatherization improvements, FmHA and HUD loan and grant packaging, and other services, and

- Assisting 27,534 people with direct client services.

Projecting these figures over the total 84 Rural Preservation Companies, an economic impact of over $165 million (leveraged public and private monies, rental income, value of jobs, etc.) was generated by these nonprofit organizations for the State of New York in 1989. Further, every Rural Preservation Company dollar generates over $30 in capital and administrative funds.

AHRNY PROGRAM

Affordable Housing for Rural New York (AHRNY) is a program developed and administered by the Coalition since 1985. As of January 1991, 2,402 rural New Yorkers were living in 912 safe, affordable homes because of the AHRNY program. The program matches $8.7 million in New York State funds with $28.5 million in other public and private funds for the rehabilitation or development of affordable housing. Leveraging matching funds makes it possible to improve and construct a greater number of housing units in a wider geographic area.

AHRNY combines these public and private financial resources with the skills of more than 30 nonprofits, local government and for-profit housing developers in 24 counties. Options available under the program include:

• Improving owner-occupied substandard homes;

• New construction of energy-efficient single-family homes, townhouses or condominiums; and

• Acquisition, rehabilitation and resale of homes currently inventoried by public bodies and financial institutions, or available through the open market.

For the 912 units completed so far, AHRNY expended a total of $17.8 million. Of this total, $5.1 million was provided by the New York State Affordable Housing Corporation, a subsidiary of the New York State Housing Finance Ag-

ency, a public benefit corporation which raises revenue for affordable multifamily housing by lending proceeds from the sale of long-term tax-exempt bonds.

The Coalition, in tandem with AHRNY local project managers, raised the additional $12.7 million as matching funds. Sources of matching funds included Community Development Block Grant (CDBG), FmHA conventional bank financing, private revolving loan funds and homeowner contributions. Administrative funds are provided by the New York State legislature's Neighborhood Development Demonstration Program.

AHRNY provides subgrantees with administrative and technical assistance from the time a project is conceived to the time it is funded and developed. Subgrantees carry out actual development, construction, or rehabilitation activities with appropriate technical assistance from the Coalition.

The Coalition's final goal is to improve and construct 1,517 units of rural housing under the AHRNY program. The Coalition will draw upon its experience with AHRNY to access more dollars from private lending institutions for rural affordable-housing development. The leveraged private dollars help maximize the benefit of limited state resources; it also teaches nonprofit agencies to work independently with banks, increasing the effectiveness of CRA requirements and the ability of the government to enforce them.

Photo Exhibit

"An Abiding Place" is a photo project designed to give faces, names and meaning to statistics on rural poverty and substandard housing. This exhibition of 57

Figure 30.1   Household Income Percentages

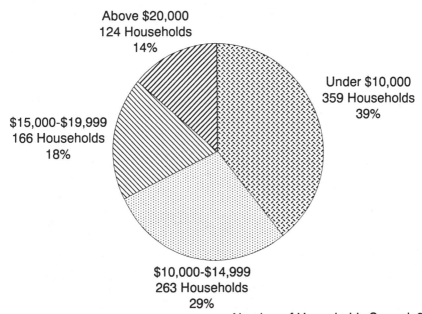

Above $20,000
124 Households
14%

$15,000-$19,999
166 Households
18%

Under $10,000
359 Households
39%

$10,000-$14,999
263 Households
29%

Number of Households Served: 912
Average Annual Income: $12,651
Average Household Size: 2.6

The Coalition is highly successful in serving very-low income families under the Affordable Housing for Rural New York (AHRNY) program. The household income statistics shown in the pie chart are less than the federal Department of Housing and Urban Development (HUD) income guidelines for low-income housing programs such as Section 8, Section 235 and Section 236.

black-and-white photographs will tour New York until March 1992, presented in public facilities and private galleries throughout the state. Created and sponsored by the Rural Housing Coalition, the exhibition was in part intended to counter the popular misconception that homelessness and dangerously deficient housing are primarily urban phenomena. The photograph of Leo, for example, speaks volumes: an elderly man smiles for the camera as he stands in front of his home of many years—an abandoned school bus with no heat and no electricity.

However, many of the photographs focus on the end results of affordable-housing programs—such as the "after" shot of a family of seven who moved from a converted chicken coop into an apartment.

While the struggle for safe and affordable housing was an ongoing one for most of the families photographed for the

Leo is 74 years old. He lived in this abandoned school bus for many years with no running water, no toilet and no lights. For heat, he'd build a wood fire in a small metal box.

"It was dark. I had my hat pulled down way over my ears and my coat all buttoned up and I put my gloves on. I was sitting right next to the heater but I couldn't feel any heat. It was cold outside, it was cold inside and I told myself that I couldn't spend another winter here."

(Photo by Jon Crispin for the New York State Rural Housing Coalition)

exhibit, some were able to find at least partial solutions through the work of community-based housing organizations.

The Rural Housing Coalition worked with photographer Jon Crispin to create the exhibit by photographing and interviewing more than 100 low-income families in 28 rural New York counties. The exhibit was intended to raise the awareness of policy makers as well as the general public. The exhibition's opening ceremony in Albany, the state capital, occurred as part of the New York State Rural Advocate's legislative conference.

This family of seven (the husband is not pictured) lived in a converted chicken coop for five years. It rented for $170 per month, and was so structurally unsound that the children's friends were not allowed to visit for fear they would be injured in the home.

They now live in a two-bedroom apartment with federally-subsidized rent. Finding an apartment was difficult; even landlords who allowed pets were unwilling to accept five children.

SUMMARY

Thousands of rural New Yorkers live in deficient and unsafe housing. Their needs are often overlooked in favor of those of the more visible poor in urban areas, particularly in New York City.

At present, one in four rural children lives at or below the poverty level. Yet at least one person works in the majority of impoverished rural families, making those families less likely to qualify for government assistance.

The New York State Rural Housing Coalition grew from a grass-roots effort to establish a "power base" to serve the state's rural poor and their housing needs. Formed in 1979 as a nonprofit organization, the Coalition was also charged with creating a network of Rural Preservation Companies (RPCs) to develop affordable housing at the local level.

The New York State Rural Advocates, formed in 1981, is the advocacy arm of the Coalition, bringing the problems of the rural homeless and impoverished to the attention of policy makers, funders, and state agencies. The Rural Advocates successfully lobbied to create and expand the state's Rural Preservation Program.

The Rural Housing Coalition now offers technical assistance, training, and up-to-date information to over 200 member organizations, including RPCs, for-profit developers, financial institutions, planners, architects, government agencies and others. This diverse membership base meets on the common ground of a shared concern for developing rural areas of New York State to ensure a higher quality of life for its residents.

Organization Contacts

National Alliance to End Homelessness
1518 K Street, N.W., Suite 206
Washington, D.C. 20005
(202) 638-1526
Thomas L. Kenyon

United Way
701 North Fairfax Street
Alexandria, VA 22314
(703) 836-7112
Ellen Gilligan

Coalition for the Homeless
500 8th Avenue, Room 910
New York, NY 10018
(212) 695-8700
Mary Brosnahan

People's Emergency Center
3902 Spring Garden Street
Philadelphia, PA 19104
(215) 382-7523
Gloria Guard

Architectural League
457 Madison Avenue
New York, NY 10022
(212) 753-1722
Rosalie Genevro

National Association of Homebuilders
15th and M Streets, NW
Washington, D.C. 20005
(800) 368-5242
Barbara Bryan

Progressive Redevelopment Inc.
127 Peachtree Street, NE, Suite 622
Atlanta, GA 30303
(404) 577-2901
Bruce C. Gunter

Bridge Housing Corporation
82 Second Street, Suite 200
San Francisco, CA 94105
(415) 989-1111
Don Terner

Habitat for Humanity International
121 Habitat Street
Americus, GA 31709
(912) 924-6935
Millard Fuller

Bertrand Goldberg Associates, Inc.
60 West Erie Street
Chicago, Illinois 60610
(312) 280-5300
Bertrand Goldberg

National Association of Realtors
777 14th Street, N.W.
Washington, D.C. 20005-3271
(202) 383-1023
Richard Koller

General Electric Mortgage Insurance Co.
6601 Six Forks Road
Raleigh, NC 27615
(919) 846-4100
Stuart Lopes

Chase Community Development
Corporation
101 Park Avenue, 15th Floor
New York, NY 10081
(212) 551-2220
Mark A. Willis

Community Preservation Corporation
5 West 37th Street, 10th Floor
New York, NY 10018
(212) 869-5300
Michael Lappin

Fannie Mae
Public Information Office
3900 Wisconsin Avenue, NW
Washington, D.C. 20016
(202) 752-7124

Neighborhood Housing Services
of America
1970 Broadway, Suite 470
Oakland, CA 94612
(415) 832-5542
Mary Lee Widener

AW Housing Group
225 Franklin
Boston, MA 02110-2803
(617) 261-9000
Amy Anthony

Resolution Trust Corporation
801 17th Street, NW, 6th Floor
Washington, DC 20434
(202) 416-6900

Muriel Watkins
Maine State Housing Authority
295 Water Street
Augusta, Maine 04338-2669
(207) 626-4600
Dwight Sewell

Neighborhood Reinvestment Corporation
1325 G Street, NW, Suite 800
Washington, DC 20005
(202) 376-2400
George Knight

Enterprise Foundation
505 American City Building
Columbia, MD 21044
(301) 964-1230
Rick Cohen

The Housing Partnership, Inc.
First Trust Center, 200 South Fifth Street
Atrium Level North
Louisville, KY 40202
(502) 585-5451

HANDI
P.O. Box 310
Mount Vernon, NY 10551
(914) 668-9126
William Jones

Lake County Community Action
Program
106 S. Sheridan Road
Waukegan, IL 60085
(708) 249-4330
Barbara Gordon

Keith Rolland
334 South 43rd Street
Philadelphia, PA 19104

New York State Rural Housing Coalition
350 Northern Blvd., Suite 101
Albany, NY 12204
(518) 434-1314
Judith A. Calogero

Index

About the Publisher

PROBUS PUBLISHING COMPANY

Probus Publishing Company fills the informational needs of today's business professional by publishing authoritative, quality books on timely and relevant topics, including:

- Investing
- Futures/Options Trading
- Banking
- Finance
- Marketing and Sales
- Manufacturing and Project Management
- Personal Finance, Real Estate, Insurance and Estate Planning
- Entrepreneurship
- Management

Probus books are available at quantity discounts when purchased for business, educational or sales promotional use. For more information, please call the Director, Corporate/Institutional Sales at 1-800-998-4644, or write:

Director, Corporate/Institutional Sales
Probus Publishing Company
1925 N. Clybourn Avenue
Chicago, Illinois 60614
FAX (312) 868-6250